SOCIETY AND KNOWLEDGE

SOCIETY AND KNOWLEDGE

Contemporary Perspectives in the Sociology of Knowledge

Edited by
NICO STEHR and VOLKER MEJA

Transaction Books
New Brunswick (U.S.A.) and London (U.K.)

Library of Congress Catalog Number: 83-5043
ISBN: 0-87855-493-9 (cloth); 0-87855-950-7 (paper)

Printed in the United States of America

Library of Congress Cataloging in Publication Data
Main entry under title:

Society and knowledge.

    Includes index.
    1. Knowledge, Sociology of—Addresses, essays, lectures. I. Stehr, Nico.
II. Meja, Volker.
BD175.S63 1984   306'.42   83-5043
ISBN: 0-87855-493-9
ISBN: 0-87855-950-7 (pbk.)

To Sebastian

Contents

Acknowledgements

The majority of the essays assembled here were first commissioned by us for a collection entitled *Wissenssoziologie* published by Westdeutscher Verlag in 1981 as special issue 22 of the *Kölner Zeitschrift für Soziologie und Sozialpsychologie*. We have asked all contributors to update their essays, but we have also considerably altered the selection of essays itself. In particular, we have included several additional essays by French sociologists, as well as an interview with Norbert Elias and an essay by W. Baldamus, which were both commissioned for this book, and we have excluded those contributions contained in the German collection which concern the various aspects of the *history* of the sociology of knowledge.

We gratefully acknowledge permission to reprint in translation and in revised form the essays by Luhmann, Dux, Namer, Knorr-Cetina, Corradi, Weiss, Forman, and Böhme, which were first published in Nico Stehr and Volker Meja, eds., *Wissenssoziologie*, Special Issue 22 of the *Kölner Zeitschrift für Soziologie und Sozialpsychologie* (Opladen: Westdeutscher Verlag, 1981), and the essays by Gabel, Ansart, Stourdze-Plessis and Strohl, which first appeared in Jean Duvignaud, ed., *Sociologie de la connaissance* (Paris: Payot, 1979). The essays by Bloor, Mulkay, and Barnes, which were published in the German collection, have appeared in somewhat different versions in English elsewhere as well: David Bloor, "Durkheim and Mauss revisited: classification and the sociology of knowledge," *Studies in History and Philosophy of Science* 13,4 (1982): 267-97; Michael J. Mulkay, "Knowledge and utility: implications for the sociology of knowledge," *Social Studies in Science* 9 (1979): 63-80; Barry Barnes, "On the conventional character of knowledge and cognition," *Philosophy of the Social Sciences* 11 (1981): 303-33.

We would like to thank the contributors to this volume for their efforts and for their prompt responses to our many requests for assistance. We are also grateful to Judith Adler, Cecilia Benoit, Juan E. Corradi, Richard Ericson, F.A. Johnstone, David Kettler, Juliet Flower MacCannell, Dieter Misgeld, Ronald D. Schwartz, Rosalynd Sydie, and Kurt H. Wolff for their support, and to the various translators who have done their best to produce readable English texts from the French and the German, an often exceedingly difficult task, which is rarely acknowledged as what it in fact is: a genuine intellectual accomplishment. In order to assure the terminological consistency and to further improve the readability and the accuracy of the texts, we have participated in the task of translation by editing the translated essays. Thanks are also due to Juan E. Corradi and Caterina Pizanias for their contribution to the mini- introductions to the four parts of this book; to Dalia Buzin and Danielle Salti for their thorough copyediting of the manuscript; and to Laura C. Hargrave, who was of enormous help in the textprocessing and typesetting stages of this book.

We have had, in addition, the capable assistance of the staff of the departments of sociology at the University of Alberta and at the Memorial University of Newfoundland. We are particularly grateful to Linda Abbott, Marilyn Furlong, and Judi Smith. The manuscript was produced with the help of the University of Alberta's computerized textprocessing facilities, an extraordinary technical aid which permitted the rapid production of this book. Memorial University of Newfoundland awarded a SSHRC General Grant to one of the editors. The University of Alberta provided a grant which helped defray the cost of translation. We are grateful to Dr. Gordin Kaplan, vice-president (research) for this financial support.

Introduction:
The Development of the Sociology of Knowledge

Nico Stehr and Volker Meja

The sociology of knowledge is even now often regarded as a rather atypical and in some respects unique speciality of sociology;[1] in the North American context, for example, it still retains a strong "European" flavor and influence.[2] Though a recognized sociological *speciality* since the late 1920s, its subject matter has always been a major part of the intellectual domain of sociology itself. Moreover, it has, perhaps to a greater degree than other sociological specialities, also met with considerable interest from scholars in other social and human sciences. This may be because the sociology of knowledge has at times been regarded as representing a kind of Copernican revolution in the analysis of cultural products.[3]

The Classical Sociology of Knowledge

The recognition that knowledge in the *broadest sense*[4] is context-dependent and somehow constrained by social factors is of recent origin, as is sociology itself. Sociology could only arise after the dogma of a congruence between natural and social inequality had fallen into disrepute. The French philosophers of the Enlightenment and the Scottish moral philosophers were among the first to recognize that all social differences also had social origins and were thus the result of factors subject to human control.[5] They were also aware that a wide range of social, economic, and political factors shape the genesis, structure, and contents of human consciousness. However, these early reflections on the effect of social conditions on consciousness did not crystallize into a more systematic examination of the questions that later became a focus of the sociology of knowledge. Nevertheless, some of these early writings, which either denied the very possibility of a *sociology* of knowledge or which represent

1

first tentative steps in the direction of a sociological examination of knowledge, must be acknowledged as intellectual precursors of the sociology of knowledge.

The histories of science and philosophy, but also of philosophy and epistemology more generally, can be read as an effort to demonstrate that any *sociological* analysis, especially of the "higher" forms of knowledge such as scientific knowledge, is inevitably seriously flawed. Philosophers have extended considerable effort in order to demonstrate that a sociology of knowledge is neither possible, necessary, nor desirable. Immanuel Kant, for example, argued that while there cannot be perception without conception, the constitutive components of conception remain a priori. Similarly, empiricists of various persuasions have maintained that (scientific) knowledge is warranted by direct experience which is unaffected by social conditions. At best, these philosophies maintain, extratheoretical factors influence the genesis of ideas but not the structure and the content of thought. In short, otherwise quite different philosophies of knowledge have often shared an explicit rejection of the kind of doubt and suspicion which sociological approaches to knowledge are believed to invariably generate and perpetuate, and they have instead aimed at overcoming doubt by placing knowledge on a firm foundation, frequently outside the realm of sociohistorical existence. But these efforts, in their very concern with the possibility of knowledge about knowledge, have nonetheless provided a significant impetus for a sociology of knowledge.

Among its precursors we must count Karl Marx, whose famous sub- and superstructure scheme, i.e. his assertion that there is, at least under certain historical conditions, a primacy of economic realities, a determination of the "ideological superstructure" by socioeconomic processes, has been particularly influential. Perhaps the sociology of knowledge represents even today, as has occasionally been argued, a struggle with this Marxist assertion. But even if this is an exaggeration, Marx's conception of a close affinity between social structure and culture continues to constitute the primary theme of the sociology of knowledge. The distinctly Marxist response to the basic sociology of knowledge assertion has resulted in some outstanding sociological analyses of problems of cultural production, for example in the works of Georg Lukács.

The French sociologist Emile Durkheim is usually regarded as a pioneer of the sociology of knowledge, even if he failed to develop a general model of the classificatory process from his assertions about the basic categories of perception and the ordering of experience (space, time, causality, direction), which he saw as derived from the social structure of simpler societies. Durkheim and Marcel Mauss, but also Lucien Lévy-Bruhl, examined the forms of logical classification of "primitive" societies and concluded that the basic categories of cognition have social origins. They were not prepared, however, to extend this kind of analysis to more complex societies. Their inquiry into the social foundations of logic generated considerable criticism of their guiding assumptions, and much of this criticism has withstood the test of time and continues to be invoked against a sociologically informed inquiry into knowledge. However, attempts are now underway to reconstitute, on a new theoretical basis, Durkheim and Mauss's central proposition that the classification of things reproduces the classification of men.[6]

Although Max Scheler, in the early 1920s, appears to have first used the term *Wissenssoziologie* (translated as "sociology of knowledge")[7] it was Karl Mannheim, only a few years later, who provided the most elaborate and ambitious programmatic foundation for a sociological analysis of cognition.

Max Scheler extended the Marxist notion of substructure by claiming that different "real factors" (*Realfaktoren*) condition thought in different historical periods and in different social and cultural systems in specific ways. Scheler's "real factors" have sometimes been seen as basically institutionalized instinctual forces and as representing a de-historized concept of substructure.[8] While Scheler is one of the major early figures of the sociology of knowledge, his insistence on the existence of a realm of eternal values and ideas nevertheless limits the usefulness of his notion of "real factors" for the notion of social and cultural (i.e. historical) change.

Mannheim, like Scheler, extends the Marxist concept of substructure by referring to the possibility — provided that they are conceived of as contexts of meaning — that biological elements (such as race), psychological elements (such as "drive for power") and spiritual or even supernatural phenomena, among others, may take the place of primary economic relations.[9] But Mannheim's contribution to the sociology of knowledge also represents exemplatory research into the social conditions associated with different forms of knowledge.[10] His analyses of competition as a cultural form, of conservative thought, of the problem of generations, and of economic ambition, for example, remain even today examples of the kind of first-rate analysis which the sociology of knowledge is capable of. For Mannheim, the sociology of knowledge, as general social inquiry, is destined to play a considerable role in the intellectual and political life of society, particularly in an age of dissolution and conflict, by examining sociologically the very conditions which have given rise to competing ideas, political philosophies, ideologies, and diverse cultural products. According to Mannheim, the sociology of knowledge must also be a *diagnosis of its time* and provide practical solutions in an age of disenchantment and disorientation.[11]

The widespread and controversial appeal of the sociology of knowledge at the time of its inception owes much to this ambitious formulation of its aims, which go far beyond anything a sociological speciality has ever claimed for itself. But Mannheim's project, while achieving considerable critical acclaim,[12] nevertheless also foreshadowed the subsequent reception and transformation of the sociology of knowledge into a sociological speciality, as sociology itself evolved increasingly into a professional activity clearly differentiated from philosophy, history, anthropology, economics, and linguistics,[13] and as it became transplanted into other societies and reflected the commitments of disciplinary traditions considerably different from those found in the Germany where it had first formulated its intellectual and political mission.

The Intellectual Status of the Sociology of Knowledge in Sociology

Even now, long after the originally rather ambitious program of the sociology of knowledge has been moderated or even abandoned, and in spite of its recognition as a legitimate sociological discipline, this recognition itself remains impeded by the pervasive perception of the sociology of knowledge as a relatively marginal sociological speciality.[14]

This observation can be corroborated, for instance, by the fact that the percentage of sociologists with interests in the sociology of knowledge had actually declined by 1970,[15] reflecting a perception that it had somehow exhausted its intellectual resources long before its extensive program was realized. This situation has recently changed rather dramatically, however. We are now witnessing a renewal of interest in the sociology of knowledge, perhaps even a kind of renaissance. The contributions in this volume are themselves a part of this renewal and transformation of the sociology of knowledge, its established boundaries, issues, and solutions.

It might therefore be beneficial to devote the remaining sections of this introduction to some brief observations, which may help to explain why the sociology of knowledge is presently experiencing a renewal and change of direction. While we have so far referred to significant work in the contemporary sociology of knowledge, we shall now focus upon some issues associated with the unusual history and status of the sociology of knowledge within sociology.

Rather than adhering strictly to one of the contending theories of the development of science, scientific disciplines or specialities,[16] we prefer to take up several themes which may help to illuminate the peculiar development and the intellectual status of the sociology of knowledge. The following five themes are especially significant here: (1) the origin of the sociology of knowledge and its intellectual development and institutional establishment within sociology; (2) closely related to this, its dogmatic history as presented, for instance, in textbooks, articles, and essays reviewing its development and status; (3) the paradigm of the sociology of knowledge;[17] (4) its limits; and (5) its possibilities.[18] Our primary concern here is to critically review the representative attitudes of social scientists with sociology of knowledge interests, since these views have until recently largely determined the characteristic evolution and status of the sociology of knowledge.[19]

Reconstructions of the Development of the Sociology of Knowledge

Karl Mannheim has provided us with a detailed description of the social conditions and processes which contributed to the emergence and differentiation of the sociology of knowledge. A comparable reflexive examination is absent from virtually all subsequent efforts in the sociology of knowledge, although there are occasional indications of a recognition that this may indeed be an important problem. Robert K. Merton, for instance, raises the question how such a speciality as the sociology of knowledge, with its deep roots in German society and culture, was able to establish itself in North America in the first place, particularly in view of the fact that the receptiveness of North American social scientists and philosophers to the sociology of knowledge cannot be explained merely in terms of the immigration of German sociologists to the United States. Merton argues that

American thought proved receptive to the sociology of knowledge largely because it dealt with problems, concepts, and theories which are increasingly pertinent to our contemporary social situation, because our society has come to have certain characteristics of those European societies in which the discipline was initially developed.[20]

However, Merton does not give us a detailed description of the social crisis conditions of the American society to which he refers, and one might argue that the immediate postwar period in North America, far from being characterized by conditions of social, economic, and political crisis, was rather a period of continuous economic growth with few if any major societal upheavals. It should also be pointed out that the process of dissemination and acceptance of the sociology of knowledge in North America involved its *transformation*. While it is well known and perhaps even self-evident that the Nazi era in Germany represents a decisive turning point for the sociology of knowledge, the precise nature of its transformation has received far less attention, particularly in the United States.

The North American transformation of the sociology of knowledge during the process of acceptance mentioned here begins in the mid-thirties with influential reviews of the English edition of Karl Mannheim's

Ideologie und Utopie, by Hans Speier in the *American Journal of Sociology*, and by Alexander von Schelting in the *American Sociological Review*, as well as with Talcott Parsons' review in the *American Sociological Review* of Alexander von Schelting's book *Max Webers Wissenschaftslehre* (Max Weber's Theory of Science), which deals at length and critically with Karl Mannheim's sociology of knowledge. These reviews are an initial (and, in retrospect, successful) attempt to "normalize" the sociology of knowledge, that is, to argue that a genuine *sociology* of knowledge must be what Parsons called a positive sociology of knowledge by restricting itself to *sociological* inquiries into the formation of knowledge.

While standard texts on the history of sociology tend to disagree about such issues as when and where sociology originated, who the major theorists are, which results are significant, which issues warrant investigation, and how they can be resolved, it is also evident that the reconstructions of the development of the sociology of knowledge are, by and large, fairly unproblematic. The development of the sociology of knowledge itself may roughly be described as having gone through three different phases.

The first phase includes the theoretical approaches of the *forerunners* of the sociology of knowledge proper. Francis Bacon, Auguste Comte, Karl Marx, but also Friedrich Nietzsche, Vilfredo Pareto, and Sigmund Freud are commonly counted among these intellectual pioneers of the sociology of knowledge.[21]

The second phase consists of the process of establishing the sociology of knowledge as an identifiable, independent speciality of the human sciences. Max Scheler and Karl Mannheim in Germany and, even earlier, Emile Durkheim, Lucien Lévy-Bruhl, and Marcel Mauss in France, are the most significant figures here.

This phase is followed by another phase which is still recognizable in some of the essays contained in this book. It might be called the phase of *normalization*, since during this period the cognitive domain of the sociology of knowledge is defined much more narrowly, the external relations of the sociology of knowledge are now mediated by disciplinary traditions, issues initially considered relevant are no longer considered *sociologically* significant, and, last but not least, a "solution" to a number of initially unresolved questions is thought to have been found.

Such a normalization of the sociology of knowledge was achieved to a considerable extent by assimilating the sociology of knowledge to the then predominant conception of science in sociology, which interpreted the cognitive processes of science primarily in terms of a logical rather than sociohistorical point of view. The special epistemological status attributed to scientific knowledge led, of course, to the fact that sociologists for the longest time refrained from examining scientific knowledge sociologically.[22] Only recently has a radical reorientation in the sociology of knowledge taken place in this regard, once again on the basis of philosophical reflections. Foremost is a revision of the traditional concept of scientific knowledge and of the theory of scientific progress. As a result, the epistemological vocabulary has become increasingly sociological. The effect of these developments in the philosophy of science, the history of science, and in a variety of substantive social science disciplines and specialities (for example, anthropology and linguistics) on the sociology of knowledge is likely to lead to a reevaluation of its history and of the whole program of the classical sociology of knowledge.[23]

The Paradigm of the Sociology of Knowledge

Nearly all reconstructions of the paradigm of the sociology of knowledge agree that it is concerned with "existentially connected" thinking (*seinsverbundenes Denken*) or, even more generally, with an "investigation of the relations between knowledge and society."[24] In view of this comprehensive characterization of the scope of the sociology of knowledge, it is rather surprising that it should ever have been regarded as a mere "specialty" among so many other sociological specialties. Downplaying the actual and the possible significance as well as the implications of the sociology of knowledge has apparently been one of the strategies of sociologists in attempting to achieve the legitimation of the sociology of knowledge as *sociology*. If, just like other sociological specialties, the sociology of knowledge is legitimated by its specialized topic of inquiry, any far-reaching claims are precluded from the outset. Karl Mannheim's attempt to transcend specialized sociology in the direction of a philosophically oriented sociology is, by contrast, an example of a more comprehensive understanding of both sociology and the sociology of knowledge.[25] Mannheim writes:

But what is decisive is that in Germany this possibility, which exists for almost all men now living — namely, to enlarge one's view of the world and to this end avail oneself of the method of sociology — eventually exceeds the problem area of this special discipline. The sociological problem constellation in the narrower sense transcends itself in two directions — in the direction of philosophy and in the direction of a politically active world orientation.[26]

And in regard to the epistemological relevance of the sociology of knowledge Mannheim claims:

The sociology of knowledge, however, is in a position to provide a peculiar kind of factual information concerning the various truth concepts and epistemologies — factual information which itself has epistemological implications that no future epistemology may overlook.[27]

The reconstruction of the sociology of knowledge by sociology of knowledge specialists in the post-Mannheim period, by contrast, is characterized by an increasing renunciation of the *general* claims of the sociology of knowledge. This has sometimes led to difficulties. It is, for instance, hardly justified to maintain, on the one hand, that the sociology of knowledge is merely another sociological specialty, and to insist, on the other hand, that its general objective is the analysis of the relations between knowledge and society, and that the relationship between thinking or culture and social processes in the broadest sense is constitutive of human thought and action. Questions about such issues as the social causes of deviant behavior or the evolution of bureaucratic organizations can therefore hardly be granted similar status and have comparable implications for sociological theory and research generally. The sociology of knowledge can only be successful if the delimitation of the paradigm of the sociology of knowledge is overcome. Mannheim argues pointedly:

It is out of the question that a certain analysis should be stopped short once and for all at the most crucial point merely because the recognized domain of a different scientific department allegedly begins there (a mode of procedure typical of the bureaucratized organization of science).[28]

It is of course possible that the observed stagnation of the sociology of knowledge in the past few decades may, at least in part, have resulted from the fact that its original concerns became those of general sociological theory or of the theoretical perspectives of other sociological specialties and, thus, are no longer explicitly interpreted and identified as issues of the sociology of knowledge. This is precisely what Lewis Coser observes for the situation in the United States:

As the sociology of knowledge has been incorporated into general sociological theory both in America and in Europe, it has often merged with other areas of research and is frequently no longer explicitly referred to as sociology of knowledge. Its diffusion through partial incorporation has tended to make it lose some of its distinctive characteristics. Thus, the works of Robert K. Merton and Bernard Barber in the sociology of science, the works of E.C. Hughes, T.H. Marshall, Theodore Caplow, Oswald Hall, Talcott Parsons, and others in the sociology of the professions and occupations, and — even more generally — much of the research concerned with social roles, may be related to, and in part derived from, the orientation of the sociology of knowledge. Many practitioners of what is in fact sociology of knowledge may at times be rather surprised when it is pointed out that, like Monsieur Jourdain, they have been "talking prose" all along.[29]

The incorporation and integration of the issues of the sociology of knowledge into other sociological specialties,[30] as assessed by Coser, also indicates that the sociology of knowledge cannot easily be seen as merely one sociological specialty among many others. The partial incorporation of sociology of knowledge issues by other areas, in particular by specialties with a history of extensive empirical research, is associated with a neglect of foundational issues initially considered extremely important, in particular the neglect of epistemological issues.

Among the central issues of the sociology of knowledge are, according to Merton,[31] the following:

1. Where is the existential basis of cognitive products located?
2. Which cognitive products are subjected to sociological analysis?
3. What is the correlation between cognitive products and existential basis?
4. What are the manifest and latent implications of such correlations?
5. Under what conditions *or* at what point in time can these assumed correlations be observed?

It is hardly surprising that the attempts to define existentially connected knowledge in concrete terms are, on the whole, characterized by a relative lack of consensus. The sociology of knowledge is, at least in this respect, self-exemplifying. To the comprehensiveness of its domain corresponds an abundance of proposed solutions to those central issues identified by Merton.

Limitations of the Sociology of Knowledge

We have referred to the general thesis concerning the characterization of the research interests of the sociology of knowledge, the thesis of the existentiality of knowledge.[32] Most reconstructions of the sociology of knowledge are in nearly unanimous agreement about the assumption that its analysis of human thought and ideas has to be limited to the evidently shrinking section of knowledge which might be called "pathological knowledge,"[33] i.e. to knowledge which does *not* deserve the distinction of being called scientific knowledge. As Hans-Joachim Lieber[34] puts it, in the sociology of knowledge the subject of inquiry ought to be limited to "ideological knowledge." Furthermore, as has been pointed out by Dietrich Rüschemeyer, for example, the investigation of the relationship between ideas about reality and the existential processes toward which the sociology of knowledge strives,

does not question the validity of these ideas, although the beginnings of the sociology of knowledge may indicate otherwise, since its interest was focused on the study of the social conditions of distorted and false knowledge and on a critique of ideology.[35]

Coser finally refers to a third basic limitation of the sociology of knowledge typically mentioned in critical assessments of the discipline: the issue of relativism and the logical contradiction in which a "radical" "general" sociology of knowledge inevitably becomes entangled. Referring explicitly to Mannheim's program for the sociology of knowledge, Coser explains that

to him all knowledge and ideas, although to different degrees, are "bound to a location" with the social structure and the historical process. . . . From its inception, Mannheim's thesis encountered a great deal of criticism, especially on the grounds that it led to universal relativism. . . . If it is assumed that all thought is existentially determined and hence all truth but relative, Mannheim's own thought cannot claim privileged exemption.[36]

This indicates, in spite of Mannheim's repeated attempts to protect his own program from the charge of relativism, that this very charge has usually also been levelled against Mannheim himself. His work on the sociology of knowledge demonstrates that "even where a dissociation from the Marxist suspicion of ideology is attempted, a radical sociologizing of thought can easily succumb to relativism."[37] Generally, however, it may be said that most authors discuss the problem of epistemology, if at all, extremely superficially. This is of particular significance once we take into consideration how much emphasis the founders of the sociology of knowledge, Karl Mannheim in particular, placed on questions related to this issue. Furthermore, it is precisely because of its epistemological implications and claims that the sociology of knowledge initially achieved much of its admittedly negative resonance.[38] Part of the phase of normalization as a marked characteristic of the development of the sociology of knowledge in the past three decades is therefore also its intentional separation from such issues. However, the traditional division of labor in science — epistemology here, substantive scientific disciplines and specialties there — thus sanctioned and implied, at the same time, that the majority of *sociologists* of knowledge fully agreed with the critique levelled against it by philosophers, epistemologists and others. The critique is thereby taken for granted and considered as not needing closer scrutiny, for the sole reason that it also deals primarily with issues which are of no direct importance to the sociology of knowledge as a sociological specialty. Niklas Luhmann has emphasized the sterility that can result from such a turning away from philosophical reflections. Screening out philosophical considerations

[becomes], in turn, too confining. Introduced as a safeguard for unrestricted research against an overwhelming tradition, the impermeable boundary between science and philosophy creates, now that the power of tradition is abating, thought barriers and provincialism, and frequently a too narrow interpretation of that which, indeed, is already being thought.[39]

The openly neutral reconstructions of the sociology of knowledge are, of course, not the result of an unbiased attitude, but rather an acknowledgement of widespread criticism of the sociology of knowledge as conceived by its founders. However, it becomes increasingly obvious that the separation of important issues from the sociology of knowledge contributes to the undesirable consequence of a stagnant, unreceptive attitude toward significant intellectual developments in other disciplines. To screen the sociology of knowledge from philosophy, though, is quite compatible with the status of a sociological specialty. The new developments in the sociology of knowledge, in which most contributors to this book participate to a greater or lesser extent, represents the beginning of a new phase. This new phase is characterized, in particular, by a gradual lifting of certain taboos which had been part of the phase of normalization. Developments in epistemology, which questioned the traditional concept of science and of the development of scientific knowledge, have been a crucial factor in this phenomenon.[40] One of the results of the emerging concept of scientific knowledge is that in the sociology of knowledge the analysis of human knowledge is no longer necessarily restricted to one limited area of human thinking. A sociology of scientific and formal knowledge, still questioned by the founders, is now increasingly considered a real possibility.[41] Similarly, the critique of the sociology of knowledge, which for a long time had remained unchallenged, has in the course of these new developments itself become an issue for the sociology of knowledge. The problems of relativism, of self-refutation and of the necessity for a distinct separation of the context of discovery from the context of the justification of human knowledge is once again being seriously discussed. While there is even now bewilderment at hearing the term *absolute*, which continues to fascinate, it is beginning to lose, once again, its status as an unassailable conception in the philosophy of science.[42]

The renewed interest in the sociology of knowledge transcends the classical sociology of knowledge program in other respects as well. Importantly among these new interests figures a concern with what had been a shortcoming of the classical sociology of knowledge, which was frequently pointed out by its critics,[43] namely the absence of a satisfactory theoretical solution to the question of how the relation between the structure of human groups and consciousness arises, is maintained or evolves, and therefore changes in the course of social evolution.[44] One of the significant areas of inquiry within the contemporary sociology of knowledge is therefore concerned with this very issue. Barry Schwartz, for example, has proposed an ingenious solution to the "missing link" in the Durkheimian sociology of knowledge by advancing a theory that accounts for the linkage between social conditions and classificatory systems.[45] These developments in turn coincide with analogous attempts in other disciplines or related intellectual traditions, for example with the attempts by Mary Douglas[46] in anthropology and by Mary Hesse[47] in the philosophy of science, to specify, often on the basis of empirical research in a variety of social science disciplines, what the nature of the relation between perception and social structure exactly is.

But quite aside from these efforts, which often occur at the level of a micro-sociology of knowledge, another set of genuinely new themes is beginning to emerge as an important set of issues within the contemporary sociology of knowledge. Significant among these are the assertions about the growing power of knowledge in industrial or postindustrial society (Daniel Bell, Norbert Elias), about the emergence of a new class (Alvin Gouldner), and about the increasing influence of a new caste of priests (Helmut Schelsky).[48] All these writings share a common emphasis on the growing importance of specialized forms of knowledge for modern society and on the corresponding power which the carriers of this knowledge may exercise in it.

Possibilities of the Sociology of Knowledge

Lewis Coser is one of the few commentators on the sociology of knowledge who considers the ambitious original claims of its founders a challenge rather than an obsolete burden. In his survey of the history of the sociology of knowledge he comes to the following pertinent conclusions:

The sociology of knowledge was marked in its early history by a tendency to set up grandiose hypothetical schemes. These contributed a number of extremely suggestive leads. Recently its practitioners have tended to withdraw from such ambitious undertakings and to restrict themselves to somewhat more manageable investigations. Although this tendency has been an antidote to earlier types of premature generalizations, it also carries with it the danger of trivializations. Perhaps the sociology of knowledge of the future will return to the more daring concerns of its founders, thus building upon the accumulation of careful and detailed investigations by preceding generations of researchers.[49]

The very question, however, whether such a return to issues that may have already been raised by the founders of the sociology of knowledge, and the related question of whether a transformation of the sociology of knowledge is in fact possible or fruitful, is not only the result of purely intellectual efforts but also, according to the theory of the sociology of knowledge, itself a development influenced by societal conditions. Merton, for example, emphasizes that an interest in the sociology of knowledge is determined by certain cultural and social conditions of society. One factor among these conditions is that

with increasing social conflict, differences in the values, attitudes and modes of thought of groups develop to the point where the orientation which these groups previously had in common is overshadowed by incompatible differences. Not only do these develop different universes of discourse, but the existence of any one universe challenges the validity and legitimacy of the others. . . . Thought becomes functionalized.[50]

It must therefore at least be *indicated* that the reconstruction of the sociology of knowledge by the generation of sociologists succeeding the generation of the founders discussed here coincided with economic, political, and social conditions as well as academic and disciplinary circumstances which in their relative tranquility stood in marked contrast to the crisis conditions of the 1920s. The present new and renewed interest in certain issues first articulated by the classical sociology of knowledge, in contrast, "reflects," as in the earlier period when it was first developed, the experience of a crisis in contemporary society. The present transformation of the sociology of knowledge in its third phase is therefore not entirely surprising.

Notes

1. Specialties of a scientific discipline do not develop simultaneously. That is, the influence of important intellectual developments for instance may be quite direct and immediate on one specialty, yet greatly delayed or nonexistent in the case of other specialties. The receptiveness of a specialty, which is of course often highly differentiated internally, to cognitive innovations of neighboring specialties or even other disciplines depends, on the one hand, on the existing cognitive state of the specialty, e.g. on the degree of intellectual consensus among its members, but also on the existing social organization of the specialty. The apparent delay in responding to relevant developments in other social science specialties (for example, linguistics, the history of science, the philosophy of science, cultural anthropology) by sociologists interested in various forms of knowledge, which is still evident even in the sociology of knowledge, shows that the specialty had reached a point in its intellectual development which for the most part prevented further development. The uneven intellectual development of specialties represents also a challenge. In the case of the sociology of knowledge it requires a critical reexamination of the history of the specialty in light of relevant cognitive developments of other fields and it also requires a sociological perspective on knowledge that is capable of transcending the apparent shortcomings of the classical formulation of the sociology of knowledge. For a sociological examination of the development of scientific specialties, which is a prominent research site of the contemporary sociology of science, compare, for example, David Edge and Michael J. Mulkay, *Astronomy Transformed: The Emergence of Radio Astronomy in Britain* (New York: John Wiley & Sons, 1976), especially ch. 10.

2. See Robert K. Merton, "The sociology of knowledge," in *Social Theory and Social Structure* (New York: The Free Press, 1957), pp. 457-60; Bernard Barber, "Toward a new view of the sociology of knowledge," in *The Idea of Social Structure*, ed. Lewis A. Coser (New York: Harcourt Brace Jovanovich, 1975), pp. 103-16.

3. As Merton points out: "The 'Copernican revolution' in this area of inquiry consisted in the hypothesis that not only error or illusion or unauthenticated belief but also the discovery of truth was socially (historically) conditioned" (cf. Merton, ibid., p. 459).

4. We concur with Berger and Luckmann's contention that the sociology of knowledge must "concern itself with whatever passes for 'knowledge' in a society, regardless of the ultimate validity or invalidity (by whatever criteria) of such 'knowledge.'" See Peter Berger and Thomas Luckmann, *The Social Construction of Reality: A Treatise in the Sociology of Knowledge* (New York: Doubleday, 1967), p. 3; see also Gérard Namer's essay in this volume.

5. Cf. Ralf Dahrendorf, "On the origin of social inequality," in *Politics and Society*, ed. P. Laslett and W.G. Runciman (Oxford: Blackwell, 1962).

6. See David Bloor's essay in this book, as well as the book by Barry Schwartz, *Vertical Classification* (Chicago: University of Chicago Press, 1980).

7. A discussion of the problems associated with this translation of the German *Wissenssoziologie* as "sociology of knowledge" may be found in Kurt H. Wolff, "The sociology of knowledge and sociological theory," in *Symposium on Sociological Theory*, ed. L. Gross (New York: Harper & Row, 1959), p. 568.

8. See Kurt Lenk, *Von der Ohnmacht des Geistes* (Tübingen: Hopfer, 1959).

9. Karl Mannheim, "The ideological and sociological interpretation of intellectual phenomena," in *From Karl Mannheim*, ed. Kurt H. Wolff (New York: Oxford University Press, 1971).

10. The formulations chosen here to characterize Mannheim's conception of the nature of the relation between consciousness and society is intentionally ambiguous because Mannheim himself wanted to avoid the impression that he viewed the connection between ideas and social conditions in a simple, straightforwardly *causal* manner. The deliberate ambiguity of many of Mannheim's formulations, which recognize the complexity of the relation in question, has been the object of serious criticism, especially in North America, where assessments of the classical sociology of knowledge tend to prefer a deterministic and mechanistic language. See A.P. Simonds, *Karl Mannheim's Sociology of Knowledge* (Oxford: Clarendon Press, 1978), pp. 23-48.

11. More extensive accounts of the history of ideas in the sociology of knowledge and its forerunners may be found in Werner Stark, *The Sociology of Knowledge* (London: Routledge & Kegan Paul, 1958); Gunter Remmling, *Road to Suspicion* (Englewood Cliffs, N.J.: Prentice-Hall, 1967); Peter Hamilton, *Knowledge and Social Structure* (London: Routledge & Kegan Paul, 1974). A collection of readings which includes a number of selections relevant to the classical sociology of knowledge is James E. Curtis and John W. Petras, eds., *The Sociology of Knowledge* (New York: Praeger, 1970).

12. As a matter of fact, Mannheim's conceptions prompted the "sociology of knowledge dispute" in German social science toward the end of the Weimar Republic, in which some of the most influential social science scholars of the time participated. See Volker Meja and Nico Stehr, eds., *The Sociology of Knowledge Dispute* (London: Routledge & Kegan Paul, 1984).

13. Robert K. Merton sums up one of his early reviews of the accomplishments and faults of the sociology of knowledge with these remarks: "If this discipline is to bear fruit, if it is to provide insights and understanding of the complex interrelations of thought and society, it would seem advisable that its investigations be restricted to problems which lend themselves to test of fact." See Robert K. Merton, "The sociology of knowledge," *Isis* 32 (1939): 502-3.

14. See also Barber, op. cit.

15. North American data for the year 1970 indicate that the sociology of knowledge ranks relatively low in comparison to a number of other sociological specialties. These data may not be conclusive, since the members of the American Sociological Association, the source of these data, were questioned about their interest in the sociology of knowledge as well as the sociology of science; nevertheless, it can be generally inferred that the number of sociologists claiming interest in the sociology of knowledge corresponds roughly to the number of sociologists interested in small groups, rural sociology, or industrial sociology (cf. Nico Stehr and Lyle Larson, "The rise and decline of areas of specialization," *The American Sociologist* 7 [1972]: 3, 5-6). The same applies to the situation in other countries. Data re-

cently presented by Günther Lüschen show that in West Germany between 1948 and 1977 the number of articles fully devoted to the sociology of knowledge in such major sociological journals as *Kölner Zeitschrift für Soziologie und Sozialpsychologie, Soziale Welt* and *Zeitschrift für Soziologie* came to a total of seventeen. Even if those articles which deal with such subjects as "ideology" or "culture" are added to this list, the impression remains that since the postwar era the sociology of knowledge seems to have been a rather neglected area of inquiry in Germany as well. Lüschen's classification of sociological publications by period and subject matter shows, furthermore, no significant trend in the degree of interest in the sociology of knowledge during this time period. Similar observations apply to book publications included in the investigation (cf. Günther Lüschen, "Die Entwicklung der deutschen Soziologie in ihrem Fachschrifttum," in *Deutsche Soziologie seit 1945. Entwicklungsrichtungen und Praxisbezug*, ed. Günther Lüschen, Special Issue 21 of the *Kölner Zeitschrift für Soziologie und Sozialpsychologie*. (Opladen: Westdeutscher Verlag, 1979), pp. 169-92. Rolf Klima's analysis of the development of the teaching of sociology at West German universities between 1950 and 1975 gives a similar picture (cf. Rolf Klima, "Die Entwicklung der soziologischen Lehre an den westdeutschen Universitäten 1950-1975," in Günther Lüschen, ed., ibid., pp. 221-50).

16. See Michael J. Mulkay, "Drei Modelle der Wissenschaftsentwicklung," in *Wissenschaftssoziologie*, ed. Nico Stehr and René König (Opladen: Westdeutscher Verlag, 1975), pp. 48-61.

17. The term paradigm is used in this context in the same sense in which it is used by Robert K. Merton in his survey essay on the sociology of knowledge, first published in 1945 (Robert K. Merton, "The sociology of knowledge," in *Twentieth Century Sociology*, ed. Georges Gurvitch and Wilbert E. Moore (New York: 1945), pp. 366-40. Also in Robert K. Merton, *Social Theory and Social Structure*, op. cit. In the context of this survey of the major contributions to the sociology of knowledge, which has been particularly influential for the reception and the status of the specialty in North America, Merton introduces a "paradigm of the sociology of knowledge" essentially consisting of a brief catalogue of the most important issues which can be raised in connection with the basic thesis of the sociology of knowledge, that knowledge is affected by social conditions.

18. One of the striking features of the reconstructions of the history and the status of the sociology of knowledge is the consensus which emerges from these writings undertaken by different authors at different times and in different societies. The consensus extends to a wide range of issues significant in the sociology of knowledge, for example, the boundaries of the specialties, its accomplishments or lack thereof, its limits and pitfalls, its characteristic features and excessive ambition. Part of the same consensus is that the sociology of knowledge, in Mary Hesse's formulation, "is a notorious black spot for accidents both sociological and philosophical. The theses connected with it are regarded by some as so clearly subversive of all good order and objectivity as to be beyond the pale of rational discussion, and by others as part and parcel of a variety of nonscientific commitments in ideology, morals and politics" (Mary Hesse, *Revolutions and Reconstructions in the Philosophy of Science* (Brighton: Harvester Press, 1980), p.30. Another common emphasis is on attempts to incorporate sociology of knowledge issues into other sociological specialties, for instance, into role theory, mass communications, sociology of labor, sociology of organizations and social psychology, in order to demonstrate how *sociological* its issues are. And this of course means that there is agreement in these reconstructions that a number of themes which were once an integral part of the classical sociology of knowledge are now outside of the proper domain of a *sociology* of knowledge; for example, questions which pertain to the validity of knowledge-claims or the problem of relativism are generally seen as outside the domain of the sociology of sociology (cf. Nico Stehr and Volker Meja, "The Classical Soci-

ology of Knowledge Revisited," *Knowledge: Creation, Diffusion, Utilization* 4(1982): 33-50.

19. The prevailing reconstruction of the sociology of knowledge can be ascertained by examining selected but nevertheless representative (encyclopedic) essays whose explicit objective it is to give a comprehensive overview of the sociology of knowledge. See Robert K. Merton, op. cit.; Hans-Joachim Lieber, "Wissenssoziologie," in *Wörterbuch der Soziologie*, ed. Wilhelm Bernsdorf and Friedrich Bülow (Stuttgart: Enke, 1955), pp. 629- 33; Dietrich Rüschemeyer, "Wissen," in *Soziologie*, ed. René König (Frankfurt am Main: Fischer, 1981), pp. 352- 59; Lewis A. Coser, "Sociology of Knowledge," in *International Encyclopedia of the Social Sciences*, vol. 8 (New York: 1968), pp. 428- 35. An earlier but similar version of Coser's article appeared in Lewis A. Coser and Bernhard Rosenberg, eds., *Sociological Theory* (New York: Macmillan, 1964), pp. 667- 84.

20. Merton, "Sociology of knowledge," (1945), p. 386.

21. Ibid., p. 367; Dietrich Rüschemeyer, op. cit., p. 353; Hans-Joachim Lieber, op. cit., p. 631; Lewis A. Coser, op. cit., pp. 428-31.

22. It is true that many of the contributors to the classical sociology of knowledge were equally reluctant to extend the boundaries of the sociology of knowledge to scientific knowledge. Karl Mannheim, for example, was characteristically ambivalent insofar as he both disassociated himself but also endorsed a restrictive conception of the specialty (see Michael J. Mulkay, *Science and the Sociology of Knowledge*, [London: George Allen & Unwin, 1979], for a discussion of past and present efforts by sociologists of knowledge to either refrain from or defend a sociology of scientific knowledge). Joseph Ben-David, on the other hand, has argued that sociologists have rejected a "general" sociology of knowledge from the point of view of the "epistemologies prevailing among sociologists (at the time), according to which 'rationality' as conceived by scientists is a sufficient basis for the acceptance or rejection of theories, requiring no further social underpinning," and therefore not, as indicated here, primarily on the basis of the then prevailing epistemology which denied any significant impact of extraneous factors on the "context of justification" of knowledge claims advanced by the scientific community (see Joseph Ben-David, "The sociology of scientific knowledge," in *The State of Sociology*, ed. James F. Short, Beverly Hills, Calif.: Sage, 1981, p. 43).

23. Part of the renewed interest in the history and the nature of the classical sociology of knowledge are the publication of previously unpublished manuscripts from this era, for example Karl Mannheim's *Structures of Thinking*, ed. and intro. by David Kettler, Volker Meja, and Nico Stehr (London: Routledge & Kegan Paul, 1982), and *Konservatismus*, ed. and intro. by David Kettler, Volker Meja, and Nico Stehr (Frankfurt am Main: Suhrkamp, 1984).

24. Hans-Joachim Lieber, op. cit., p. 629.

25. Karl Mannheim, "Zur Problematik der Soziologie in Deutschland," *Neue Schweizer Rundschau* 22 (1929), reprinted in *Der Streit um die Wissenssoziologie*, vol. 2, ed. Volker Meja and Nico Stehr (Frankfurt am Main: Suhrkamp, 1982), pp. 427-37. A similar programmatic statement of Mannheim's can be found in his "Announcement" written on the occasion of taking over the editorship of the series *Schriften zur Philosophie und Soziologie* originally founded by Max Scheler and published by Friedrich Cohen, Bonn. In the "Announcement" (1929) Mannheim writes: "Collaboration between the two disciplines [philosophy and sociology] should not obliterate boundaries, yet mutual stimulation should be one aspiration. Neither displacing the initially philosophical context of inquiry with sociology, nor burying empirical methods under empty speculation in the social sci-

ences can be desirable. Co-operation can have but one purpose, namely that philosophical questions can become a part of this newest level of world orientation in science and life, and that sociology in the attempt to permeate reality empirically keeps its investigative impulses always uniformly centered. Philosophy gives up on itself if it does not deal with contemporary problems, sociology if it loses the center of its inquiry."

26. Kurt H. Wolff, ed., *From Karl Mannheim*. (New York: Oxford University Press, 1971), p. 263.

27. Ibid., p.259; see also Nico Stehr, "The magic triangle," *Philosophy of the Social Sciences* 11(1981): 225-29.

28. Ibid., p. 259.

29. Lewis A. Coser, op. cit., p. 432; see also Dietrich Rüschemeyer, op. cit., pp. 354- 59.

30. Robert K. Merton's influence on this development in the United States was instrumental, especially through his works on mass communications (in connection with Paul F. Lazarsfeld) and the sociology of science; see, for example, his comparison of *Wissenssoziologie* and mass communications research in *Social Theory and Social Structure*, op. cit., pp. 440-55.

31. Robert K. Merton, "Sociology of knowledge" (1945), p. 372.

32. For example Lewis A. Coser, op. cit., p.428, or Hans-Joachim Lieber, op. cit., p. 629.

33. Mary Hesse, op. cit., p. 32.

34. Hans-Joachim Lieber, op. cit., p. 633.

35. Dietrich Rüschemeyer, op. cit., p. 352.

36. Lewis A. Coser, op. cit., p.430.

37. Hans-Joachim Lieber, op. cit., p. 633.

38. The sociology of knowledge dispute centering on Mannheim's work at the end of the 1920s and the beginning of the 1930s is presented and discussed in our two-volume book: Volker Meja and Nico Stehr, eds., *Der Streit um die Wissenssoziologie* (Frankfurt am Main: Suhrkamp, 1982). An abridged English edition is forthcoming: Volker Meja and Nico Stehr, eds., *The Sociology of Knowledge Dispute* (London: Routledge & Kegan Paul, 1984).

39. Niklas Luhmann, *Zweckbegriff und Systemrationalität* (Frankfurt am Main: Suhrkamp, 1977), p. 9. See also Luhmann's essay in this volume.

40. Among the contributions which have been highly critical of the dominant concept of science and its conception of progress of scientific knowledge, as represented for example in the work by Carnap, Hempel, Nagel, and Popper, are: Thomas S. Kuhn, *The Structure of Scientific Revolutions* (Chicago: University of Chicago Press, 1962); Paul K. Feyerabend, *Against Method* (London: NLB, 1975); Imre Lakatos, *The Methodology of Scientific Research Programmes* (Cambridge: Cambridge University Press, 1978); Stephen Toulmin, *Human Understanding* (Princeton: Princeton University Press, 1972). Some of the writings in which these ideas are reviewed from the point of view of the sociology of knowledge are: Barry Barnes, *Scientific Knowledge and Sociological Theory* (London: Routledge & Kegan Paul, 1974); Barry Barnes, *Interests and the Growth of Knowledge* (London: Routledge & Kegan Paul, 1977); David Bloor, *Knowledge and Social Imagery* (London: Routledge & Kegan Paul, 1976); and Michael Mulkay, *Science and the Sociology of Knowledge* op. cit.

41. Such an extension of the sociology of knowledge domain has not gone unchallenged either within the philosophy or the sociology of science (for instance, Joseph Ben-David, op. cit.). However, the removal of some of the intellectual barriers against the possibility of a sociology of scientific knowledge has, for the time being, merely opened up an area of inquiry but has not decided how the relation, and how the possible sociohistorical changes in the very nature of the relation, are best examined or, for that matter, detected in the first place.

42. As Fritz Mauthner observes in his dictionary of philosophy first published at the beginning of this century: "Only those good people and bad musicians among the philosophers whose intention it is to defend and discover the absolute and eternal moral truths, will not hear of a relativity of *all* knowledge; thither is their reward" Fritz Mauthner, *Wörterbuch der Philosophie*, vol. II (Zürich: Diogenes, 1980), p. 308. First edition 1910/11.

43. For instance, Robert K. Merton, "The sociology of knowledge " (1945) in *Social Theory*, op. cit.

44. Norbert Elias, in particular, has referred to the gap in theory in the sociology of knowledge concerning the long-term development of knowledge and therefore of empirical or theoretical inquiry into the possible evolutionary changes in the relationship between consciousness and society. However, Elias not only identifies such a gap but actually proposes an interesting theoretical solution. See Norbert Elias, "Sociology of knowledge: new perspectives," *Sociology* 5(1971): 149-168, 335-370.

45. Barry Schwartz, *Vertical Classification* (Chicago: University of Chicago Press, 1981).

46. Mary Douglas, *Implicit Meanings* (London: Routledge & Kegan Paul, 1975).

47. Mary Hesse, op. cit.

48. Daniel Bell, *The Coming of Post-Industrial Society* (New York: Basic Books, 1973); Alvin W. Gouldner, *The Future of Intellectuals and the Rise of the New Class* (New York: Continuum, 1979); Helmut Schelsky, *Die Arbeit tun die anderen* (Opladen: Westdeutscher Verlag, 1975). See also Rudolf Bahro, *The Alternative in Eastern Europe* (London: New Left Books, 1978); and Radovan Richta, *Politische Ökonomie des 20. Jahrhunderts* (Berlin: Makol, 1971).

49. Lewis A. Coser, op. cit., p. 433.

50. Robert K. Merton, "The sociology of knowledge," op. cit., p. 368.

Part I
Fundamental Issues

Introduction

The contributions in this part update the classic debate on the possibility of overcoming the distorting effects of ideology upon thought. Gabel, Ansart, Bloor, and Mulkay vindicate the central tenet of the sociology of knowledge, to wit: that there is no privileged site of speech but instead a field of perpetual conflict between partial perspectives wherein consciousness is socially rooted yet capable, under special cirumstances, of transcending social constraints.

Joseph Gabel tackles the question of whether nonideological consciousness is possible, that is, whether there are groups with a special vocation for undistorted thought, and, beyond that, whether we may envisage an historical stage in which discourses of power have withered away. After reviewing the inadequacies of the Marxist answers to this question, Gabel defends Mannheim's argument for the possibility of political disengagement as a path to greater objectivity. Mannheim, Gabel insists, deposited his hopes with the intellectuals — not as a class but as a pool of individuals potentially capable of overcoming conformism, utopianism, and ethnocentrism. Viewed from this angle, Mannheim's thesis does not lack empirical support (witness the persistent relation between sociocultural marginality and critical insight in the development of social science). For Gabel, Mannheim managed to turn anomie into a positive factor in the growth of objectivity and creative thought. As for the reality or the possibility of an end to ideology, Gabel's skeptical remarks are pertinent. He argues that such a thesis — whether in its Marxist or its technocratic version — favors elite control over public life and fails to realize how scientific debates are often also ideological disputes. Gabel's position is clearly supported by the work of other sociologists of knowledge, such as Bloor and Mulkay. In short, ideology will stay with us in some form or another

— a perpetual parasite to the feats and the feasts of thought.

Pierre Ansart's essay takes Gabel's remarks one step further by showing how, despite the impossibility of ever attaining a "postideological" knowledge of the social world, sociology is perpetually engaged in the deconstruction of dominant world-views and in the reconstruction of knowledge through conceptualization and quantification procedures. Ansart proposes a tripartite classification of ideologies, according to their degree of generality and diffuseness. He thus distinguishes between political, social, and societal ideologies. This distinction allows us to show how social theory may, at any given time, be radical on one level of discourse and conformist on another. Ansart's essay is an original critique of all cumulative notions of social science development. He prompts us to inquire into the nature of creative ruptures and into various modes of interaction between science and ideology, so as to situate those moments of lucidity in which societal ideologies are challenged and recast.

David Bloor reexamines the classical claim of Emile Durkheim and Marcel Mauss in *Primitive Classification* that the classification of things reproduces the classification of men. Such a reexamination is timely since the empirical, theoretical, and logical criticisms of the Durkheim-Mauss thesis continue to be widespread and even now are endorsed by most social scientists. Durkheim and Mauss had argued that the sevenfold classification of space in Zuni cosmology was the outcome of a sevenfold Zuni social organization, in particular of a sevenfold arrangement of Zuni camps. The anthropological evidence for this claim was soon challenged, and the question was raised, how this thesis could possibly help in accounting for *successful* knowledge. It was argued that Durkheim and Mauss's claim contained inherent logical flaws.

To the list of objections Bloor adds the lack of an adequate and systematic model of the classificatory process itself in the Durkheim-Mauss thesis. Bloor contends, however, that the latter formula may be reconstituted on a new theoretical base by linking it to a general model of classification. He proposes the use of the network model developed by the philosopher of science Mary Hesse. Following an elaboration of this model, first formulated as an analysis of scientific inference, Bloor shows how empirical material from the history of science strongly supports the network model.

Finally, Bloor reexamines the standard objections to the Durkheim-Mauss thesis, and demonstrates how these can be overcome. He argues that Durkheim's work not only continues to be of central significance for the sociology of knowledge but that the scope of this significance has actually been considerably extended since Durkheim's work can now be regarded as applying not merely to "primitive" classification but to classificatory processes in general.

Michael Mulkay presents a well-argued defense of the sociology of knowledge against its own inhibitions to treat the exact sciences as topics of sociological investigation rather than as idealized role models. The first section of his essay presents two contrasting sociological perspectives on science: the standard view, which treats science as a special sociological case and regards scientific knowledge as epistemologically unique; and an alternative perspective, which argues that the procedures and conclusions of science are the contingent outcome of interpretive social acts.

Mulkay confronts us squarely with a case of interdisciplinary cultural dependency. There has been a persistent effort on the part of sociologists of knowledge and science in particular, and of sociologists in general, to exempt the "hard" sciences from the taint of sociological determination. This phenomenon is itself a topic for the sociology of knowledge. Perhaps as a result of a deep need to legitimate itself, sociology developed a mythical self-understanding, according to which it appeared as a "young discipline" following the trail blazed by the advanced sciences. This mythical self-understanding led to the fetishism of scientific method and to the "sacralization" of natural science, as if, by following the latter's recipes, one could earn solid credentials in social science research. Sociologists of knowledge, like Karl Mannheim, sought to contain the self-relativization of thought by restricting epistemological consequences of their approach to domains outside the natural sciences. Sociologists of science, for their part, sought to reconstruct social science after the model of natural science, reinforcing instead of deflating idealized versions of the latter.

Until quite recently, the specialty of sociology of science has been a sort of fan club of natural science. Its basic questions have been: How could this marvel of objectivity that is natural science develop? What are its normative warrants? Under which cultural conditions does it thrive? How are vocations pursued inside its universe? In their search for answers, sociologists of science sought to demonstrate the elective affinities between natural science and the ethos of modernity. Science appeared as an enterprise that was fully rational, correctible, public, nonconstrained, open-ended, liberal, and meritocratic. In short, as a world of truth that was also a world of freedom, reason, and justice. Today we treat this corpus of statements with a sort of bemused and critical distance, as when we sometimes watch old movies. The merit of Mulkay's paper lies in presenting and synthesizing the reasons for this current skepticism. The standard view of science does not stand serious scrutiny, which has been coming from philosophers, historians, and scientists themselves. Sociological enthusiasts of the standard view of science — very much like modernizing elites in some underdeveloped countries — are thus left with an obsolete piece of equipment that they had purchased as the latest novelty.

A major question addressed by Mulkay concerns the relationship between knowledge and practical application. Mulkay demonstrates that there is little empirical evidence of any clear or close links between both basic and applied scientific research and the great mass of technical developments. It is consequently hardly possible to maintain that the practical success of a scientific theory validates the theory. Mulkay's conclusions about the consequences and the status of scientific knowledge support the second sociological perspective on science, which maintains that scientific knowledge is in principle open to sociological analysis because it too is context-dependent, i.e. constituted differently in different social contexts and groups according to varying interests, purposes, conventions, and criteria of adequacy.

1

Is Nonideological Thought Possible?

Joseph Gabel

Ideology can be defined either as an ensemble of doctrinal theses pertaining to a group (the neutral concept of ideology), or as a form of political thought exhibiting a coefficient of distortion or occultation (P. Ansart), or, finally, as a discourse of power (the critical or polemical concept). The last two definitions are corollaries, since distortion and occultation are among the techniques of domination and, more generally, the techniques of political struggle. In the last sense the concept of ideology is inseparable from that of *false consciousness*. This clarification is necessary because the observation that a given social system is resistant to the discussion of ideas does not at all imply that it is immunized against the danger of false consciousness. In what follows, we will employ the second (polemical) concept of ideology except where another concept is specifically indicated. According to this second concept, the "ideological" perception of sociopolitical data is essentially a degraded perception, a *Depravat*, in the expression of a German author of the Weimar epoch, which is easier to understand than to translate.[1] Formulated from a sociological rather than an epistemological perspective, the problem is: are there any social groups (classes, strata, or organizations) that possess a specific vocation for nonideological thinking and, on the other hand, can humanity sooner or later achieve a stage of social evolution at which ideology, defined as the discourse of power (as a factor of occultation or distortion), has lost its reason for being? These are two aspects (one synchronic, the other diachronic) of the same problem.

The Marxist response is well known: it is bound up with Engels' famous theory. In a future and supposedly egalitarian and noncoercive society, ideology as the "discourse of power" will wither away along with the state; on the other hand, even before the beginning of the process of constructing socialism, the proletariat in struggle elaborates its class consciousness by transcending the reifying mystifications of capitalist ideology. This theory thus situates itself in a *historicist* perspective; the dominant class consciousness is false to the extent that this class refuses to become conscious of the historicity of social phenomena, a historicity which indicates the historical limits of its domination. "Heir to the future," according to the expression of a contemporary socialist author, the working class has no need to mistrust history; its consciousness is nonideological to the extent to which it is historicist. However, it is apparent that for some time now a tendency has been developing on the Marxist side which discards the historicist interpretation of this doctrine despite the textual evidence; in tandem, we observe attempts to "rehabilitate" ideology, the concealing and distorting character of which is scotomized.[2] Finally, the historical emergence of the "Stalinist phenomenon" and the tenacious persistence of its effects offer a persuasive demonstration of the vulnerability of proletarian consciousness to the danger of ideology. This vulnerability is the consequence of two factors: the utopian factor and the sociocentric one. In fact, the psychological conditions of class struggle simultaneously favor and presuppose the illusion of fighting for definitive solutions (the utopian factor); on the other hand, the instrument of this struggle (the party), and similarly the country or countries where this ideal is supposed to be in the process of realization, tend to occupy a privileged place in the logical universe of activists (the sociocentric factor). As an ideology, Stalinism is the extreme crystallization of this double tendency. It is thus by no means a matter of a simple "deviation," as Louis Althusser believes not without a certain naivety.[3]

When Mannheim attempted to substitute the intelligentsia for the proletariat as the potential bearer of a nonideological consciousness, he did not merely displace the solution of the problem from one social stratum to another; his approach has implications for epistemology. For Marx — and still more for Lukács — *political involvement* (*umwälzende Praxis*) is the source of authentic consciousness — and correlatively, the condition for the transcendence of ideology; for Mannheim, on the contrary, it would be noninvolvement, a contemplative attitude; one detects in his approach a faint whiff of a remote oriental influence. But Mannheim also persists in seeing himself as an *uncompromising historicist*, which leads to the unexpected and even paradoxical consequence that according to Mannheim's view the historicity of the historical process is better comprehended by a spectator than by an actor. Mannheim had no luck with the French public. His work, which had a real influence in Germany and the Anglo-Saxon countries, reached France in a mutilated and deformed version, thus becoming a predestined target of every sort of misinterpretation. Georges Gurvitch maintains that, according to Mannheim, "the intellectual elite would free knowledge from all social frameworks,"[4] doubly betraying Mannheim's thought with this reflection. Mannheim was a much too skillful sociologist of knowledge — and also much too close to Marxism — to seriously imagine that belonging to "the intellectual class," or even to the professoriate, could enable someone to think *outside of all social frameworks*; in addition, it is simply wrong to translate *"freischwebende Intelligenz"* as "intellectual elite."[5] But it should be added that Gurvitch quotes the (rather poor) English translation of *Ideologie und Utopie* and that Mannheim's notorious lack of conceptual precision is largely responsible for these misunderstandings.

In my opinion, the problem is essentially *axiological*. Ideology belongs simultaneously to the ontological and the axiological spheres (the *Sein* and the *Sollen*),[6] and this very admixture, unless disentangled, is undoubtedly one of the major causes of ideological distortion. It is quite obvious that persons belonging to the *freischwebende Intelligenz* are hardly in the position to abolish, as Gurvitch claims, the social determination of thought. It is impossible to imagine anyone capable of thinking outside of social frameworks; on this point the Durkheimian analyses (including those of M. Halbwachs) remain valid. But it is to some extent possible to attenuate the *axiological contamination of cognitive processes*. Furthermore — and this is a personal extrapolation of Mannheim's thought — the purported political noninvolvement of the intelligentsia is supposed to free the consciousness of this stratum from the burden of utopianism, which is an indispensable ferment of political action ("Il ne faut pas désespérer Billancourt," Sartre) and a source of false consciousness at the same time. In short, this outstanding work, which has been misunderstood if not ignored, offers an anticipatory critique not so much of the Stalinism of 1929 as of what it *would become a few decades later*. It should perhaps be added that it is an error to see in Mannheim's theory a sociology of the *intellectual class*. A social scientist of Mannheim's stature could not have been unaware of the existence of as many "intellectual classes" as there are social contexts, nor could he have been capable of overlooking the fact that a significant number of intellectuals participate (to a different degree depending on the country) in social struggles on the side of the proletariat. Mannheim's approach belongs more to a sort of political phenomenology than to a sociology of the intellectuals; the *freischwebende Intelligenz* is thus less a social stratum than an *ideal type* symbolizing the highest possible degree of freedom from alienating influences such as sociocentrism, conformism, and utopian spirit.

This theory, which has been so often criticized, is by no means absurd when interpreted in this manner; it even possesses a certain explanatory value for the present. Certain aspects of student contestation seem to confirm Mannheim's intuitions, and at the same time reveal their limitations.[7] The relatively high percentage of sociologists of Jewish origin has often been noted. But this observation holds primarily true for sociologists of historicist orientation — sociologists of knowledge and of ideology; in addition, this characteristic orientation is certainly not the consequence of an educational or biological ("racial") factor, but an effect of marginality.[8] The "demystifying" sociologist is ordinarily perceived as a *man of the Left*, essentially because of the Marxist influence to which he has often been subjected. However, two of the great figures of this tendency — Pareto and Sorokin — are neither Jewish nor leftists, but, curiously, somewhat *freischwebend* nevertheless: a Russian sociologist teaching at Harvard, and a Franco-Italian sociologist holding a chair in Switzerland.[9] In the case of Marx, the demystifier has often been contrasted to the utopian, the sociologist to the ideologue, with the somewhat facile explanation that the first element of each pair results from his commitment to the cause of a class which is the architect of the future, and which, consequently, is immunized against the danger of ideology. But Marx was to some extent also a *freischwebende* personage: a poorly converted Jew who had ceased to be Jewish without becoming Christian, a commoner married to an aristocrat, an intellectual who had failed in his university career, the eternal emigré, an accomplished polyglot. There remains little to add to what has already been said about the transformation of Marxism into an ideology, and about the roots of this transformation in the work of Marx. It is appealing to explain the demystifying dimension of his thought by his *freischwebende* personality and the ideologico-utopian dimension by his total commitment to a value system different from that of his original milieu.

It is obvious that the city is a natural reality and that man is by nature an animal destined to live in a city (a political animal); he who is without a city is, by nature and not by chance, a being either inferior or superior to man: he is like the one whom Homer reproached for having neither clan, nor law, nor home.[10]

This is a pioneering insight which applies to a large extent to Aristotle himself. Simplifying a little, one might say that there is a "bad" anomie which generates criminals and suicides and a "good" anomie which, by facilitating the bracketing of the axiological element in the perception of sociohistorical data, makes it possible to conjure the pitfall of ideologizing. I do not believe that it is worthwhile to look for more than this in Mannheim's thesis, which refers to a method of deideologization rather than to an actual social stratum.

   This question of a social stratum that is privileged in its relation to the trap of ideology has as a corollary the question of a social regime — whether imaginery or real — capable of reducing its "ideological consumption" to the point of reaching zero at the limit.

The distinction suggested above between the "neutral" and the "polemical" concept of ideology reveals its usefulness in this connection. A recent and most important historical event comes to mind: the Cultural Revolution in China. Despite the massive literature it has inspired, the historical significance of this revolution has so far hardly been elucidated, and it is an oversimplification to see it exclusively as an antibureaucratic reaction accompanied by egalitarian nostalgia. The antiintellectualist orientation of the Cultural Revolution, which was expressed in the campaign against the academics, is however undeniable, and so is the exceptional centralization of ideological production: the cult of Mao Tse Tung Thought, Mrs. Chiang Ching's "model operas," etc. The Chinese leaders of the period must have reached the not altogether unreasonable conclusion that ideologues were a luxury for a country confronted with urgent technological, economic, and medical problems. A simplistic Marxism is tempted to diagnose this as the forerunner of the "withering away of ideologies" corresponding to that of the class state. But the China of the Cultural Revolution was far from being free of false consciousness[11] and a country *without ideologues* is not necessarily a country *without ideology*.

Generally speaking, the theory of the withering away of ideology, conjoined with the hypothetical withering away of class society, suggests several observations:

1. Although following logically from a Marxist thesis, this theory is compatible with various non-Marxist interpretations of social evolution. "Even a qualified decline of ideological tensions," Jean Meynaud writes,

appears likely to facilitate the technicians' rise to power. The conditions of efficiency win out the more easily as partisan passions diminish. Even if they deny it, the techno-bureaucrats and experts contribute to reinforcing this tendency by their actions and sometimes by the mere desire to better serve the state. The "de-ideologization-technocratic" connection thus possesses a high degree of verisimilitude. Since technicist expansion has the reciprocal effect of creating the bases of a new decline of ideology, one wonders if the movement does not become self-perpetuating once a certain threshold has been crossed.[12]

It is noteworthy that a process of declining ideological tensions can be spontaneous in an affluent society, but may also be artificially induced in a totalitarian regime with identical results; the idea of a government of technicians is familiar to the Right; it played a certain role in the ideology of Vichy. Right-wing totalitarianism has an ambiguous position on this issue: on the one hand, it is a favorable terrain for the rise of false consciousness (racist consciousness being one example), and on the other hand, it provides a privileged status to scientific experts, especially as an irreplaceable auxiliary in the military effort.[13]

2. The displacement of the emphasis in public debate from the ideological toward the scientific *favors the dominance of elites in public life*, no matter what the general orientation of the political context, whether it be socialist, liberal, or conservative. Every moderately well-educated citizen can form a valid opinion on questions such as the advantages or disadvantages of the vote by district or the appropriateness of abolishing the death penalty; he can thus cast an informed vote. Only specialists with a sophisticated scientific education are able to cast a valid vote concerning the best solution to the problem of energy. Thus the scientific and technical knowledge of the elite takes on an ideological function since it becomes the instrument for maintaining a privileged position.

3. The example of contemporary political life shows clearly to what extent a supposedly scientific debate can be vulnerable to ideological parasitism;[14] even now the ecologists form a *political* party that must be reckoned with during electoral campaigns. In a society freed from its own internal tensions — as is supposed to be the case in a socialist society — this risk would no doubt tend to diminish, but external tensions can also become a source of ideological parasitism. Nuclear energy doubtless threatens the environment — to what extent must be left to the evaluation of scientists — but it also threatens the privileges of those who intend to monopolize the world's energy resources as an instrument of political power. Antinuclear movements can thus take on an ideological significance as the discourse of a power situated beyond the borders.

This notion of ideological parasitism leads us to a final problem, that of the possibility of a *scientific* thought free of all trace of ideology. Just like political ideology, scientific ideology is an instrument of legitimation and struggle; G. Canguilhem notes, however, that it is neither a *false consciousness* nor a *false science*.[15] In contradistinction to political ideology, it seeks a model and a reference in the scientific domain. Thus,

evolutionary ideology functions as a self-justification of the interests of a type of society, industrial society in conflict with both traditional society and with social demands. We find here once again the Marxist concept of ideology as a representation of natural or social reality, the truth of which resides not in what it says but in the silences it imposes.[16]

He who follows the path of Spencer's thought in the progressive development of his work, will discover that at first von Baer's biology and later Darwin's offered him a patron and a scientific guarantee for a project of social engineering in the English industrial society of the nineteenth century: the legitimation of free enterprise, and of the corresponding political individualism and competition. The law of differentiation ends up bringing support to the individual against the State. But if it ends up there explicitly, perhaps this is because that is where it began implicitly.[17]

This demonstration is seductive. Its weak point is that it applies equally well to *theoretical Darwinism*, which can also be considered as a legitimation of free enterprise, individualism, or competition. The criterion distinguishing between a scientific theory and a scientific ideology would seem to be situated at the level of the scholar's unverifiable intentions, and the boundary which Canguilhem believes to have drawn with precision[18] threatens to prove vague indeed.

At this point two ideas help us to clarify the problem: that of "ideological parasitism," discussed above, and the Marxist theory of reflection. The influence of the social context on the formation of scientific theory operates through many channels; the mechanism of "reflection," considered by a certain Marxism as exclusive, is certainly one of these channels. Darwinism "reflects" and projects onto the biological sphere the rough and ready marketplace of capitalist accumulation in that period; in doing so it offered a scientific justification for the latter and served an ideological function. But so it is every time reflection intervenes as a mechanism of mediation between society and knowledge. Thus the theory of social roles, first formulated around 1950 in a still highly conformist America and taken up later in a Europe fascinated with the American model, can be interpreted as an ideology of the *American way of life* as it was conceived in that period.

As for ideological parasitism, this is a phenomenon which few theories can avoid in a period of social tension and struggle. The most typical example is the debate on the heredity of acquired characteristics, which began in the laboratories but was rapidly contaminated by parasitic ideologies, both those of racist origin and their opponents.[19] In a crisis period this phenomenon can affect every discipline, including the most exact sciences. Could the hypothetical arrival of a classless society remedy this state of affairs? The spectacle of scientific life in those societies supposedly building socialism hardly inspires an optimistic response to this question.

Notes

Translated from the French by Andrew Feenberg

1. Gottfried Salomon, "Historischer Materialismus und Ideologielehre," *Jahrbuch für Soziologie*, vol. 2 (Karlsruhe, 1926).

2. *Pour Marx* (Paris: Maspero, 1972), p. 238, "ideology, as a system of representations, is distinguished from science by the fact that the practico-social function predominates over the theoretical function (or function of knowledge)." This definition scotomizes the distorting and concealing components of the ideological phenomenon while maintaining its character as an instrument of struggle (the "instrumental" concept of ideology). It thus contains the premises of a *rehabilitation of ideology*.

3. For more details on these two questions, the role of collective egocentrism in ideology and the Althusserian "critique" of Stalinism, I must refer to my two works, *Ideologies* (Paris:

Anthropos, 1974), pp. 14, 79ff; and *Ideologies II: Althusserienne et stalinisme*, passim (Paris: Anthropos, 1978).

4. G. Gurvitch, "Le problème de la sociologie de la connaissance," *Revue philosophique* (1958):444.

5. The German term *"freischwebende Intelligenz"* has been left untranslated throughout this paper; "Intellectual elite" as well as the even more common "free-floating intelligentsia" are misleading. A better, though still unsatisfactory, rendering is "socially marginal (or unattached) intelligentsia." (Eds.)

6. "Political ideologies always mix together judgments of fact with judgments of value, sometimes with greater, sometimes with lesser success. They express a perspective on the world and a will that is turned toward the future." Raymond Aron, *L'opium des intellectuels* (Paris:Calmann-Lévy, 1955), p. 246. Of course, there is no question of denying the reality or the importance of values in social life, but merely of criticizing the axio-cognitive confusion. In the Stalinist period, the overvaluation of Soviet reality hid the "Gulag phenomenon" from the eyes of sympathizers despite the existence of converging testimony (Kravchenko, Margarete Buber-Neumann, etc.) which we now know to have been worthy of confidence. "A well comprehended ideology critique would thus not aim to *destroy value systems* but simply to bring to the fore the fact that such systems do not belong to the sphere of rationality and are not scientifically verifiable." Tibor Hanák, *Ideológiák és korunk* (Ideologies and Our Time), (London: Szepcsi Csombor Kör, 1969), p. 18. To valorize one's fellow beings is a normal and respectable tendency; it becomes ideological only once this subjective valuation claims a borrowed rationality from biological science, thereby arrogating to itself both the status of a scientific approach and the right to devalorize what is other than itself. This helps to understand why *freischwebende* individuals are particularly well placed to take on the axio-cognitive confusion of ideological discourse. But it is also clear that, from a partisan standpoint, they may appear to be destroyers of traditional values and poisoners of the public spirit.

7. The movement of May 1968 was simultaneously demystifying and egalitarian. The first tendency has left lasting and positive traces, notably in the domain of sexual taboos (the struggle over discrimination against homosexuals) and also in the relations of teachers and students. The second tendency, the ideological character of which is underlined by the nonegalitarian orientation of the Eastern countries, led to openly antidemocratic demands, such as the suppression of standard national recruiting tests.

8. "Ideology is a global system of interpretation of the historical-political world. Because it expresses and valorizes a society or a group at a given time and place, it has a definite historical character. But it is ahistorical in that it idealizes a regime, a situation, and wishes to freeze the phenomena it expresses and interprets for all eternity. All ideology is reifying: it aims at the prolongation of a given state of affairs. In this sense, it is antihistorical." Jean Lacroix, *Le personnalisme comme anti-idéologie* (Paris: Presses Universitaires, 1972), p. 21. Deideologization is thus often dereification. But, on the other hand, since reification consists essentially in a "naturalistic" perception of social data (the Victorian economist Jevons explains the periodicity of economic crises by the periodic appearance of sun spots!), it turns out that a certain marginality accompanied by polyculturalism can facilitate the grasp of the autonomy of the social fact in distinction from Nature. Spencer's biologism, Comte's "social physics," the experimentalists of our day all represent the type of the "rooted" sociologist in the face of somewhat marginal "demystifying" thinkers such as Marx, Mannheim, Pareto, Veblen, and even Durkheim.

9. For more details, see my *Ideologies*, ibid., pp. 255, 291ff., as well as *Ideologies II*, ibid.

One of these examples concerns the Emperor Frederick II of Hohenstaufen, a *"freischwebende* intellectual" on the throne, master of nine languages, torn between the German, Italian, and Arab cultures, the true "inventor of the Renaissance" according to the expression of a German historian (Kantorowicz), and whose political and *scientific* work (*De arte venandi cum avibus*) contains a specific disalienating nuance. In the same spirit, I have tried to interpret the disalienating tendency of the Hungarian Marxist school (Lukács, his epigones, and Mannheim himself) as a consequence of the *freischwebende* situation of the intelligentsia of Budapest, at the crossroads of various cultural, religious and other influences ("Marxisme de carrefour").

10. Aristotle, *Politique* (Paris: Coll. Bude, 1968), p. 14. The same idea reappears in a somewhat different form on p. 15. As a resident without political rights, Aristotle was himself to some extent a *"freischwebende* intellectual," and one may well wonder if his exceptional political lucidity — he created political sociology practically from nothing — did not owe much to this situation.

11. This false consciousness of the Chinese Cultural Revolution was manifested especially in the *magical* aspects of the cult of Mao, aspects that were practically absent in the cult of Stalin.

12. Jean Meynaud, *Destin des idéologies* (Lausanne: l'auteur, 6 chemin de Mornex, 1961), p. 41.

13. Cf. in this regard rightist-inspired critiques of the teaching of philosophy in the high schools and of sociology in general.

14. Cf. Jean Baechler, *Qu'est-ce que l'idéologie* (Paris: Gallimard, 1976), pp. 160 and passim.

15. Georges Canguilhem, *Idéologie et rationalité dans l'histoire des sciences de la vie* (Paris: Vrin, 1977), p. 39.

16. Ibid., p. 43.

17. Ibid., p. 42.

18. Peter Kropotkin dedicated an entire work (*Mutual Aid*, 1912) to showing the importance of cooperative support in nature, in opposition to the Darwinians. This is the work of a great scientist and it is based on a strictly scientific method. His intention is, however, ideological; we know this to be the case because the author is also one of the outstanding figures of the libertarian movement. Is this theory or scientific ideology?

19. The debate over the heredity of acquired characteristics has been the object of positive parasitism by partisans of racism who believed they could find in it a scientific proof of their ideology, but also of a negative parasitism on the part of certain progressive biologists who reject a priori any critique of such acquisition precisely because it might lead to racism. Despite the generous inspiration of these latter, this is still a form of ideological parasitism, because a debate of this type should be settled in the laboratory and nowhere else.

2

Is All Social Knowledge Ideological?

Pierre Ansart

The question is of finding out whether thought, when its object is so-cial life, can avoid the trap of ideology, can serve as an introduction to an epistemological critique of sociology. This question is both irritating and necessary: irritating because it formulates suspicion, whereas the very thing the sociologist proposes to do is to confound the illusions and sur-mount the limitations imposed by the ideologies of his time; necessary be-cause only when we begin to ask this question do critical examination and verification force themselves upon us. In the realm of the social sciences, the suspicion of ideology plays a permanent role, which may be compared to the role played, in the realm of the natural sciences, by the recourse to verification procedures: it is a permanent weapon for purposes of control, of raising doubts, and of rectification.

To piercing suspicion of this sort, sociologists have quite often re-sponded in messianic style: Saint-Simon, Marx, and Durkheim proclaim that the official discourse on social and political life grows inside illusion, and that the first task is to break this yoke of ideology in order to consti-tute that positive science from which Auguste Comte expected the crown-ing completion of positive knowledge. In a variety of ways, sociology has, from its beginnings, lived off this myth of disillusion, this myth of demythification, with the distant goal of escaping ideological bias, with the immediate objective of reaching an epistemological break on the basis of which to develop, if not absolute knowledge then at least a body of knowledge accepted by all those who have been initiated into the same in-tellectual procedures.[1] "Our knowledge is not yet free from ideological bias, but it will be, as the critical efforts and the research process pre-sented here testify" — in such terms does the sociologist introduce his dis-course.

I shall propose here to set aside this messianic hope (the efficacy of

35

which should be questioned within the dynamics of research) and instead consider only the past of sociology and the monumental works which it has bequeathed. The history of this production is vast and imposing enough to permit a restating of the question in the following manner: has sociological science, in the past 150 years, realized the hopes of its founders? Has this body of knowledge — or have these bodies of knowledge — avoided ideological bias, and, if so, to what extent? It is, of course, impossible to answer this question exhaustively, but at least it offers us the opportunity to take up a fundamental problem once again, and to suggest a certain number of hypotheses.

Two aspects need to be emphasized. First, it is essential that we reflect upon the fact that sociological thinking is a kind of thinking which has been and continues to be constituted in an indirect manner, through a critical analysis that breaks down the spontaneous understanding of social reality and brings about not a total break between ideology and knowledge but a constant negation of their conjunction, thus permitting the emergence of a different type of knowledge. Second, now drawing upon research results rather than upon criticism, we shall be bound to suggest new hypotheses about the role of ideologies in sociological creation, for it seems to us that, in its conclusions, no sociological creation has been able to escape what Georges Gurvitch has called an "ideological coefficient."[2]

Any generalizing critique that discloses the persistence of schemes unconsciously reproduced in sociological constructs, and that uses them as a pretext for confusing sociological production with ideological reiteration, hides the fact that revolt against imposed models is, initially, an essential aspect of sociology. Beginning with the innovations of Proudhon, Marx, and even Herbert Spencer, even if to different degrees and with very different consequences, an opposition to imposed schemata and an intellectual destructuration of models suddenly emerges. Proudhon, in his *Premier Mémoire*, provides a list of the economic and legal dogmas which he proposes to deconstruct; Marx inaugurates the development of dialectical materialism with his denunciatory analysis of the "German ideologies"; Spencer, in his *Introduction to Social Science*, lists the ideological obstacles with which anyone aspiring to create a scientific work will have to struggle. The initial revolt combines two intentions, which indeed share in the foundation of this branch of learning: the intention to break with the schemata of the dominant body of knowledge, and, on the other hand, the intention to produce a scientifically founded body of knowledge. This dual intentionality must not be belittled; it is plainly expressed, and it encourages the work of breaking away from received notions and sustains its continuity.

What is important to emphasize here is not so much the manifest revolt as such but the methodologically reinforced character of this criticism and the employment of these methods and means. We shall have occasion to call to mind the fact that the revolt against the dominant ideology takes place within the much broader framework of sociopolitical conflicts; the sociology of social knowledge warns us of the constant interrelations between social contradictions, the dynamics of revolutions, and the discontinuities in the history of this type of knowledge. The historical aspects of the rejection of ideology are contained within the dynamics of social conflict, and, in the cases of Proudhon and Marx, but also in that of Durkheim, we can detect behind the epistemological revolt the confrontations to which that refusal is one response. The specificity of the break does not lie in that inaugural revolt but rather in the establishment and pursuit of procedures of deconstruction. The image of an "epistemological break" may lead to a split representation of the creation, as if there were a time of illusion and a time of science separated by the happy, heady moment of invention. The essential thing here is not the inaugural gesture of refusal, but the elaboration of efficient procedures for sustaining the break, making possible the uninterrupted practice of criticism. Hence the pages in which Saint-Simon or Auguste Comte speak of the urgent need for observation, however inadequate they may appear to be today, were historically important insofar as they gave shape to a new intellectual practice, dissolved traditional lines of reasoning, scrutinized the objects of experience in a new manner, and forced thought to deal with new objects. The proclamations of Saint-Simon, calling for the introduction into the "moral sciences" of the methods of observation proper to the natural sciences, symbolized this new work, whereby the dominant line of reasoning was suspended and replaced by the establishment of new procedures of investigation on new objects: social classes and their conflicts, the development of "productive faculties," and industrial society.

This undertaking of deconstruction is best illustrated by two examples: the process of sociological concept-formation, and the development of quantification. The point is not that this work has met with full success, but rather that it was carried out methodically and in an exemplary fashion, pressing the need to pursue it further and to take it up again. Marx's *Grundrisse der Kritik der politischen Ökonomie* does not complete the critique of the concepts of ordinary political economy but traces the movement of this work, and, indeed, one may argue that the entire Book I of *Das Kapital* is a sustained break, a work of a deconstruction of the concepts of commodity, price, wage, labor. Likewise, it matters little, as far as the history of sociology is concerned, that Quetelet was striving toward an unattainable goal in attempting to render the notion of the average man pertinent;[3] what does matter is that he dared to quantify what was considered nonquantifiable, thus furnishing an example, if not a model, of a methodological break at the very level of objects.

To our question, whether sociological thinking is inevitably ideological, our initial response is to contrast with this suspicion of ideology the continual efforts of those individuals determined to produce a break with tradition through observation, reconceptualization, and quantification. As early as in the nineteenth century, and without prejudging the results of this work, the major inquiries provide us with models for the deconstruction of ideologies, models that determine on which basis a body of knowledge can be constituted that could be defined as scientific. Moreover, these major and exemplary works are hardly typical of their time. Like great philosophical writings, which cannot be completely reduced to the context of their period insofar as they touch on problems that transcend the historical conditions of their production, these great sociological writings are exemplary in regard to the work manifested in them, exemplary also in going beyond received systems and ideas, and in attempting to counteract ideological constraints. This or that page from Auguste Comte on method, this or that passage from Marx, this or that rule by Durkheim are exemplary for this work of dismantling false knowledge and today constitute devices in deconstructing ideologies.

However, one can hardly be satisfied with our initial response. Even if it is conceded that sociological thinking has been built up through the assiduous work of deconstruction, there nevertheless remains the question whether the results and responses have corresponded to the ambitions, and whether or not the ideology which was banished from the premises has not reappeared, in another form, in the conclusions.

Before pursuing this matter any further, it is necessary to clarify briefly the meaning of ideology and to distinguish its various forms. As might well be imagined, creative sociological activity confronts us with three systems of knowledge/ignorance: the political ideologies proper, the social ideologies, and the ideologies which, for lack of a better term, we shall call *societal*. By "political ideologies" we understand those most visible systems of discourse that are today constituted and reconstituted by political movements and, even more visibly, by the parties and their representatives. By "social ideologies" we understand those less apparent but more meaningful systems that participate in the regulation of conduct in all forms of societal life, from the production of goods to individual private behavior. This distinction between political and social ideology makes it possible to inquire into the presuppositions of critical work, for an apparently radical break on the political level might have reproduced or reinforced models of conformity to accepted standards in domains that are not directly political. Finally, let us call "societal" those ideological forms most durable and least perceptible of all, those that Marx located in the different modes of production, whose continuity we can observe more clearly today behind political shake-ups and military conflicts: ideologies, for example, of history as progress, of the nation states, and of industrialization, which were first constituted at the end of the eighteenth century and to which the great majority of contemporary symbolic constructions subscribe.

These distinctions permit us a more varied response. If one admits that ideological structures and their practical implications are not limited to the sphere of politics alone but affect, in ways that vary with the circumstances, all social practices and share in their control, one will be ready to admit the possibility that a particular sociology may have been able to achieve a genuine deideologization in one domain, while remaining enclosed within the limits of its period in other domains. To take an extreme example, we see Proudhon, almost alone in his lifetime, accomplish an impressive denunciation of the ideology of statism, and demonstrate how the ideology of the state actually adopts the models of religion even while appearing to challenge them. Yet Proudhon also upholds or rather reinforces the cult of the traditional family and vindicates patriarchal power. It would be illusory to believe that a critique of ideology should, like some supreme sovereign, be capable of making a clean break with all ideological models, even those whose articulation is difficult to detect. John Stuart Mill, who wrote one of the liveliest critiques of phallocratic ideology in the nineteenth century, nevertheless proves to be a great deal more moderate on the issue of political systematizations.[4]

And it would be similarly naive to believe that a work, whether produced by a single individual or by an entire school, should have been able to unfold, continuously and in all of its parts, at that place where ideologies are deconstructed. An entire imagery, which is more political than historical, imposes a representation of the sociologist as liberator, who, through his or her triumphant genius, continuously dispels the illusions and the paradigms of his or her century. Marx or Durkheim would thus have triumphed in every page of their writings over the temptations of ideology. An attentive reading will show, however, that a great creator may achieve a most rigorous deconstruction in some places, yet remain satisfied with repeating ideological messages elsewhere. The work of Marx is a good example, even if political image-makers have taken great pains to obscure the profound difference in scientific status of his various writings. Marx himself quite consciously introduced in his epistemological writings elements supportive of a cognitive break and hoped to forestall the return of ideology in social analysis; yet in his *Manifesto* he equally consciously produced a synthesis of revolutionary messages aimed at political practice and employed the usual procedures of ideological persuasion. The movement and the chain of reasoning are completely different in the two cases.

This is not a problem we can afford to neglect. Here the question is no longer whether sociological research has been responsible for bringing about a break with ideological models but rather how, in an analytical work taken in its entirety, it has been possible for deideologizations and ideological reiterations to follow in quick succession or juxtaposition. How, in the very center of a work, can things which ought to be separated be brought together?

A first response consists in isolating the various parts of a work or the various problems considered, and in distinguishing those subjects, to which the practices of effecting a break are applied, from others, in which the old ideological patterns are reiterated. On the basis of such a distinction one could say that the work reveals that the author deconstructs collective illusions in some places, and reproduces them, or proposes new ones, in others. However limited such an answer might be, it is nevertheless not without pertinence. One may indeed say that in a great endeavor like that of Auguste Comte, the author exemplifies these epistemological "breaks" but, on the other hand, reconstructs an ideology based on the claim that philosophical problems can be solved by science. In his late writings, this ideology leads him to contradict his premises. It is this patient work of making careful distinctions which Marx invites his readers to undertake when he criticizes traditional political economy, and when he points to the "empty spaces"[5] in the writings of the economists which he proposes to fill in with new concepts. And likewise one may say that Marx constructs an eminently critical model of capitalist society while, on the other hand, a new grid is constituted in *Das Kapital*, which is not altogether free from the attempt to keep some things well out of sight. Thus, in each great work, such as *Suicide* or *Economy and Society* for example, and at the various stages of a work, the critical reader rightly exercises his powers of discernment which permit him to separate the successful deconstructions from the reiterations of imposed grids. This patient work is not done in vain, since it outlines the very movement of research by detecting the locked-in patterns.

But, once again, this answer too is inadequate. One might be tempted to rewrite the history of sociology in order to present the reassuring image of a cumulative body of knowledge constantly being rectified by a rational detection of ideologies; here one would place in proper context a few great salutory crises, in which the illusions by which the predecessors had been held "prisoners" would collapse under the impact of criticism. But history, as is well known, is heavy with conflicts and social contradictions.

This sketch of a progress achieved through critique, however, leaves the question of the enunciation of the critique unanswered. It might be supposed that a scientific consciousness that contains within itself all necessary conditions for the detection and criticism of error could be put to work. This model of thought is indeed applied to all secondary critiques in which the established body of knowledge, as long as it remains unchallenged, provides the instruments for detecting inadequacies in the application of the methods or any negligence with respect to the norms of "normal science."[6] But beyond these critiques — which remain within the limits of verification understood as conformity to the norms admitted by the scholarly community — there still remains the need to inquire into the dynamics of the creative "break," which is not reduced to the application of norms but, on the contrary, overturns them.

We may regard as symptomatic that all the big names we have just mentioned — Saint-Simon, Proudhon, Marx, Quetelet, Durkheim, Weber (and the list can be extended) — very overtly adopted, at various stages of their work, either a political position or a position with respect to politics in their time. It should also be noted that adopting such a position was not merely accidental, something external to the thought of these men, but that, on the contrary, the adopted position was intimately related to the contents of their writings, as if these two dimensions — scientific analysis and adoption of a political position — had been much more tightly connected than we previously assumed.

We know that the birth of sociology occurred gradually within an ideological movement that associated social science and socialism in an organic relationship. Durkheim emphasized that this link was so intimate that it was, in his opinion, impossible to dissociate these two orientations, the theoretical and the practical.[7] Indeed, as far as these founders of the "science of society" are concerned, one cannot separate their effort to break the yoke of old beliefs from their attempt to promote a new type of political thinking. The early writings of sociology are imbued with enthusiasm and with an ideology claiming to solve philosophical problems with the aid of science, an ideology according to which, as Auguste Comte stated unambiguously, the new body of knowledge would have the practical task of taking the place of the declining religions. If Marx makes this "pious" wish the object of satire, he does not do so out of an indifference toward political practice, since, on the contrary, he intended to forge the theoretical instruments for transforming the world. Moreover *Das Kapital*, though written with entirely different conceptual tools than the *Manifesto*, does not disown its political objectives. The two dimensions we have isolated as distinctive, the work of effecting a break by setting up suspensive procedures and the possibility of a conciliation between the scientific and ideological lines of reasoning, are denoted here without ambiguity. *Das Kapital*, while confirming the labor of deconstruction of political economy, represents a complete break with conventional views, and Marx even goes so far as to think that this work and its conclusions will remain inaccessible to the crowd, since it is removed from ordinary experience and from the expectations of the collective consciousness.[8] The *Manifesto*, on the contrary, bypasses this theoretical labor and situates the receiver immediately in the closed and mobilizing universe of political persuasion. From the point of view of the task of suspending ideologies, no relation can therefore be established between these texts of opposite intellectual status. But the second dimension, that of the possible conciliation between the scientific line of reasoning and the ideology, is here no less clearly marked. For if there is nothing in *Das Kapital* of a precise political program like the one which Marx inserts in the last few pages of the *Manifesto*, there is a perfect continuity between these two texts in the theses concerning the analysis of capitalist society and the dynamics of its contradictions.

A comparison of these two writings, the one analytical and the other persuasive, makes it possible for us to formulate a hypothesis which we would like to examine and which can be stated initially in the form of a question: Might not one's adhesion to an ideology and the will to promote it constitute in certain situations one of the prerequisites of foresight and knowledge? Marx's work is the best illustration of this hypothesis. The fundamental inspiration for all his writings after the winter of 1844-45 stems not only from the theoretical critique of liberal ideology, but also from commitment to a social movement, where practice and reasoning challenged the established economic order. It is on the basis of such a commitment that the theoretical analyses of the historical role of social classes and of the contradiction inherent in the mode of capitalist production are formulated. And it is known that this matrix of interpretation was, in its broad outlines, constituted in the workingmen's press of the 1840s. This basic inspiration was not in contradiction with the effort to deconstruct liberal ideology; on the contrary, it stimulated it. It made it possible to systematically analyze the structure and the conflict of social classes and to focus the analysis on labor and economic relations of production as the decisive area for scientific investigation.

The example of Proudhon is no less enlightening. Here again, a distrustful attitude toward politics and its infringement upon workers' autonomy is not just the outcome of scholarly criticism or the final accomplishment of an epistemic break with official ideologies. The denunciation of the dominant classes' monopoly powers and the satire against the state and bureaucratic centralization, can be traced back to Proudhon's commitment to the working-class movement of revolt which he analyzes theoretically as a threefold revolt against economic inequality, political subjection, and religious delusion. What we can call an ideological perspective characterized by a knowledge and a practice, by a global approach and conceptual closure, provides Proudhon with the instruments that enable him to achieve a different kind of lucidity. Never abandoning the quest for emancipation, Proudhon perceives the scope of the sociopolitical apparatus of subjection and he also perceives the extent to which a new distribution of productive wealth might leave the political relationship of subjection unchanged. He discerns, inside the workers' movement, the possibility of a new political alienation and the reconstitution of a power which would call itself popular but which would be no less oppressive than capitalist power. The historian of today cannot untangle what one may call the ideological coefficient and the cognitive aspect of these analyses since it is indeed his political aim to defend working-class autonomy which makes Proudhon sensitive to the relations of political domination and teaches him to recognize the progressive extension of state controls and the potentialities of authoritarianism in the midst of the working classes. And from this new point of view, the similarities that appeared at the epistemological level between Marx, Spencer, and Durkheim cannot be sustained. Spencer does indeed give a strong warning against imposed ideological models, but his commitment to the values and political ideologies of his time prevents him from availing himself of his own insights and from discovering the historical character of his conformity to established patterns.

One might comment upon these examples by resorting to a consciously paradoxical formula, proposing that political ideology is not an obstacle to discovery and knowledge but rather a prerequisite for any effort to get to their bottom. Can any explanation of that relationship be advanced? One reassuring answer would be to substitute for ideology the movement of social revolt, and the two preceding examples lend themselves to such an interpretation. The hypothesis of Lukács, that an increase in lucidity comes not from any elucidation by intellectuals but from the proletariat and from the consciousness of the totality, would solve the problem we are presenting here.

Indeed, from these two examples one may conclude that the conciliation between ideological audacity and the breadth of knowledge is assured, behind the author's back, by the cognitive privilege of an illuminating social situation. Lukács's general hypothesis, according to which an oppressed class that is nevertheless productive of social life would be an outstanding locus of social consciousness, must be provisionally retained. Through revolt, the possibility is gradually constituted, as many of the liberation movements have confirmed, of a global consciousness which perceives, beyond the circumstances and vicissitudes of the struggle, the social system in its oppressive totality. Within that totality the insurgents discover themselves as exploited and as agents of the revolution. This general hypothesis would make it possible to affirm, by applying it to the history of sociology, that the works which come closest to revolutionary positions ought also be closest to scholarly knowledge and that, inversely, any position of withdrawal from revolutionary attitudes would doom us to a merely partial analysis.

Applied to the history of sociology, this thesis is nevertheless insufficiently explanatory. If one may, for polemical purposes, define Durkheim, Weber, and Mannheim negatively, in terms of what they did not discuss, one is forced to recognize that they opened up certain avenues of research precisely because they managed to keep a relative distance from the social struggles of their immediate time. And, once again, one can claim that for these authors there is a certain relationship between their ideological adherence and their scientific perspective. Did not Durkheim need both a cautious sympathy for socialism and an unreserved adherence to the new ideology of professional social science in order to establish that observation post which French sociology became through his school? Was a morose resignation to the universe of capitalism not essential for Weber, in order to rethink the incorporation of actors and their actions into this system and to propose a scientific model of bureaucracy? Was the political questioning of socialist experiments not essential for Mannheim, in order to spell out the sociologically crucial question of the historical functions of ideology, and to lay the foundations for new inquiries in this domain?

In that intermediate area in which ideological risk sustains research and the production of a body of knowledge while at the same time establishing its boundaries, it seems impossible to reiterate the dissociation of ideology from scientific creation. Later criticism must perform the indispensable task of critique and analytic differentiation, but it cannot be applied to the creation of a body of knowledge without first appreciating its creative dynamics. It is precisely in the area of scientific creativity where the thrust and impact of ideology is most likely to be detected; it is therefore the undefined intermediate area between the various forms of ideology and sociological creativity that should be studied.

The problem here is no longer one of rigor and of respect for the rules of scientific production. Quite to the contrary, it may well be that in this domain more than in others scrupulous respect for rigor and precision may have the effect of blocking the innovative processes. Sociological creativity essentially presupposes two theoretical practices: forcing a break with imposed models of thought and pursuing a sustained and audacious elaboration of the new hypotheses proposed. These two dimensions must coexist and find a way of translating themselves into production. The great sociological creations can be reduced neither to a cry of revolt nor to the rigor of scientific construction. Moreover, genuine sociological creativity does not consist merely in insolent remarks on the established system but is rather a double movement, which is accomplished only rarely and with difficulty, in which the initial deviance translates itself into the power to construct. The historical production of a new sociological perspective will be all the more creative, the further away from imposed intellectual structures it is located, and the further it is extended in a rigorously sustained theory. This creativity is not located, therefore, in the originality of the initial propositions alone but rather in the exceptional conjunction of originality and a rigorous logic of theoretical construction. The conflict between the boldness of invention and the routinization of exacting rigor is precisely what is overcome in the creations of Marx, Weber, or Durkheim.

Creativity bears essentially on the construction of new, hitherto unseen social objects, which the creative effort makes visible even against the resistance of prevailing illusions and concealments. The creation seeks to construct a new object with its own logic and internal relations, a latent object that cannot give rise to an exhaustive experience, e.g. a theoretical object. Marx seeks to destroy the traditional social representation that opposes rich and poor, and to put in its place the knowledge of a system of necessary relations based on the notion of property and that is reproducing itself through internal contradictions. Durkheim seeks to destroy the established representation of the causes of suicide, and to substitute for them a set of social regulations sharing in the determination of behavior.

Apparently, the object construction that comes about in the innovative phases of social science is not so different from the constructions that appear periodically throughout the history of the natural sciences, and one would be tempted to consider sociological creativity as an instance of these historical reorganizations of knowledge. But to do so would be to ignore both the specificity of the object-domain and the special nature of the relation of sociology to its objects.

If, in the physical sciences, object construction has a purely theoretical character, in the social sciences it has a politically scandalous character, since it calls into question, to varying degrees, the symbolic cohesion of the established order. The sociologist does not come on the scene ready to post his constructs in a neutral area and simply to fill in a mere absence of knowledge. Before his arrival, political and social ideologies have constructed representations of social arrangements and contributed to ensuring the functioning and the reproduction of society. Should the sociologist refuse to go along with this, should he claim to remain innocent and indifferent to social organization, the political forces participating in the support of the established order would not fail to register the aggression and to detect in this different line of reasoning a symbolic threat. The sociologist may wish to avoid such a debate, but he cannot succeed, since substituting his construction of what is "real" for the models already in place and which set beliefs and norms in action, is precisely what he claims to be doing. One of the essential contributions of the dominant ideology is precisely this: it constructs social representations, designates groups and functions, and organizes that representation in agreement with the dominant interests. The deconstruction of social objects attacks the symbolic system at one strategic point, at that junction in which mental structures are adapted to the social order in an attempt to ensure its renewal. Should the sociologist choose to remain indifferent, his message will be perceived as an aggression by the official definers of social reality.

This is indeed a question of a symbolic aggression with unforeseeable repercussions. The construction of the new object attacks a system of representations which is highly endowed with power and clothed with authority. By discovering other social relations, by constructing other regularities and other relations of power, the sociologist strikes at the values defended by the agents of the established system and by the representations that grant them recognition. In fact, the new construction, scientific as it may claim to be, calls into question the values and ideology of the system; it constitutes a denunciation of the established scheme of things and a symbolic threat to the provisionally dominant forces. It is therefore necessary to anticipate that this new construction might experience a more or less repressive rejection on the part of the established forces and might be designated a fallacious, i.e. ideological production. By a necessary reversal, the production that claims to be scientific and founded in reason is perceived as a symbolic aggression, and is denounced as ideological by the champions of "common sense" and of the "reasonable." The mobilization of the forces of repression against nonconformist sociological productions stems from a social logic that stigmatizes new constructions as ideological and as contrary to the collective interests. The repression of new sociological constructions in totalitarian political systems carries to an extreme the predicament in which the sociologist finds himself, whether he wants it or not: a situation in which he is accused of being in collusion with the critical ideologist. His aggression may be tolerated if it only strikes at a limited sector of the established ideologies, e.g. at a social ideology; it will be repressed all the more severely if it appears to be an aggression with multiple consequences, involving the deconstruction of all established symbolic systems.

Sociological creativity thus finds itself in an extremely ambiguous situation that is symptomatic of the status of sociological knowledge and of its contradiction. The condition that makes creativity possible in this domain is not found in mere detachment, in a lack of commitment to the established system, but in an act of refusal of the established values. The creator finds himself not in front of an object that he can manipulate at will, but in the heart of a total system, rich with rationalizations, seductive strategies, and power relations. At the onset of sociological creativity we find a relinquishment of values and of established ideology, a refusal which is not motivated by scientific curiosity alone. The deconstruction of the received object entails a rejection of the system and its legitimations, a negative attitude, the best illustration of which is the refusal of political ideology. All great sociological constructions have these two characteristics in common: a critical liveliness and an enterprising spirit aiming at breaking the spell of ideology and at destroying conformist attachments.

Moreover, the new object produced by a great sociological mutation corresponds, in a more or less adequate way, to new relations, to new social forces which are emerging and which find a new sociological representation. Alexis de Tocqueville does not construct an exhaustive model of democracy in America. Marx does not exhaust the many facets of capitalism, but constructs as best as he can a model of the class struggle characterizing its history. It is this effective connection with history that characterizes the relationship between sociological creation and ideology. Sociological creation is rooted in history, and its greatest achievements designate, imperfectly, the new changes, the new integrations or disintegrations that evolve in the womb of the old society. In the case of historically crucial creations, sociology designates more than a change, it announces an entire social system, and it may foreshadow the values and essential traits of that system. One may dream of a sociology that would have the aseptic function of analyzing the formation of new social forms and that would assume the responsibility of announcing them without adhering to them. Since we are here limiting ourselves to what has hitherto been the history of sociology, we observe that such neutral foresight has never occurred, and that the great sociological creations have been sustained by a more or less profound adherence to the new social relations which they explored. Alexis de Tocqueville does not adhere unreservedly to the new world he discovers, but his liberalism sustains his understanding and interest. Marx draws the energy needed for his analysis from his adherence to the values and to the aspirations and efforts of the European labor movement. One has trouble seeing how mere intellectual curiosity could have animated the breadth of these constructions. More profoundly, the construction of the new sociohistorical object is indeed creation within history and within the limits of history. To a certain degree, the sociologist escapes from the limits of his own present but not from the limits of his future, and he shares in the values and misunderstandings of the new social system, whose constitution he designates.

One would therefore be tempted to respond that sociological creativity has indeed brought about the deconstruction of yesterday's ideology, but that has not been accomplished merely by assuming new values and new representations of the social scheme of things. But, once again, the ambiguity of sociology is deeper and more productive than this schematic reduction would suggest. Sociological creativity cannot be reduced to being an ideological response to the provisionally dominant ideology. The genuine creation finds itself in collusion with a faceless movement, a movement without a definite fixed form, and, at the time of creation, the new ideology has not yet become the framework of knowledge. If creation in fact shares in the new modes of thought, the latter are in a process of constitution, in a fully mobile condition, and at a point in time in which they are prompting the appearance of a new reality. Great sociological creation shares in this history and brings to the social movement elements of knowledge which the historical movement will possibly use. Nevertheless, here again, the movement will take over the conclusions rather than the creation, the letter rather than the spirit, transforming what was essentially a process of research into a language of defense, into ideology.

Thus, in order to understand this history of sociology, it does not seem necessary to set aside the school room disjunction that separates the ideological from the scientific as it separates error from truth. For the reasons we have just recalled, we must not only recognize that political and ideological commitments have not prevented creations from being realized, but also understand how passionate adherences have sustained exceptional discoveries. A history of sociology worth its salt would be based not on contents alone but on the moments of exceptional foresight, moments in which creation attains not only the level of political ideologies but also the level of all-inclusive, societal ideologies located in the long sweep of history. It is precisely on this level that the power of intellectual creativity finds its sustenance in the passion for the imaginary.

Notes

Translated from the French by Pierre Ansart and Juan E. Corradi

1. Max Weber, *Essais sur la théorie de la science* (Paris: Plon, 1965). *Gesammelte Aufsätze zur Wissenschaftslehre* (Tübingen: Mohr, 1922).

2. Georges Gurvitch, "Problèmes de la sociologie de la connaissance," *Traité de sociologie* (Paris: PUF, 1960), pp. 103-36.

3. Adolphe L.J. Quetelet, *Sur l'homme et le développement de ses facultés, ou Essai de physique sociale* (Paris: Bachelier, 1835), 2 vols.

4. John Stuart Mill, *The Subjection of Women* (London: Longman, 1869).

5. Louis Althusser, *Pour Marx* (Paris: Maspero, 1965).

6. Thomas S. Kuhn, *La structure des révolutions scientifiques* (Paris: Flammarion, 1972). *The Structure of Scientific Revolutions* (Chicago: University of Chicago Press, 1962).

7. Emile Durkheim, *Le socialisme, sa définition, ses débuts, la doctrine saint-simonienne*, 2nd édition (Paris: PUF, 1971).

8. Karl Marx, *Lettres à Kugelmann*, 28 décembre 1862 (Paris: Éditions Sociales Internationales, 1930), p. 41.

3

Durkheim and Mauss Revisited: Classification and the Sociology of Knowledge

David Bloor

In 1903 Emile Durkheim and Marcel Mauss formulated one of the central propositions of the sociology of knowledge. They said that the classification of things reproduces the classification of men.[1] In proposing that our classificatory activities reproduce the pattern of social inclusions and exclusions, Durkheim and Mauss offered us a bold, unifying principle. If the claim were true it would be of the utmost importance for a whole range of disciplines: not only for anthropology and sociology but also for the history of science and for philosophical speculations on the nature of knowledge.

Unfortunately Durkheim and Mauss's monograph *De quelques formes primitives de classification* raised more doubts than it settled. It was criticized in an influential series of papers by Gehlke, Dennes, Goldenweiser, Schaub, Benoit-Smullyan, and Worsley.[2] Their arguments have been endorsed and elaborated by Lukes in his massively comprehensive and scholarly analysis of Durkheim's life and work,[3] and by Needham in the introduction to his valuable translation of *De quelques formes*.

The criticisms can be grouped under three heads: empirical, theoretical, and logical. First, in accordance with their central claim, Durkheim and Mauss argued that the sevenfold classification of space in the Zuni cosmology was the consequence of their sevenfold social organization with

My debts in the writing of this paper are too extensive to describe in detail. Various drafts have received valuable criticism and comment from: Michael Barfoot, Barry Barnes, Celia Bloor, Peter Caws, Mary Douglas, David Edge, Jon Harwood, Mary Hesse, Stephen Jacyna, John Law, Donald MacKenzie, Rodney Needham, Malcolm Nicolson, Martin Rudwick, Steven Shapin, Peter Worsley, and Brian Wynne. I am extremely grateful to them for the time and trouble they have taken. I need hardly add that they are not responsible for, or necessarily in agreement with, the argument that I have tried to develop.

its corresponding sevenfold arrangement of their camps.[4] The ethnography of this, and other similar examples, was quickly challenged.[5] Second came a more theoretical objection. How could Durkheim and Mauss's claim possibly apply to practical and successful knowledge? Surely genuine knowledge must reproduce the pattern of things themselves, of nature — how could it do this if, instead, it was reproducing the pattern of social arrangements?[6] Third, Durkheim and Mauss were trying to provide an account of the major "categories" of thought. Their work was offered as an empirical development and correction of the Kantian tradition in the philosophy of mind.[7] Here Durkheim and Mauss's claims have been criticized on the grounds that they contain logical defects. How can social occasions of joining and separating people explain the wider practice of classification when they themselves depend on the exercise of a classificatory ability?[8]

To these objections I shall add a fourth, which has not perhaps been sufficiently stressed. Durkheim and Mauss failed to give an adequate theoretical underpinning for their central claim. Neither *Primitive Classification* nor *The Elementary Forms of Religious Life* provided a general picture or model of the classificatory process. They gave valuable hints but no systematic account. In consequence the precise meaning of Durkheim and Mauss's proposition is unclear.[9]

I claim that we can reconstitute the Durkheim and Mauss formula on a new theoretical base. This will allow us to infuse fresh significance into it and then relate it to a new range of factual material. To do this we need a general model of classification. Fortunately such a model exists. It is called the *network model* and has been developed by the philosopher of science Mary Hesse following the work of Duhem and Quine.[10] Originally offered as an analysis of scientific inference, it applies as much to myth or common sense as to science. The importance of the model and its being thoroughly understood will justify a careful account of its main features, though of course not all of its details or implications can be discussed. I shall show how Durkheim and Mauss's thesis, when expressed in terms of the network model, is strongly supported by material from the history of science. Finally, I shall reassess and answer the standard objections mentioned above.

Hesse's presentation of the network model starts with a simple account of naming or labeling. A language learner — for example a child — has his attention drawn to conventionally discriminated objects or features in the environment and learns to associate a word with them. Let us call these conventional foci of attention *exemplars*. We must assume the learner to be endowed with a disposition to generalize, so any occurrence of what appears to be the same sort of object or feature is brought under the same heading. Hesse calls this our primitive recognition of similarity. More refined discriminations are then built up by the learner's responses receiving positive or negative sanctions from competent language users. With these assumptions it is possible to explain how words like *cup* or *hot* are first learnt.

A similar account can then be given of how competent language-users extend a classificatory scheme to cope with new objects. New cases are bracketed with precedents to which they bear some intuitive resemblance. Even the esoteric practice of scientific thinking proceeds in the same way. Scientific theories make new phenomena intelligible by showing us how to see them as instances of more familiar processes. The role of models, analogies, metaphors, and exemplars in science has been clearly demonstrated and described. Thus we can grasp the nature of sound by picking out similarities in its behavior to the more accessible and visible properties of water waves. Coclassifying them as "waves" initially depends for its plausibility on being able to discern a likeness in the two cases.[11]

So far we have described a simple "language" consisting of names applied on the basis of subjective similarity to exemplars. Hesse calls this an initial classification of the environment. It is, however, only an expository device, not a historical phase in the growth of knowledge. Our primitive sense of similarity is a necessary part of the transmission, use, and extension of knowledge; it is ubiquitous but, by itself, insufficient to explain the working of a real classificatory scheme. This is because its promptings frequently have to be overruled. The pattern of similarities that can be detected in the environment is so rich and so contradictory that these similarities have to be treated selectively. How this is accomplished will emerge as the rest of the model is described. Already, though, it is clear that the model depends at every point on the cooperation of a psychological (dispositional) factor and a sociological (conventional) factor; and that their joint operation only makes sense if we think of knowledge as a working relationship with our material surroundings.

The different sorts of object in a system of classification can be thought of as related together by elementary laws, like "fire is hot" or "wood floats." In one respect the laws may be said to assert the copresence or coabsence of those features of the world to which we have selectively attended. They could be arrived at by the brain keeping a probabilistic tally of the (conventionally classified) stimuli that impinge on it. But the laws may also be thought of sociologically rather than psychologically. They will then have the status of conventional typifications: for example, "foxes are sly" or "diamonds are hard." Those maxims may be confirmed in the experience of the individual, but usually they will be learned from accepted authorities. Such laws will still structure individual expectations and serve the general end of adaptation to the environment, but they will differ from the probability estimates mentioned above. They will be uniform and stereotyped and act as reference points and shared resources for framing explanations. They will be common property and belong more to the public domain than the psyche of the individual learner. From now on I shall focus my attention on laws in this second sense in which they are, as Durkheim would say, "collective representations."

Two facts about laws are important. First, they extend the range of circumstances in which a classification can be confidently applied. Knowing the law that fire is hot, the cues which prompt the application of the word *fire* can now prompt the application of *hot*. No direct experience of the case in hand is needed to serve as a justification. (It is in this way that laws enable us to talk about the objects that science postulates, even though we have never directly confronted them.) Second, it must not be thought that laws can only perform these functions if they are true. A false law can be the basis for action and inference just as effectively as a true one. It is a point of logic that false premises can yield true conclusions, and that we can get the right answers for the wrong reasons. And when things do go wrong, the circumstances of practical action are so complicated that the source of the error can always be disputed.[12]

The next step is to show that just as predicates and classifications are organized into laws, so laws themselves exist within systems of a still higher order. They form networks. The simplest network comprises two or more laws referring to the same classification. It is here that the model comes into its own, because networks have some interesting properties.

Imagine a very primitive system of classification where it is said that "fish" live in the sea; "birds" fly in the air; and various classes of "animals" live on the land. Of the land animals a subgroup of "mammals" has been discriminated on the grounds that they suckle their young. This little system of knowledge possesses the properties that have so far been described. It consists of a number of names or classes that can be taught by pointing out accepted instances. The names are joined by laws which sometimes give crossreferences to the same classification. These could be said to form a network if one thinks of the crossreferences as the knots of the net, and the laws as the strings that connect them. Furthermore, this network could be entirely adequate for many practical and important dealings with the environment.

Suppose now that the users of this network come into contact with a new creature, say, the whale. This has the habitat and appearance of a huge fish but it suckles its young — facts which could be established by the routine use of the labels of the network. It is clear that the whale can be seen in a way that creates problems for the network. It could be used to force a choice between saying (1) that not only mammals suckle their young but some fish do as well; or (2) that not all mammals live on the land. The proper application of the predicates "mammal" and "fish" depends on which law of the network is retained. Resemblance alone pulls us in opposite directions, so the choice cannot be resolved by experience. Retaining either law will do justice to what is known and will restore an acceptable form of correspondence with the world.

The lesson to be learned from this example is that the functioning of a name or a predicate cannot be explained fully by similarity relations but depends on the laws into which they enter. Conversely, the laws will depend on conventions about the boundaries of the classes they relate. This reciprocal dependency, the discretion it allows, and the choices it forces upon us are completely general phenomena. They do not apply only to new and problematic cases which — like the whale in the example — have yet to be assigned to a class; they apply to existing classifications as well and can lead to their reassessment. New contingencies can always prompt retrospective revisions.

In order to demonstrate this I shall look at the cases where the claim might seem least plausible: the exemplars of a class. Because they are defining instances or paradigm cases, it might seem that they are in no way beholden to the laws into which they enter. How could an exemplar of the class of Xs be anything but an X, since being an X just means "being like the exemplar"? Because exemplars seem to be known directly by experience, it might appear that the only reclassification they can suffer would be a trivial change of name, e.g. being called by the symbol Y rather than X. To see what is wrong with this, let some object be used to introduce a class, say, the class of Xs. At first other objects are counted as Xs by virtue of their similarity to the exemplar. Suppose that it then emerges that most members of the class of Xs are also members of the class of Ys. All that stands in the way of this law are the few Xs which are not Ys. A variety of strategies may be employed to create such a law in the face of this residue. It may be decided that being a Y is to be a defining characteristic of being an X, as obeying the law of constant proportions became part of the definition of a chemical compound. Or, more interestingly, the anomalous Xs may be examined and found to possess another property, Z, which differentiates them from the "well behaved" Xs. This allows the anomalies to be excluded on the grounds that they are not "sufficiently similar" to the other Xs, where the criterion of similarity now involves the previously insignificant property Z. Or again it may be found that being an X is a matter of degree, like being more or less hot, or more or less intensely red. If the anomalous Xs can be said to possess the property of "Xness" to a different degree from the others, then this could become the reason for excluding them and so preserving the law. Mary Hesse refers to these various expedients as methods of adjusting the threshold of a classification.

Clearly this argument applies even if one of the anomalous Xs happened to be an exemplar. There is no a priori reason why this should not happen; there is nothing in the above sequence of steps that applies less to the exemplar than to any other member of the class. The argument is completely general. The exemplar may turn from being central to the class, to being peripheral and problematic, and end up by being excluded altogether. These changes in status show that even exemplars depend on the surrounding network of laws, and conversely that laws involving exemplars are no more secure than any others.[13]

The argument can be taken even further in order to bring out the holistic way in which laws relate together. The fate of a classification can depend on extremely remote contingencies. In principle an alteration or innovation in one part of the network might have repercussions in any other part. Stating the argument formally, as before, let us begin with a classification of the environment that suggests that most Xs are Ys. Assume that being accounted an X has nothing to do with being accounted a Y. Then the suggestion is made that *all* Xs are Ys. To perfect the law that appears to relate X and Y — or for that matter to undermine it — our assignment of objects to the class X comes to be made with an eye to their character as Ys as well. The relationship becomes an "internal" one. But the same story that has been told about X could have been told about Y. This has no greater claim to be treated as stable or unproblematic or fixed in its scope. It too can have its threshold adjusted or its exemplary cases cast out. The relationship of Y with other classes apart from X will also have suggested laws and prompted adjustments. These might easily bear upon our first law, the one connecting X and Y. The original rough correlation between X and Y might be high or low because of prior decisions designed to alter another correlation involving Y. And of course decisions about the scope of Y might make it more or less difficult to alter the threshold of X, because different Xs will be rendered anomalous. The problem of justifying their exclusion from the class of Xs will take on different forms, depending on what has happened elsewhere in the network. Clearly this argument can be reiterated for each class that Y is related to, and then in turn for each class to which these are related.

The general picture is now emerging. The appropriate verbal description of an object is always a matter of context as well as direct confrontation. There is no "direct" verbal rendering of experience: it is always mediated through a network of laws. Like analogies and metaphors, which are but special cases, laws repair the fragmentary character of experience; they highlight real or imagined patterns in it, and prompt and justify threshold adjustments. They act as selective filters while permitting us to impute an inner nature to things — in the way that the analogy with water flow captured for a while the essence of heat and defined the laws that it was said to obey. All the elements of this network of classifications are equally open to negotiation, and equally the outcome of such processes. At any given time the network will be finite in extent and organize a very limited range of experience. It will therefore be at the mercy of unknown contingencies and may undergo profound changes as a result of the decisions that are made in response to them. Every law will have a historical dimension, for the network is just a register or an index of the predicates that have been introduced, the particular comparisons that have been made: the metaphorical redescriptions and glosses that have gone into its creation, and the options that have been exercised over which laws to protect or to sacrifice.

Despite all this scope for internal adjustment the network is not a free-floating system of thought. Classificatory decisions are made with reference to the world and in light of experience. The strength of this connection to the world resides in habit and the routine application of predicates based on similarity to current exemplars. These considerations are brought together by Mary Hesse under the heading of the "correspondence postulate."

In the context of the network model, however, the word *correspondence* refers to any viable relationship that can be established with the environment. All the usual connotations of structural identity, or the perfect reflection of reality in knowledge, have to be dropped. This is because the model proceeds from the assumption that reality is indefinitely complex. All systems of classification simplify what they portray, and this destroys the possibility of a "oneness" between knowledge and the world. There are therefore always endless possibilities for reclassification. So whilst Hesse's correspondence postulate asserts a connection between knowledge and the world, it also emphasizes its looseness. The word *correspondence* was perhaps an unfortunate choice. *Adaptation* would be better. We are used to the idea that there is more than one way of being adapted to the world.

At this point a query may be raised. In some of our dealings with familiar objects we have surely become so intimate with their ways that it can be said that we simply and decisively know their characteristics. The demands of reality will filter out erroneous habits of thought and leave behind a reliable pattern of responses. Similarly it is tempting to believe that in some circumstances our sensory experience of the world gives us a direct apprehension of the properties of things. If these claims are correct then not everything in our network of knowledge is liable to alteration. Some parts will so closely intermesh with the world that its laws can be said to be the laws of things themselves. This suggests that a stronger sense of correspondence might be needed after all.[14]

It does seem plausible to insist that there are stable elements in our cognitive relation to the world, and to locate these in our sensory motor experience and practical handling of the environment. They derive, no doubt, from the evolution of our eyes, hands, and nervous system. But it will suffice to say that at the very least the sociologist can use the network model in a totally unrestricted form to describe any *explicit definition* of reality or any developed system of *verbalized* theoretical knowledge.

For instance, consider our practical commerce with the world. This can be looked upon as a purely mechanical interaction: certain forms of behavior work certain effects. Such a behavioral repertoire may indeed have stable and repeatable features, but it hardly rises to the level of explicit knowledge until it acquires a form of self-consciousness. In what categories is the technical lore encoded? How is it internally mediated and verbally transmitted? What relations are believed to connect it with other patterns of thought and action? How is failure accounted for? How does it stand with regard to affirmations of truth and falsehood? How is it rationalized and explained in relation to an accepted picture of reality? When we ask and answer questions such as these we can be sure that we are dealing with knowledge in the full sense of the word, with collective representations, and that an unqualified form of the network model is appropriate. For, so deep are the changes that have taken place in our thinking about causality, force, matter, body, and soul, that we can be sure that none of those ideas is immune to change or held fast by reality alone.

This answer only makes another question all the more pressing. What is it that can then account for the known stability of our explicit theoretical knowledge? For the sociologist the answer is simple. Such stability as there is in a system of knowledge comes entirely from the collective decisions of its creators and users. It derives from the active protection of parts of the network. That is to say: from the requirements that certain laws and classifications be kept intact, and all adjustments and alterations carried out elsewhere. The rest of the network then becomes a field of resources to be exploited to achieve this end — a place where thresholds can be moved with relative ease; where complexity or blame can be conveniently located, or troublesome cases relegated. We need not assume that a protected law or classification is singled out because of any intrinsic properties like truth, self-evidence, or plausibility. Of course, such properties will be imputed to them, but this will be a justification from their special treatment rather than the cause of it. On those occasions when prior belief in the truth of a law is responsible for its being given protection, it is the state of belief which is the cause rather than any property that belongs to the law itself.

The specially protected, and therefore stable, parts of the network can be divided into two related types. First there are favored theoretical models, metaphors, and analogies. Their repeated application confers unity on the network and makes one part resonate with another. Second, there are favored boundaries or distinctions. These separate off the different models or metaphors, marking their proper limits of application. Think, for example, of the determined defense of the distinction between the organic and the inorganic, the living and the nonliving. In different European countries, and at different times, this boundary assumed different degrees of importance. In conservative France of the Second Empire the spontaneous generation of life, which would have violated the boundary between the living and the nonliving, was rejected as theologically mischievous, politically dangerous, and scientifically false. The network of knowledge was duly adjusted to sustain the desired effect. Whenever life appeared to emerge spontaneously from some laboratory preparation of nonliving matter it was postulated that unknown, invisible living creatures were already present or had intruded themselves, so as to account for the observation. Indeed the nonappearance of life in such experiments became the measure of whether they had been properly performed. This is clearly illustrated in the way that Pasteur was able to dismiss Pouchet's "incompetent" experiments when they appeared to show spontaneous generation.[15]

There is thus no need to explain stability by appealing to truth or reality. Active protection is a well-documented phenomenon and yields a sufficient account. The history of science is replete with examples. When faced with problems it is a routine procedure in science, as elsewhere, to protect accepted theory and practice by elaborating the network — hence the continuity of research programmes and theoretical traditions.[16]

It would be desirable to know more about the factors that determine which parts of a network its users want to keep stable. What is it that we are protecting when we selectively manipulate our network of knowledge and shield certain of its laws? Part of the answer is that we are protecting our hard won ability to cope with our environment. But we must not have an unduly narrow picture of this activity. The network has shown that all classificatory schemes, however much oriented to practice, require sustaining at every point by social processes. A continual stream of decisions is called for about classificatory boundaries: what laws are to be retained when the promptings of experience are in conflict; or when we are tempted by rival interpretations. Conventional elements are present and necessary throughout the network, and strategic decisions must superintend the many tactical decisions. Whilst some of those decisions, conventions, and strategies may be explicable in terms of the technical advantages that they secure for the creators of a network, we must not assume in advance that this always provides a sufficient explanation.

In order to acknowledge and explain our protective strategies, Mary Hesse introduces the notion of "coherence conditions." These are conditions imposed upon a network of laws without being laws themselves. It is in the treatment of this topic that we might expect to find a fuller answer to our question. Unfortunately, *The Structure of Scientific Inference* only contains one paragraph on the origin and nature of coherence conditions. We learn that they are of two types: "physical constraints ... which may have been selected during the evolution of learning organisms" and "perhaps culturally conditioned metaphysical principles."[17] Without denying their reality I shall leave the biological contribution aside and confine myself to the socially generated coherence conditions.

The words "culturally conditioned metaphysical principles" were obviously meant as no more than a pointer to things social. Nevertheless they have all the wrong overtones. Metaphysical principles are as much in need of explanation as the cognitive preference they are said to bring about, and the same can be said for the cultural factors that are then cited as *their* cause. Again, reference to the process of conditioning, although meant loosely, suggests that metaphysical principles are passively imbibed and then dominate and determine our thinking. This is an implausible picture of human action, creating a problem about the origin of the conditioning.

Fortunately there is an approach to the subject that avoids all these traps. The anthropologist Mary Douglas has suggested that metaphysical principles and conceptions of nature are used as polemical weapons in the attempt to control our fellows.[18] Nature and its workings provide us with a repertoire of legitimations and justifications, sources of danger for threatening and blaming, and images of order around which we can muster support. In the pursuit of our social goals it is expedient to deploy nature in this way as a symbol, and within any given context certain natural laws will be especially appropriate for the task. The wish being the father to the thought, these laws will be invested with high a priori probability and treated as if they are self-evident or necessary. Mary Douglas suggests that:

Apprehending a general pattern of what is right and necessary in social relations is the basis of society: this apprehension generates whatever *a priori* or set of necessary causes is going to be found in nature.[19]

Here is a way of explaining how coherence conditions can be generated. They can come from nature being put to social use as well as practical use. Certain laws are protected and rendered stable because of their assumed utility for purposes of justification, legitimation, and social persuasion. Because these activities are meant to further interests, we can say that interests *are* coherence conditions. And since interests derive from, and constitute social structures, it will be no surprise to find that putting nature to social use creates identities between knowledge and society of the kind predicted in *Primitive Classification.*

To show these ideas in action I shall look at a sequence of events that are central to the historical development of Newtonian physics. The choice of an esoteric science is deliberate. It emphasizes that a concern with the prediction and control of nature is not automatically sacrificed by giving nature a moral employment. At the same time we shall see that interests in social control intimately affect the particular way that a body of natural knowledge is developed. The issues involved in the examples are not themselves technical although their implications cut deep.

Historians of science have given us a fascinating account of the development of what is called the corpuscular or mechanical philosophy.[20] Robert Boyle and the group that was to become the nucleus of the Royal Society of London adopted and refined this theory in the late 1640s and early 1650s. According to the corpuscular philosophy, nature was to be understood in terms of particles of inert matter blindly obeying laws of motion and operated on by forces such as gravity.[21] The point insisted on by these theorists was that particles of matter did not contain with themselves the active principle of motion. Matter was brute, inanimate and irrational, and could neither move nor organize itself. Commenting critically on Lucretius, Boyle said:

He supposes his eternal atoms to have from eternity been their own movers, whereas it is plain that motion is in no way necessary to the essence of matter. . . . Nor has any man, that I know, satisfactorily made out how matter can move itself.[22]

The corpuscular philosophy was an answer to the vulgar or received views of nature.[23] Boyle largely identified these with the doctrines of Aristotle, but he also had two other important targets in mind. As we have seen, one of these was the form of atomism developed by the pagan thinkers of antiquity. The other was the popular alchemical teaching of Helmont and Paracelsus. Boyle asserted that all of these theories rested on the same mistake. Each in their own way assumed that the cause of motion lay within matter. They all treated nature as if it were intrinsically active and self-organizing.

Boyle took as an example the accepted explanation of why water would rise in a straw when the air was sucked out. This was based on the principle that nature "hated" a vacuum, hence the water moved in to fill the undesirable space. But, objected Boyle, this supposes that there is a kind of *anima mundi*, furnished with various passions, which watchfully provides for the safety of the universe; or that a brute and inanimate creature, as water, not only has a power to move its heavy body upwards, contrary (to speak in their language) to the tendency of its particular nature, but knows both that air has been sucked out of the reed, and that unless it succeed the attracted air, there will follow a vacuum; and that this water is withall so generous, as by ascending, to act . . . like a noble patriot, that sacrifices his private interests to the publick ones of his country.[24]

The proper approach, said Boyle, is to avoid any hint of this soul of the world and speak only of the weight or pressure of the air. More generally we must only appeal to the size, figure, and texture of particles of matter, and construe sources of activity and motion so that they are always said to be impressed on matter from the outside. They do not belong to matter as such.

How are we to understand the preference that developed in certain quarters, rather suddenly, for an inert and passive, rather than an active and self-moving matter? There was nothing innately repugnant to reason about the rejected opinions. Indeed Boyle and other corpuscular philosophers like Charleton had only a short time before embraced such theories and continued to use them in a selective and unsystematic way.[25] In order to explain the change historians have found it necessary to look at the social context.

From the civil war of the 1640s to the Restoration, England experienced a breakdown in the machinery of social control. It also witnessed the proliferation of radical religious groups and sects, such as the Diggers or True Levellers, the Ranters, Seekers and Familiasts. These disruptive and sometimes bizarre "enthusiasts" derived their religion and morality from their own revelations and conscience. Drawing their support from the growing number of "masterless men" and the remnants of Cromwell's army, and moved by their inner light, they threatened to turn the world upside down.[26] For, despite the intensely personal character of their sources of knowledge, their revelations carried a disturbingly uniform message: resistance to church tythes, the disestablishment of the church, redistribution of property, political and social equality — and the practice of lay preaching. They would organize themselves as they saw fit.

The theological justification for this unprecedented claim to autonomy was the immediacy of the sectaries' contact with God. Divinity, they preached, was potentially within all men and women and within nature. It was in the soil they tilled, the common land they claimed as their own; and it could be directly experienced. It was visible to the eyes.[27] God had become identified with the natural world and the natural world had become divine. This emerges clearly in the writings of Gerrard Winstanley, the Digger leader, but it was not peculiar to him. "All the creatures of the world's," said one sectary, "are but one entire being. Nothing that partakes of the divine nature, or is of God, but is God." Another said: "He does not exist outside his creation."[28] For the sectaries, God is the soul of the world.

The Honorable Robert Boyle and the future leaders of the Royal Society had other social goals in mind and possessed very different interests from the sectaries. Their personal fortunes were deeply involved in the quest for stable social forms. In 1646 Boyle had noted with alarm that London "entertains ... no less than 200 several opinions in points of religion," and wanted to "put a restraint on the spreading impostures of the sectaries, which have made this distracted city their rendezvous."[29] Boyle had suffered financially during the civil war (his Irish estates had been lost), but he had thrown in his lot with the new republic and was now reaping the benefits that were threatened by the continuing turbulence. For many years, even after the Restoration, he continued to be preoccupied by the sectaries and the danger of their resurgence, just as he continued to be worried by the threat of the Roman Church. For example, the crisis generated by the failure to exclude James from the throne and the possibility that the king would grant general toleration to Catholics and Dissenters alike, prompted Boyle's publication of his *Free Enquiry into the Vulgarly Received Notions of Nature*.[30] There he wrote:

There is lately sprung up a sect of men, as well professing Christianity, as pretending to philosophy, who . . . do very much symbolize with the ancient Heathens, and talk much indeed of God, but mean such a one, as is not really distinct from the animated and intelligent universe.[31]

In the place of this animated and intelligent universe Boyle put the mechanical philosophy, with its inanimate and irrational matter. This was then used to bolster up the social and political policies that he and his circle advocated. This was called "latitudinarianism." The aim was neither complete toleration of dissent nor outright repression. The latter policy would fail and therefore be as disastrous as the former. A middle way was required that would contain dissent and comprehend it within the church. Enthusiasm was to be discouraged by an ethic of diligent, time-consuming work, while inspiration was to give way to the slow accumulation of knowledge through study and experiment. In this way the initiative would be taken out of the hands of the sectaries and put back where it belonged. The church would prosper, it would be acknowledged as the agent of providence and accorded a dominant role in the conduct of social affairs — and so, therefore, would the group who made this policy their own.

Sensitivity to the ideological use of nature was commonplace in Boyle's time and played a central role in contemporary polemics. Thus the sectarian supporters of Paracelsus and Helmont were attacked because of the "Familiasticall-Levelling-Magicall Temper" of their doctrines.[32] As

Boyle said, God has not merely contrived the world for the provision of necessities and delights, but for our instruction too. Nature carries a moral message. "For each page of the great volume of nature is full of real hieroglyphicks, where (by an inverted way of expression) things stand for words, and their qualities for letters."[33] If we follow Boyle's invitation — as we were surely meant to — and read the corpuscular philosophy as a "real hieroglyphick," we should be able to link together his latitudinarianism with his preference for inert matter rather than an active self-organizing nature.

The sectaries had so arranged the cosmos that it provided no role for professional mediators or interpreters of God's will. By making reality directly accessible through the experience of the senses, and the experience provided by revelation, they provided themselves with all the knowledge and guidance they needed. And the assertion of self-activity in nature reinforced the claim to autonomy because it put all the sources of activity in the world where they could grasp them. It put activity, so to speak, at the bottom rather than at the top. Collapsing natural hierarchies justified them in collapsing social hierarchies. To say that matter could organize itself carried the message that men could organize themselves. By contrast, to say that matter was inert and depended on nonmaterial active principles, was to make nature carry the opposite message. Here the world was made to prefigure the dependence of civil society on an involved, active and dominant Anglican church. The church was presented as the agent of providence in the social realm. It was the controller of social motion, just as the spiritualized forces and active principles in nature were the controllers of material motion.[34]

The dictionary that tells us which things stand for which words in the great volume of nature is therefore simple and short. For inert matter read "people"; for active principle and force read "Anglican church"; for natural hierarchy of matter and spirit read "social hierarchy." To deny that matter can move and organize itself is to deny that (certain) men can organize themselves.

This reading is reinforced if we follow the career of the corpuscular philosophy and see how it was elaborated for both scientific and social purposes by Newton and his followers.[35] For example, in 1667 Sprat's *History of the Royal Society* provided a timely explanation of how science induces humility in a prince's subjects. In the course of this discussion the analogy between natural and social hierarchies is made explicit. The mass of men are likened to particles of matter, and the forces of social order to the forces governing atoms. Science, says Sprat, "shows us the difficulty of ord'ring the very motion of senseless and irrational things; and therefore how much harder it is to rule the restless minds of men."[36]

A famous series of lectures, financed by Boyle's will, was used by Newton's followers to press the corpuscular philosophy into service. The Boyle lectures were a platform for the latitudinarian cause. The aim was still to combat enthusiasm and Catholicism, but by now it was necessary to justify the Glorious Revolution of 1688. There was also the need to come to terms with the increasingly influential men of "business and dispatch" — the rising capitalist class. The revolution was therefore shown to be the work of divine providence, while capitalists were encouraged and courted, provided only that they allowed a prominent place for the Anglican church. This meant, for example, resisting the Hobbesian belief that economic rationality constituted a self-organizing and self-sufficient system. Significantly Hobbes was also convicted of error in his underlying metaphysics of matter and motion, for he too thought that the system of matter could move itself.[37] The message is clear. As Newton's friend Samuel Clarke said in his Boyle lecture, "the generality of men must not by any means be left wholly to the workings of their own minds, to the use of their natural faculties."[38]

If we look at Newton we find that he too insisted that God is the Lord of creation, not the soul of the world. As he said in the General Scholium to *Mathematical Principles*:

The word *God* is a relative Term, and has Reference to Servants, and *Deity* is the Dominion of God, not (such as a Soul has) over a Body of its own, which is the notion of those who make God the Soul of the World; but (*such as a Governor has*) over Servants.[39]

He too thought that

we find almost no other reason for atheism than this notion of bodies having, as it were, a complete, absolute and independent reality in themselves.[40]

Again, Newton always insisted in his scientific work that matter could not move itself. In *Opticks* he said:

The *Vis inertiae* is a passive Principle by which Bodies persist in their Motion or Rest, receive Motion in proportion to the Force impressing it, and resist as much as they are resisted. By this Principle alone there never could have been any Motion in the World. Some other Principle was necessary for putting bodies into Motion; and now they are in Motion, some other Principle is necessary for conserving the Motion.[41]

A recent study devoted to tracing the shifts and complexities in Newton's scientific thinking has identified the passivity of matter as one of his central commitments, concluding that: "he sought one means after another to avoid attributing activity and agency to matter."[42] In our terminology the passivity of matter was a protected law shared by the mechanical philosophers. Behind it must lie a coherence condition, that is to say, an interest and a social purpose. We know of the involvement of Newton and his followers in low-church politics, their concern for the Whig cause, and the ideological continuity from Boyle's latitudinarian stance to theirs. As Newton said when helping his protégé Bentley, who was preparing to give a Boyle lecture: he "rejoiced" to see his natural philosophy put to such uses, for "when I wrote my treatise upon our system, I had an eye upon such principles."[43]

Of course, neither Boyle and Newton, nor their freethinking opponents will be found saying that they believe what they do just because of the political implications, though they were deeply concerned with these. Both sides will say that they believe what they do because experience, reason, or the Bible make it plain to them. Nevertheless, we know enough of the divergent interests of both sides to explain why all these sources of rational evidence lead to such opposing conclusions. Both groups were arranging the fundamental laws and classifications of their natural knowledge in a way that artfully aligned them with their social goals. The political context was used to construct different pictures of the physical world, and the resources of the network of laws were exploited to sustain it in the face of new tasks and new facts. As we have seen, the effect in each case was to ensure that the classification of things reproduced the classification of men.[44]

To consolidate these conclusions I shall now return to the standard criticisms of Durkheim and Mauss. First, I have not tried to dispute the empirical objections raised by the anthropological critics. Instead, I have exhibited a new domain of facts that confirm the thesis of *Primitive Classification*. Given a secure empirical bridgehead of this kind the question then becomes one of finding the scope of the claim. It would certainly be easy to produce much more factual evidence than has been given here.[45]

Nevertheless, the most striking thing about the standard objections is the extent to which they rely on matters of principle rather than fact. Consider for example the theoretical objection urged by Benoit-Smullyan. He says that the primary aim of our concepts is to enable us to adapt to the world, and "if they simply reflected the organization of a particular society, they would not so well fit the physical world."[46] The assumption underlying this objection is that nature and society are forces pulling in opposite directions. A concession to one is a denial of the other. Durkheim was aware of this problem. In the first and last chapters of *Elementary Forms* he asks how it is that concepts modeled on social structures apply to nature as well. His answer is that society is, after all, "part of nature" and must therefore share in its general characteristics. The premises of this argument are true, but the principle is too vague to provide a convincing answer to the worry.[47]

Given the inadequacy of this response it is perhaps no surprise that Durkheim permitted himself to exempt "scientifically elaborated and criticized concepts" from the scope of his analysis.[48] Having only this flimsy basis for saying that concepts could simultaneously reflect nature and society, a respect for science would naturally suggest attenuating the social connection. Thus scientific concepts are said progressively to escape the grip of society as they become responsive to nature alone.[49] Durkheim then simply claims that these exceptions to his theory do not matter, because scientific concepts represent only a "very slight minority."[50]

Of course it does matter. It represents a concession of principle. It also debars the sociology of knowledge from those cases of knowledge that we take most seriously. However, Durkheim's concession was premature. The examples I have given from science, and the network model, both show that it is perfectly possible for systems of knowledge to reflect society and be addressed to the natural world at the same time. Put simply, the answer to the problem is that the social message comprises one of the coherence conditions, while the negotiability of the network provides the resources for reconciling those demands with the input of experience. The idea that knowledge is a channel that can convey two signals at once requires us to drop the assumption that nature and society are polar opposites. It also requires us to become less complacent about what it is to "fit the physical world." This is where the network model is crucial.

The final logical objection is directed at the very heart of Durkheim's sociological theory of knowledge. It concerns his treatment of the so-called categories of thought. By the word *category* Durkheim means those ideas which "dominate all the details of our intellectual life." Because they "correspond to the most universal properties of things," they naturally include such ideas as space, time, class, force, cause, and personality. He calls them "the molds of mental life." They "are like the solid frame which encloses all thought." Again, they "constrain our intelligence" and it seems as if thought would destroy itself without them. While "other ideas are contingent and unsteady," the categories possess "a special sort of moral necessity which is to the intellectual life what moral obligation is to the will."[51]

From Durkheim's description we can see at once that his categories are parts of the network which are held stable by coherence conditions. For these are the parts of our system of knowledge that are made to dominate over its details, which provide a framework and signalize the constraints upon it.[52] They cannot be merely constructed out of experience, and their independent guarantee of stability gives them a special kind of necessity. From now on I shall take it for granted that when Durkheim uses the word *category* it refers to a specially prominent and protected law, like Boyle's and Newton's assumption that matter is passive.[53]

In 1915 Gehlke argued that Durkheim's whole treatment of this question is vitiated by a confusion of the capacities of the mind with the content of mind.[54] A *capacity* is an ability or competence or faculty, while *content* refers to a definite belief, idea, or representation. For example, the ability to think in spatial terms and the potential to organize experience spatially is quite different from some specific belief about the nature of space, e.g. the theory that is Euclidean. Gehlke's point is then driven home by Dennes who argues that

Durkheim's theory of the origin of the categories depends upon his ambiguous conception of mind. If he takes mind in the Kantian sense, the sense usual in epistemology, as the subject's system of cognitive faculties, it is ridiculous to say that the categories of the mind are in any sense transferences from social organization. The category of quality would have to exist and to operate in order that an individual mind should even recognize the one, the many and the whole, of the divisions of his social group. And again, it is only by the mind's perceiving its data in the form of succession that the periodicity of religious rites could have been known at all. . . . If, on the other hand, Durkheim means by mind a mere aggregation of representations or ideas, there is sense in supposing that the first ideas of time may have been of the periodicity of primitive religious rites, the first ideas of quantity, of the divisions of the tribe, etc. But the supposition is then of merely historical importance. . . . It has no direct bearing upon either the epistemological or the psychological study of the nature or status of the categories of mind.[55]

The argument is that Durkheim's theory of the categories is circular because it presupposes a set of social actors already equipped with these very categories. This charge is totally unfounded.

To begin with, the critics are at cross purposes with Durkheim. They are using the word *category* in one way — he in another. The critics take it for granted that categories are properties or possessions of the individual mind. They are counted amongst the *capacities*, or as part of the explanation of these capacities. For Durkheim, however, the categories are something social. In his discussion of the difference between our subjective sense of time and the objective category of time, he tells us that a category is "in itself . . . a veritable social institution."[56] He uses the word *category* when describing public systems of knowledge: "They are, essentially collective representations."[57] It refers to a property of our shared knowledge, indicating the special status that is imputed to one part of the system relative to the rest. The categories are the parts that are accorded the role of being a priori. Despite his evolutionary and historical speculations Durkheim is quite clear that the a priori in knowledge is not to be equated with the biologically innate or psychologically prior.[58] The priority in question is impersonal and objective, and is always thought of as timeless.[59]

No wonder the critics think Durkheim is presupposing what he should be proving when they treat his investigation as if it is an inquiry into the nature of the individual mind. For instance we are told that although *Primitive Classification* is subtitled "a contribution to the study of collective representations," Durkheim and Mauss's "real concern throughout is to study a faculty of the human mind."[60] In fact Durkheim and Mauss are quite explicit about the capacities they allocate to individuals, and are absolutely definite that what they want to explain is something other than this. When the confusions of the critics' own making have been removed, a perfectly consistent line of argument can be found, which in no way muddles capacities and content. It is indeed precisely the line of argument that has been followed in the development of the network model. Durkheim and Mauss tell us that the individual mind is capable of drawing rudimentary distinctions in the flux of experience; it can detect resemblances; it possesses a sense of spatial and temporal orientation; and it can develop expectations which prefigure theories of cause and effect.[61] This much — which is shared with the mentality of other animals — is indeed presupposed by social life and cannot be explained by it. But then, ask the critics, what is there left to explain "when so much is admitted"?[62]

As Durkheim and Mauss are at pains to point out, there is a great deal to explain. Their point is that "what truly constitutes a classification" possesses properties that could not possibly arise from individual cognitive achievements of the kind that have just been "admitted." As the network model shows, public systems of knowledge possess laws and principles of organization that are binding and authoritative.[63] These have the property of being "an external norm, superior to the flow of our representations"[64] and they function as rules or standards.[65]

To overlook these facts is to make the same mistake as those who would explain specifically moral concepts by appeal to individual psychological dispositions. To assume that individual classificatory inclinations could endow any of their products with authority is like assuming that an isolated individual could generate for himself a moral obligation, as if desiring to do something prefigures being duty bound to do it, or as if abhorrence were an embryonic form of being forbidden. Just as the argument about morality applies whatever our supposed natural inclinations, so the argument about the necessary and a priori parts of knowledge applies whatever capacities we possess. Any natural cognitive propensities can be overruled and declared to be an error or illusion, as the network model has shown. The celebrated charge of circularity therefore rests on a blunder, and an elementary one at that. It confuses properties of the individual with what is specifically social.[66]

The main strands of my argument can now be summarized. The material from the history of physics has shown us cases where Durkheim and Mauss's claim is true. In the corpuscular philosophy we have seen the classification of things reproducing the classification of men. The idea of nature being put to social use then shows us how it comes about that the formula is true. It gives us the cause of which Durkheim and Mauss's homologies are the effect.[67] Finally, the network model has shown us how it is *possible* for the Durkheim and Mauss formula to be true. It has provided us with an account of what knowledge is that makes the previous results natural and comprehensible. It also allows us to overcome the theoretical reservations that have dogged *Primitive Classification*. In fact, it performs the vital function of giving the sociologist a workable account of knowledge that orients him to all its main social features, showing not merely how society influences knowledge, but how it is constitutive of it. All the different strands of the argument therefore complement and reinforce one another.

It is time we stopped treating *Primitive Classification* as a museum piece. Rather than condescending to it we should take it seriously. This means being selective and revisionary. For this reason I have not dwelled on its shortcomings or equivocations, but concentrated on the main thrust of the argument and asked myself what can be learned from it. Whatever seems unserviceable has been discarded without a second thought.[68] Approached in this way, the machinery of the theory can be made to work. The importance of Durkheim and Mauss's formula for the sociology of knowledge should no longer be in doubt.[69]

Notes

1. E. Durkheim and M. Mauss, "De quelques formes primitives de classifications," *Année Sociologique* 1901-2 (1903); trans. and intro. by R. Needham, *Primitive Classification* (London: Cohen and West, 1963), p. 11.

2. E. Benoit-Smullyan, "The Sociologism of Emile Durkheim and his School," in *An Introduction to the History of Sociology*, ed. H.E. Barnes (Chicago: University of Chicago Press, 1948), ch. 27; W.R. Dennes, "The methods and presuppositions of group psychology," *University of California Publications in Philosophy* 6(1924):1-182; C.E.E. Gehlke, "Emile Durkheim's contributions to sociological theory," *Columbia University Studies in History, Economics and Public Law* 62(1915):1-188; A.A. Goldenweiser, "Methods and principles," *American Anthropologist* 17(1915):719-35; E.L. Schaub, "A sociological theory of knowledge," *Philosophical Review* 29(1920):319-39; P.M. Worsley, "Emile Durkheim's theory of knowledge," *Sociological Review* 4(1956):47-62.

3. S. Lukes, *Emile Durkheim, His Life and Work: A Historical and Critical Study* (London: Allen Lane, 1973).

4. Durkheim and Mauss, *Primitive Classification*, ch. 3.

5. For a summary of the main empirical objections, see: Needham, ibid., sect. II; and Lukes, op. cit., ch. 22.

6. Benoit-Smullyan, op. cit., p. 533.

7. E. Durkheim, *The Elementary Forms of Religious Life*, trans. J.W. Swain (New York: Collier Books, 1961). (First French ed., 1912), pp. 23, 494. Cf. Lukes, op. cit., p. 435.

8. Dennes, op. cit., p. 39; Schaub, op. cit., p. 336.

9. Although there are hints of a better theory in *Primitive Classifications* (e.g. on p. 15), Merton is surely right to complain that Durkheim's use of the word "reproduce" suggests a naive reflection or projection theory; cf. R.K. Merton, "Paradigm for the Sociology of Knowledge," in *The Sociology of Science: Theoretical and Empirical Investigations* (Chicago: University of Chicago Press, 1973), p. 31.

10. M.B. Hesse, *The Structure of Scientific Inference* (London: Macmillan, 1974), chs. 1, 2; P. Duhem, *The Aim and Structure of Physical Theory*, trans. P.P. Weiner (Princeton: Princeton University Press, 1954). (First French ed. 1906.); W.V.O. Quine, "Two Dogmas of Empiricism," in *From a Logical Point of View* (Cambridge, Mass.: Harvard University Press, 1953).

11. M. Black, *Models and Metaphors* (Ithaca: Cornell University Press, 1962); M.B. Hesse, *Models and Analogies in Science* (London: Sheed & Ward, 1963); M.B. Hesse, "The Explanatory Function of Metaphor" in *Logic, Methodology, and Philosophy of Science*, ed. Y. Bar-Hillel (Amsterdam: North-Holland, 1965); D. Schon, *Displacement of Concepts* (London: Tavistock, 1963).

12. I am not saying that any alleged law would work in any circumstances. The point is that we cannot test each law in isolation, and the practical demands that we impose on our beliefs bear upon groups of laws. The crucial fact about the equivocal location of error is called the Duhem-Quine thesis. If the joint premises A and B imply the conclusion C, and C is false, then all we know is that either A is false, or B is false, or both are false. Thus far we are free to lay the blame where we will.

13. For a real life example see G. Allen, "Hugo de Vries and the 'Mutation Theory,'" *Journal of the History of Biology* 2(1969):55-87. (I am grateful to Barry Barnes for drawing my attention to this example.)

14. This criticism has been levelled at the network model by E. Nagel, "Theory and Observation," in *Observation and Theory in Science*, ed. E. Nagel, S. Bromberger, and A. Grunbaum (Baltimore: Johns Hopkins University Press, 1971). A particularly interesting example is provided by the stability of color categories. For example, B. Berlin and P. Kay, *Basic Color Terms: Their Universality and Evolution* (Berkeley: University of California Press, 1969). Berlin and Kay arranged the natural languages in a sequence depending on the number of basic color terms they contain. It emerges that there is a regular order in which the colors appear in sequence: first black and white, then red, then yellow or green, then blue, etc. The color terms are all focused on similar places on the spectrum, so that exemplars of "red" in all cultures are roughly the same.

15. J. Farley, *The Spontaneous Generation Controversy from Descartes to Oparin* (Baltimore: Johns Hopkins University Press, 1977); J. Farley and G.L. Geison, "Science, politics, and spontaneous generation in nineteenth-century France: the Pasteur-Pouchet debate," *Bulletin of the History of Medicine* 48(1974):161-98.

16. Cf. the concept of *normal science* in T.S. Kuhn, *The Structure of Scientific Revolutions* (Chicago: University of Chicago Press, 1962). Recent attacks on Kuhn, for example by Lakatos, have not succeeded in discrediting this concept. On the contrary, they have simply recast Kuhnian insights into a more rationalistic and inferior idiom. I. Lakatos, "Falsification and the Methodology of Scientific Research Programmes" in *Criticism and the Growth of Knowledge*, ed. I. Lakatos and A. Musgrave (Cambridge: Cambridge University Press, 1970); D. Bloor, "Two paradigms for scientific knowledge?" *Science Studies*, (now *Social Studies of Science*) 1(1971):101-15.

17. Hesse, *Structure of Scientific Inference*, p. 52.

18. M. Douglas, *Purity and Danger: An Analysis of Concepts of Pollution and Taboo* (London: Routledge & Kegan Paul, 1966), ch.5; idem, *Natural Symbols: Explorations in Cosmology* (Harmondsworth: Penguin, 1973); idem, *Implicit Meanings: Essays in Anthropology* (London: Routledge & Kegan Paul, 1975), pt 3; idem, *Cultural Bias* (Royal Anthropological Institute of Great Britain and Ireland, Occasional Paper No. 34, 1978).

19. Douglas, *Implicit Meanings*, p. 281. The context makes it clear that the word "apprehending" refers to an active rather than a passive process.

20. P.M. Rattansi, "Paracelsus and the Puritan revolution," *Ambix* 11(1963):24-32; idem, "The intellectual origins of the Royal Society," *Notes and Records of the Royal Society of London* 23(1968):129-43; J.R. Jacob, "The ideological origins of Robert Boyle's natural philosophy," *Journal of European Studies* 2(1972):1-21; idem, "Robert Boyle and subversive religion in the early Restoration," *Albion* 6(1974):175-93; idem, "Boyle's circle in the Protectorate: revelation, politics and the millenium," *Journal of the History of Ideas* 38(1977):131-40; idem, *Robert Boyle and the English Revolution: A Study in Social and Intellectual Change* (New York: Franklin, 1977); idem, "Boyle's atomism and the Restoration assault on pagan naturalism," *Social Studies of Science* 8(1978): 211-33. Throughout this and the next section I am greatly indebted to S. Shapin, "Social uses of science" in *The Ferment of Knowledge: Studies in the Historiography of Eighteenth-Century Science*, ed. G.S. Rousseau and R.S. Porter (Cambridge: Cambridge University Press, 1980), pp. 93-139.

21. Robert Boyle, "Some considerations touching the usefulness of experimental natural philosophy," in *The Works of the Honourable Robert Boyle*, vol. 1 (London: 1744). On p. 446 Boyle says: "God . . . having resolved, before the creation, to make such a world as this of ours, did divide . . . that matter, which he had provided, into an innumerable multitude of variously figured corpuscles, and both connected those particles into such textures or particular bodies, and placed them in such situations, and put them into such motions, that by the assistance of his ordinary preserving concourse, the phenomena, which he intended should appear in the universe, must as orderly follow, and be exhibited by the bodies necessarily acting according to those impressions or laws, though they understand them not at all. . . ."

22. Ibid., p. 448.

23. Hence his: "A free enquiry into the vulgarly received notion of nature"; Ibid., vol. 4, pp. 358-424.

24. Ibid., vol. 1, p. 445.

25. Rattansi, "The intellectual origins of the Royal Society," p. 139.

26. C. Hill, *The World Turned Upside Down: Radical Ideas during the English Revolution* (Harmondsworth: Penguin, 1975).

27. As Gerrard Winstanley said: "I tell you, this great mystery is begun to appear, and it must be seen by the eyes of flesh: and those five senses that is in man shall partake of this glory." Quoted, ibid., p. 149.

28. Quoted, ibid., pp. 206, 219.

29. From a letter by Boyle dated October 22, 1646, quoted by Rattansi, "The intellectual origins of the Royal Society," p. 136; Jacob, "The ideological origins of Robert Boyle's natural philosophy," op. cit., p. 3.

30. The detailed circumstances and political context are described by Jacob, "The ideological origins of Boyle's natural philosophy," op. cit.

31. Boyle, *The Works of the Honourable R. Boyle*. vol. 4, p. 376.

32. Rattansi, "Paracelsus" (1963), p. 29.

33. Boyle, *The Works of the Honourable Robert Boyle*, vol. 1, p. 439.

34. A general summary of the evidence connecting sectarians and supporters of Paracelsus, and the story of the rift between them is given in Rattansi, "Paracelsus," 1963. Interestingly, the Boyle circle was haunted by the fear of a subversive alliance between the sectaries and the Catholics.

35. The argument that follows is derived from M.C. Jacob, *The Newtonians and the English Revolution, 1689-1720* (Ithaca: Cornell University Press, 1976); J.R. Jacob and M.C. Jacob, "The Anglican origins of modern science: the metaphysical foundations of the Whig constitution," *Isis* 71(1980):251-67. Obviously, only the main outlines of this detailed and sustained piece of sociology of knowledge can be given here.

36. Quoted, Jacob, *The Newtonians* p. 184.

37. This was suggested to Boyle as a way of refuting Hobbes' dangerous opinions on matters of religion. Cf. Ibid., p. 24.

38. Quoted, ibid., p. 184.

39. I have used William Whiston's translation given in F.E. Manuel, *The Religion of Isaac Newton* (Oxford: Clarendon, 1974), p. 16.

40. A.R. Hall and M.B. Hall, eds., *Unpublished Scientific Papers of Isaac Newton* (Cambridge: Cambridge University Press, 1962), p. 144.

41. I. Newton, *Opticks*, 4th edition 1730. Query 31. (Reprinted by G. Bell, London, 1931, p. 397.)

42. E. McMullin, *Newton on Matter and Activity* (London: University of Notre Dame Press, 1978), p. 103. It is a significant comment on the present state of academic boundaries that McMullin's excellent book makes no mention of the work of either J.R. Jacob or M.C. Jacob on the ideological significance of the passivity of matter. Instead of referring to the social use of this principle it is simply related to a metaphysical "influence" and theological "tradition," as if these were in some way self-explanatory or self-perpetuating.

43. Quoted, Jacob, *The Newtonians*, p. 156. The quotation continues "I had my eye on such Principles as might work with considering man for the belief of a Deity, and nothing can rejoice me more...." It would be a mistake to think that Newton had in mind any kind of sincere profession of belief in God. Many such professions were for Newton no better than atheism, e.g. believing in God as the soul of the world. His concern, like Boyle's, was to direct men to a *specific* religious stance, viz. the worship of the God of the latitudinarians.

44. A very similar debate occurred right at the end of the Newtonian Tradition, around 1900. By that time the role of Newton's active principles and forces had been taken over by the luminiferous ether. For the Cambridge School of Stokes, Rayleigh, J.J. Thomson, Larmor, Tait, Stewart, Lodge, and Fitzgerald, the ether not only played a technical role but also had an intense theological significance. For the description and documentation of this fascinating case in which the classification of things again reproduces the classification of man, see B. Wynne, "Physics and Psychics: Science, Symbolic Action and Social Control in Late Victorian England," in *Natural Order: Historical Studies of Scientific Culture*, ed. B. Barnes and S. Shapin (London: Sage, 1979), ch. 7.

45. See S. Shapin, "History of science and its sociological reconstructions," *History of Science* 20(1982):157-211.

46. Benoit-Smullyan, op. cit., p. 533.

47. Durkheim, *The Elementary Forms of Religious Life* (1912), pp. 31, 488. The idea that society is part of nature might be called the materialist version of Durkheim's answer. On p. 490 he gives the answer an idealist twist by saying that nature is part of society, part of its "interior existence." But neither principle is sufficiently precise to solve the problem.

48. Ibid., p. 486.

49. Ibid., p. 493.

50. Ibid., p. 486. After this betrayal of his own theory it is refreshing to see Durkheim swing back with a forceful discussion of the way science rests upon opinion, pp. 486-87.

51. Ibid., pp. 22, 30, 488.

52. Notice that it is not the network that constrains. This only signalizes constraints by its stability. Knowledge does not constrain, people do. What limits our freedom to change category boundaries are the countervailing interests that other people have invested in them. What gives knowledge its coherence lies outside knowledge. We must never appeal to the network to *explain* its own application, employment or development: it is a *description*. The point is nicely made in D. MacKenzie and B. Barnes, "Scientific Judgement: the Biometrician-Mendelism Controversy," in *Natural Order: Historical Studies of Scientific Culture*, ed. Barnes and Shapin, ch. 8.

53. This is, of course, a perfectly proper use of the word "category." It is a notion that has had a vexed history in philosophy and takes on special meanings within the context of each philosopher's system. Durkheim's use and my gloss upon it corresponds closely to the meaning of category as it occurs in present day analytical philosophy. Here it refers to any classification that is deemed so important that a violation must be specially sanctioned, for instance by making it out to be nonsense or unintelligible, rather than merely wrong. (For Durkheim the notion of nonsense is relative: it *seems* as if thought would destroy itself if categories are violated. Durkheim, *The Elementary Forms of Religious Life*, op. cit., p. 22). For the diverse uses of the word "category" and the difficulties philosophers have in justifying their intuitions that certain ideas they do not like are "category mistakes," see M. Thomson, "Categories," in *The Encyclopedia of Philosophy*, ed. P. Edwards (London: Collier Macmillan, 1967), vol. 2, pp. 46-53; J. Passmore, "Allocation to Categories," in *Philosophical Reasoning* (London: Duckworth, 1961), ch. 7.

54. Gehlke, op. cit., pp. 52-3.

55. Dennes, op. cit., p. 39.

56. Durkheim, op. cit., p. 23, n. 6.

57. Ibid., p. 28.

58. Ibid., p. 28, n. 16.

59. Ibid., p. 484. "Logical thinking is always impersonal thinking, and is also thought *sub species aeternitates* — as though for all time." It could be said that Durkheim was offering a theory of the objective mind, or an epistemology without a knowing subject. This explains the obvious parallels between his conception of knowledge and Popper's account of the so-called world three of objective knowledge. For an explanation of these similarities and a sociological transformation of Popper's highly reified theory, see D. Bloor, "Popper's mystification of objective knowledge," *Science Studies* (now *Social Studies of Science*) 4(1974):65-76.

60. Needham, op. cit., p. xxvi. It becomes quite clear on p. xxviii that these "innate faculties" are properties of "the individual mind."

61. Durkheim and Mauss, op. cit., pp. 7, 81, n. 1. Durkheim, op. cit., pp. 411, 489, 491.

62. Needham, op. cit., p. xxviii.

63. Durkheim and Mauss, op. cit., p. 8.

64. Durkheim, op. cit., p. 410.

65. Ibid., p. 482, n. 10.

66. The individualism and empiricism of Durkheim's critics is marked. Thus Gehlke, op. cit., pp. 105- 06 , argues that the properties of the "social mind" are just augmented features of individual minds. The common areas of overlap are "mutually strengthened," so the difference is one of quantity rather than quality. Goldenweiser, op. cit., p. 73, says that "categories come into being within the mental world of every single individual," and have their "sources in experience or the psychological constitutions of man." Similarly, Schaub, op. cit., p. 333, sees the categories as "rooted in instinctive responses and sense experience." Worsley, op. cit., p. 59, although allowing a role for social interests, says that "the universality and necessity of the categories . . . arise from common, but not necessarily collective, experience of the external natural order." But how could the categories so arise? We are never told. I suspect that Durkheim's critics reject his solution because they do not understand the problem. (It is only fair to add that Professor Worsley's empiricism is considerably modified in later publications, e.g. P. Worsley, "Groote Eylandt totemism and Le Totemisme aujourd'hui," in *The Structural Study of Myth and Totemism*, ed. E. Leach, A.S.A. monographs, 5 [London: Tavistock, 1967], pp. 141-59.)

67. In the present theory the two structures related by Durkheim and Mauss's formula do not stand to one another precisely as cause to effect. Rather, the similarity of structure between knowledge and society is itself the effect of the social use of nature. This is the real cause. As interests vary, we have seen the resulting patterns of social relationship vary and also the resulting pattern of knowledge. If there were no expressions of interests through the social use of nature, then perhaps no homologies would be generated between social and cognitive structures. Vary the cause, vary the effect; remove the cause, remove the effect.

68. For example, I have rejected Durkheim and Mauss's "intellectualist" approach. They stress the "purely speculative purpose" of primitive cosmologies and say that they are not instituted "with a view to regulating . . . conduct." They do this because they say that it will help their case when arguing for the continuity of primitive and scientific classifications, op. cit., pp. 81- 2 n. 1. I would reverse their argument and see continuity in the fact that they *both* have a role in regulating conduct.

69. The next step is to generalize the theory. For example, is it possible to develop a typology of all possible structures of interest? If so, then we have at the same time stated a typology of coherence conditions for knowledge. For such a theory to work it is necessary to hit upon a way of describing social structures so that they fall into a small number of recurrent types. Then it will be possible to detect regularities and frame laws. Such a theory is currently being developed by Mary Douglas in her grid and group dimensions of social structure. For a brief account of this theory applied, speculatively, to material from the history of mathematics, see D. Bloor, "Polyhedra and the abominations of Leviticus," *British Journal for the History of Science* 11(1978):254- 72, and, more generally, D. Bloor, *Wittgenstein: A Social Theory of Knowledge* (London: Macmillan, 1983).

4

Knowledge and Utility:
Implications for the Sociology of Knowledge

Michael J. Mulkay

In recent years there has been much discussion of whether it is possible to have a sociology of scientific knowledge as distinct from an analysis merely of the social relationships and moral ethos of science. This debate has necessarily raised issues which are epistemological as well as sociological in character. The most obvious of these issues is that of the relativity of knowledge. This problem has been prominent in the main tradition of the sociology of knowledge and has received most attention in the recent debate. There is, however, at least one other topic which has had a major influence on sociologists' thinking about science and which, if my experience is at all representative, is seen by most students, as they draw on their stock of "common knowledge" about science, as showing most clearly that scientific knowledge must be exempt from sociological analysis. This second topic or issue is that of the supposed connection between scientific knowledge and utility or practical effectiveness. Let me try to show that this issue, which has not so far been systematically explored by sociologists of knowledge, deserves a place in the current debate.

Two Sociological Perspectives on Science

In the literature which considers the place of science within the sociology of knowledge, two contrasting perspectives are to be found.

Perspective One

This is the dominant perspective which treats science as a special sociological case. Scientific knowledge is regarded as epistemologically unique — as consisting basically of observation statements that have been

77

firmly established by the controlled, rigorous procedures of scientific method. The corpus of certified scientific knowledge is thought to represent, with increasing accuracy and completeness, the truth about the physical world. Because scientific knowledge is seen as an objective account of the real world, it is assumed that sociological analysis must stop when it has shown how the social organization of science enables scientists to observe and report the world objectively, with little sign of the bias and distortion that are thought to arise in other areas of cultural production through the impact of social and personal factors.

Within this perspective, the close analysis of the development of scientific knowledge can be left almost entirely to philosophers of science and to historians of ideas. Sociologists will be able to contribute directly to analysis of the conclusions of science only in cases where social factors have helped to remove impediments which have previously hampered scientists' perception of the truth,[1] or where there has been some mistake. Werner Stark expresses this view when he writes that

social developments do not determine the content of [genuinely valid] scientific developments, simply because they do not determine natural facts, but they may well open the eyes of the scientists to natural facts which, though preexistent and always there, had not been discovered before.[2]

Within this perspective it appears that social influences can intrude into the actual intellectual content of science only when science has been distorted by nonscientific pressures. Sociologists interested in the creation of scientific knowledge, as distinct from scientific error, have therefore come to concentrate not on the intellectual content of science, but on the normative structure which is thought to make objective knowledge possible.

The norms of science have customarily been conceived as a defensive barrier which protects the scientific community from intellectually distorting influences, and which thereby enables scientists to assess research results solely in accordance with the clear-out, preestablished technical criteria appropriate to the validation of empirical knowledge-claims. General conformity to such normative principles as impartiality, emotional neutrality, and, particularly, universalism, is seen as necessarily implied by the nature of scientific knowledge. Insofar as scientists deviate from such prescriptions, it is argued, they will be influenced in their observations and judgments by considerations that do not originate in the physical world itself. From this perspective, then, sociological analysis of science is built upon the promise that the firm conclusions of science are determined by the physical, and not the social, world; that the content of scientific knowledge is not amenable to sociological investigation; and that the cohesion and effectiveness of the scientific community depend on the maintenance of a highly universalistic ethos without which "object-centered" knowledge could not be regularly produced.

Perspective Two

There is, however, an alternative perspective which argues that the procedures and conclusions of science are, like all other cultural products, the contingent outcome of interpretative social acts.[3] It is argued that the empirical findings of science are intrinsically inconclusive and that the factual as well as the theoretical assertions of science depend on speculative and socially derived assumptions. It is also suggested that the general criteria by which scientific knowledge-claims are assessed (such as consonance with the evidence, replicability, and the like) have no meaning until they are interpreted in terms of scientists' particular intellectual commitments and in relation to specific interpretative and social contexts. In addition, it is argued that scientists' actions within the research community are not governed by the universalistic social norms traditionally assumed by sociologists. Rather, it is proposed that what have been taken to be the institutionalized norms of science are merely one part of a much broader repertoire of social formulations, which scientists employ as resources in negotiating the acceptance of specialized knowledge-claims.[4]

The central contention, then, of this perspective is that although the physical world exerts constraint on the conclusions of science, it never uniquely determines those conclusions.[5] Scientific research is never merely a matter of registering an objective world. It always involves the attribution of meaning to complex sets of clues generated by scientists' actions on the physical world; and such attribution of meaning is not carried out in a social vacuum maintained by a set of rigid moral prescriptions. Rather the attribution of technical meaning is always inextricably bound up with those processes of social interaction whereby the social attributes of participants and their claims are negotiated.

The conclusions established through scientific negotiation are not taken to be definitive accounts of the physical world. Nor is it accepted that they have been demonstrated to be valid for all groups at all times through the application of unchanging technical criteria, although, of course, scientists may often appear to treat their conclusions in this way. Instead, the propositions advanced by scientists are regarded, sociologically, as claims which have been deemed to be adequate by particular groups of actors in specific social and cultural contexts. Within this second perspective, it is accepted that there are good grounds for including science fully within the sociology of knowledge and for examining in detail how objects present themselves differently to scientists in different social settings, how scientists in different social positions devise and accept different kinds of knowledge-claims, and how social (that is, nontechnical) considerations enter into the structure of scientific knowledge.[6]

The Two Perspectives and the Problem of Relativity

Until very recently the first of the two perspectives I have briefly outlined was quite clearly dominant — and indeed virtually unchallenged — within the sociology of knowledge. In the last few years, however, the alternative perspective has been gaining ground. Consequently, some attention has been given by its proponents to showing that adoption of such an approach need not lead, as has been customarily assumed, to intractable analytical difficulties — in particular, that it does not founder on the problem of relativity. Within this perspective, all assessments of knowledge-claims, as well as the very meaning of such claims, are viewed as contingent products of social processes. In the past, most sociologists of knowledge have regarded such a position as relativistic and, therefore, as self-refuting: they have seen it as a "trap" to be avoided, not least because of the threat it seemed to pose to their own knowledge-claims. They have generally accepted without question that, unless they can retain a special epistemological status for a certain class of propositions which are not socially or existentially determined, their own analyses will have to be treated as mere byproducts of social processes and, consequently, as invalid. Thus any extreme version of the sociology of knowledge which fails to define some knowledge-claims as beyond its scope, appears to lead to intellectual chaos.

In the last few years, however, this form of argument has been reexamined.[7] It has been pointed out that this vicious circle only operates as long as one presupposes that socially determined ideas are necessarily invalid. Thus, if we have been led to conclude that all ideas are socially contingent, we can avoid the trap of relativity simply by abandoning this presupposition. Once a firm commitment has been made to the idea that all knowledge is socially created, this traditional presupposition comes to appear as "a gratuitous assumption" and to embody "an unrealistic demand. If knowledge does depend on a vantage point outside society and if truth does depend on stepping above the causal nexus of social relations, then we may give them up as lost."[8] In short, when faced with the trap of relativity, we can always choose to revise our conception of validity instead of abandoning a sociological approach to the creation of knowledge.

In the passage from which I have just quoted, David Bloor asks us to reconsider the assumption that if ideas are a product of social causation they must be false. It is, however, difficult to abandon this assumption as long as we continue to use the kind of causal terminology traditionally employed within the sociology of knowledge. Within this tradition, sociologists have written of ideas (or knowledge-claims, etc.) as being determined by social factors in much the same way that the movement of a billiard ball may be seen as determined by the impact of a cue. Given such a causal metaphor, it is particularly difficult to accept that an idea can be socially determined and yet valid, for the nature of the idea appears to depend solely on the character of the cause and to have little or nothing to do with the subject dealt with by the idea. But this kind of causal language need not necessarily play any part in a sociological account of knowledge-production.

Thus in my brief description of the second sociological perspective on science I made no mention of causes or social determinants, but referred instead to social actors using cultural resources to interpret socially produced observations in specific contexts. The metaphor here relies on a notion of actors negotiating meanings rather than the impacts of billiard balls and cues. It inclines more toward some form of hermeneutic analysis than the kind of causal analysis that traditionally gives this problem a misleading appearance of insolubility.[9] An interpretative formulation of the second perspective on science does not lead us into intellectual chaos. We are not impelled to abandon all criteria of validity, nor to accept that all knowledge-claims are epistemologically equal. What we do have to accept is that criteria of validity are neither preestablished, eternal or universal. They are cultural resources whose meaning has to be reinterpreted and re-created constantly in the course of social life.[10]

Knowledge, Utility, and Perspective One

I will not pursue the topic of relativity any further here. I have mentioned it partly in order to suggest that the "problem of relativity" does not necessarily eliminate the second perspective from consideration; and also to show that the discussion that follows contributes, from a different angle, to the same debate. I turn now to an equally fundamental issue, which, although it also has major implications for the sociology of scientific knowledge, has so far received much less attention. This is the question of the relationship between knowledge and practical application.

This issue has as much bearing on our choice between the two perspectives as that of relativity, for a reluctance to attempt to carry out sociological analysis of scientific knowledge is often linked to an unquestioned conviction that such knowledge must be epistemologically unique and independent of social context because it is such a fruitful source of successful technological application. To put this another way, whereas the problem of relativity has led sociologists to seek a class of knowledge-claims which is epistemologically privileged and therefore exempt from sociological analysis, the supposed connection between science and technology has often led them to identify this class of privileged propositions with scientific knowledge. Let me give three illustrative examples of sociologists presenting this kind of argument.

The first is Werner Stark, who, writing some twenty years ago, maintained that:

So far as nature is concerned, the main guiding value has ever been the same, namely, to achieve an understanding and control over her. . . and hence in all ages attention has been paid to the same aspects of the realm of nature — those which promise us a foothold in and a whiphand over her. . . . Whether [man] likes it or not, he must, under all cultural circumstances, pursue, among others, the economic and technological values, the values of science.

Accordingly,

Whereas man has more than once shifted his vantage-point for the consideration of social facts so that these facts appear to him in ever new and often surprising, outlines he has always kept to the same spot for surveying the facts of nature . . . so that these latter have always offered to him the self-same surface. He has merely learned to look more closely. . . .[11]

Stark concludes, therefore, that in our dealings with the physical world there has been cumulative intellectual progress, as sources of bias and distortion have been steadily eliminated, and as selection of knowledge-claims on the basis of their capacity for providing effective practical control has been generally established.

A second, and more recent, example is provided by Elias, who claims that human knowledge of the physical world "has reached a comparatively high degree of object-orientation, of fitness to [its] objects . . . and men have acquired a correspondingly high capacity for controlling the course of events in that sphere."[12] He goes on to argue that if we are to develop a general sociology of knowledge, we must recognize that our analysis of the production of such relatively objective knowledge must differ markedly from our analysis of subject-centered knowledge. Central to this analysis, he stresses, must be the fact that scientific thought has become progressively separated from social influences and its conclusions thereby rendered independent of variations in social context. Elias's argument is particularly interesting, because the only criterion he gives to identify object-centered knowledge is its "capacity to control the course of events"; and because object-centered knowledge is treated as being synonymous with science and technology. In this formulation, then, effective practical control is seen as the defining characteristic of the body of properly validated and socially autonomous scientific knowledge.

It is important to recognize that neither Elias nor Stark is referring exclusively to the kind of control over events which is exercised by laboratory scientists in the course of experiment and systematic observation. The point these authors stress is that the universal validity of scientific conclusions can be established for us, as laymen, by the success of science in everyday practical affairs. Thus Elias emphasizes that the object-centeredness of scientific knowledge becomes evident in the contribution it makes to its possessors' efforts in the struggle for survival. Presumably he has in mind the contribution of science to economic technology, to military hardware, and to the control of disease. This view of the practical effectiveness of science is most clearly expressed by Johnston:

> When we say that science "works," what we mean is that it provides us with the capability to manipulate and control nature   The enormous attainments of modern natural sciences, which are supported not only by the work of the scientists themselves, but, even more importantly, by the millions of experiments going on in the real world when objects are constructed or predictions made based on scientific theories, represent a fairly conclusive proof of their mastery of a segment of reality and a clear demonstration of their superiority over all other knowledge systems invented by man.[13]

This line of argument can be used to pose a major challenge for the second sociological perspective on science, and for its central claims that scientific knowledge is socially contingent, that its content is influenced by variations in social context, and that the interpretation of the criteria used to validate scientific knowledge is also socially variable. For we have just seen that it can quite reasonably be argued that there is an objective, socially invariant criterion which can be and is used to certify the validity of scientific knowledge-claims — the criterion of practical utility. Scientific knowledge can be seen to be valid because it works, irrespective of changes in social context, in a way which everyone must accept: it seems to be objectively valid in the sense that it gives us efficient control over many aspects of the physical world. It is difficult to see how context-dependent formulations would do this. Thus it seems that "every new technology bears witness," not only "to the integrity of the scientist,"[14] but also to the objectivity of his knowledge and to his freedom from social influences. In short, the practical effectiveness of scientific knowledge establishes its special epistemological status; and its special epistemological status then establishes its independence of social context, and its exclusion from the scope of sociological analysis.

In the next two sections I shall subject this line of argument to critical appraisal, in order to try to discern how far it does undermine the second sociological perspective on science. I do not imagine that the brief comments which follow will resolve the complex issues involved. My aim, therefore, is the relatively modest one of drawing attention to the fact that discussion of the relationship between science and technology has important implications for the sociology of scientific knowledge, and of showing

that the view of this relationship, which is contained in the dominant tradition of sociological thought about science, is at least open to question.
My intention, then, is to generate discussion of these issues, rather than to
forestall further argument by means of a final, conclusive analysis.

How Far is Modern Technology Dependent on Science?

When we argue that the special epistemological, and therefore sociological, position of science is established by the technological productivity
of modern society, we appear to be assuming that most effective practical
techniques created today are a fairly direct product of scientific knowledge, and also that most scientific knowledge actually generates such
techniques. The very terminology which sociologists, and others, have
used to describe the relationship between science and technology clearly
expresses these assumptions. Thus the processes whereby knowledge is
produced and put into operation have typically been depicted as taking
place along a continuum from "basic" (or "pure" or "fundamental") research, to "applied" research, to "technological development." As we have
seen, sociologists of knowledge have been inclined to take it for granted
that the conclusions reached at the "basic" end of the continuum are in
general validated by practical activities occurring at the "development"
end. Yet when we come to look at the empirical evidence relevant to this
issue, we find little indication of any clear or close links between basic scientific research and the great mass of technical developments. Let me
refer briefly to several different kinds of evidence to illustrate this point.

If we begin with the results of citation analysis we find, first, that in
any given scientific field, most knowledge-claims do not appear to work in
any sense at all (except perhaps as items on a curriculum vitae). The majority of claims are not cited by (and appear to receive virtually no attention from) other scientists. They seem to exist merely as archival material.[15] Moreover, certain areas of scientific inquiry (for example, stellar
spectroscopy) are never seen by participants or outsiders as having any
relevance to practical application. Consequently, when we talk of scientific knowledge demonstrating its objectivity through successful application, we are at most referring to a minority of scientific knowledge-claims
within a limited number of research areas. We cannot, therefore, use this
argument to show that the intellectual products of science in general enjoy
a special epistemological status. This negative conclusion is strengthened
by the fact that the literatures of science and technology tend to remain
distinctly separate, with little cross-reference and with significantly different patterns of internal citation. As far as we can tell from citation analysis, science seems to accumulate mainly on the basis of past science, and

technology primarily on the basis of past technology.[16]

The view that the relationship between academic research and practical application is weak and indirect receives further support from various case studies of technological development. For example, in the early 1960s a number of studies of recent innovations in "materials" were carried out, under the sponsorship of the Materials Advisory Board of the U.S. National Academy of Sciences.[17] The Board constructed a seven-stage model of the process of technological innovation, which depicted an orderly sequence from basic science to practical application. It proved, however, to be impossible to interpret the empirical findings consistently with this model. In none of the cases studied could the innovation be seen as a direct consequence of advances in basic science. In most instances, the innovation appeared to derive directly from prior technological activity. Similar conclusions were reached in a later British study of the eighty-four technological innovations granted the Queen's Award in 1966 and 1967. The authors write:

We have paid particular attention to the relation of basic science to innovation. . . . Our failure to find more than a small handful of direct connections is the more striking for the fact that we set out deliberately to look for them.[18]

In a recent review of the literature bearing on this issue, Layton sums up its implications with the statement that "the old view that the basic sciences generate all the knowledge which technologists then apply will simply not help in understanding contemporary technology."[19]

Layton and others have stressed that practical application and what has traditionally been called "basic research" take place in different social contexts. It seems that the social separation and divergent internal dynamics of these contexts operate to prevent any marked social or cognitive interaction. This is evident in the findings of a study by Blume and Sinclair of the reward system among chemists in British universities.[20] These authors show that only a minority of British academic chemists are concerned with problems of practical application, and that those who are so concerned are neither particularly productive nor highly regarded by their colleagues. Furthermore, those with strong industrial interests tend to receive appreciably less recognition in the university setting for a given amount of published work. It seems that the British chemical industry has the attention of a small and relatively unproductive sector of the university research community — at least partly because the allocation of academic rewards directs participants' interests away from practical application. This, it should be noted, is within that scientific discipline which has the longest history of contact with industry.

We must not exaggerate the line of argument being proposed here. There have been some notable and well-documented cases where aca-

demic research undertaken in pursuit of fundamental scientific knowledge
has led directly to successful practical application. There is also the phenomenon of "embodiment." This occurs when scientific knowledge becomes embodied in a specific procedure or device, such as a transistor,
which is then used in the production of further techniques. There is a
tendency in such cases to treat the second generation of techniques as
growing out of prior technology alone and to ignore the original scientific
contribution. There is also the difficulty of estimating the extent to which
basic science contributes to technological advance by means of informal
interaction and as a result of the basic training which most applied scientists obtain in an academic setting. Nevertheless, the kind of evidence I
have summarized makes problematic the simple view that in general the
abundant technology of industrial societies is a direct by-product of a
growing corpus of basic scientific knowledge.

It is, of course, true that there is an increasing number of technological sciences which are explicitly organized around problems arising in the
pursuit of practical objectives. These subdisciplines are often located
mainly within the academic community, while retaining close links with
industry. However, these technological sciences are intellectually as well
as socially distinct from the autonomous generalizing sciences that sociologists have considered to be the main repositories of certified scientific
knowledge. In particular, they are

... less abstract, less idealized. Thus, the theory of structures is less abstract than physics, for
example, in incorporating idealized versions of manmade devices. But in turn, structural design, which has become scientific in some respects, is much less abstract than structural theory. That is, the designer must take into account a more complex reality. The theorist may assume that the materials are uniform, but the designer must be aware of nonuniformities in his
materials and make due allowances for them.[21]

In other words, insofar as this kind of technological science approaches
practice, so its cognitive content appears to diverge from the universal
formulations of the basic scientific disciplines. Whenever basic science is
used as the foundation for technological science (and hence for the production of technology), it requires a considerable amount of
reformulation. In order to make basic science work, it has to be radically
reinterpreted in accordance with the requirements of the social context of
practical application.[22] This seems to illustrate not that practical utility
furnishes an objective criterion of the universal validity of scientific propositions, but rather that judgments of cognitive adequacy vary with social
context. It certainly makes it far from obvious that we can treat the practical success of technology or applied science as validating the
formulations of basic science; for the latter actually undergo major transformations of meaning as they come nearer to the realm of application.

So far I have concentrated on the connection, or lack of connection, between technology and basic science. But even if we leave basic science aside for the moment, and focus instead on the contribution to practical technique made by applied science, it is still doubtful whether the bulk of modern technology derives in any direct fashion from scientific knowledge.

> The rapid growth and the scientific glamour of research-intensive industries tend to obscure the fact that most industries are not research-intensive, and that much technological work is relatively unsophisticated. . . . The first design in a new field of industry may be quite crude and totally outside science. R.G. LeTourneau, the inventor of the bulldozer, quite typically was a practical mechanic without formal technical education. The prototype machine was assembled from known components using an acetylene torch. . . . [As in this example], a major portion of modern industry is quite unrelated to the science-technology complex. . . .[23]

When we consider those practical applications which do appear to originate in scientific research, it is important to remember that most (and possibly all) knowledge systems have produced successful practical applications — even systems like Babylonian mythological astronomy,[24] whose general principles we now regard as clearly falsified. Given this, and given that industrial societies have devoted an ever increasing proportion of their immense "surplus product" specifically to the production of systematic knowledge, we would expect a dramatic growth of knowledge-related technology in modern society, without having to assume that the epistemological character of knowledge has altered with the advent of modern science. There is no need to assume that scientific knowledge is different in kind from prescientific or craft knowledge, or that the "rate of practical return" on scientific knowledge is remarkably high.[25] It may simply be that there is now much more systematic knowledge; that it is much more detailed and precise; and that there are many more people actively concerned to exploit it for practical purposes.

A notable consequence of the cumulative increase in the rate of knowledge-production has been that more and more previously unsuspected phenomena and realms of investigation have been identified and explored in detail.[26] Many of the most obvious and influential practical successes of science have come from exploiting the findings of these new fields; this is true, for example, in relation to electricity, bacteria, and subatomic particles. Such practical applications have seemed particularly dramatic because there has been little or no knowledge previously available of the phenomena involved. Consequently, even the crudest kind of practical intervention, as in the early attempts at vaccination, could be and were interpreted as testifying to the special efficacy of scientific knowledge. Scientists and scientific popularizers used these discoveries to promote an aura of wonder and infallibility, which served to strengthen their claims for ever more men, money, and social support. But, given that most bodies of systematic thought about the natural world have engendered successful practical applications, the practical exploitation of new areas of scientific inquiry generated by the increasing scale and intensity of the scientific enterprise provides no grounds for treating scientific knowledge as epistemologically unique or as occupying a privileged sociological position.

It is also important to realize that in most areas where scientific research is maintained as a basis for practical application, technological failure, unlike technological success, usually remains invisible to and unconsidered by the outsider. If we wish to argue that practical success validates scientific knowledge, we have to accept that practical failure is an indication to the contrary. Unfortunately, we know very little about the incidence or circumstances of technological failure — perhaps partly because its possible significance for traditional sociological assumptions about scientific knowledge has not previously been noted. However, what little we do know seems to suggest that unexpected failure to bring about technological advance through the exploitation of scientific knowledge is far from uncommon.[27] Without sufficient evidence we cannot reach a firm conclusion about the frequency of technological failure. But without a systematic attempt to balance success against failure, we can hardly use the technological productivity of modern society as grounds for exempting scientific knowledge from sociological analysis. Finally, it is worth documenting the fact that in areas where science has made a significant contribution to practical action, this contribution can become greatly exaggerated, thereby providing spurious support for common sense assumptions. We have already seen how sociologists tend to take for granted that the effectiveness of modern medicine provides one of the clearest illustrations of how science pays off in practical terms. Indeed, this view is very widely held. For instance, until recently it was accepted, almost without question, that the massive decline in mortality from infectious diseases which has occurred in Western societies since the middle of the last century, was brought about by improvements in medical therapy deriving directly from the findings of scientific research.[28] This view is so well entrenched that it is worth examining the systematic evidence closely. Let us look briefly at some of the more significant infectious diseases.

Consider first tuberculosis, which was the largest single cause of death in the nineteenth century, and the virtual elimination of which has contributed nearly a fifth of the total reduction in mortality since then. It is clear that the death rate in England and Wales from respiratory tuberculosis declined steadily from 1850 to 1970. But effective chemotherapy did not begin until 1947, with the introduction of streptomycin, and immunization was used on a substantial scale only from 1954. "By these dates mortality from tuberculosis had fallen to a small fraction of its level in 1848-54; indeed most of the decline (57%) had taken place before the beginning of the present century."[29] This pattern is repeated in the case of virtually all the major infectious diseases. "Of the total decline of mortality between 1848-54 and 1971, bronchitis, pneumonia and influenza contributed nearly a tenth; of the fall in the present century they contributed a fifth. Most of this decrease occurred before the introduction of sulphapyridine."[30]

Mortality from whooping cough began to decline from the seventh decade of the last century. Treatment by sulphonamides and, later, antibiotics was not available before 1938 and even now their effect on the course of the disease is doubtful. "Clearly almost the whole of the decline of mortality from whooping cough occurred before the introduction of an effective medical measure."[31] Mortality from cholera and related diseases began to fall from the late nineteenth century and, by the time that intravenous therapy was introduced, 95 percent of the overall improvement had taken place. Similarly "mortality from typhus fell rapidly towards the end of the last century and there have been few deaths in the twentieth. It can be said without hesitation that specific medical measures had no influence on this decline."[32]

The decline in mortality from infectious diseases is the most significant medical achievement of modern times. It is commonly assumed that this achievement is primarily a product of applied science, and this assumption about the impact of medical science has strengthened sociologists' conviction that scientific knowledge is a special type of knowledge. Detailed examination of the historical evidence, however, seems to show unambiguously that medical science has made only a marginal contribution to this practical achievement. If this realm of practical action is at all representative, much of what we take for granted about the practical efficacy of science may be quite illusory. Given that the production of scientific knowledge-claims has grown steadily and cumulatively in modern times, any secular trend in the realm of practical action will be correlated with the growth of scientific knowledge; and given our conception of the special character of scientific knowledge, it will be only too easy to interpret the former as a consequence of the latter. But the example of the infectious diseases should lead us to beware of taking this kind of connection for granted, and to treat seriously the evidence and arguments (presented earlier in this section), which challenge common sense by insisting that the links between scientific knowledge and practical application are relatively weak.

In this section I have concentrated on the strength of the connection between science and technology, and have commented only in passing on the question of whether, even where there is a direct link, the practical application of knowledge can actually serve to validate that knowledge. In the next section I will take up this latter issue in more detail.

Can Successful Practical Application Validate a Scientific Theory?

As we have seen, it has customarily been taken as self-evident that when a theory is actually used as the basis for successful practical action, this necessarily validates the theory. There are, however, strong grounds for maintaining that effective practical application is insufficient to provide such validation. This issue has been examined with particular reference to modern science and technology by Mario Bunge, and the discussion which follows takes his analysis as its point of departure.[33]

The central question with which we are concerned can be restated as follows: is it possible for a false or a partly false theory to be successful in practical terms? Bunge argues that it *is* possible for several reasons. In the first place, we must recognize that any theory is composed of a number of propositions. It is always possible that only some of these propositions contribute significantly to its successful practical application. It therefore appears that the most we can conclude from using a theory to good practical effect is that some part of that theory is valid, or approximately so. But this conclusion must be further qualified. The complexity of everyday practical situations and the impossibility of controlling all relevant variables make it much more difficult to establish clear theoretical inferences on the basis of practical success, compared with the relative clarity of inference attainable in the laboratory or its equivalent, where some close approximation can often be made to the idealized relationships between phenomena with which scientific theory deals.

A careful discrimination and control of the relevant variables and a critical evaluation of the hypotheses concerning the relations among such variables is not done while killing, curing, or persuading people, nor even while making things, but in leisurely, planned, and critically alert scientific theorizing and experimentation. Only while theorizing or experimenting do we *discriminate* among variables and *weigh* their relative importance, do we *control* them either by manipulation or by measurement, and do we *check* our hypotheses and inferences. This is why factual theories, whether scientific or technological, substantive or operative, are empirically tested in the laboratory and not in the battlefield, the consulting office, or the market place.[34]

It follows that it is usually impossible to identify by means of successful practical action alone which elements of a theory have been responsible for, and hence validated by, the successful achievement. It is, therefore, misleading to talk of scientific knowledge being validated by "the millions of experiments going on in the real world."

Another important consideration that strengthens these conclusions is that the idealized formulations of scientific theory have always to be not only reformulated, but also combined with other cognitive elements when they are brought to bear on the "chunks of everyday reality" with which men deal in their practical affairs. For example,

the relativistic theory of gravitation might be applied to the design of generators of antigravity fields ... which in turn might be used to facilitate the launching of spaceships. But, of course, relativity theory is not particularly concerned with either field generators or astronautics; it just provides *some of the* knowledge relevant to the design and manufacture of antigravity generators.[35]

The construction of effective antigravity generators, therefore, would not necessarily provide conclusive support for any part of the initial academic version of relativity theory, partly because that theory will have been revised, reinterpreted and, probably, considerably simplified in accordance with the specific requirements of this field of practical endeavour; and also because many supplementary conceptions will have been introduced which may well have been crucial in bringing about practical success.

It is also important to realize that the accuracy requirements of practice are very different from, and usually far less stringent than, those applied in research undertaken with no immediate practical objective. An approximate and simple theory will often be sufficient for practical purposes, even when it is known to be scientifically inadequate. For instance, applied physicists today concerned with designing optical instruments can get by for the most part with optical theories dating from the middle of the seventeenth century. In many cases, the crudity of the theories employed for practical purposes will be hidden from the outsider by the wide margins of error which are allowed for in the technological product.

Safety coefficients will mask the finer details predicted by an accurate and deep theory anyway, and such coefficients are characteristic of technological theory because this must adapt itself to conditions that can vary within ample bounds. Think of the variable loads a bridge can be subjected to or of the varying individuals that may consume a drug. The engineer and the physician are interested in safe and wide intervals centered in typical values rather than in exact values. A greater accuracy would be pointless since it is not a question of testing. Moreover, such a greater accuracy could be confusing because it would complicate things to such an extent that the target — on which action is to be focused — would be lost in a mass of detail. Extreme accuracy, a goal of scientific research, is pointless or even encumbering in practice in most cases.[36]

The considerations identified above — that is, reformulation of theories in practical contexts, use of only part of a theory, low accuracy requirements and the complexity of practical situations — show that "infinitely many possible rival theories" can yield results that are identical in practical terms, and that it is undoubtedly possible for a false theory or a partly false theory to be practically effective. In other words, we seem to have decided that successful practical application has no conclusive validating force. However, we might still wish to object to this conclusion, on the grounds that knowing how to do something is itself valid knowledge. As Bunge puts it, it might yet "be argued that a man who knows how to do something is thereby showing that he knows that something."[37] Let us examine this claim in connection with the following example of a successful practical act. The example will help us see that the claim is either a tautology or demonstrably false.

An African tribal remedy, using strips of paw-paw fruit, successfully cleared postoperative infection in a kidney transplant patient after antibiotics had failed, doctors disclosed yesterday. The remedy for infection was suggested by Dr. Christopher Rudge, a junior member of the transplant team, who had seen it used in the South African bush on ulcers and wounds. The fruit was bought from Fortnum and Mason, the Piccadilly grocers. He said he had used it before in difficult cases, and felt it could be useful in treating routine healing problems. "It is not awfully scientific: I do not know why it works."[38]

One might wish to argue that Dr. Rudge's knowledge of the curative effects of paw-paw was shown to be valid by his practical success. It is certainly clear that Dr. Rudge did have the prior knowledge that the act of laying paw-paw strips on a wound was sometimes followed by a reduction of infection. It is also clear that the act was deemed to have been successful in this instance. But "success" and some form of "knowledge that" are presupposed in the kind of case we are considering, for, if either of these elements were lacking, the issue of validation would not arise. Thus the claim that "a man who knows how to do something must know that something," when applied to such cases, can become a mere tautology. It can be used to mean only that, in the kind of case being examined, a man described a practical act which, when carried out, was judged to have been successful. By the nature of such cases, however, there must be a correspondence between the original description and the practical outcome. Interpreted in this minimal sense, then, the claim is vacuous. But if we interpret the claim more strongly, as requiring that the actor must state not only that something works, but also present some appropriate account of how it works — that is, some form of theoretical or scientific knowledge — then this example appears unambiguously to refute the claim.

We are quickly led to a similar conclusion if we reverse the formulation of the claim above and present it as: "If a man knows X, then he must know how to do or make X." This statement appears not to apply to all cases. For example, we know (or think we know) how geological formations are produced by natural processes, but we are unable to reproduce them ourselves. Likewise, astronomers are confident that they have an enormous body of validated knowledge about the nature of stars, the distribution of galaxies, and so on, without being able to influence these objects in any way at all. Our practical incapacity in no way weakens our confidence in the validity of either geological or astronomical knowledge. Furthermore, not only can we use our knowledge in these areas to show why practical intervention is impossible, but earlier theories could also be used in this way, such as those of medieval astronomy, which we now regard as false. It seems that our ability to control, regulate, or reproduce natural phenomena is not decisive in enabling us to claim valid knowledge of such phenomena; nor is the capacity to explain this lack of practical effectiveness, within a theory's own framework of analysis, crucial in distinguishing false from true theories.

We can, then, conclude that the successful use of scientific theories establishes neither their validity nor their privileged epistemological status. This conclusion strengthens the case of the second sociological perspective on science, by weakening one of the main presuppositions of the dominant framework: it is also more consistent with the analysis of science provided by the second perspective. From the dominant perspective, validated knowledge is conceived as being established as universally valid by the application of invariant criteria of adequacy; it is, therefore, rather hard to understand why it should prove to be so difficult to validate theoretical knowledge by means of the apparently invariant criterion of practical success. In contrast, the second perspective proposes that knowledge is constituted differently according to varying interests, purposes, conventions and criteria of adequacy, in different social contexts or groups, and that judgments of cognitive "correctness" will necessarily be context-dependent; it follows that judgments of practical efficacy cannot serve unproblematically to validate knowledge-claims which are proposed in connection with different interpretative contexts and in relation to different socially defined objectives.

Concluding Remarks

I have sought to widen the scope of the current debate about the possibility of subjecting scientific knowledge to sociological analysis. I have tried to show that in identifying scientific knowledge as epistemologically special, and as exempt from sociological analysis, sociologists have tended to make two basic assumptions which have so far received little systematic investigation; namely, that scientific theories can be clearly validated by successful practical application, and that the general theoretical formulations of science do regularly generate such practical applications. I have argued that both these assumptions are very doubtful. In developing this argument, I have been led to defend the second sociological perspective on science, which treats scientific knowledge as open to sociological analysis, and to show that it can cope with the basic issues which arise when we consider the relationship between science and practical application.[39]

There is at least one important respect in which my argument remains incomplete. I have avoided raising the question of whether or how *practical effectiveness* is itself socially constructed. Throughout the analysis above I have used *practical success* as a sociologically unproblematic notion — an unexamined interpretative resource. To this extent I have stayed within the main sociological tradition, where it has generally been assumed that the effectiveness of certain kinds of practical action is self-evident and is not open to negotiation or subject to social variation. Despite my reticence on this question, it does seem to me that there are areas where the technical meaning of given practical actions can be shown to be socially constructed, socially variable and context-dependent.[40] This is well illustrated in Michael Bloor's study of the diagnosis of cases for adenotonsillectomy.[41] Nevertheless, there are very few studies of this kind and none at all which consider how the technical meaning of hard technology is socially constructed. Until this kind of analysis is forthcoming, the second sociological perspective will remain incomplete; for it is clearly implied in that perspective that no area of knowledge (whether formal, scientific, or practical) is closed to sociological interpretation. I suggest that this area of discourse should also be introduced into the debate, although at the moment I intend to offer nothing more concrete on the topic than this broad exhortation.

Notes

1. Barry Barnes, *Scientific Knowledge and Sociological Theory* (London: Routledge & Kegan Paul, 1974).

2. Werner Stark, *The Sociology of Knowledge* (London: Routledge & Kegan Paul, 1958), p. 171.

3. See, for example, J. Law and D. French, "Normative and interpretive sociologies of science," *Sociological Review* 22(1974):581-95; H.M. Collins, "The seven sexes: a study of the sociology of a phenomenon or the republication of experiments in physics," *Sociology* 9(1975):205-24; G.N. Gilbert, "The transformation of research findings into scientific knowledge," *Social Studies of Science* 6(1976):281-306; B. Wynne, "C.G. Barkla and the J phenomenon: a case study in the treatment of deviance in physics," *Social Studies of Science*, 6 (1976): 307-47.

4. M.J. Mulkay, "Norms and ideology in science," *Social Science Information* 15 (1976), 637-56.

5. Barry Barnes, *Interests and the Growth of Knowledge* (London: Routledge & Kegan Paul, 1977).

6. This is a paraphrase of Karl Mannheim's general formula in *Ideology and Utopia* (New York: Harcourt, Brace & World, 1936), p. 265.

7. See Barnes, op. cit., note 1; David Bloor, *Knowledge and Social Imagery* (London: Routledge & Kegan Paul, 1976); H.M. Collins and Graham Cox, "Recovering relativity: did prophecy fail?" *Social Studies of Science* 6(1976):423-44; J. Law, "Prophecy failed (for the actors): a note on 'Recovering Relativity,'" *Social Studies of Science* 7(1977): 367-71; H.M. Collins and G. Cox, "Relativity revisited," *Social Studies of Science* pp. 372-80; Hugo Meynell, "On the Limits of the Sociology of Knowledge," *Social Studies of Science* pp. 489-500; Eric Millstone, "A framework for the sociology of knowledge," *Social Studies of Science* 8(1978):111-26.

8. Bloor, *Knowledge and Social Imagery*, nn. 7, 14.

9. A similar point is made by Millstone, op. cit., n. 7. It is worth noting that both Barnes and Bloor, when actually engaged in sociological analysis, clearly interpret social causation in terms of active agents employing various kinds of interpretative resources to pursue socially defined ends.

10. See Barnes, op. cit., n. 5.

11. Stark, op. cit., p. 166, n. 2.

12. Norbert Elias, "Sociology of Knowledge: New Perspectives, pt. 1," *Sociology* 5(1971):163; see also Ibid., pt. 2, pp. 355-70.

13. Ron Johnston, *Science and Rationality*, pt. 2 (Manchester: SISCON/Department of Liberal Studies in Science, Manchester University, 1977), pp. 23-4.

14. R.K. Merton, *Social Theory and Social Structure* (New York: The Free Press, 1957), p. 560. Revised and enlarged edition.

15. See, for example, S. Cole and J. Cole, *Social Stratification in Science* (Chicago and London: University of Chicago Press, 1973).

16. Derek J. de Solla Price, "Is technology historically independent of science?" *Technology and Culture*, 6(1965):553-67; and "The Structures of Publication in Science and Technology," in *Factors in the Transfer of Technology*, ed. W. Gruber and G. Marquis (Cambridge, Mass.: MIT Press, 1969), pp. 91-104.

17. Materials Advisory Board, *Report of the Ad Hoc Committee on Principles of Research-Engineering Interaction* (Washington, DC: National Academy of Sciences, 1966). Similar remarks could be made about the well-documented studies known as "Project Hindsight" and "TRACES." For a very apposite commentary, see K. Kreilkamp, "Project Hindsight and the real world of science policy," *Science Studies* 1(1971):43-66.

18. J. Langrish et al., *Wealth from Knowledge* (London: Macmillan, 1972), p. xii.

19. E. Layton, "Conditions of Technological Development," in *Science, Technology and Society*, ed. I. Spiegel-Rösing and D.J. de Solla Price (London and Beverly Hills, Calif.: Sage, 1977), p. 210.

20. S. Blume and R. Sinclair, "Chemists in British Universities," *American Sociological Review* 38(1973):126-38.

21. Layton, op. cit., p. 210, n. 19.

22. For a general discussion of how the findings of research are continually reinterpreted, see J. Ravetz, *Scientific Knowledge and Its Social Problems* (Oxford: The Clarendon Press, 1971), pp. 182-208.

23. Layton, op. cit., p. 215, n. 19.

24. See S. Toulmin and J. Goodfield, *The Fabric of the Heavens* (Harmondsworth, Middx.: Penguin, 1963), ch. 1.

25. H. Inhaber, "Scientists and economic growth," *Social Studies of Science* 7(1977):517-24.

26. M.J. Mulkay, "Three models of scientific development," *Sociological Review* 23(1975):509-26.

27. H.M. Sapolsky, "Science, Technology and Military Policy," in *Science, Technology, and Science,* ed. Spiegel-Rösing and Price, pp. 452-53, n. 19.

28. T. McKeown, *The Modern Rise of Population* (London: Arnold, 1976). I have assumed that the figures for other Western countries will resemble those for England and Wales.

29. Ibid., p. 93.

30. Ibid., pp. 94-5.

31. Ibid., p. 97.

32. Ibid., p. 102.

33. M. Bunge, "Technology as applied science," *Technology and Culture* 8(1967):329-47.

34. Ibid., p. 336. (Emphasis in original)

35. Ibid., p. 331. (Emphasis in original)

36. Ibid., pp. 334-35.

37. Ibid., p. 336.

38. The Daily Telegraph (London), 14 April 1977, 3.

39. See also M.J. Mulkay, *Science and the Sociology of Knowledge* (London: Allen & Unwin, 1979).

40. It is important to recognize that the difficult task facing the sociologist here is that of providing an analysis of the technical as opposed to what we might loosely call the social meaning of technology. Thus, it is fairly easy to show that the social meaning of television varies with and depends upon the social context in which it is employed. But it is much more difficult to show that what is to count as a "working television set" is similarly context-dependent in any significant respect.

41. M. Bloor, "Bishop Berkeley and the adenotonsillectomy enigma," *Sociology* 10(1976):43-61.

Part II
Theoretical Perspectives

Introduction

In times of uncertainty such as ours, the need to make knowledge both legitimate and certain increases dramatically. Consequently there is in contemporary societies an increasing reliance on technical or scientific knowledge and an emphasis on its evermore rapid and varied dissemination. What are the limits of society's capacity to know and to learn? The old questions regarding the relationship of a knowing subject and knowable object surface once again, are reexamined, and new answers are sought.

All authors in this section emphasize the importance of a reexamination of the role of epistemology and of method in sociological theory as well as the contribution of science to its formation. Though the authors' theoretical perspectives are different, they all assign to the sociology of knowledge a special role in this task of reexamination. For Niklas Luhmann, knowledge is of two kinds — knowledge of the life world and scientific knowledge. Truth is understood as but one of many generalized media of communication and science as but one self-referential system among others. He sees the task of the sociology of knowledge as providing us with the discourse necessary in the explication of the different approaches. Luhmann arrives at this conclusion by reviewing various theories of reflection from the seventeenth century onwards within the context of a general systems theory.

By contrast, Barry Barnes views knowledge, whether logical or natural, as a social phenomenon existing as a restricted (institutionalized) form of cognition of a particular culture. By using the Hesse net he demonstrates the two processes employed by people to classify the world around them — ostension and generalization. Ostension is the process by which we associate a term with an object or event in our immediate environment; it is primarily an element of verbally mediated learning. Generalization is the process by which associations are made between objects, events, and processes within the larger environment or culture. Barnes claims that it is not necessary to differentiate and choose between different bodies of knowledge; all classifications (rational or not) are socially sustained as parts of the reality or experience of a given culture. Decisions are made at any given time based on open-ended conventions which in turn are influenced by special interests. A body of knowledge is used because it serves a particular interest and not because it is inherently more rational. There are not different kinds of knowledge but merely different kinds of interests and uses. For Barnes, the sociology of knowledge should be in the forefront of sociological theory by explicating the ways in which knowledge is a social phenomenon. The appropriate question should be: Why this institution, in this context?

Günter Dux observes that sociology was established as a discipline in order to do away with idealist epistemology. Since it has so far failed to do so, it is important and timely that sociological theorists review and reconstruct the discipline's history in order to learn from the difficulties of the past and avoid the mistakes of the past in their theoretical reconstructions. After tracing Descartes' argument on the origin and conditions of human cognition, Dux discusses its variations in the work of Feuerbach, Marx, Plessner, and Gehlen. He concludes that sociology's inability to formulate a materialist epistemology is not a failure of the discipline but rather a historical inevitability. By utilizing and improving on Piaget's genetic epistemology a new scientific epistemology can be established, which takes into account that human cognition is social in origin. The sociology of knowledge, Dux argues, can play an important role in determining the means by which different life-worlds are created by human beings.

Gérard Namer proposes a model for a triple legitimation and suggests that the sociology of knowledge can greatly gain in substance and status by associating itself with the sociology of science. He describes Ziman's "itinerary" of scientific knowledge where knowledge gains legitimation only after it has acquired social significance, and traces the process in which a knowledge-claim achieves legitimate status first within the scholarly community, then in the media, and finally acquires social recognition. For Namer, the role of the media is of extreme importance. The various media have historically played a dual role, not only by making scholarly knowledge more easily accessible to a larger audience, but also by fragmenting historical knowledge. The media have thus created new facts, a new logic, and a new history. As a result, a new hierarchy of knowledge has emerged, creating an uncertainty which the scholarly community in general and the sociology of knowledge in particular must come to terms with.

Karin Knorr-Cetina examines how scientific knowledge is created and assessed. She focuses upon the problem of facticity — the nature of facts — which has preoccupied philosophers for centuries and which has been the underlying reason for the proliferation of epistemological theories. There has been a tendency recently to move the search for facts away from the knowing subject to other locations within the social process of production, in particular the laboratory. Knorr-Cetina has discovered in her macrosociological studies of scientists at work that research results or knowledge claims are constructed in a laboratory within an indeterminable context which both directs and promotes the construction and reconstruction of scientific facts. Her studies demonstrate that laboratory operations are results of actual or potential discursive interaction and communication among the inhabitants of a laboratory. Knowledge about facts is located within social processes of production formation found in the laboratory.

The five articles in this section propose new directions for the sociology of knowledge which take into account modern developments in epistemology and in the production of scientific knowledge. The authors' suggestions, however tentative, often involve issues which, while not concerns of the founders of sociology, appear to promise for the sociology of knowledge a prominent place in the tradition of sociological inquiry.

5

The Differentiation of Advances in Knowledge: The Genesis of Science

Niklas Luhmann

I

There are many reasons why one should take up the question of a sociological theory of knowledge once again and reformulate it with the means available today. One reason already lies in the irritatingly unresolved status of the classical problem of the sociology of knowledge: the question of the truth value of the sociological explanation of knowledge that lays claim to truth. A second reason lies in the fact that epistemology is becoming increasingly sociological: this is especially striking where it includes historical analyses of the development of theory — tying itself to historicism.[1] Other empirical disciplines have in the meantime attempted to establish an epistemology with a claim to universal validity — above all neurophysiology, biology, and evolutionary theory.[2] The work of Gotthard Günther, which belongs to a completely different domain of inquiry, should be mentioned here: it concerns the history of the principle of bivariateness and the problems of multisubjectivity which undermine it.[3] This approach makes appear as superficial, or at least as in need of clarification, the currently widespread use of such concepts as discourse or dialogue in characterizing the process which constitutes knowledge.[4]

There is a close affinity between this form of inquiry in logic and the recent interest in self-reference in both the field of logic and in systems theory.[5] From this perspective, traditional epistemology, in all its substantive, temporal, and social variants — as the apriorism of principles, of process, of sociality — appears to have been shaped by the (logically based) fear of the self-referential circle. Some apriority appeared to it as indispensable on the basis of the assumption that, in Kantian terms, the very conditions of the possibility of experience cannot themselves be objects of experience and cannot be located in that domain. But did this not also mean that there could be no rational answer to the inquiry into the conditions of the possibility of reason? Whatever the case may be, it seems to be precisely this well-founded and apparently compelling resistance that renders the classical problem of the sociology of knowledge unsolvable, requires an introduction of the concept of discourse in a theoretically unexplicated manner, and is the reason for basing epistemology on problematic apriorisms (Kant) or long-range hopes (Popper).

This approach to the problem, "avoidance of self-reference," has been supported and complemented by the assumption that self-reference only appears in consciousness. It was therefore possible to declare consciousness on the basis of Cartesian self-analysis to be the "subject," locate the binary schematization of logic in the subject, and therefore limit and restrict the dangerous problem of self-reference at this point. But in the final analysis positing this subject as the foundation of both itself and everything else did not succeed. The fact that this attempt was unsuccessful apparently has to do with the limitation (*Engführung*) caused by the link to consciousness. This association of self-reference and consciousness, highly susceptible of being anchored in the modern individual's experience of himself, produced transcending ("transcendentalizing") strategies as attempts to avoid an exclusively subject-immanent (hence a consciousness-immanent) foundation of knowledge. The history of these attempts indicates a succession of substantive, temporal, and social apriorisms: it tries out principles of orientation (Kant), the subjectivity (better: the "subjectity") of the historical process which works itself upward (Hegel), and finally the thesis of the social a priori immanent in all reason (Adler, and no doubt also Habermas). This a priori reasoning, presented from the viewpoint of the subject, has replaced the older distinction between self-consciousness and self-maintenance[6] and forced conservative connotations on the concepts of "existing conditions" and "maintenance." Sociologists interested in epistemology have always initially sought reconstructions of the a priori.[7] Today this entire network of concepts and theories has its own historically grounded significance. But it is dependent on a version of the problem which begins to lose its persuasive force once alternatives arise.

Once it is recognized that this semantic, accumulated in the history of epistemology, runs into difficulties which it can no longer solve on its own — and once it is realized that this foundation is in the way of an adequate sociology of knowledge — a renewed concern with the problem that initiated this development might seem attractive. I have called this "the avoidance of self-reference." This is the point at which the following considerations begin, which do not attempt to seek a remedy by formulating a counterthesis or by simply negating the classical premises and asserting their opposite. In the end it cannot be ignored that pure self-reference corresponds to arbitrariness and does not provide specific limits. But the changes in the potential of contemporary theories which I have mentioned do suggest a far-reaching recontextualization of the precept of avoidance. I will move away from the association of self-reference and (subjective) consciousness; more specifically, I will reduce it to a special case among many others and begin instead with a theory of self-referential systems which allows for several quite different realizations. Of particular interest as a realization will then be the domain of social systems and here, in turn, specifically the case of modern society with its subsystem specializing in science.

II

In the context of a general systems theory we must distinguish between three different meanings of "self-reference," depending on what it is that functions as the "self" of the "reference." The first meaning arises when we start with the elements (or, more particularly, the elementary events) that constitute the system by way of interrelation, for example if we start with individual actions, information, decisions. We can speak of self-reference at this level if the event can only participate in system formation by referring back to itself by way of its relationship to other events — thus if it requires a context to identify itself and select its relations to others. In this sense I will speak of "basic self-reference."

A second meaning arises when events are linked to form processes over time by means of reciprocal selection. If processes are directed and identifiable, they can, for their part, function as a "self" of the "reference." In this case I will speak of "reflexivity" or "reflexive processes."[8] Reflexive processes refer to themselves before they are directed toward an object and thereby acquire steering capability. Examples here are: thinking about thinking, knowledge about knowledge, research about research.

To be distinguished from this is the case where the system in which events and processes take place functions as the "self" of the reference. I will call this "reflection," since in this case the system uses the orientation toward its own identity to steer itself. Indispensable for this is the separation from an environment which does not belong to the system, hence the system-internal use of the difference between system and environment. Not all basic self-referential systems develop an identity by means of reflection. For example, while the neurophysiological system of the brain is endowed with a basic self-reference and reflexivity with which it can increase sequences and frequencies and let them be effective as such, it cannot as a means of self-selection make reflections about its own difference from the environment.[9] To this end it must produce consciousness. (The theory that only starts here, i.e. with consciousness, therefore had initially regarded it unnecessary to distinguish clearly among the different forms of self-reference and separate them conceptually). The different forms of self-reference are related to problems of complexity. Complexity compels a system toward selection once a system contains so many elements that it can no longer link each element to every other one. The selection which is then necessary can be controlled by means of self-reference in that the (possible) reference back to the self is used as the criterion of discrimination. The greater the demands, the greater the need to employ more exacting forms of self-reference. The demands become greater with increasing selectivity because selections then become riskier and must prevail against a larger number of alternatives. It can therefore be assumed (and I shall try to demonstrate this by way of the example of science as a differentiated subsystem of society) that as complexity and consequently selectivity increase, the other forms of self-reference must be employed as well. In other words, reflexivity and reflection must subsequently be developed if control complexity is not to trail too far behind design complexity.[10]

A circular context of reference is at the root of all self-reference. The element active within it gains access to itself again by locating itself vis-à-vis other elements. In systems with temporalized complexity and elements fixed in time (events),[11] this occurs by using time (permanence) by way of an orientation which anticipates or recalls.[12] Following Alfred Korzybski we may speak of "time binding."[13] For the occurrence of events (information, actions, decisions), such a temporal binding requires a number of processors and in this sense a multiple, "mutualistic," dialogue-like system. In the case of simplified models one occasionally starts with an (illusory) minimum of two processors as the condition of self-reference.[14] In the theory of social systems such a minimal requirement is symbolized by the terms *ego* and *alter*. This terminology can be used without difficulty when it is made clear that neither institutionalized roles nor even concrete persons are intended, but rather minimal conditions for the constitution of self-referential systems in the special domain of social systems.

To produce a self-referential organization of the system's elements, the processors must be linked in a circular fashion. This structure has frequently been represented with regard to ego and alter; we can therefore confine ourselves to a description of well-known theoretical assumptions. The circle arises *within* each processor *by way of the other*, because each processor produces its own events. In its selections of action, ego adheres to that which it expects from itself and that which, according to its expectation, alter expects of it. In order to realize these complementary expectations, it experiences alter as alter ego. It can therefore be assumed that alter also functions as ego, since the figure of the ego duplicates itself in alter. Hence ego can expect that its alter ego will experience it as alter and likewise attempt to take its bearings from both itself and the other. The circle does not merely consist in knowing that one depends on the preferences of the other, but rather that one depends *on* the awareness of the dependency *of both*. Only in this way, viewed chronologically, does it have a moment-like (and not already a "sequenced" and thereby asymmetrical) existence, and in each processor impresses itself upon events from moment to moment.

<h1 style="text-align:center">III</h1>

It might be useful to conceive of this now common model of circular "sociality" more concretely by way of a historical example. In the seventeenth-century literature concerning social behavior, especially conversation, in addition to detailed prescriptions and certain ideal figures (*honnête homme*, etc.), the maxim of "pleasing" (*plaire*) was emphasized above all.[15] It is important to please others by putting aside one's own impulses. In this context one particular prescription acquired central significance: it is especially important to please another by offering him the possibility to please.[16] The *doux commerce* of social behavior thereby turns in a circle to optimize the reciprocal "passing to the other" of opportunities to please. To this end both a facility in the management of themes and the constant change of themes are required. Thus we can find in the *Encyclopédie* the following passage, which codifies a long development:

Les lois de la conversation sont en général de ne s'y appesantir sur aucun objet, mais de passer légèrement, sans effort et sans affectation, d'un sujet à un autre. . . en un mot de laisser, pour ainsi dire, aller son esprit en liberté et comme il veut ou comme il peut.[17]

At the same time, according to contemporaries, this circle of pleasing eliminates some incompatible elements — for example, exalted individuality, knowledge that must be discussed precisely and intensively, or delicate topics of another sort (such as religion or politics) that might give rise to conflict. Although the circle is self-referentially closed, it behaves selectively and thereby produces a system. It actually constitutes the difference between system and environment, i.e. that which is admitted as *bienséance* as opposed to that which is rejected.

Social conversation has peculiar features and makes demands which (just like the consciousness that one thinks) stand in opposition to the true/false dichotomy. This parallel has hardly been noticed until now. As Descartes's analysis shows, self-consciousness reaffirms itself by way of true and false ideas. But conversation is likewise bound to the necessity of keeping silent about certain truths or even of practicing the art of disguise so that it can remain possible as communication and is not broken off.[18] Thus the differentiation of social communication as such does not lead to advances in knowledge; it only permits a keener awareness of what must be taken into consideration if interaction and reciprocal pleasing are to be continued.

The problems of a restricted self-referential circle, that is, the problems of a dual relationship which is only concerned with itself, have been duly noted. Self-reference — including social self-reference — leads to boredom if it cannot "extract its wine from the grapes of life":

L'union de deux personnes attachés entièrement l'une avec l'autre, cette belle union a besoin des choses étrangères qui excitent le goût du plaisir et le sentiment de la joie. . . . C'est dans le monde, et dans un mélange de divertissement et d'affaires, que les liaisons les plus agréables et les plus utiles sont formés.[19]

But this world still seems to exist in an unproblematic way, and any world is sufficient to provide the indispensable environment for friendship as long as it accords with the requirements of pleasant company. Within the general context of class-specific requirements, such a system, together with its environmental prerequisites, specializes in being unspecialized.

This first circular model[20] already possessed clearly formulated, but also clearly antiscientific, features. It selected what was essential for maintaining the readiness to continue contact and (to this end) for changing the topics of the conversation continually. What mattered with respect to topics was not the attainment of conclusions; the imposition of either/or demands could therefore be avoided, and, because they were socially uncomfortable,[21] also had to be avoided. Disagreement with beliefs expressed in a conversation was regarded as problematic, or even as an instance of unacceptable behavior.[22] No articulated thought could be criticized, for it must never be forgotten that vulnerable persons were behind such thought; it must therefore only be commented upon, reviewed from another perspective, cautiously examined, and circumvented. What was permissible as a discourse was determined by the fact that the discourse itself was the sole reason why the most diverse persons took part in it.

If this is the purest form of sociability, a self-contained sociality which perpetuates and maintains itself — then how is knowledge possible? Viewed historically, it was already clearly recognized in the second half of the seventeenth century that an advance in knowledge and especially in scientific knowledge was beyond the ability of the individual and required a collective undertaking.[23] The differentiation of special contexts of communication conducive to promoting advances in science was consciously supported. Whereas social communication rejected scientific communication as incompatible, for scientific communication it was above all the relationship to religion which constituted a problem. For in questions of truth it could accept neither clerical mediation nor instant revelation to the individual; it preferred to let its own approach decide.[24] From this a number of requirements derive, especially: (1) empirical proof intelligible to everyone; (2) certainty, not necessarily rigidly logical, but to a considerable extent merely "moral" (i.e. socially plausible) as a criterion;[25] (3) clarity as a requirement of linguistic presentation; (4) the hypothetical but not apodictical sense in which theories and system outlines are advanced;[26] and (5) measures for organized cooperative efforts, especially in scientific societies and academies. This way of formulating the problem was determined by the very inquiry into the conditions of an *advance* in knowledge.[27] Within this perspective there was no reason to go back and inquire into the possibility of knowledge as such, let alone to seek these conditions in the social domain. The development of science had to occur initially within the context of already existent knowledge and objects of knowledge, for therein lay the justification for its existence.

This did not change fundamentally in the eighteenth century. On the contrary, the social component in the understanding of science receded to the extent that it was now recognized that common sense and object-bound empiricism were not a sufficient basis for science, and reflection began to take place about already consolidated scientific knowledge and about the very conditions of its possibility. To formulate this in the terminology offered above, the eighteenth century switched from basic and communicative self-reference to theories of reflection. By inquiring how knowledge concerning the conditions of knowledge was possible in the first place if it must presuppose itself in every endeavor, an attempt was made to determine the identity of the system of science and at the same time develop a theory of operative methods for scientific research. In this context the problem of the unity in the difference between knowledge and object had to surface. The question about the bearer of knowledge as a process and as possession was provisionally and satisfactorily answered by reference to the subject.

Certain questions which remain unanswered can clearly be discerned by looking at the avoidances that developed at approximately the same time in the form of the model of social conversation. These questions inevitably reappear in recent developments in sociological theory where the "double contingency" in the ego/alter social relationship is recognized and elaborated as the fundamental problem of the general theory of social systems. These questions begin with the problem of self-reference in social relationships, not with the classical theme of the relation of all knowledge to its object. Given the insight, it should be asked, that all sociality must be structured self-referentially if a "talking-past-one-another," with its consequence of terminating the relation is to be avoided — how is knowledge possible in the first place if ego merely says what alter wants to hear and alter says what ego wants to hear?

IV

Until now investigations into the origin of modern science, into the question of what distinguishes it from earlier efforts to acquire knowledge and whether there was a kind of "scientific revolution" in the period from Galileo to Newton, have been conducted chiefly by comparing theories and methods. One could therefore inquire whether and to what extent the consciousness of contingency characteristic of late medieval nominalism and its tendency toward a kind of singular empiricism prepared the way for modern science. The question whether the *expectations* linked to theories, and above all to methods, changed primarily in the transition to the modern age takes us a step further.[28] A change at this level can even be compatible with continuity and discontinuity at the level of theories and methods itself, because the selective attitude toward this material is then altered. In addition to the theories and methods, whose variety could be tolerated, the claims to certainty and the decision-making possibilities connected with these theories and methods — and they above all! — were controversial in the sixteenth and seventeenth centuries. What remains to be explained is why the expectations and claims changed, and what had to happen in order to make these changes possible.

Extending the basis of inquiry in this manner requires recourse to a theory of society on the one hand, and a more thorough understanding of the epistemological process itself on the other, a process which is not adequately grasped if it is merely characterized in terms of the application of theories and methods. The decisive change here is a greater differentiation of those contexts of communication specifically aimed at advances in knowledge, and which increasingly judge on their own what can be expected from theories and methods.

The familiar thesis of the increasing differentiation and autonomy of those discourses specialized in the acquisition of knowledge[29] initially only names formal boundary conditions that emerge from the general process of the functional differentiation of the system of society. But this does not yet explain how such a differentiation itself is possible by simultaneously altering the societal conditions that sustain it. To account for this we must return to the fact of self-reference, which on the one hand is the condition of all sociality and, on the other, is a circular, short-circuiting, and thereby unproductive tautology. Reduced to its pure form and left to its own resources, this implies that it is arbitrary and inconclusive, which was precisely the meaning and purpose of conversation. If this is to be avoided, the system must be "detautologized": specific conditions must be built in that break the interdependency without terminating it. Put differently: the use of self-reference must be conditioned, but this in turn does not preclude introducing the conditions self-referentially and justifying them in terms of their function.

Conditioning is a very general and perhaps even the most general form of the system-internal management of self-reference.[30] It can be characterized as the repression or inhibition of possibilities — in our case as the inhibition of the immediate and unproblematic return to oneself. Making use of the possibilities offered becomes contingent on conditions which are themselves not unconditionally valid but which may, for example, be valid only up to a certain threshold. Conditions which prevent the emergence of such a short-circuited tautology of self-reference can therefore be self-referentially legitimated in turn.

This "detautologization" by way of acts of conditioning occurs in very different ways. We have already presented one model: *un mélange de divertissement et d'affaires* has been used to save friendships from the boredom of pure self-reference.[31] The same problem directs the differentiation of function-specific subsystems in society. If systems are to be developed that specialize in advancing knowledge, their "detautologization" must focus on this function. The acts of conditioning that are supposed to safeguard this process must then be selected accordingly. The question of *how* this occurs discloses the material and historical conditions of the possibility of scientific knowledge.

In the classical tradition this task was assigned to logic and its metaphysical foundation. For every operation employed in acquiring knowledge there were specific axioms: the principle of identity for the formation of concepts, the principle of the forbidden contradiction for judgments, and the principle *tertium non datur* for arriving at conclusions. Later on the principle of sufficient reason was added, which reflects this axiomatization as a closed system in the legitimation of knowledge.[32] Conditions were thereby stated which were to prevent arbitrariness and increase sensitivity toward positive facts. This achievement was and remains indispensable. The form in which it was made axiomatic nevertheless presupposed the distinction between being and thinking (and between metaphysics and logic) and considered as its only problem the problem of taking charge of negation in thinking. Hence the maintenance of the identity of concepts, particularly in the transition to negation; the avoidance of contradictions, although they can occur in thinking; and the regulation of syllogistic forms to avoid logical "errors." Dependency on external factors was presupposed and not expressly problematized. Accordingly, axiomatization had to take account of two kinds of distinctions: being and thinking; "true" and "false." It did this with one instrument: the binary schematism of logic.[33] To this corresponded on the side of thinking a concept of reflection which was too simple and which did not distinguish clearly between self-reference, process-reflexivity, and identity-reflection — an amalgamation which rested on the possibility of its opposition to being (or even to the world at large). On this basis the metaphysics of the subject then proceeded from the assumption that, in its relation to being, the subject could only be concerned with finding its way back to itself. This it called "reflection."

If (rather than starting with "thinking" or the self-conscious "subject") one starts with a structural analysis of self-referential systems with a number of processors, a logic with such a set of axioms may still retain its technical significance. But it does not provide sufficient information about how (1) the system uses its self-reference to remain capable of operation, and how (2) it posits conditions which "detautologize" and functionally specify this self-reference in a manner compatible with this. If our analysis has pointed to the place where the approach of the traditional set of axioms is too compact, a clearer distinction emerges at this point. This concerns the relation of being and thinking on the one hand and truth and falsity on the other. Both dichotomies must be distinguished more clearly and presented as system-internal strategies with regard to the fundamental problem of self-reference. In this sense I will therefore distinguish between *externalization* and *binary schematization*, and will attempt to demonstrate that one strategy serves to interrupt, the other to facilitate the operation of self-referentiality.

The first principle of self-conditioning and specification introduces *externalizations* and thereby *asymmetries*. The requirement for externalizations is above all based on the subject/predicate structure of language. It is, in communication, responsible for the impression that the object (the subject of the sentence) is itself responsible for its properties — and not he who speaks about it and ascribes properties to it.[34] In the process of communication the impression of external references is thus consolidated to such an extent that very extensive communication about communication would be necessary to counteract this process.

Aided by such linguistic forms, information processes can become dependent on something other than themselves and which they have not created. They project an environment from which they can then proceed, although it is merely their projection! This is the case for all processors in the system, for ego as well as alter, so that one is always already in agreement if one acts within the system. If the goal is knowledge acquisition this cannot mean that the environment is presupposed in the form of facts, circumstances, and data. Too much is determined by ontology. It is just as inadequate to oppose one's own subjectivity (which, after all, one hopes to establish vis-à-vis others) to being, and to stress one's own participation in the projection of the facts. Even the "transcendental" or "dialectical" reconciliation of objectivity and subjectivity does not bring us further if both versions are inherently wrong. The problem is rather expressed in the question of *what* the externalization *refers to.*

If we link the problem to the imputation of selections, this would lead beyond the traditional distinction between being and thinking, or object and subject.[35] Factual assumptions of all kinds are potentially dissolved and are permitted to recombine — without this ending up in mere subjectivity. What is decisive is the fact that the selection (or, as it is often referred to as well, the information) — i.e., that this or that is the case — is imputed to the environment and not to the system, and that the selection is therefore perceived system-internally as *experience* and *not as action.* The fact that the semantics, language, and conceptual apparatus in which experience is grasped and which serves as the vehicle of system-internal understanding is only "valid" internally, is beyond question here. The system is also involved in the production of a surplus of possibilities which could potentially be realized. But only the selection among these possibilities is imputed to the environment — and this without regard for the fact that the meaning of this selection cannot be fixed independently of the categories the system provides for this purpose, or independently of the alternatives considered, or independently finally of whether the system itself initiates and brings about or merely observes the selection.

In the historical changes semantics has undergone, such an adaptation to the (merely) experience-oriented imputation of selection was expressed as "disenchantment" or, more precisely, as a demythologization of the world. The interpretation of occurrences and events as action and their representation, in model form, in myths, epics, and legends is deconstructed, since this representation as action too strongly invites a commitment to action by way of imitation or consensus. The mythical action models are dismantled and then reconstructed as something that was "only meant symbolically": as allegory, as a symbol for something else, as metaphor.[36] In this way both science and mythology can, for example in the fifteenth and sixteenth centuries, be considered as successors of myth. Mythology moved from narrative action models to an action-oriented understanding of the world with direct correspondences, situational constellations, sympathies, and antipathies.[37] It was in this form that an attractive and apparently promising alternative was initially established to Aristotelianism as the dominant school oriented toward universalistic concepts. But then the newly emerging natural sciences rejected this path as dark and mystical, precisely to the extent to which imputations of action played a role. The distinction between action and experience determined the course which the differentiation of science then took. The means for action were withdrawn from the world during the seventeenth century and the differentiation of action systems increasingly presupposed experience. Science in turn also pursued this differentiation and thereby attained positions from which it could decide whether it was faced with experience or action. It did not project a world which called for action through action, for obedience through norms, for love by way of love. Rather, it projected at best a society in which certain general responsibilities could be insisted upon, even for the differentiated enterprise of science.

As an abridged version of this analysis we may say that the differentiation of specifically scientific discourses is attained through a reduction to the form of imputation of experience. Ego and alter reciprocally assert types of behavior for the other by way of this externalizing mode of imputation. A symbolically generalized medium of communication, specially designed for this, is constructed for truth, and thus provides an orientation for the reciprocal assertions.[38] By way of this form of externalization truth is distinguished from all other media of communication which permit imputations of action to ego, alter, or both.[39] At the level of interaction the differentiation is supported by that of a corresponding medium and generalized beyond the specific interaction among those present.

The mode in which experience is imputed prevents the short-circuiting of self-reference by making the relation to the object asymmetrical. Only in this form can ego offer its experience to an alter without having to face the objection: I only see what I see; you only see what you see; I only see that you see what you see, and only I see this. Reference to the mutually assumed form of experience solves this problem. By no means does it thereby ensure an agreement about experience in the sense of intersubjectively compelling certainty; but it is a prerequisite for the very possibility of achieving such agreements in experience. The basic self-reference is not abandoned. Short-circuiting remains possible. But it is now employed in the form of criticism and reserved for special situations — for example, when it must be demonstrated that the experience of another stands and falls with his premises and that the same information can also be interpreted differently.

Whereas externalizations of this sort interrupt tightly constructed interdependencies in the self-referential system, binary schematizations have the opposite function: to facilitate short-circuits and put them into an

omnipresent, continuously present form. To this end the topics are dupli-
cated in their entirety: everything acquires a yes-version and a no-version.
Every adoption of a yes-version is set against the no-version associated
with it, and thereby becomes a selection. The same is true in the opposite
case of the no-versions. We call this duplication "coding" and the correspondingly prepared symbolic constructs "codes." Codes make it possible
to expect "yeas" and "nays" as being *possible* in *every* context associated
with them (hence in the entire domain of competency of the schematism),
and by permitting the expectation of possible orientations in this manner
can they deal with double contingency. In this sense language is already a
code, even though it is not always and not only used in this way. Media of
communication arise through a repetition of this process of coding at the
level of the "values" or preferences which determine selections.
Yes-versions and no-versions can be either true or false. Here too the binary schematism can be universally practiced and be ever present. As a
duality it is constructed so simply that it does not overtax the attention, so
that every ego can also assume that both values are simultaneously present for every alter.[40] *Only on this basis can the selectivity of experience
be a socially functioning assumption.*

Accordingly, the function of binary coding and its more extreme version of easily manageable schematisms requires that opposites are moved
closer together, thereby facilitating the transformation of one into the
other. In contrast to what might perhaps be expected as a result of the
qualitative privileging of truth over falsity, the relationship is in fact made
logically *symmetrical*, and negation becomes the operator which technically guarantees this symmetry in the form of interchangeability.[41] This
amounts to a condensation of basic self-reference in the sense that the affirmation of a topic sees itself reflected in the negation of the same topic
and recognizes and finds itself confirmed in this negation. The proof for
the "yes" then moves by way of the impossibility of the opposite.[42] Not
only is basic self-reference permitted, it is actually encouraged, provided
that it accommodates itself to binary schematism and can be absorbed in
it.

Viewed from the perspective of the theoretical model, specifications
concerning the relation of self-reference and the function of binary
schematization have occupied the traditional place of metaphysics, which
had hoped to locate, above all dichotomies, an ultimate and superior perspective in the form of an interpretation of being. For this reason we can
also speak of a sociological epistemology, since we assume that it must be
possible to organize, within science, a functional equivalent of metaphysics restricted to science. Viewed in terms of the sociology of knowledge,
this corresponds to the assumption that the hierarchical form of problem

solving by superimposing a particular idea is in our society no longer convincing.[43]

Finally a remark concerning the technization (*Technisierung*) of binary codes — technization in the sense of facilitating the execution of self-referential operations. At the beginning of their development and in more concrete societal situations the two values of the code are usually qualitative, and therefore cannot be translated into one another by mere negation. In this way the difference between pleasure and displeasure is already established at the organic level as a behavioral code — but in such a manner that pleasure can be acquired by simply negating displeasure as displeasure by negating pleasure.[44] Qualitative dualities of this sort refer at once to the environment, organize the system's contact with the environment, and thus function as externalizations. They are therefore not reversible, because they also corepresent external reasons. The behavioral systems of externalization and binarization cannot be achieved independently; this brings to mind what was earlier observed about the classical axioms in logic. Advances in formalization and technization of the sphere in which self-reference is applicable can only be expected if externalization is taken care of elsewhere. For this reason developments in logic have, since the Middle Ages, inevitably also generated inquiry into the status of the objects of knowledge and finally led to theories of knowledge which must attend to this kind of inquiry, and no longer need to concern themselves with logic.

If, however, motivation is only possible by way of qualitative dualities — if, in other words, the logically technicized distinction between true and false assertions is no longer a motivating force — there develops a motivational deficit which makes special arrangements necessary if the attempt to advance knowledge is to progress further. Here the modern enterprise of science is generally dependent on financial incentives. But it also makes use of an independent secondary code of reputation, in which values of reputation are a substitute for truths and produce motivational consequences which can no longer be achieved by way of truth itself.[45]

This first series of considerations concerning a theory of self-referential social systems specialized in advancing knowledge can be summarized in the following diagram:

externalization   binary schematization
(asymmetricalization)   (symmetricalization)

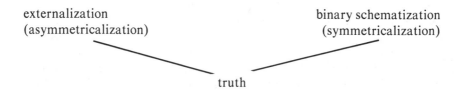

truth

The code of truth is composed of two functions which must be distinguished because of their different relationship to the question of self-reference, which is present in the form of a double contingency. Such a distinction is on the one hand an element of the differentiation of specialized systems of interaction, but also of a specialized societal subsystem for the advance of knowledge. It leads, on the other hand, to the technization of binary schematism, the articulation of problems which thence emerge in the relation to the object, and to the development of peculiar motivational resources based on an exploitation of gains in knowledge for the sake of reputation. If we retained an emphatic concept of truth or a notion of the subject which emphasizes "meaning," this entire development might appear as a "crisis," or even as the miscarried development of a specifically European rationality.[46] But what compels us to base our evaluation on such a point of departure?

V

As soon as the fact can be counted upon that a system of discourse is able to distinguish itself from the environment of its objects and begins to produce decisions by way of questions structured in a binary manner, complications become probable. In the way the question is formulated, a consensus with alter is sought concerning the environment under the condition of "experience." This means that only the environment can provide an answer to the question and that alter will consent for precisely this reason. But the environment does not answer easily. Therefore the system must be able to vary the theme and move toward concerns to which the environment can respond. The various themes must be decomposed until questions have been formulated which can be resolved. The system moves in the direction of analytical abstraction.

The first tangible differentiation of self-referential inquiry uses as its mode of organization the social situation and the self-reference built into it. This was called "dialectic" in antiquity. It presupposes someone who questions and someone else who answers. It further assumes that the one who answers addresses the questions and that the questioner raises questions with the answers in mind and in response to them. This is sufficient to set into motion a process of self-limitation which leads to truth if the questioner is a philosopher, and to falsehood if he is a sophist.

At first, then, as tradition demonstrates,[47] the question is still directed toward the partner. The original communality in the experience of the world is dissolved in a social direction. The partner is moved toward the social environment by way of a pregiven alternative constructed in a hinary manner. Someone who already knows persuades someone who does not yet know.[48] The technique of persuasion is conducted "alongside" the social environment and therefore presupposes expert knowledge. But for the "philosophy" dedicated to the things themselves this is still just sophistry, or rather, for teaching purposes, dialectic.[49] With the general availability of (alphabetized, universally applicable) writing, an instrumental attitude begins to dominate,[50] and the technique of persuasion seeks out its own domain, for example in the education of the nobility. Dialogue becomes a literary form. Dialectical logic, which makes possible dialogue and which still presupposes differences between the partners, and hence an ego/alter schema, produces the proper logic to the extent that it is clarified with regard to its own forms of thought.[51] It is substantially a matter of gaining knowledge by way of a method of deconstruction — in metaphysics, for example, by way of the deconstruction of "being" into what later came to be called "categories."[52]

Following this trend of decomposition into yes/no decisions, the emerging system of science differentiates *theories* and *methods*. This distinction is no longer located at the constitutive level which permits differentiation itself, but rather concerns the programming of the operative execution under conditions requiring correctness of action.

Theories are linked to the condition of externalization. They refer to information that can be externalized as features of objects. They "bind" information to permanently available and reproducible meaning. The decisive step in the differentiation of a special theoretical consciousness might, long before transcendental philosophy, have consisted in the fact that intelligibility and constructibility were no longer seen as *the condition for the existence of things* in the context of theories — hence that the notion of an all-embracing continuum of rationality was abandoned. This does not mean, of course, that every relationship between theory and reality is disputed. But the externalization of self-referential theoretical contexts is only possible when it is not already certain from the start that only that can exist which is then merely examined by the theory. Boyle "see[s] no necessity that intelligibility to a human understanding should be necessary to the truth or existence of a thing."[53] The world thereby opens itself up to a limitless complexity which can no longer be represented; on the other hand, it is now possible to give up the assumption that there are secrets in the world which will forever remain concealed from human eyes.

Inquiry concerning knowledge and science is also subject to this constraint toward externalization; therefore it must transfer the act of knowing itself into the world of its objects and postulate that knowing can encounter itself in the domain of its objects, "experience" itself in the strict sense of the word, and associate itself with other experiences. Only once it meets this condition can theory become universally applicable.

Yet this alone is not sufficient. Provisions must also be made for a binary "potential for schematization." For it must be possible to distinguish, according to the theory's assumptions, between what is the case and what is not. At the level of theory this general imperative acquires, in addition, the form of "limitationality" (*Limitionalität*): a limited number of possibilities is postulated against all probability, so that the negation of one possibility increases the probability of the others.[54] A theoretical method directly stemming from this employs dichotomized cross-tabulations and assumes that all possible cases are covered by the table (on grounds that must be explained by way of the marginal variables).[55]

One of the most dramatic analyses achieved with this binary and therefore classificatory theoretical method is Aristotle's justification of self-reference in the form of the thinking of thinking.[56] Thinking might be thought of as something that either thinks of nothing or thinks of something — and, when it thinks, as something which either thinks itself or something else. The examination of these alternatives leads to the mode of self-reflection (which Plato still questioned). But by way of the approach to questions which classifies in a binary manner a concept is produced which transcends this very method of questioning: a relational concept. Despite this result, no other theoretical means were available at first and for a long time thereafter, and one therefore became accustomed to defining and accepting self-reference as a kind of final and limiting paradox.

This example demonstrates how the science of method operates in the service of theory, and this leads us on to the second domain, to methodology in the narrower sense. A consciousness of method arose in connection with a specialization of the efforts and communications concerned with the acquisition of knowledge. If we proceed step by step here, the context in which this process occurred needs to be considered. A greater differentiation of this aspect can nevertheless be observed since the seventeenth century. Methodology is differentiated above all vis-à-vis epistemological premises, vis-à-vis epistemology in general. Rather than being based on certain concepts of human nature, human abilities, and universal human characteristics, the proper method is now based on practical problem situations and notions concerning attainable research goals (and is connected at this level with object-related theories, though not with epistemology). The result of this development can be formulated as follows: methods are operational instructions linked directly to a binary schema and which transform it into sequences of decision. Unlike theory, they require time to rid themselves of complexity by means of sequential operation, in that they themselves adopt the peculiar nature of the binary structure: each selection produces a specific result.[57] By now it is known, of course, that a multiplicity of viewpoints (and in this sense complexity) can only under very improbable conditions be expressed in a yes/no decision;[58] but in our context this only points to the fact that method is always dependent on theory, and that only jointly can they improve on and replace intuitive knowledge.

Methods cannot be satisfied with merely expressing a self-reference reconstructed in a binary manner, which would only make the system vulnerable to arbitrariness — in opposition to which one must be able to create structures and make choices. To attain results, methods must also presuppose limits as a condition for the operative productivity of their procedures. In this respect they are dependent on theoretical considerations or, to put this more precisely, on fundamental notions applicable in the context of both theory and method. In the classical understanding of science this was true above all for the concept of causality. Today it is especially true for the distinction between independent and dependent variables in all research designs and for the distinction between the problem of reference and the (functionally equivalent) alternative solutions, a distinction which reflects reality and is also presupposed in the methodology of comparative analyses.

If we continue the sketch started above, we arrive at the following diagram:

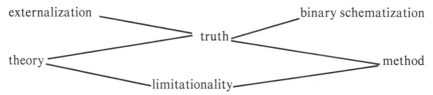

Just as truth establishes the unity in the difference of externalization and binary schematization, and just as a social system can only be differentiated by way of this medium of communication if this linkage succeeds, so do theory and method function as an operative unity when they employ common premises of limitationality. The first relationship makes differentiation possible, the second the operationalization of a self-referential system which is directed toward advances in knowledge.

VI

Theories and methods consequently presuppose limitationality and thereby reciprocity. It can thus be assumed that the relationship between theories and methods is regulated as well, and in particular that the degree of possible mutual differentiation is determined by the manner in which limitationality is understood. I have discovered a high degree of interdependence through the traditional procedure of classifying by way of binary schemes, as well as through its result, that the problem of self-reference had to be marginalized. Is this and will this remain the only possibility?

This leads us to consider more precisely the concept of limitationality, for which there are few models. We can speak of limitationality with regard to opposites or alternatives[59] if the determination of one element of the relation contributes to the determination of the other; or, formulated in another way, if the determination of one element of the relation restricts the scope within which the other element is determined. Thus the problem of limitationality is already posed at the level of basic self-reference. The determination of an element, for example a decision, must reflect itself as something which restricts the latitude of others. From the perspective of the function, limitationality ensures that either the selections or the combinatory relations (for example, the combination of means of production) must deal with only a limited number of possibilities. But how can this limitation be justified if the likelihood that there are other possibilities cannot be excluded?

In earlier thought the world itself — as *congregatio corporum*, as finite quantity of finite matters — contained a kind of guarantee of limitationality. Even as late as 1700 it was still assumed that the number of living beings and possible forms were limited and unalterable. When there was talk of the contingency of everything that exists, what was implied was that the world could have been created differently. Hybrid forms belonged to the pathology of the world and, in the form of "monsters," attracted interest as "falls from grace" in nature.[60] Fontenelle already noted, however, that the history of monsters is "infinic et peu instructive."[61] The problem of infinite possibilities of variation which lies concealed behind this becomes evident and is initially warded off by rejecting an inquisitive interest in monsters. The self-reference that opens itself up to arbitrariness is experienced as monstrous in other ways.[62] The result of self-diagnosis — not being able to accept limits — is called "monstrous." The notion of the monster made plausible the limitationality of the world in terms of its pathological cases.

Yet the closer self-reference moves toward becoming the precondition of the very possibility of knowledge (just as, in another domain, self-love is a precondition for the possibility of loving), that is, the more important this condition becomes for a differentiation of a system which specializes in knowledge acquisition, the greater the pressure to thematize the introduction of limitationality itself. One must then distinguish between suppressed and comprehended, bracketed and admitted possibilities, and shoulder responsibility for the difference. "One need not accept the conceptual opposition based on the notion of limits," we can read in a recent text, "unless a proof for certainty is desired; it is a speculative opposition. And to this extent it is and remains a function of the object of theory."[63] From now on it is explicitly a matter of limiting what is possible vis-à-vis a blueprint of possibilities which transcends this limitation, a blueprint also produced by the self-referential system and which is in fact the precise correlate of circular self-reference.

Every determination of meaning which achieves such a demarcation can generally be characterized as a *formula of contingency*. Formulae of contingency arise in the process of the differentiation of functional systems which require on the one hand a universalization of all relations to the world (*Weltbezüge*) and on the other instructions for respecification.[64] They operate in a dual manner: on the one hand in the direction of an infinite number of increasing and always different possibilities, and on the other in the direction of programs for operations that can be completed within the system. What the "horizons" of meaningful experience and action achieve in an even more general sense (namely to be or not to be a boundary) is here expected from a formula, and it is the purpose of such a condensation to guide function-specific differentiations. From this result two hypotheses: that formulae of contingency develop in connection with the differentiation and increasing autonomy of functional systems of society, and that for each particular functional domain this development is aimed at an increasing specification of the function of switching from what is arbitrary to what is ascertainable.

I will use the concept of limitationality as a term describing the contingency formula specific to science.[65] In the history of science, generic or typological constructs have been employed above all to guarantee limitationality at the level of phenomena. Moreover, there has been the retreat to lawlike or statistical regularities compatible with a limitless realm of phenomena but which are not themselves explained, although they are employed in the search for an explanation. During the past two centuries, at least in the natural sciences, the emphasis has shifted in favor of this technique, and toward the close of the nineteenth century it also became clear, above and beyond all "epistemological" positions, that this too was a matter of excluding unlimited contingencies.[66]

In recent decades, this classical repertoire of techniques has been extended by two new variants: the methodological principle of falsification, which assumes some kind of limitationality but does not specify which kind, and functional-comparative analysis. Apparently these two additions are a response to an intensified differentiation of the system of science with respect to the distinction between methods and theories. The principle of falsification is a methodological principle which does not prejudice (or only minimally prejudices) theory formation. Functional analysis, on the other hand, has proven itself to a greater degree in the area of theory formation, while as a method its achievements remain unclear and disputed.[67] Theory construction in functionalism, which proceeds from the assumption that there are problems behind the appearances which may be solved in another way (but not arbitrarily in just any way), is able to reflect upon its own procedure. But despite all attempts it is still far from having developed a methodology of comparative analysis, if we mean by methodology the theory of methods which, by way of binary schematisms, attains results which permit further advances.

Hence there are five different possibilities for introducing limitationality: generic logic, typology (especially cross-tabulation), lawlike or statistical regularities, the principle of falsification, and functional comparisons. In the course of historical development these possibilities overlap, but they do not follow one upon the other in the sense that a later one is only activated when its predecessor has stepped aside. And apparently the simultaneous use of several ways of setting limits is advisable because the domains of individual scientific disciplines offer quite different prospects and contain different difficulties, and because theory formation and methodology have distinctly different requirements.

VII

All knowledge presupposes knowledge and can only be knowledge in the first place by applying this basic premise to itself. Knowledge is and remains bound to self-reference at the levels of individual events, of processes, and of systems. This state of affairs inheres in the structure of meaning: it cannot be overcome anywhere, and it has no exceptions. For a self-referentially closed system, "truth" is therefore always already presupposed as a banality which is on hand. It is thus always initially probable that the knowledge already on hand and already established stabilizes "around itself," associates other things with itself, and rejects or isolates disturbances. This probability of continuation cannot be negated because it inheres in the meaningful self-reference itself;[68] negation is after all merely one of its instruments. Yet the fact that the thereby established expectations of normality and continuity cannot be directly negated does not mean that change is not possible. The change must overcome the threshold of improbability which inheres in normality. In the development of societal structures this occurs through evolution, and indeed through the differentiation of self-referential systems within self-referential systems. At the levels of knowledge representation and motivation of action, the same process appears as an improvement or as an advance of knowledge. Only recently can we observe rearrangements in *both* respects: there are attempts to replace evolution by planning, while at the same time the belief in progress is shattered in the depiction of changes as improvements. These still immature innovations, however, uneven also in relation to one another (are they in turn improvements of knowledge resulting from evolution?), I will leave aside for the time being.

It can be presupposed that occasions for an interest occur often enough to permit evolution, since contingency is after all corepresented in all meaningful experience and especially in all linguistic coding. But under which conditions can such occasions bring forth a coherent advance in knowledge — a process in which a gain in knowledge is accumulated in such a way that it makes further gains possible; a process which can construct itself, react to itself, accelerate itself?

It is likely that an evolution in the direction of a differentiation of social systems specialized in advancing knowledge presupposes certain technical means of communication. We have already mentioned the emergence of the alphabet and the wide dissemination of writing as an accomplishment of the Greeks and as a precondition of an approach to topics which is no longer merely narrative. In the transition to the modern age the invention of printing must be added to this, since it made for the first time possible a literary integration of communication in many areas (for example with regard to "technologies"),[69] and which above all increasingly offered an opportunity for contrasting the new with the old — initially in the sense of catching up but, after the middle of the sixteenth century, also in the sense of surpassing. But further preconditions had to join these technical prerequisites of communication. In actual situations one must be able to experience in a reasonably attractive fashion the possibility of deviating from already existing knowledge or the possibility of acquiring not yet existing knowledge. These possibilities, furthermore, must apply not only to things ("Where did I leave my glasses?") but also to structures of expectation. They must concern the types and ideas by way of which it is possible to inquire and establish what is in fact the case. These preconditions in turn cannot exist independently of the knowledge that is already known. Thus theory, in this respect as well, must take into consideration the self-reference of the object to which it refers and try to clarify how what is on hand can nevertheless go beyond itself.

I want to characterize the first and perhaps most important complex of conditions as *the differentiation of cognitive vis-à-vis normative expectations.*[70] This distinction applies in the case of disappointment. Expectations can be fashioned in such a way that they are also expected to be valid in and beyond the case of disappointment; their counterfactual validity is anticipated and endurance from oneself and others is expected even in the event of occurrences contrary to expectation. Such a normative attitude toward expectation obstructs the readiness to learn. The opposite is true when expectations are explicitly established as cognitive ones; here the very form of the expectation already implies permission to oneself and others to alter the expectation if it should be refuted by contradictory evidence. The distinction between normative and cognitive expectation does not divide the horizon of expectations absolutely. It can only develop in the first place where disappointments are anticipated and where attitudes are kept in reserve which can cushion the disappointment, although commitment to a specific direction of expectation is made at the same time. For the normal way of life this is an exceptional case which presupposes unusually specific expectations. The horizon of normality of everyday life — the basis of the life-world, as Husserl would say — is always already assumed in every one of these specifications and therefore, as a whole, it cannot be divided into a cognitive and a normative aspect. For the large number of disappointments which would correspond to the actual and infinite horizon of "living-in-the-world" (*In-der-Welt-Lebens*) cannot even be anticipated. Specific sensibilities can only be developed and heightened on this basis, and only these are available for a differentiation of the normative and cognitive manner of expectation.

The differentiation of specifically cognitive attitudes of expectation — which imply a specific readiness to learn — develops in two directions. On the one hand it is a differentiation *from* the domain of normal expectation which experiences contingency only marginally and does not make any specific provisions; on the other hand it is a differentiation *against* the normative manner of expectation, which assumes and articulates the opposing function, that of obstructing learning. Only if both aspects are considered simultaneously can an adequate sociological understanding of these problems be achieved which had to be solved in the course of the evolutionary differentiation of social systems specializing in the development of knowledge up to the point at which a corresponding subsystem of society specializing in "science" had been established.

In the late medieval European tradition it was above all the concept of nature which served as the semantic correlative of this development and as the point of reference for its differentiations.[71] The original meaning of this concept, which referred to that which has grown by itself, permitted to give expression both to the basic foundation which sustains all differentiations and to the unity of the principle that makes them possible. The Christian representation of nature as the (contingent) creation of

God did not alter anything here. The modern age initially intensified this appeal to nature by way of its intention of wresting the necessary warranty of unity from the ecclesiastical-religious dogma and by way of offering this interpretation to religion for its own use.[72] Nature, after all, in the context of science, has since Bacon not so much been an end in itself as the point of departure for change, for "improvement."[73] As a countermovement, the romantic natural science of the nineteenth century, by way of the concept of nature, attempted once again to revitalize a principle of the unity of opposites and to derive from it normative postulates for the control of the already dominant, cognitively specialized natural sciences or, as they were thought of at the time, of the mechanistic natural sciences.[74] Since then both the successes of the "natural" sciences — based on very specific theoretical assumptions — and the epistemological neutralization of their ontological interpretability, have contributed to the elimination of this concept of nature. If one wants to express something similar and stress normative "background postulates," one may, for example, refer to the "environment." This establishes at the same time that normative constraints upon a kind of inquiry which is driven by purely cognitive considerations require a special foundation which is not the result of an ultimate sacredness of the domain, but of particular problems of the societal system with its environment.

A second viewpoint concerns the possibilities for the legitimation of what is new. As long as the new must legitimate and assert itself in terms of its deviation from what is generally accepted, the prospects are poor. The idea of the new retained this meaning of "deviation" until well after the Middle Ages.[75] In the seventeenth century the concept of fanaticism still expressed this resistance to innovations in terms of a deviation from proper opinion; but in the eighteenth century it was already expressed in the sense of resisting the employment of an inadmissible method (appealing to private insights and intuitions) whenever innovations were introduced.[76] These few examples demonstrate that in the course of the differentiation of science the temporal dimension is also increasingly relied upon in the efforts to advance knowledge. The new is no longer merely related to the old in terms of a contradiction in the substantive assertion; as a knowledge which for the first time "is possible only now," which can appeal, for example, to intervening discoveries, reports, and experiments, it acquires a temporal distance from the knowledge that is already on hand. He who asserts something new thereby does not necessarily destroy the merits of earlier thinkers and researchers; he does not necessarily behave disrespectfully, even if he cannot avoid calling into question the authority which had been granted to the earlier thinkers vis-à-vis more recent ones.[77]

On the basis of these conditions, and perhaps of others as well which emerge in the process itself, it becomes possible for advances in knowledge to react upon themselves. In the temporal dimension this means acceleration; the speed of change can be changed. For example, as was already recognized and advocated in the sixteenth century, the speed of learning can be changed through printing.[78] But above all, the advance in knowledge itself takes control of the acquisition of new knowledge. This is particularly true for the task of formulating those problems to be solved by research. They draw on the conceptual apparatus and the level of knowledge of science itself. For this reason, approximately since the time of Bacon, the necessity of justifying the search for new knowledge in terms of its (social) benefits becomes an issue, thereby invoking the relation to society.

As a result, the structure of self-reference changes; it is multiplied. Knowledge presupposes knowledge — this fact remains unchanged. But now, in addition, growth in knowledge presupposes the process of knowledge growth in which it participates and which it codetermines; and all this is kept in motion by anticipating future growth which, according to all experience up to this point, one believes oneself capable of delivering. Theories are revaluated with regard to their capacity to generate new knowledge,[79] and one also wants to become independent of chance[80] and build the driving force into the system itself.

VIII

What in the seventeenth century was still only a promise for the future has now become reality. This fact in turn reacts, as experienced reality, on the semantics with which science comprehends its own increasing differentiation. From a sociological viewpoint, self-diagnosis is not necessarily already reliable knowledge. But it is interesting to note how it has varied with success.

In the seventeenth century, problems of differentiation were current at two levels. The most pressing questions referred to avoiding or evading a theological monopoly of important concepts. Theoretical dispositions had to become independent of religious and dogmatic presuppositions, and in the same way the scientist's personal religiosity had to be warranted independently of the conceptual dispositions emerging from his research. Relief from far too many reciprocal implications was necessary. The increasing speed of scientific advance, furthermore, was incompatible with a religion anchored in dogmatic concepts, and for this reason as well distancing was a requirement of the moment. I will leave unconsidered here this frequently discussed dissociation of religion and science,[81] since this problem has not been taken up again today. I will instead confine myself to a second and deeper level: the question of the status which the specifically scientific communication claims for itself vis-à-vis the communication typical throughout society.

In the seventeenth century this question was regarded as a problem of the persuasive demonstration and dissemination of new knowledge. For a long time there had been experiences with scientific idealizations intelligible as such, without reference to persons or communicative relations. Yet such idealizations of Galilean-Cartesian science, typically offered by mathematics, were limited in two ways. On the one hand the binary schematism of truth presupposed a decision maker. Since Descartes he was identified, in a new sense, as the "subject." On the other hand it was not possible to represent the entire domain of science in mathematical terms. For this reason Descartes was forced to distinguish between *certitude morale* and *certitude plus que morale*.[82] The first, *suffisant pour régler nos moeurs*, refers not only to morality itself, but to all knowledge to which the conduct of life can orient itself free of doubts (for example: "Rome is a city in Italy"), but without being able to prove it in a compelling manner and without reference to the knowledge of other persons. Leibniz connects this concept to the problem of induction.[83] As a result, "moral certitude" becomes the point of departure for demands on the conduct of scientific communication, specifically with regard to an orientation to common sense, a comprehensible language, and a proximity to empirical reality. Organizational efforts to encourage cooperation in scientific research also have their basis here. The criterion according to which the subject is supposed to distinguish between truth and falsehood is therefore still embedded in communication regulations unwarranted by science itself but which must be presupposed as the basis of social life.[84]

If this situation is viewed retrospectively, with Husserl's eyes,[85] the perspectives shift in a characteristic manner. Husserl depicts the current situation of the mathematically idealizing science of Galilean origin as a "crisis." Perceived as a crisis is precisely that which constituted the once celebrated *certitude plus que morale*: the ability to express something without reference to the subject and, in this sense, its technical utilization. It arises during the conversion of the formal sciences into forms of interaction with the real world. And this conversion, since not properly understood, leads to a "transformation of a formulation of meaning which was originally vital,"[86] to an emptying of meaning through "technization," to a loss of the original meaning of the truth content of the real world. The original meaning is the meaning for the subject which lives bodily and personally in the real world. The world that is initially given to this subject is called the "life-world." The crisis of the European sciences consists therefore in the neglect of its foundation in the life-world as the basis for every idealization, mathematization, and technization. A return to the original meaning-constituting achievements of concretely living subjectivity is demanded and, in this sense, a return to the life-world.[87] For "what is primary in itself is subjectivity, understood as that which naively pregives the being of the world and then rationalizes or (what is the same thing) objectifies it."[88]

If we ignore the fact that subjectivity, which should be the domain of philosophers, is here declared to be primary — what is the life-world? As a new term the formulation has done well,[89] although no one has succeeded in clarifying the concept. It is striking that, especially in sociological usage, the concept of the "common-sense world" appears as an alternative.[90] Does this indicate a return to the seventeenth-century concept of certainty? That one now regards as the proper foundation what was then merely the second-best solution?

This kind of consideration indicates the direction of the change in a precise manner; however, it does not go far enough conceptually, and it therefore cannot comprehend even itself. Crisis consciousness is the awareness that the specialized systems alone are not adequate, neither each by itself nor in concert. The sum total of the functional systems is not equivalent to the sum total of the existential conditions; this is already true for the sole reason that communicative interaction in general cannot be explained in terms of merely one functional system. There remains a residual sphere of everyday action that cannot be classified unambiguously, but also, and in spite of all emphasis on functionality, a sphere of a "residual consciousness" (*Sonst-noch-Bewusstsein*). This is because no functional specification of meaning can altogether eliminate references to other possibilities. Although the process itself was never sufficiently clarified when the concept of the life-world was carried over from transcendental phenomenology to sociology, it appears to have been merged with this notion of unspecialized everydayness. This, at any rate, is the only way in which a "translation" of the concept makes sense in sociology. The concept of the life-world accordingly brings together all of these meanings in everyday life which are not intended to associate such action with the differentiated functional subsystems of society.

Thus understood, the concept becomes useless as a basis for a critique of functional systems, if "critique" is to refer to a reminder that expectations for improvement should be fulfilled. The tradition of such a critique thereby reached the end of its rope. The critique had begun with the anthropocentrism of the eighteenth century and its dissolution of the assumption of a teleological unity between a service for the glory of God and its benefits to human beings. On the basis of this anthropocentrism and against the background of the differentiating functional systems, an opposition emerged for the first time between that which is due to humans as humans and the problem of utility and usefulness in society.[91] This opposition, initially conceived as one which could be communicated by way of pedagogy, was then, in the critique of political economy by Hegel and Marx, projected onto the historical process and at the same time focused on one of the functional systems, the economic system. Husserl, finally, changed the theme of the critique; he attacked science rather than the economic system, but without calling into question the form of the critique itself on the basis of a transcending set of opposing concepts. On the one hand the theory of a final solution must become increasingly questionable the more functional systems are represented as inadequate for humans. On the other hand, sociology has matured in the meantime. Its concepts of everyday life orientation, of the life-world, of common sense, and of the "always having already been informed" (*Immer-schon-Verständigt-Seins*) as a basis for all peculiarities and extravagances, is certainly inappropriate as the focus for a critique of functional systems. But it does relativize the evaluation of the functional orientations by raising the question of how and to what extent such improbable specializations are possible in the first place on the basis and within the forms of corporate social life.

These intervening thoughts on the life-world's concept of reflection help to make plain the extent to which the situation has changed since the seventeenth century as a result of greater differentiation of functional systems. The semantic correlate of the structural development of society reorients itself from promotion to critique — a critique directed toward the (utopian) maximal promotion of human self-realization, which in turn promotes the growth of the functional systems without being able to realize itself in them. Sociology initiates a new line of thought, which for a time remains secondary. Already Vilfredo Pareto contrasted nonlogical action and its residues — derivatives and derivations — with those spheres of action favored by the style of rationality of the modern age.[92] Talcott Parsons saw this contrast as an indication of a "transindividual" character of emergent social rationality[93] — with the consequence that this notion could enter into the analytical system of functional differentiation without difficulty.[94] The new romanticism of the life-world came upon vacated territory; it could not and does not have to come to terms with Parsonian theory.[95] If the concept of functional differentiation could be successfully connected with the theoretical traditions represented by such concepts as nonlogical action, residues, common-sense orientation, and life-world, sociology would be able to formulate a position in its theory of society which could guide a self-analysis of modern society as a functionally differentiated system — without committing this analysis to (1) a measurement of the subject's expectations of self-realization or (2) dichotomized concepts (*Gesellschaft/Gemeinschaft*, rational/nonrational, formal/material) and thereby ending the analysis.

This broader theoretical background must be kept in mind because it can help to show that a critique of the specifically scientific mode of knowing (1) is only one among many cases of a general critique of function-specific special achievements, and that (2) as a critique it reflects the development of society in a historical situation in which *neither* advances of knowledge *nor* the complete humanization of humankind (either aided or opposed by knowledge) offers an adequate standard of reference. The analysis then moves on to the question of if and how a society, in which structural forms have been developed to such an incredible extent, is even possible, if by its very success it erodes its environment and the forms of interaction in its life-world, or at the very least alters them so dramatically that the consequences of these changes can no longer be controlled by the very means which triggered them in the first place.

IX

If we want to do justice to this sociohistorical situation and to the theories which are a response to it, it is necessary to distinguish two different concepts of truth, according to whether knowledge of the life-world is addressed scientific knowledge. The distinction is not focused on the question of whether truth is dependent on the social context of its discovery or on its validity. Hence it does not accept the traditional distinction between dialectical (topical) and analytical logic, nor the distinction between *certitude morale* and *certitude plus que morale*. The distinction refers rather to social, communicative behavior.[96] Truth, for this sort of behavior, is a matter of the probability of success (i.e. of the probability of the acceptance) of communications. Depending on what this probability rests upon, a distinction can be made between truths warranted by the life-world and which are therefore self-evident (Descartes's example: "Rome is a city in Italy") and truths that are (or are to be) warranted scientifically. The boundary is far from precise and over time many scientific truths turn into self-evident truths belonging to the life-world.

Such a dual concept of truth would not have been acceptable within the framework of the traditional logical-ontological conception of the world because here truth was understood as the relation of thought to being, as *adaequatio intellectus ad rem*, and according to the rules of logic this relationship could only be either affirmed or rejected. Every dual notion of truth would by definition have admitted to contradictions in the concept of truth and thereby dissolved truth as truth. At most it could be accepted that truth was a result of object-specific thought and that the different sorts of objects also led to different forms and "levels of certainty" of truth. But this view — that the sphere of being (*Sein*) itself offers various truths — has vanished along with the view that open possibilities (in the sense of *actus*, *habitus*, and *potentia*) are specified by their object. This kind of certitude is neither possible nor necessary once there is a greater differentiation of scientific communication. The concept of truth itself changes with the evolution of the social system and must finally acquire a form in which even the very fact of its variation can be grasped as true.

It is the task of a cognitive sociology to provide a kind of semantics that is still possible in this situation. If the theoretical proposals put forward here are accepted, such a sociology does not rest primarily on a reflection of the reflexive achievements of epistemology[97] itself, but rather upon those parts of theory that have proven themselves outside of the specific sphere of epistemology: the theory of symbolically generalized media of communication and of self-referential systems.[98] Truth is understood as only one differentiated, symbolically generalized medium of communication, and science as only one differentiated (and thereby self-referential) social system among others. The concept of differentiation (which refers to an increased independence from arbitrariness and a greater dependence on positive facts, or to an increase in indifference and sensibility) constitutes the basis on which epistemology (among other things) must be constructed. Truth that functions in the life-world bases the expectations of its acceptance on presupposed agreement.[99] This presupposition serves to safeguard everyday processing from one situation to the next. The source and contents of communication are not strictly separated as a basis for the validity of truth, thus making it possible that dubious things can still be believed out of consideration for the communicator, and that errors can be interpreted with reference to him (his motives, his stupidity, his insincerity). Similarly, the social status of its source gives a communication a greater chance of being accepted as true. For stratified societies, this is an indispensable and even necessary means of ensuring communicative successes. The motives for questioning the cognitive contents of a communication are accordingly diverse and not necessarily determined by a theoretically informed cognitive interest. Even well into the modern period the preciousness of a substance, for example, was sufficient for regarding it as especially valuable in the research process. Newly emerging problems could consequently usually be dealt with by restoring the general sense of plausibility from which one had proceeded.

Every scientific activity employs and reproduces such truths of the life-world in its actual practice. Writing on the typewriter does not require a calculation of the necessary pressure of the finger, an understanding of how muscles work, nor of how the machine manages to deflect the direction of the pressure. What is decisively important is that specific meanings can be isolated vis-à-vis uncontrolled interferences from the sphere of truths generally accepted in the life-world. This is exactly what takes place by way of the establishment of self-referential circles which are initially closed but eventually become detautologized in the specified manner. Both the source and the contents of the communication are thereby differentiated in that they in different ways are made dependent on the self-referential treatment of the problem.[100] Only such a new and independent foundation makes it possible to detach the constitution of the object from the premises of the life-world[101] and, in scientific terms, to "objectify" it.

What takes place here can be made clear only by referring to self-reference and thereby to the circular structure of the scientific way of proceeding. Science neither retreats to a mere treatment of its own artifacts (concepts) nor does it constitute special objects in the life-world which did not previously exist.[102] To the self-referential discourse under the specific conditions of the system of science corresponds, in the environment, *a dissolution of unities into relations.*[103] What in the life-world initially exists as a solid thing (*dinghaft*) or as event (*ereignismässig*), thus ensuring consensus in a diffuse manner, is now reconstructed as a set of relations. This dissolution and recombination increases the potential for variation because in a relational structure it is often possible to change some things while holding others constant. But the environment will above all become more complex from selective points of view if ever newer unities and eventually even souls and atoms are dissolved by theoretical perspectives into relations among yet simpler elements.

Since the seventeenth century — and it is no accident that this development coincides with an increase in the functional differentiation of science — the traditional concept of the world as a *universitas rerum*, as an *aggregatio corporum*, has gradually been dissolved, and the world is conceived in a new way as an infinite horizon of the possible progressive advances of meaningful thematization. For science this means an advance in possible dissolutions and recombinations. At the same time, reason — which once referred to the hierarchically superior ability to possess knowledge — is in the domain of science now reduced to the ability of establishing relations[104] from which one can no longer expect any confirmation of the circumstances themselves.

The assumption of "ultimate" elements is thereby relativized in terms of the latest state of research,[105] and the establishment of elements and relations becomes dependent on the level of emergent reality — and there is no lowest one! — which one has in mind.[106] This openness is not restricted by its object, which proves resistant to further intellectual decomposition; its limit lies, in a purely pragmatic way, in the possibility of a further dissolution of unities by way of the current state of research and its technical instrumentation and in postulating underlying relations that can be subjected to research techniques.[107]

Late medieval European metaphysics had made a last minute attempt to prevent this dissolution into arbitrariness by way of the principle of sufficient reason, which insisted that even the choice between being and nonbeing must have a reason since nothing is without cause.[108] Yet this question does not pose itself on the basis of the life-world, which is itself always cause enough since its inquiry has already answered the question. An inquiry into causes can nevertheless be respected as the concern of first philosophy. For science the basic problem is not that of sufficient reason, but rather the question of establishing the life-world and increasing its capacity for dissolution. Science must (although it thereby assumes its capacity for dissolution) in the final analysis (in the case of philosophy: in the first place) also understand its relation to objects *not as a unity* (and even if this were the unity of reason) but rather *as a relation*, and indeed as the *relation between the tautological self-reference of the system and the arbitrariness of its environment*. Driving dissolution back to this ultimate relation always remains an operation of the life-world, and it always provides a reason because it is unstable; because it presents the greatest redundancy, namely the functional equivalence of all information; and because it ascribes to every event which occurs in the life-world the function of detautologization.[109]

X

We can summarize all this by saying that the capacity of scientific discourse for dissolution and recombination is aimed at a closed, self-referential system ("I think what you think, if you think what I think") in any given environment. But in the real world closed self-reference is just as impossible as an arbitrary environment.[110] The formulation that cybernetics concerns itself with systems "that are open to energy but closed to information and control"[111] indicates that a differentiation of levels is presupposed in the structure of the world which makes possible a distinction between the flow of energy and the reception of information, and that all organization of closure can only refer to processes specific to particular levels. For the domain of meaningfully constituted systems — in which all meaning refers beyond the system boundaries and in which closure can thus only exist by way of rules that govern the management of these references — operation in self-referential relations is bound in a special way to an order that must be presupposed. How does one locate and identify this order, which distinguishes and mediates between the closure and openness, between the self-reference and the reference to the other of the process of knowing?

On the basis of our initial guiding assumptions these questions as well as the possibility of answering them belong to the sphere of scientific efforts, and hence are in turn dependent on the evolutionary social process in general and the differentiation of a functional system for scientific knowledge in particular. Efforts of this sort concern themselves with the identity of a socially differentiated system. As was indicated above,[112] I am proposing to call such efforts "reflection" and their result "theories of reflection."[113]

The efforts at reflection which are important for our purposes begin in the eighteenth century, *after* the differentiation of an autonomously operating system of scientific research had already become evident and made itself felt as a fact. The controversies conducted in the seventeenth century between the more dogmatic and the more skeptical notions pale in comparison because both are unable to do justice to the concern and successes of research. The long disputed concept of "innate ideas," furthermore, is now generally recognized as untenable, owing to Locke's critique. The natural warrants of unity for what is (possibly) rather complex are thereby eliminated in the process of knowing. Research shows further that the world beneath the moon is also accessible to mathematical calculations, that it can be dissolved into relations. There is no longer a division in the world that separates perfect domains from corrupt ones, and there appear to be no fundamental, but at best methodological limits to the possibility of mathematization which result from the stage of the inquiry itself. But the shift from unity to relation gives the problem of epistemological certainty even greater relevance. At the same time all the qualities of assent which had been linked to noble birth and social status become now inoperative for the advances of knowledge. All persons are in principle equally valued in reaching consensus, and personally achieved understanding is demanded from all. Science prepares itself for an inclusion of the entire population and in so doing can recognize only itself, its scientific knowledge as a differentiating factor. All extrascientific supports along the lines of "moral certitude" become inoperative. Thus for the eighteenth century the critical question was to become: What can still warrant that which is fundamental, that which provides unity in diversity, and, above all, that which constitutes the unity of the difference between knowledge and object?

That which appears to this way of seeing as a problem of induction or synthesis is subjected to two conditions which direct the strategies which aim for an acceptable solution. The first condition reproduces the difference between life-world orientation and self-evident perception as the difference between the two subjective capabilities of experience and reason.[114] The second condition establishes as a rule the avoidance of self-referential legitimations of knowledge. These theoretical notions together lead to the thesis that the conditions of the possibility of experience cannot be grounded in experience itself, i.e. to the Kantian concept of a priori. If one adheres to this line of thought, there must be an a priori because there is after all experience, hence something which makes experience possible and which is not itself experience. It is then only a matter of grasping and locating the a priori in such a way that its achievement of grounding knowledge can be made understandable. Here the object reference of knowledge first comes to mind. Its temporal structure remains relatively unelaborated, if one ignores the chapter on schematism in the *Critique of Pure Reason*, and its social dimension is covered by the generalization of such terms as subject, consciousness, reason, that is, by way of generic concepts.

The narrower conception of the a priori introduced by Kant[115] has prevailed and has itself become a model, although the assumptions which guided it were not kept open. Instead, the difficulties which epistemology now had to deal with were met with an inflation of a prioris. Here begins the impressive methodological dispute concerning the psychologization of the foundations of knowledge; here enter the unconscious (Fichte), the emotional (Scheler), the religious (Otto), the historical (Simmel), the social (Adler), and the valued (Rickert, Scheler). The development of theory transcends a strictly epistemological framework without being able to contribute anything essential to epistemology (or even to the self-reflection of the scientific system). Only in this sense are the temporal and the social dimensions also included, based on their own apriorisms. But its inflation finally deprives the concept of all distinctive contours and permits in the end to elevate to the place of a priori the counterconcept of the "always already" experienced a posteriori, the life-world. The concept produces out of itself the self-reference that it was supposed to avoid by identifying itself with its counterconcept.

Even for the purposes of sociological analysis it is not insignificant to note in which direction a mode of thinking is developing which starts precisely with the problem of identity and thus concerns itself with reflection in the strict sense. The history which has run its course under the rubric of "epistemology" has kept little contact with the development of science.[116] The merit of the ongoing epistemological discussion has consisted in supporting a state of consciousness which has precluded a relapse into unreflexive objectivism, at least as a general concept for science. In this way it has again and again been possible to translate research experiences which demonstrate the researcher's own participation in the constitution (and not merely the selection!) of his subject matter and make them available at a more general level of discussion. One need only think of the uncertainty principle formulated by Heisenberg, the problems of undecidability in logic, or the everyday experiences of social-scientific research. Owing to epistemological conceptions, all this has been more than just a temporary methodical dilemma. It could and had to be experienced as the nuisance of self-reference which cannot be eliminated from one's own practice.

Notes

Translated from German by Steven Roesch and Volker Meja

1. Compare especially with Thomas S. Kuhn, *Die Entstehung des Neuen: Studien zur Struktur der Wissenschaftsgeschichte* (Frankfurt: Suhrkamp, 1977); also Werner Diederich, ed., *Theorien der Wissenschaftsgeschichte: Beiträge zur diachronen Wissenschaftstheorie* (Frankfurt: Suhrkamp, 1974); Volker Bialas, "Grundprobleme der Wissenschaftsgeschichte," in *Wissenschaftssoziologie: Studien und Materialen, Sonderheft 18 der Kölner Zeitschrift für Soziologie und Sozialpsychologie*, ed. Nico Stehr and René König (Opladen: Westdeutscher Verlag, 1975), pp. 122-34. For an empirical investigation with epistemological claims see Karin D. Knorr, *The Manufacture of Knowledge* (Oxford: Pergamon, 1981).

2. Here for example on the basis of the theses of Maturana Peter Hejl, Wolfram K. Kock, Gerhard Roth, eds., *Wahrnehmung und Kommunikation* (Frankfurt: Suhrkamp, 1978); further, for example, Donald T. Campbell, "Evolutionary Epistemology," in *The Philosophy of Karl Popper*, ed. Paul Arthur Schlipp (La Salle, Ill.: Open Court, 1974), vol. 1, pp. 412-63.

3. See the collection *Beiträge zur Grundlegung einer operationsfähigen Dialektik*, 3 vols. (Hamburg: F. Meiner, 1976-80).

4. See also Günther himself in Gotthard Günther, "Kritische Bemerkungen zur gegenwärtigen Wissenschaftstheorie," *Soziale Welt* 19(1968):328-41; reprinted *Beiträge zur Grundlegung*, vol. 2, pp. 157-70.

5. See Francisco J. Varela, "A calculus for self-reference," *International Journal of General Systems* 2(1975):5-24; Heinz von Foerster, "The Curious Behavior of Complex Systems: Lessons from Biology," in *Futures Research: New Directions*, ed. Harold A. Linstone, W.H. Clive Simmonds (Reading, Mass.: Addison-Wesley, 1977), pp. 104-13.

6. But notions of a primacy of self-maintenance could not be entirely suppressed. Here see especially Dieter Henrich, "Die Grundstruktur der modernen Philosophie" (with a supplement concerning self-consciousness and self-maintenance), in *Subjektivität und Selbsterhaltung: Beiträge zur Diagnose der Moderne* ed. Hans Ebeling (Frankfurt:

Suhrkamp, 1976), pp. 97-143. A more detailed analysis would have to take into consideration the countermovement which, since the late seventeenth century, has been characterized by the concepts of "pleasure" and then "existence."

7.   Compare this for example with Georg Simmel, "Exkurs über das Problem: Wie ist Gesellschaft möglich?" in *Soziologie: Untersuchung über die Formen der Vergesellschaftung*, 2nd. ed. (Munich-Leipzig: Duncker & Humblot, 1922), pp. 2lff.; Karl Mannheim, "Die Strukturanalyse der Erkenntnistheorie," in *Kant-Studien, Ergänzungsheft Nr. 57* (Berlin: Reuther & Reichard, 1922); Max Adler, *Das Rätsel der Gesellschaft: Zur erkenntnistheoretischen Grundlegung der Sozialwissenschaften* (Vienna: Saturn, 1936).

8.   See also Niklas Luhmann, "Reflexive Mechanismen," in *Soziologische Aufklärung*, vol. 1, 4th ed. (Opladen: Westdeutscher Verlag, 1974), pp. 92-112.

9.   It is interesting that Maturana, whose work is oriented to this model, therefore regards a consciousness of the environment as generally impossible in closed systems and thus ascribes *every* perception of a difference between system and environment to an observer. See Humberto R. Maturana, "Cognition," in Hejl et al., pp. 29-49.

10. With regard to this distinction see Hans W. Gottinger, "Complexity and information technology in dynamic systems," *Kybernetes* 4(1975):121-34; "Notes on dynamic systems and social processes," *General Systems* 20(1975):121-34; "Problems in large-scale social economic systems," *Journal of Peace Research* 15(1978):131-51.

11. Compare Niklas Luhmann, "Temporalization of Complexity," in *Sociocybernetics*, ed. R. Felix Geyer, Johannes van der Zouwen, vol. 2 (Leiden: Nijhoff, 1978), pp. 95-111.

12. I have tried to show that this assumes complex temporal structures, especially the distinction between two kinds of present. See Niklas Luhmann, "Temporalstrukturen von Handlungssystemen: Zum Zusammenhang von Handlungs-und Systemtheorie," in *Verhalten, Handeln und System: Talcott Parsons' Beitrag zur Entwicklung der Sozialwissenschaften*, ed. Wolfgang Schluchter (Frankfurt: Suhrkamp, 1980), pp. 32-67.

13. See Alfred Korzybski, *Science and Sanity: An Introduction to Nonaristotelian Systems and General Semantics* (Lancaster, Pa.: Science, 1933). Here too in close connection (one that is only rarely mentioned these days) with an analysis of self-referential relations. In addition see also Robert P. Pula, "General Semantics as a General System which Explicitly Includes the System Maker," in *Coping with Increasing Complexity: Implications of General Semantics and General Systems Theory*, ed. Donald E. Washburn and Dennis R. Smith (New York: Gordon & Breach, 1974), pp. 69-81.

14. Explicitly for example in W. Ross Ashby, "Principles of the Self-Organizing System," in *Modern Systems Research for the Behavioral Scientists: A Sourcebook*, ed. Walter Buckley (Chicago: Aldine, 1968), pp. 108-18.

15. The reasons for the generalization of this particular principle would require more precise clarification. A very suggestive hypothesis can be found in Christoph Strosetzki, *Konversation: Ein Kapitel gesellschaftlicher und literarischer Pragmatik im Frankreich des 17. Jahrhunderts* (Frankfurt: Suhrkamp, 1978), pp. 95ff. The maxim is generalized because in courtly society it was no longer only ladies who had to please the men, but rather, on the contrary, the efforts of men on behalf of women took priority. This, argues Strosetzki, imposed the symmetricalization of the relationship.

16. Strosetzki, p. 105, provides references to literature from the last two decades of the seventeenth century. In the German *Moralischen Wochenschriften* of the early eighteenth century this topic is encountered repeatedly.

17. "Conversation," *Encyclopédie, ou Dictionnaire raisonné, des sciences, des arts et des métiers*, vol. 4 (Paris: Briasson, 1754; reprinted Stuttgart: Fromman, 1966), p. 165.

18. See for example the section on conversation in Jacques du Bosq, *L'honnête femme* (Paris: Billaine, 1633), pp. 50ff.

19. Saint-Evremond, "L'amitié sans amitié," in *Oeuvres*, vol. 1 (Paris: Didier, 1927), p. 74. Only after the relationship between two people has become intimate and after the discovery of the inexhaustible inner depth of the individual does there appear the opposite thesis: two people reciprocally guarantee enough reality for each other and for precisely this reason can bring the "as well" (*Ausserdem*) closer to the "marginal value zero," as Simmel, (p. 26), puts it.

20. A detailed analysis of the historical development can be found in Niklas Luhmann, *Gesellschaftsstruktur und Semantik: Studien zur Wissenssoziologie der modernen Gesellschaft*, vol. 1 (Frankfurt: Suhrkamp, 1980), pp. 72-161.

21. Here see George A. Kelly, "Man's Construction of His Alternatives," in *Assessment of Human Motives*, ed. Gardner Lindzey (New York: Rinehart, 1958), pp. 33-64; see also G.E.R. Lloyd, *Polarity and Analogy: Two Types of Argumentation in Early Greek Thought* (Cambridge: Cambridge University Press, 1966).

22. See Claudia Henn-Schmölders, "Ars conversationis: Zur Geschichte des sprachlichen Umgangs," *Arcadia* 10(1975):16-33.

23. See Robert K. Merton, *Science, Technology, and Society in Seventeenth Century England*, 2nd ed. (New York: Harper & Row, 1970), pp. 216ff.; elaborating the specialization of this development and its understanding of sociality, see Wolfgang van den Daele, "Die soziale Konstruktion der Wissenschaft: Institutionalisierung und Definition der positiven Wissenschaft in der zweiten Hälfte des 17. Jahrhunderts," in *Experimentelle Philosophie: Ursprünge autonomer Wissenschaftsentwicklung*, ed. Gernot Böhme, Wolfgang van den Daele, and Wolfgang Krohn (Frankfurt: Suhrkamp, 1977), pp. 129-82.

24. Impressive evidence for the extensive and intensive restoration (felt to be very necessary) of compatibility between science and religion on the basis of great communicative differentiation is offered by Robert Boyle, *Of the Usefulness of Natural Philosophy* (1663, esp. part 1) written circa 1650, long before the foundation of the Royal Society, cited according to the edition in *The Works*, vol. 2, ed. Thomas Birch (London: 1772; reprinting in Hildesheim: 1966), pp. 1-246. See p. 61 for the view that God hardly reveals the secrets of chemistry by dispatching good angels or through nocturnal visions, as followers of Helmont or Paracelsus believed; but that he does favor human communication and makes those who possess knowledge ready to share it with others, "by whose friendly communication they may often learn that in a few moments, which cost the imparters many a year's toil and study." Here it is also evident that scientific communication must be distinguished from economic behavior in the utilization of one's own lead in knowledge.

25. See Henry G. van Leeuwen, *The Problem of Certainty in English Thought, 1630-1690*, 2nd ed. (Den Haag: Nijhoff, 1970).

26. This point of the merely subjective and "draftlike" nature of all theoretical claims and systemics has strong points of contact with the conversational ideal of "not being binding." It is also not a coincidence that this aspect is cultivated more in France than in England (Newton rejected it explicitly). See Friedrich Kambartel, "'System' und Begründung als wissenschaftliche und philosophische Ordnungsbegriffe bei und vor

Kant," in *Philosophie und Rechtswissenschaft: Zum Problem ihrer Beziehungen im 19. Jahrhundert*, ed. Jürgen Blühdorn and Joachim Ritter (Frankfurt: Klostermann, 1969), pp. 101ff.

27.   And this against the background of the question which arose around 1600 whether modern developments could surpass the culture and level of knowledge of antiquity. See Richard F. Jones, *Ancient and Moderns: A Study of the Rise of the Scientific Movement in Seventeenth-Century England*, 2nd ed. (St. Louis: Washington University, 1961).

28.   Thus Ernan McMullin in "Empiricism and the Scientific Revolution," in *Art, Science, and History in the Renaissance*, ed. Charles S. Singleton (Baltimore: 1967), p. 332. See also Ernan McMullin, "Medieval and modern science: continuity or discontinuity?" *International Philosophical Quarterly* 5(1965):103-29.

29.   See Gernot Böhme, "Die Ausdifferenzierung wissenschaftlicher Diskurse," in *Wissenschaftssoziologie: Studien und Materialien, Sonderheft 18 der Kölner Zeitschrift für Soziologie und Sozialpsychologie*, ed. Nico Stehr and René König (Opladen: Westdeutscher Verlag, 1975), pp. 231-53.

30.   See also Ashby, pp. 108ff.

31.   See n. 19.

32.   In the depiction (but not in the use of the concept of reflection) I am following Gotthard Günther, "Metaphysik, Logik und die Theorie der Reflexion," *Archiv für Philosophie* 7(1957):1-44; reprinted in Günther, *Beiträge zur Grundlegung*. vol. 1, pp. 31-74.

33.   Gotthard Günther objects with justification to this metaphysical overexertion of bivariate logic and also sees correctly that this axiomatized structure is not suitable for a system with multiple processors (a plurality of "subjects"). This objection is still based on transcendental theory and only tries to formulate the specific significance of the subjective identity of reflection. Helmut Schelsky was the first to suspect the sociological relevance of this criticism.

34.   There are also cases in which this normal deflection does not work, and even where it does not work in line with one's expectation. For example, when one feels oneself obliged to inform someone that his clothing is disorderly, or that something else of an embarrassing nature is noticeable. These are cases in which the imputation to the object (the subject of the sentence) is turned back to the person who finds it necessary to communicate about this topic.

35.   This has moreover the advantage that epistemology can bring its basic categorial apparatus into direct contact with empirical research and thus locate itself vis-à-vis existing reality in this manner. There is extensive research on attribution. See Niklas Luhmann, "Erleben und Handeln," in *Handlungstheorien interdisziplinär*, vol. 2, ed. Hans Lenk (Munich: Fink, 1978), pp. 235-53.

36.   This process to is then again available for reconstruction, for "elaborating myths," to take up the guiding thought of Hans Blumenberg, *Arbeit am Mythos* (Frankfurt: Suhrkamp, 1979).

37.   With regard to the hermetic tradition, which is important in this context, see Frances A. Yates, *Giordano Bruno and the Hermetic Tradition* (London: Routledge & Kegan Paul, 1964); P.M. Rattansi, "The Social Interpretation of Science in the Seventeenth Century," in *Science and Society, 1600-1900*, ed. Peter Mathias (Cambridge: Cam-

bridge University Press, 1972), pp. 1-32; Thomas Schnelle and W. Baldamus, "Sociological Reflections on the Strange Survival of the Occult within the Rational Mechanistic World View," *Zeitschrift für Soziologie* 7(1978):251-66. See further Robert Lenoble, *Mersenne, ou La naissance du mécanisme*, 2nd. ed. (Paris: Vrin, 1971) esp. pp. 83ff.; Brian P. Copenhaver, *Symphorien Champier and the Reception of the Occultist Tradition in Renaissance France* (Den Haag: Mouton, 1978).

38.   Concerning the context of the general concept of symbolically generalized media of communication see Niklas Luhmann, "Systemtheoretische Argumentationen," in Jürgen Habermas and Niklas Luhmann, *Theorie der Gesellschaft oder Sozialtechnologie: Was leistet die Sozialtechnologie?* (Frankfurt: Suhrkamp, 1971), pp. 342ff.; Niklas Luhmann, "Einführende Bemerkungen zu einer Theorie symbolisch generalisierter Kommunikationsmedien," in *Soziologische Aufklärung*, vol. 2 (Opladen: Westdeutscher Verlag, 1975), pp. 170-92.

39.   It may be asked how self-references can be treated if, as in the case of political power, ego and alter are engaged with the imputation of action. In this case externalizations are replaced by an expansion of the circle, a diversion of power which assigns power over the government to the politician, power over the public to the government, and power over the politician again to the public, so that in each phase of this circle the other two can be assumed to be externally given. The theories of reflection are distinguished accordingly. In the case of science their problem is the identity in the difference of perception and object; in the case of politics, their problem is the identity in the difference between those with power and those subject to it.

40.   Even in a trivariate profile, ambiguities would arise time and again about the alternative against which a partner primarily orients his selections. It is obvious that the prescribed bivariateness does not solve this problem once and for all. Countless (and also fruitful) misunderstandings arise in scientific discourse in that the partners' horizons of comparison — with which their statements are contrasted — diverge.

41.   Viewed psychologically, it remains true that the negation of falsehoods is not a complete equivalent of truths. Concerning this see P.N. Johnson-Laird and Johanna Tagart, "How implication is understood," *American Journal of Psychology* 82(1969):367-73; David E. Kanouse, "Language, Labeling and Attribution," in Edward E. Jones et al., *Attribution: Perceiving the Causes of Behavior* (Morristown, N.J.: General Learning, 1971), pp. 121-35, contains interesting considerations about the countereffects on the process of attribution.

42.   For Pascal this detour by way of the opposite was still a sign of deficiency, not a principle of advance, namely a desperate solution in the face of the fact that man lacks the direct intuition of truth. See "De l'esprit géométrique et de l'art de persuader," in *Oeuvres*, éd. de la Pléiade (Paris: Éditions de la Nouvelle Française, 1950), p. 369.

43.   See also the critique of this "ideological attitude, which is slowly disappearing today," in Gotthard Günther, "Das Janusgesicht der Dialektik," in *Hegel Jahrbuch 1974*, ed. W.R. Beyer (Cologne: Pahl-Rugenstein, 1975), p. 90: reprinted in Günther, vol. 2, op. cit., p. 308.

44.   See for example Neal G. Miller, "Central stimulation and other new approaches to motivation and reward," *American Psychologist* 13(1958):100- 08.

45.   Concerning this see especially Niklas Luhmann, "Selbststeuerung der Wissenschaft," in *Soziologische Aufklärung*, 4th ed., vol. 1 (Opladen: Westdeutscher Verlag, 1974), pp. 232-52.

46.   Here I have in mind Edmund Husserl, *Die Krisis der europäischen Wissenschaften und die transzendentale Phänomenologie*, Husserliana vol. 6 (Den Haag: Nijhoff, 1954).

47.   See in classical clarity Plato, *Sophistes* 219 A, esp. pp. 249ff. For an overview see also F. Cornford, *Plato's Theory of Knowledge* (London: Kegan Paul, 1935), pp. 170ff.

48.   This also determines the nature of the figures of reflection that are now necessary: Sophrosyne is the knowledge about knowledge and ignorance. See Plato, *Charmides* 166 E. This is not yet a matter of the reflection of identity in the difference between cognition and object.

49.   Plato in turn also constructs this distinction between sophist and philosopher in a binary manner, and indeed according to whether one is oriented to nonbeing or being (*Sophistes* 254 A), whereby the philosopher, who already knows being, comes to a position which removes the social dialectic from him and only lets him manage it. A transition to a mode of analysis which is no longer dialectical, one which will later be called "logic," is thereby prepared.

50.   See Eric A. Havelock, *Preface to Plato* (Cambridge, Mass.: Harvard University Press, 1963); id., *The Greek Concept of Justice: From Its Shadows in Homer to Its Substance in Plato* (Cambridge, Mass.: Harvard University Press, 1978). Also noteworthy is Jack Goody and Ian Watt, "The consequences of literacy," *Comparative Studies in Society and History* 5(1963):304-45.

51.   This can be easily demonstrated by the scientific biography of Aristotle, written prior to the *Analytica priora* and the *Analytica posteriora*. See Ernst Kapp, *Der Ursprung der Logik bei den Griechen* (Göttingen: Vandenhoeck & Ruprecht, 1965), pp. 7ff. See also the precisely corresponding explanations concerning Epagoge/Induction, pp. 89ff.

52.   Whereby the history of the concept, which originates in court procedure and originally meant accusation, still retains the inquisitorial nature of a bivariate scheme of questions in the form of negatable predicates, even if it is no longer the person questioned who is answerable, but rather being (*Sein*).

53.   *Works*, vol. 4, ed. Thomas Birch, p. 450, cited according to McMullin, (1967), p. 354.

54.   This in turn is a prerequisite for the symmetricalization in binary schematism, for only in this way can the effort to establish falsehoods (or "falsification") be held to be as significant as the effort to establish truths.

55.   Many variants of this procedure can be discovered from Plato to Stoic and neo-Stoic ethics, to Agrippa von Nettesheim and up to Parsons. It continues to be attractive as a framework for empirical research. Even Max Weber has recently been successfully integrated within this framework. See Wolfgang Schluchter, *Die Entwicklung des okzidentalen Rationalismus* (Tübingen: Mohr, 1979). Yet the theoretical derivation of the marginal variables still leaves something to be desired, despite its progress in comparison with the more natural initial assumptions of antiquity. See also Niklas Luhmann, "Talcott Parsons: Zur Zukunft eines Theorieprogramms," *Zeitschrift für Soziologie* 9(1980):5-17.

56.   See *Metaphysics*, Lambda 9 (1074 b 15ff.). See also Klaus Oehler, "Aristotle on self-knowledge," *Proceedings of the American Philosophical Society* 118(1974):493-506, esp. 503.

57.   For this reason the number of necessary steps is suggested as a measure of complexity (computational complexity).

58. See Kenneth Arrow, *Social Choice and Individual Values*, 2nd ed. (New York: Wiley, 1963).

59. The first variant is more common in philosophy, the second in economic theory (with regard to factors of production).

60. *Errata naturae*, which actually serve to verify the normal order, in Fortunius Licetus, *De monstris*, cited according to the new edition of Amsterdam 1665, pp. 5, 29. With regard to the widespread interest in monstrous species which extends far beyond zoology, see also François de La Mothe le Vayer, "Des Monstres," in *Opuscules, ou Petits traittez* (Paris: de Sommaville, 1647), pp. 342-84.

61. Quoted according to Jacques Roger, *Les sciences de la vie dans la pensée française du XVIIIe siècle*, 2nd ed. (Paris. Colin, 1971), p. 389.

62. "Je n'ay veu monstre et miracle au monde plus exprès que moy mesme," writes Montaigne in *Essais* III, XI, éd. de la Pléiade (Paris: Société les belle lettres, 1950), p. 1154.

63. Klaus Hartmann, "Zur neuesten Dialektik-Kritik," *Archiv für Geschichte der Philosophie* 55(1973):229.

64. For other examples see Niklas Luhmann, *Funktion der Religion* (Frankfurt: Suhrkamp, 1977), pp. 126ff., 200ff.; id. and Karl Eberhard Schorr, *Reflexionsprobleme im Erziehungssystem* (Stuttgart: Enke, 1979), pp. 58ff.

65. It could be objected that economic theory also uses this concept. Yet it does this with the goal — see Erich Schneider, *Einführung in die Wirtschaftstheorie*, 13th ed., vol. 2 (Tübingen: Mohr, 1972), pp. 172ff. — of discovering which factor of production restricts the latter in a given combination of factors. As a scientific undertaking, this theory postulates *limitationality* in the relationship of factors of production. The relation to the economy arises from the fact that what finally matters is its formula of contingency, namely scarcity.

66. This is the accomplishment of the so-called theory of contingency. See Émile Boutroux, *De la contingence des lois de nature* (Paris: Baillière, 1874), quoted according to the 8th ed. (Paris: Alcan, 1915). See also Ferdinand Pelikan, *Entstehung und Entwicklung des Kontingentismus* (Berlin: Simion, 1915).

67. This applies especially to the relation to the classical methodological goals of explanation and prognosis, but also in a very general manner to the operative use of binary schematism, which mostly appears in theoretical form in the work of the functionalists, above all Parsons.

68. Earlier there was a second concept, annihilation, which, as the opposite of creation, was supposed to depict the case that goes beyond this: the dissolution of world continuity. Today, instead of this, we can imagine a physical or chemical annihilation of the meaningfully constituted world which proceeds from other levels of system formation.

69. See Michael Giesecke, "Schriftsprache als Entwicklungsfaktor in Sprach- und Begriffsgeschichte," in *Historische Semantik und Begriffsgeschichte*, ed. Reinhart Koselleck (Stuttgart: Klett-Cotta, 1979), pp. 262-302.

70. From the viewpoint of the differentiation of specifically normative structures of expectation see Niklas Luhmann, *Rechtssoziologie*, 2 vols. (Reinbek: Rowohlt, 1972), esp. vol. 1, pp. 40ff.

71. Still lacking is an explication of the history of nature, as concept and problem, which is sufficient for these theoretical aims. The most important contributions focus on single

historical epochs. For a concise overview see Heinrich Schipperes, "Natur," in *Geschichtliche Grundbegriffe: Historisches Lexikon zur politisch-sozialen Sprache in Deutschland*, vol. 4 (Stuttgart: Klett-Cotta, 1978), pp. 215-44. Concerning newer developments, especially important for our topic, see Ita Osske, *Ganzheit, Unendlichkeit und Form: Studien zu Shaftesburys Naturbegriff* (Berlin: Dissertation, 1939); Roger Mercier, *La réhabilitation de la nature humaine (1700-1750)* (Villemonble, Seine: 1960); Jean Ehrard, *L'idée de nature en France dans la première moitié du XVIIIe siècle* (Paris: SEVPEN, 1963); Robert Spaemann, "Genetisches zum Naturbegriff des 18. Jahrhunderts," *Archiv für Begriffsgeschichte* 11(1967): 59-74; Herbert M. Nobis, "Frühneuzeitliche Verständnisweisen der Natur und ihr Wandel bis zum 18. Jahrhundert," *Archiv für Begriffsgeschichte* 11(1967):37-58; "Die Umwandlung der mittelalterlichen Naturvorstellung," *Archiv für Begriffsgeschichte* 13(1969):34-7.

72. This can be readily seen in a formulation of Joseph Glanvill, *The Vanity of Dogmatizing* (London: Eversden, 1661; reprinted Brighton: Harvester, 1970), p. 180: "Nature works by an invisible hand in all things." Benjamin Nelson also stresses this aspect of a warrant which is independent of religion, but nevertheless still quasi-religious (in contrast to straightforward skepticism) in *Der Ursprung der Moderne: Vergleichende Studien zum Zivilisationsprozess* (Frankfurt: Suhrkamp, 1977), pp. 94ff, 165ff.

73. See the interesting argument in Francis Hutcheson, *An Essay on the Nature and Conduct of the Passions and Affections* (London: Osburn and Longman, 1728), pp. viiff.: Despite false beliefs about optics one may see well; despite false beliefs about morality one may act virtuously. "*True Opinions*, however, about both, may enable us to *improve* our natural Powers, and to rectify accidental Disorders incident into them." Only progress demands as its Archimedean point a basis in a knowledge of nature.

74. The "hermetic" doctrine is also a characteristic example of such survival and revival of older traditions that seek to retain the founding notions of unity vis-à-vis "more modern" developments and are then relativized as being "occult," "mystical," and so on. See references in n. 37 above.

75. See Walter Freund, *Modernus und andere Zeitbegriffe des Mittelalters* (Cologne: Böhlav, 1957).

76. See Robert Spaemann, "Fanatisch, Fanatismus," in *Historisches Wörterbuch der Philosophie*, vol. 2 (Basel-Stuttgart: Schwabe, 1972), pp. 904-8.

77. The dispute concerning the relative merits of the older or, more particularly, the new science in the sixteenth and seventeenth centuries also referred especially to the attribution of authority, and one must consider in this connection the fact that even the very age of the "elders" was finally challenged with the argument that they have actually lived in a more recent period of historical development and are therefore younger than those now alive. (The argument *juventas mundi antiquitas saeculi* appears to have traveled from Giordano Bruno to England by way of Bacon. See also Jones, p. 44.)

78. See Louis B. Wright, *Middle Class Culture in Elizabethan England* (Chapel Hill: University of North Carolina Press, 1835), esp. pp. 134ff. The tendency to systematize the transmission of knowledge (and thereafter knowledge itself) which emerged toward the end of the sixteenth century also had this interest in acceleration (for example of education, of court trials, and so on).

79. "The Aristotelian Philosophy is inept for New Discoveries; and therefore of no accomodation to the use of life," writes Glanvill, p. 178.

80. "Most of our Rarities have been found by *casual Emergency*; and have been works of time and chance rather than of Philosophy" (Glanvill, p. 179).

81. See for example Henri Busson, *La religion des classiques 1660-1685* (Paris: PVI, 1948); Richard S. Westfall, *Science and Religion in Seventeenth-Century England* (New Haven: Yale University Press, 1958); Theodore K. Rabb, "Religion and the rise of modern science," *Past and Present* 31(1965):111-26; Rainer Specht, *Innovation und Folgelast: Beispiele aus der neueren Philosophie- und Wissenschaftsgeschichte* (Stuttgart: Frommann-Holtboog, 1972); Charles Webster, ed., *The Intellectual Revolution of the Seventeenth Century* (London: Routledge & Kegan Paul, 1974).

82. Descartes, "Principes de la philosophie," pp. 205, 206, in *Oeuvres et lettres*, éd. de la Pléiade (Paris: Gallimard, 1952), pp. 668ff. For Hobbes an analogously formulated distinction lies completely *within* communicative relationships: "The signes of Sciences, are some certain and infallible; some uncertain. Certain, when he that pretendeth the Science of any thing, can teach the same; that is to say, demonstrate the truth thereof perspicuously to another: Uncertain, when onely some particular events answer to his pretense, and upon many occasions prove so as he sayes they must." *Leviathan* I 5, quoted according to the edition of Everyman's Library (London: Dutton, 1952), p. 22.

83. "Omne quod multis indiciis confirmatur, quae vix concurre possunt nisi in vero, est moraliter certum": thus in *Opuscules et fragments inédits de Leibniz*, ed. Louis Couturat (Paris: Alcan, 1903), p. 515.

84. In this connection the knowledge that there can be no certain knowledge of causality and that all empirical science must therefore appeal to moral certitude exists long before Hume. See for example Glanvill, pp. 188ff. With this, limits were also set to the tendency to accept mechanistic philosophy as having the final word in all matters.

85. Edmund Husserl, *Die Krisis der europäischen Wissenschaften und die transzendentale Phänomenologie*, Husserliana vol. 6 (Den Haag: Nijhoff, 1954).

86. Ibid., p. 57.

87. See also Edmund Husserl, *Erfahrung und Urteil: Untersuchungen zur Genealogie der Logik* (Hamburg: Claasen & Goverts, 1948), pp. 38ff.

88. Husserl, *Krisis*, p. 70.

89. See, among others, Hubert Hohl, *Lebenswelt und Geschichte: Grundzüge der Spätphilosophie E. Husserls* (Freiburg: Alber, 1962); José Gaos, Ludwig Landgrebe, Enzo Paci, and John Wild, *Symposium sobre la noción Husserliana de la Lebenswelt* (Mexico: Universidad Nacional Autónoma de México, Centro de Estudios Filosóficos, 1963); Stephen Strasser, *Phänomenologie und Erfahrungswissenschaft vom Menschen: Grundgedanken zu einem neuen Ideal der Wissenschaftlichkeit* (Berlin: de Gruyter, 1964), pp. 61ff.; John C. McKinney, "Typification, typologies, and social theory," *Social Forces* 48(1969):1-12; Paul Janssen, *Geschichte und Lebenswelt: Ein Beitrag zur Diskussion von Husserls Spätwerk* (Den Haag: Nijhoff, 1970); Gerd Brand, *Die Lebenswelt: Eine Philosophie des konkreten Apriori* (Berlin: de Gruyter, 1971); Fred Kersten, "The life-world revisited," *Research in Phenomenology* 1(1971):33-62; Karl Ulmer, *Philosophie der modernen Lebenswelt* (Tübingen: Mohr, 1972); Lester Embree, ed., *Life-World and Consciousness* (Evanston: Northwestern University Press, 1972); Lothar Eley, "Life-world constitution of propositional logic and elementary predicate logic," *Philosophy and Phenomenological Research* 32(1972):322-40; Gerhard Funke, *Phänomenologie, Metaphysik oder Methode*, 2nd ed. (Bonn: Grundmann, 1972), esp. pp. 97ff., 136ff.; Alfred Schutz and Thomas

Luckmann, *Strukturen der Lebenswelt* (Neuwied: Luchterhand, 1975); Achille Ardigò, *Crisis di governabilitò e mondi vitali* (Bologna: Cappelli, 1980).

90. For example in the essays of Alfred Schutz, assembled in *Collected Papers*, 3 vols. (Den Haag: Nijhoff, 1962-70). See also Aaron Gurwitsch, "The common-sense world as social reality: a discourse on Alfred Schutz," *Social Research* 29(1962):50-72; Peter Berger, *Invitation to Sociology: A Humanistic Perspective* (Garden City, N.Y.: Doubleday, 1963), pp. 66ff. On the other hand, concepts such as everyday life and everyday orientation are also used outside of this theoretical context, and indeed already in the Middle Ages in the sense of that which everyone must notice (*quotidiana dispositio*).

91. Regarding the pedagogical thematization and the development linked to this see Niklas Luhmann and Karl Eberhard Schorr, *Reflexionsprobleme im Erziehungssystem* (Stuttgart: Enke, 1979), pp. 63ff.

92. Vilfredo Pareto, *Traité de sociologie générale* (Paris: Payot, 1917).

93. Talcott Parsons, *The Structure of Social Action* (New York: Free Press, 1937), pp. 178ff.

94. It is not surprising to find that Pareto becomes insignificant in the course of time as one of the "founding fathers" of Parsonian theory.

95. Concerning an unsuccessful attempt see Richard Grathoff, ed., *The Theory of Social Action: The Correspondence of Alfred Schutz and Talcott Parsons* (Bloomington: Indiana University Press, 1978).

96. This should not be understood in the sense of a superficial distinction between monologue and dialogue as one finds in Plato or Habermas (*Sophistes* 217c-d).

97. Gotthard Günther tries to pursue this path in overcoming iterative reflection through a reflection which incorporates iteration as an actual infinity. See *Metaphysik, Logik und die Theorie der Reflexion*. This also leads Günther to the social dimension — but once again only from the point of view of the subject who infers an alter ego in his reflection about reflection.

98. When I say "the" theory, this admittedly exaggerates the degree of standardization in current research. The supposed unity is only a postulate. But in the face of an open situation, one which cannot be readily altered, it can also be useful to call attention to the significance a consolidated theory would have if it in fact existed and to work "on credit" for a while.

99. Ethnomethodology is leading the frontal assault against this assumption without having significantly progressed beyond a mere identification of this assumption. See Harold Garfinkel, *Studies in Ethnomethodology* (Englewood Cliffs, N.J.: Prentice-Hall, 1967). The goal of this kind of inquiry remains vague as long as the relation between life-world and science is not clarified. The effort to explain the life-world in terms of scientific concepts seems to lead to the reduction of science to a practice in the life-world and is from then on only reflected upon as such.

100. We already indicated earlier that this dependency on sources (and therefore an assumed asymmetry) is still present in the Platonic dialogues. But at the same time a radical change becomes evident. In the process of communication the questioner is simultaneously the source of knowledge and the dialectical process moves toward truth or falsehood depending on whether he is a philosopher or a sophist. But this very difference becomes for its part the theme of dialectical (!) investigations, because the use or

misuse of the dialectic depends on it. Thus on the one hand the source is still assumed to be the status of the questioner, and on the other the self-referential system already makes itself asymmetrical in that it decides about this status — which it knows it is itself dependent upon — with its own means. But the decision then assumes the form of imputing a quality to the source which lies beyond the relations of the object: the sophist is defined as a mimic who feigns knowledge (*Sophistes* 267e-268d).

101. Gernot Böhme begins his treatment of this same topic with this process; it therefore remains too strongly dependent on the notion of "theory of discourse," i.e. that special forms of argumentation brought about a scientific attitude toward the life-world. Böhme, pp. 237ff.

102. On the basis of the *results* of scientific research, objects can be produced for which there are no models in nature. But this problem is completely different from that of the constitution of the object that is specific to science.

103. Concerning this point historically as well as substantially see Ernst Cassirer, *Substanzbegriff und Funktionsbegriff* (Berlin: Cassirer, 1910).

104. Certainly for the first time by Marin Mersenne. See Robert Lenoble, *Mersenne, ou La naissance du mécanisme*, 2nd ed. (Paris: Michel, 1971), pp. 316, 320.

105. See Ranulph Glanville, "The Nature of Fundamentals, Applied to the Fundamentals of Nature," in *Applied General Systems Research: Recent Developments and Trends*, ed. George J. Klir (New York: Wiley, 1978), pp. 401-9.

106. See Talcott Parsons, pp. 43ff.

107. One only needs to consider the problems which Parsons's decomposition of the concept of action poses for empirical research with its present methods.

108. A discussion along these lines can be found in Arthur O. Lovejoy, *The Great Chain of Being: A Study in the History of an Idea* (Cambridge, Mass.: Harvard University Press, 1936), pp. 144ff.

109. On this see also the considerations in systems theory as to the necessity of disorder in the construction of order, for example Henri Atlan, "Du bruit comme principe d'auto-organisation," *Communications* 18(1972):21-36.

110. This is not disputed even in the theory of self-referential systems. See for example W. Ross Ashby, "Principles of the Self-Organizing System," in *Principles of Self-Organization*, ed. Heinz von Foerster and George W. Zopf (New York: Pergamon, 1962), pp. 255-78. Reprinted in *Modern Systems Research for the Behavioral Scientist*, ed. Walter Buckley (Chicago: Aldine, 1968), p. 114.

111. W. Ross Ashby, *An Introduction to Cybernetics* (London: Chapman & Hall, 1956), p. 4.

112. See section II in this essay.

113. For parallel investigations in the domain of other functional systems see Niklas Luhmann and Karl Eberhard Schorr, *Reflexionsprobleme im Erziehungssystem* (Stuttgart: Klett-Cotta, 1979); Niklas Luhmann, "Selbstreflexion des Rechtssystems: Rechtstheorie in gesellschaftstheoretischer Perspektive," *Rechtstheorie* 10(1979):159-89.

114. This version is in turn anchored in the rejection of the notion that the human mind is a closed self-referential system and in the corresponding distinction between two faculties ("sensations" and "reflections" in Locke, for example). For a radical critique of the

possibility of such a decision see Edmund Husserl, *Erste Philosophie I*, Husserliana vol. 7 (Den Haag: Nijhoff, 1956), p. 78. The discussion of this question (and the gradual obsolescence of that difference) is closely connected with the transposition of the guarantee of unity from the object by way of simple ideas into intention.

115.   Instead of "originating in reason" it has been said since Kant: to "originate simply in reason and without any admixture of experience," and this intensified form is chosen with a view to epistemology. See his *Critique of Pure Reason*, B 2ff.

116.   The "dispute over methods" around the turn of the century, which could not have taken place without Kant, is an exception to this rule — and perhaps not even that. In retrospect it is clear that its consequences for the development of science require a more careful investigation. Although its significance is evident in the case of Max Weber and others, the alternative of a more or less psychological or even "depsychologized" (but nevertheless "subjective") methodology could not have advanced the social sciences. Toby E. Huff thinks otherwise in *Max Weber and the Methodology of the Social Sciences* (New Brunswick, N.J.: Transaction, 1984).

6
Toward a Sociology of Cognition

Günter Dux

The Consciousness of Convergence

The modern period has contributed an insight of strategic importance to the development of the theory of knowledge, an insight that was nevertheless long in preparation. It came to consciousness as early as the fifth century B.C., during Greek antiquity, and was soon replaced by the great metaphysical systems. It became radical as late as the sixteenth and seventeenth centuries: the world of humans converges on humans (*die Welt des Menschen konvergiert auf den Menschen*). This means that the reasons for the world being as it is must be rooted in human beings themselves. This insight into the process of convergence reaches both the sphere of nature and the social world. There are good reasons for assuming that particularly the developments in the social world led to this convergence and assisted in its success. In the social world the convergence on humans attained a very concrete meaning: domination had permeated social structure for nearly four thousand years, and the violence of the rulers, which was directed inward as much as, in the perpetual wars, toward the outside world, had inscribed it in the human mind. This affected the consciousness of the self, and here too the ancients took the lead. The class struggles of the ninth and seventh centuries B.C. contributed greatly to the formation of the historical consciousness and the philosophy that began in the sixth century.

Developmental processes in the social world that are of historical significance have always affected nature also. For ever since domination has determined history, i.e. ever since it sprung into motion at the end of the neolithic revolution, the domination of nature has increased as well. There are many reasons for this. The demand for goods which made domination enjoyable while also keeping the expropriated classes alive sufficed to produce this effect. The insatiability and the show of power contributed to this as well. By way of the diversification of the rulers' gratifications a broad range of wants arose, which, too, could only be satisfied by an increasingly more extensive and intensive exploitation of nature. In short, domination initiated the civilizing process. The more extensive use of natural resources, which is inherent in the civilizing process, was only possible in one way: knowledge of nature had to be increasingly detached from the original structures of interpretation (*Deutungsmuster*) and incorporated into a network of causal knowledge (*Gesetzeswissen*). But every increase in causal knowledge also brought with it an increase in the technological efficiency of domination.

Domination dissociates ruler and ruled, subject and object. It leads to a convergence of the object toward the subject. Every increase in knowledge, especially every increase in technologically useful knowledge, tends to strengthen the convergence of the world onto humans. At the beginning of the modern era the consciousness of convergence became radical in that it now claimed the status of a founding principle for knowledge in general. What caused this effect was the revised interpretation of nature according to the model of the machine. The process of reinterpretation of nature had far-reaching epistemological consequences, for, in principle, the growth of knowledge always implies a revision of knowledge. However, once it becomes clearly evident that what was still true yesterday is obsolete today, this revision must sooner or later lead to the recognition that knowledge is only what humans can acquire and have acquired by their own means. The naive ontological belief, that by having knowledge about an object we possess the object itself, is lost. It is exactly this consciousness that, at the beginning of the modern era, radicalized epistemology. Its first expression was a new consciousness of method. The more fundamental epistemological critique followed on its heels. It is worth noting that the occidental epistemology of the sixteenth through the eighteenth centuries emerged as an epistemology of the natural sciences, even if it had more universal pretensions. Bacon, Descartes, and Kant are our witnesses.

The Questions

The recognition of the convergence of the world upon man, in particular the convergence of nature upon man, had to lead to an inquiry into the causes of the very possibility of this convergence. Anyone who begins to reflect on the preconditions of knowledge, i.e. reliable knowledge, must be impelled to ask how it is possible to locate the preconditons of knowledge in the subject while nevertheless claiming to have knowledge of the object.

This question is disquieting, and its explosive power cannot be ignored: if the human world actually converges onto man, if the preconditions of knowledge and of its acquisition are to be found in man himself, who can guarantee that the knowledge we claim to have about an object can in fact be attained? Who, in other words, is to say that true knowledge will be incorporated into world-views? What is the status of truth under such conditions? Is there any clue that tells us why the knowledge acquired is of precisely those types which just happen to be encountered in the multitude of societies at the different stages of historical development? And can it be shown why it is precisely these particular types of knowledge that are effective in mediating reality? These questions clearly touch upon fundamental epistemological questions. And this is inevitable. Under conditions of uncertainty human beings need to make knowledge certain, i.e. provable. But uncertainty of knowledge is the stigma of the modern age. The sciences have espoused the cause of this uncertainty, which is precisely why the question of method remains and indeed should remain an issue.

It is likely that sociologists will be inclined to relegate questions of such subtlety to philosophy. But this cannot be permitted. Two reasons speak against this: First, sociology, together with its theory of knowledge, including methodology, is profoundly tied to epistemology. As long as we do not go beyond the mere assertion that the world of humans converges onto them, both nature and the social world appear as the product of a power to construct the world which is ultimately incomprehensible. The acquisition of a knowledge of nature and the constitution of society are two processes that need to be distinguished, yet are also inseparable. If we want to determine how human beings create their life-worlds, we need to discover just how they acquire knowledge in the first place. And if we want to find out how a science with its own particular methods can gain knowledge of precisely these life-worlds, we also need to determine in what manner humans create them. Second, sociology brings its own special competence to the problem. By now it has become a cliché to say that particular systems of knowledge as well as life-worlds can only be constructed as social systems and social worlds. This nevertheless remains true. If one then assumes that the conditions determine the result and that the result must be made comprehensible in terms of its conditions, it is hardly possible to avoid the conclusion that social scientists themselves must assume this task.

At the beginning of its history, sociology had indeed proclaimed this as one of its main tasks. Moreover, it promised to do away with philosophical problems by a surprise move, by turning philosophy from its head to its feet. The goal was to demonstrate the empirical foundation of knowledge in society. It is by now common knowledge that the move did not succeed. Sociological theories and theory-fragments are carried along in the stream of the philosophical tradition as much as in all other thought. Yet there is no reason for sociology to drop the claim. On the contrary, it needs to be renewed. The difficulties that have been encountered by a sociology of cognition, however, must be taken into account. The renewed attempt can learn from these difficulties by seeing them as a part of that historical process of cognitive development which itself needs to be understood.

From the very start, sociology attempted to understand the varieties of human life in terms of their historical development. Even its own viewpoint was meant to be self-reflected metatheoretically within the process of history. It was understood as a transition from an idealist to a materialist epistemology. This development has proved to be more difficult than was initially assumed, but such difficulties belong to the logic of the cognitive process. It therefore seems advisable to reconstruct this process prior to dealing with a sociological epistemology itself. This procedure has at least two advantages: (1) it will become apparent just where the difficulties lie in getting on with such an epistemology, and (2) this procedure appears most suited to showing how sociological theory must proceed today. I anticipate the result of this reconstruction in the form of a number of theses:

- All inquiry into knowledge — and this is the task of epistemology — is arrested by an absolutist logic that again and again presupposes prior knowledge.
- Although sociology assumed at its very beginning the task of discrediting idealist epistemology, it was unable to provide the foundation of a materialist epistemology.
- The foundations of such a materialist epistemology have in the meantime been achieved; they are to be found in anthropology, and their scope was first staked out by philosophical anthropology. By now the epistemological foundations have been developed with great empirical precision by way of an evolutionary cognitive theory.
- A materialist epistemology is necessarily evolutionary, and an evolutionary epistemology is necessarily genetic, i.e. reconstructive. Piaget's "genetic epistemology" has recognized this, even if it has been unable to integrate the sociological sphere.
- A reconstructed genetic epistemology holds the key to the growth of knowledge, not only for ontogenesis: the intellectual history of the species must emerge from a reconstructed ontogensis.

The intention of first establishing the present position of epistemology through the reconstruction of those antinomies and deficiencies that are the result of its historical development, also determine the direction of any future discussion. Because a critique of epistemology that follows the historical development of knowledge can only proceed by analyzing the philosophical systems of the past, I focus on those elaborations which have in the meantime achieved the status of representativeness. Hence I attempt to verify my first thesis by reaching back to that philosophy which arose at the onset of the modern era, and which most impressively demonstrates the dilemma of its inner logic — Cartesian philosophy. (The dilemma itself, however, remains characteristic of thought even beyond Descartes.)

Thinking as "first principle" (Descartes)

There are good reasons for the assumption that knowledge is built up in order to cope with the resistance of the outer world. Experiences of resistance need to be assimilated to already existing schemata and behavior, because he who experiences them could not live without this assimilation. This holds for the development of special knowledge and for the cognitive system as a whole. Though it is true that what can be incorporated into cognitive systems is dependent upon its very structure and the special knowledge that was previously integrated, cognitive systems are not altogether resistant to new experiences. In certain historical situations new experiences may even challenge the system itself. This was the situation in which Descartes had found himself. He stated that he had been promised certain knowledge as a student. However, he had come to the conclusion that even though philosophy made it possible to talk about everything while maintaining an appearance of truth, not a single philosophical proposition could any longer be considered as *certain*.[1]

What can be expected in a situation so fraught with uncertainty? Precisely what since time immemorial has been done in such situations: to recognize the need for self-reliance, and to use every means available to escape uncertainty. And this is what Descartes sets out to do. He lays out explicitly the necessary steps. The first one is to take the business of thinking into one's own hand: "et je me trouvai comme contrainte d'entreprendre moi-même de me conduire" (vol. 6, p. 16). It is hardly possible to show the convergence of knowledge in humans more forcefully than Descartes did in his first publication, *Discours de la methode*.

Thinking that resorts to its own premises continues to rely on its own logic. In the very structure of his argumentation Descartes addresses the problem of certainty very much in the manner in which the question had been approached for millenia: he searches for an absolutely certain fixed point as a way out of the uncertainty of his time, a point from which all further propositions could be explained and derived:

Archimedes, in order that he might draw the terrestrial globe out of its place, and transport it elsewhere, demanded only that one point should be fixed and immovable; in the same way I shall have the right to conceive high hopes if I am happy enough to discover one thing only which is certain and indubitable (*Works*, vol. 1, p. 149).

How does Descartes propose to find this fixed point? This question does not concern Descartes's method of presentation of his own thought processes (which I shall discuss later), but rather its underlying logic, i.e. that knowledge is problematic. Hence it is necessary to step further and further back in the search for certainty, until one discovers the original fixed point, the source from which it was derived. The logical procedure is straightforward: that which is must be derived from the source from which it came — its origin. The determination of the point of origin is prestructured in the experience of time: somehow it must be rooted in the subjectivity of the thinker. This knowledge is after all the starting point in the inquiry. Only against the background of this prestructured logic does Descartes's explicit argumentation become fully understandable. His argumentation is well known. He raises doubt to the category of method and, by doing so, rather than arriving at the certainty of doubt, arrives at the certainty of doubting as a cognitive act of the subject. Here then we have the primary source after which Descartes inquires: the subjects' cognitive action. Considered as primary source (*Ursprung*), thinking appears as essence (*Substanz*), just as the "absolute beginning" has always been thought of in terms of an essence, as *res cogitans*. The solution has been found, the dilemma is complete. But in what sense?

The movement of thought that turned upon the subject as the source of certainty proceeded from the empirical subject, from the empirical self. And it is toward the empirical subject that the inquiry is oriented — at least initially. Even in its assertion of absolute doubt, the empirical self remains at least involved in the process of ascertaining its absolute status. The reduction that is offered as an answer to the question "what then am I?" is precisely the kind of reduction that begins with the empirical self. It would thus be folly not to recognize the empirical self in Descartes's famous formula that grounds certainty in the thinking subject: "Then without doubt I exist also if he [God] deceives me" (p. 150). As long, however, as we focus upon the empirical self, it is impossible to extract out of the certainty of existence the certainty of the knowledge which the subjective self already has at hand or which it acquires. On the contrary, there is no way out of the circle of subjective knowing.

Thus Descartes has to reach beyond himself to God twice in order to achieve certainty of knowledge.[2] He requires God in order to be certain that that which is *clare et distincte* is also true. In the third "Meditation" Descartes abandons himself to the radical doubt that even the clearest, most logical insights might have been merely erroneous suggestions by a deceitful God. This doubt, to be sure, remains weak. He continues:

But, in order to be able altogether to remove it, I must inquire whether there is a God as soon as the occasion presents itself; and if I find that there is a God, I must also inquire whether he may be a deceiver; for without a knowledge of these two truths I do not see that I can ever be certain of anything (*Works*, vol. 1, p. 159).

The result is well known: God exists and he is not a deceiver. And this is also the reason for putting to rest the most radical of all the doubts that concern knowledge of the world. One can be sure that corporal things do exist: *Ac proinde res corporeae existunt* (*Oeuvres*, p. 80; *Works*, vol. 19, p. 191).

I am not concerned here to show that Descartes erred on this or that point in his argumentation. To the contrary, his reflections are entirely conclusive! If, under conditions in which knowledge has become uncertain, we attempt to ground certainty upon first principles, then we are forced to seek the certainty of knowledge in an absolute principle, which is not to be found in the empirical subject. This logic forces one to go beyond the empirical subject, even if only toward a transcendental subject in which knowledge locates both its origin and its unity.

Renunciation

Knowledge concerned with the convergence of the world on human-kind has increased even in our time. The world has become a construct. That this conceptual shift has come about with case should not surprise us, for all earlier epistemology, metaphysics, and ontology had been founded upon the same cognitive structure, that is, the structure of action. I am simplifying here, but the central idea is correct, even if the norms of action were often not clearly comprehended in the schematizations of logic. Thus, by declaring the world a construct, the epistemology of the modern period made use of the same cognitive structure, i.e. the structure of action. But this is not all; making use of the logic of action in the interpretation of the world returns the logic of metaphysics to its empirical origin.

This uninterrupted continuation of the empirical subject's logic of action has had its price, for the maintenance of an explicative matrix by way of which everything is deduced from a subject makes it unlikely that an answer to any of the questions posed above can be successfully achieved. Under the premise of this undirected relationship humans become the real creators; they truly turn into demiurges. The subject of the construct becomes the final point of reference in the analysis of what reality is and is not. It is not possible to go beyond human beings as the sub ject, because whatever partial or grand theories they invent, in the final analysis it is always they who invent them. The creator of a construct always evades the questions that refer back to himself, for even those questions point to his powers of construction. The consequences of this absolute mode of self-reflection have been disastrous. The constructor evades the question of how man's capability to possess and to gain knowledge actually works, namely, how the convergence of his world unto him is possible at all. For it is precisely this capability that has been deemed absolute. The absolute, however, does not bestow knowledge, and it is not possible to extract anything from it that had not been previously known. Kant knew this, and so did Hegel. To paraphrase the latter: In the darkness of the absolute all cats are grey. To the extent to which man, in his world-creating capacity, evades this insight, his insight in the construction of the world itself is evaded as well. What constitutes the world for human beings then becomes at best a matter of mere description; it is no longer possible to explain why the world is the way it is.

The dilemma first came to consciousness in man's relationship to nature. Ironically, it is precisely at that world-historical moment that humans secured a kind of insight into nature of which they in earlier times had not even dared to dream, i.e. that once we leave methodology behind, all epistemological warrants of the truth of knowledge fail. This deficiency is all the more consequential since nature's self-reliance requires explanation: how is interaction with nature possible when the conditions of this interaction are claimed to lie within the human being? This question has by now been put to rest. The natural sciences have learned to live with the compromise that they are not concerned with nature itself but merely with its constructs.[3] The actual practice of research, however, is dominated by the consciousness of having a grip on nature itself, and this is even more so with regard to the technological transfer of its results.

The situation is different in the social sciences. Adhering to an absolutist logic of construction there means not only that it is impossible to discern why the human world is the way it is, but it also remains a mystery how humans can gain access to foreign cultures. The appeal to an historically informed hermeneutics does not lead us very far, for hermeneutics can only assure an understanding of our own cultural tradition. Beyond the reach of hermeneutics an inaccessible world is built up that is constructed along different lines, and that constitutes reality for those who live in it. There is no bridge between their reality and ours. Strictly speaking, we should not concern ourselves with foreign cultures, e.g. with primitive societies, at all.[4] Of course, if the social sciences would take this constructive absolutism seriously, they would soon be at the end of their road.

Is there a way out of this dilemma? Sociology, as mentioned above, did promise such a way out. From its very beginnings it wanted to be more than a mere science of social structure. In fact, it would not have been able to delimit itself in such a way, because even the most substantiated relations in the realm of contradictory interests involve thought and interpretation. The subtle relationship between proposition and fact have achieved in them the hardness of social organization. The social sciences attempt to clarify the situation by means of the clarification of thinking that is involved in it. The decisive question for sociology is how this can be done. It would have been folly to expect that this question could have been resolved in a first attempt. Hence it is crucial to recognize the thrust of the argument, especially in its historical dimension.

Sociology opposed the idealist world-view and thereby turned against the tradition of a logic of argumentation that had existed for millennia. For idealism is based on the logic of action as the structure of its philosophical explanations. The overcoming of this logic was at the same time the overcoming of the epistemological aporia: why question the conditions of knowledge while making use of that very knowledge? Sociology embarked on a naturalistic and materialist counterstrategy. By dissolving the primacy of thinking, thinking was made the explicandum within a context of explanation that had nothing to do with thinking at all. It is not difficult to demonstrate that only that strategy of epistemology integrates the contemporary knowledge of humankind, especially its origin in the evolution of natural history.[5]

Yet, in the execution of this strategy, sociology fell behind for a time. Having taken recourse to society as the actual determinant only led into a new aporia: (1) society is always already based on thinking; (2) the logic of thinking is not just a mirror image of sociostructural relations. It is advisable initially to clarify the difficulties sociology encountered in its beginnings. These difficulties are still with us, even if beginnings that might lead to overcoming them have long been made.

The Displacement of Philosophy

When sociology entered the field of scientific discussion, it pronounced the end of philosophy, the end of an independent philosophy, to be precise.[6] Such a proclamation appears presumptuous. It rests upon two premises: (1) philosophy has always interpreted the world, including man, from the perspective of an absolute principle that had always been conceived in the form of a subject, or as spirit (*Geist*); (2) systems of interpretation are themselves only the product of human thinking. They derive from the hypostatization of human existence and spirit, that is, from a sort of isomorphic cosmological transformation. The absolute, the absolute as subject, is nothing else.

As is well known, Feuerbach already proposed this critique. His straightforward assertion that the secrets of theology lay in anthropology was an attempt to bring back the mighty metaphysical and ontological systems of philosophy from heaven to earth. The turn against theology included a turn against philosophy as a sort of enervated theology. Feuerbach, however, lacked a clear understanding of how the particularities of human existence and conduct were able to reach the heaven of theology and philosophy. He appears to have conceptualized this process as a sort of projection for which any number of reasons could then be given. But this need not interest us here. One thing is crucial: it is here that the consciousness of convergence is taken up for the first time in such a way that it now stands in opposition to all prior intellectual history. The very concept of critique assumes another meaning. If human thinking converges upon humans, then this convergence necessarily encompasses the fundamental forms within which philosophizing has always taken place.

That is, philosophy must be analyzed in terms of its nonphilosophical preconditions. This is exactly what the demystification of absolutist thinking made possible. Even though sociology remained uncertain about just how the mirroring of human life in the absolute subject had come about, this changed nothing in terms of the direction sociology was to take. The major thrust of the sociological argumentation was from the start directed against a logical structure that disclosed itself at the level of contents as absolute subject and absolute spirit. Marx and Engels reflect the historical development of their time when they state: "Certainly it is an interesting event we are dealing with: the putrescence of the absolute spirit" (German, p. 17; English, p. 27).

The theory of knowledge constitutes an advance from the beginning of sociology. To reflect upon causes was, after all, already the postulate of transcendental epistemology. The additional step needed was not to restrict the analysis of these conditions to a mere interpretation at the level of the subject-substance oscillating between the empirical and the absolute subject so that it could only be understood by the logic of its historical development. It was rather necessary to place human beings themselves, including their capacity to create the world, under conditions from which the creation of knowledge could be discerned. Only under this premise was it possible to assail the absolutist logic and to break the epistemological circle. Let us look at this circle once again: if the insight of the convergence of knowledge onto humans leads to the conclusion that they become the absolute source behind which it is no longer possible to reach in argumentation, this becomes a "justified conclusion" on the grounds that human knowing is itself also knowledge, and that this knowledge leads back to man. To conclude that knowledge about humans, because it is also knowledge, does not lead us a single step toward a fundamental explanation is only compelling if one assumes that insights which are directed toward other insights always carry us back to the beginning. This proposition is unsubstantiated — except by way of a metaphysical presupposition, according to which equal is equal because it emanates from a common substance, i.e. similarities are the result of similar essences. The absolutist logic is the logic of substance, but humans as empirical persons cannot in fact be construed as an absolute, not even at the level of thought. The beginning of thinking and knowledge in humans therefore necessarily points to an absolute that is beyond them, though it becomes comprehensible only in them. To ground the absoluteness of knowledge in humans remains plausible only as long as it is absorbed within a comprehensive absolutist logic. But when it is objected that (1) the absolutist assumption only mirrors human life-experience, and that (2) this life-experience can be unraveled in terms of its self-induced conditions, in which these assumptions are not even made, then epistemology is placed on a new footing. Now knowledge can be inquired into without having to posit prior knowledge first. The argumentation now proceeds in the reverse direction: whoever inquires into the conditions of knowledge, always brings along prior knowledge, but that which he brings along becomes incorporated into the entire knowledge that is to be explained. From the perspective of epistemology, this was the decisive step taken by Marx in his critique of Feuerbach, when he insisted that it was decisively important to consider the conditions under which humans conduct their demiurgical activities. What is thereby claimed is by and large merely what had already been discovered by historical consciousness: that human thinking and acting take places under the actual, empirical conditions of the life-world. However, this insight did not gain a footing in logic. As long as thinking remains committed to a particular structure of argumentation that provides proof by means of deductions out of a substance, it is necessary to posit thought, spirit, and reason as derived from a "cosmic potential" which appears to be attributed to human beings from there. It was the radicalization of historical consciousness in the modern era that also radicalized the consciousness of the conditions of knowledge in such a way that it could now at least be asserted that the foundation of knowledge should not be sought in knowledge.

However, the reference to the conditions of knowledge is little more than a very general allusion to the so-called materialist foundation that was supposed to take the place of idealist presuppositions. Materialist epistemology is, as Marx explains, "not devoid of premises. It starts out from the real premises and does not abandon them for a moment. Its premises are men, not in any fantastic isolation and fixity, but in their actual, empirically perceptible process of development under definite conditions" (German, p. 27; English, p. 37). And what are these concrete, empirical conditions? Marx mentions two: first, the physical constitution of man and the relation to the rest of nature that is thereby constituted; second, and immediately following upon the first condition, the first historical act, i.e. the production of the means of subsistence, upon which all further development depends (German, pp. 20, 23; English, pp. 31, 33). There is obviously a gap between these two conditions, but nowhere is it explained how the human physical organization leads to this first historical act. Leaving this gap open, however, meant that no explanation was given about how the sociocultural forms came into existence. This is the real deficiency of Marx's and Engels's theory and of all sociological theory ever since.

Life and Consciousness

Just as the Copernican revolution in philosophy demonstrated the convergence of the world of humans onto humans, so the sociological revolution demonstrated the emergence of humans, including their social world, out of a history which still had to be conceptualized in its own presuppositions. This is precisely why Marx and Engels recognized only one science, the science of history (German, p. 18; English, p. 28). It is hardly possible to follow with greater determination the Cartesian imperative of starting right at the very beginning and of redesigning the structure of the world from its very foundations. *The German Ideology* is a chaos of thought, and yet it remains a model in reformulating the problem and addressing the task at hand. If henceforth something is to be accomplished in epistemology, in particular with regard to a clarification of the "conditions of the possibility of thinking," this is possible only by clarifying the much more fundamental question about the "conditions of the possibility of man's intellectual and spiritual existence" in general. The radicality of the consciousness of historicity, however, converted this question into the question about the very conditions of the possibility of history. And if one intends to leave this question at the empirical level rather than pushing it in the direction of the well known speculations in terms of philosophy of history, it turns with equal stringency into an inquiry into the very possibility of its beginning.

As already mentioned, Marx and Engels indicate that human corporal organization is a first prerequisite for this. But they do not go beyond that observation (German, pp. 20ff.; English, pp. 31ff). The actual starting point of history, the whole process of its reconstruction, begins with production. Unconcerned about the intervening problems, Marx and Engels focus on an already socialized "empirical person." When they formulated the critique of ideology, they also began with already socialized men, or more precisely, with the mode of production with which men make their livelihood. Their further argumentation is transparent: if one recognizes the actual empirical conditions in the mode of production and uses them as a point of departure, one gives the mode of production, in the actual argumentation at least, the status of a primary condition, even if primary only at the historical level. Consequently everything else becomes secondary. Thoughts, ideas, theories follow: they are derivatives. This is precisely how Marx and Engels conceived it, or in any case how they presented it. They assiduously formulated the antithesis to idealist philosophy in terms of a set of opposing relationships. The passage is well known, but nevertheless deserves to be fully quoted here, not least because it has the significance of a testimonial:

The phantoms formed in the brains of men are also, necessarily, sublimates of their material life-process, which is empirically verifiable and bound to material premises. Morality, religion, metaphysics, and all the rest of ideology as well as the forms of consciousness corresponding to these, thus no longer retain the semblance of independence. They have no history, no production and their material intercourse, alter, along with their actual world, also their thinking and the products of their thinking. It is not consciousness that determines life, but life that determines consciousness. For the first manner of approach the starting-point is consciousness taken as the living individual; for the second manner of approach, which conforms to real life, it is the real living individuals themselves, and consciousness is considered solely as *their* consciousness. (German, pp. 26ff; English, pp. 36ff)

The seriousness with which Marx and Engels held this view is affirmed by the fact that Marx repeated the passage some fifteen years later. Marx here even more explicitly points to the mode of production as the truly primary condition of the entire mode of human existence:

The mode of production of material life conditions the general process of social, political and intellectual life. It is not the consciousness of men that determines their existence, but their social existence that determines their consciousness. (German, pp. 26ff.; English, pp. 36 in the Preface to *A Contribution to the Critique of Political Economy*. Moscow: Progress Publishers, 1970, pp. 20ff.)

Both formulations are so powerful that they must initially be taken literally, even if Marx and Engels were aware of all the "ifs" and "buts" that persist. If we take these passages literally, we must then see the mode of production as the determining factor, and thinking as determined. No other interpretation is possible. However, little can be done with this idealist formulation, and its mere reversal is epistemologically sterile; it leads nowhere. Rather it produces an obvious dilemma: life is always already conscious life. The mode of production of material life is always determined by already socialized individuals. Marx and Engels were of course aware of this. In the *German Ideology* they therefore also explicitly emphasized the reverse direction: the influence of intellectual and spiritual (*geistigen*) factors on the mode of existence and "the reciprocal action of these various sides on one another" (German, p. 38; English, p. 53). If this is so, then, this so strongly emphasized set of opposing relationships — i.e. being (*Sein*) determines consciousness rather than consciousness being — appears as an empty intellectual tour de force. If being is always already conscious, and if society is always constructed by already socialized individuals, then the relevant epistemological question is how being gains consciousness, and how it arrives at society in the first place. The foundation of all future epistemology must, in other words, be based precisely on that step which Marx and Engels bypassed, that is, the step from the corporal constitution of humans to their intellectual and spiritual way of life. How else can we begin to establish a materialist epistemology? Only when this step has been explicated, only after the process of the formation of spiritual structures has been reconstructed from its basis in nature, are we able to determine how knowledge is linked to the social structure, especially to its subsystems of economy and politics.

That problem was taken up in the first half of our century precisely where it had become stuck in the nineteenth century: in the sphere of the biological organization of life. This work was initially continued within the philosophical tradition, and became established as philosophical anthropology. A perspective based purely on the history of ideas (*Geistesgeschichte*) would hardly be prepared to connect philosophical anthropology, of all things, to Marxist theory. Yet the logic of intellectual progress is indifferent to the context in which solutions to problems are achieved. The question of the boundaries between the biological and the spiritual-cultural organizations had to be settled, no matter by whom or within which intellectual tradition.

Philosphical Anthropology's Achievement and Limits

It is not difficult to determine the significance of philosophical anthropology in the context of the history of ideas. Philosophical anthropology emerged in the context of that progress of knowledge that goes beyond the Cartesian opposition between mind and body or body and soul. After it had become certain that thinking, intellect, or soul could not be posited as independent, pure essences (*Substanz*), and after the conditions of their existence had begun to claim attention because these conditions appeared to have become problematic, finding a way out of the Cartesian alternative became an urgent demand. To settle accounts with Descartes was precisely what the founder of philosophical anthropology, Helmut

Plessner, wanted to do.[7]

As does all anthropology, philosophical anthropology too begins at the level of the constitution (*Organisation*) of human beings. Its intention, however, is different from that of physical anthropology right from the start. It intends to demonstrate, within the human biological constitution (*Organisationsplan*), a tendency toward spiritual, i.e. sociocultural forms of life. A misunderstanding which has been encountered by philosophical anthropology ever since, can therefore be encountered even here: The showing (*Aufweis*) of an anthropological base is not thereby meant to elevate one or another of man's cultural ways of life to the status of his "essence." As we shall see later, this tendency enters only through the back door: by way of a fear of social revolution. In terms of a systematic disposition the precise opposite is true: if the intention is to demonstrate a tendency toward a spiritual-cultural form of life even at the level of the anthropological design (*Organisationsplan*), then this is particularly the case for the historical dynamics which belongs to this form of life.[8]

Arnold Gehlen's design of a philosophical anthropology is the one best known. It documents both the contribution of philosophical anthropology to epistemological progress (*Erkenntnisfortschritt*) and its deficiencies. Gehlen sketches the human being as a creature that in his biological make-up (*Substanz*) is largely released from instincts. In their natural state, however, humans are hopelessly inadequate, unadapted, nonspecialized creatures (pp. 31ff).[9] This approach initially provides a negative evaluation (*Bestimmung*), one which is nevertheless decisively important for two reasons: on the one hand, it remains strictly at the biological level, i.e. takes up the problem of where to begin with the explanation precisely at the point at which, in terms of everything we have discussed so far, it must inevitably be taken up. On the other hand, it thereby brings into focus the enormous constructive achievement that humans must accomplish in their cognitive systems. On this basis it is possible to inquire, with expectations of positive results, how human beings are capable of accomplishing such an achievement. This is the question Gehlen asks, but his answers remain deficient. There are understandable reasons for this: his negative definition of the anthropological design in terms of a release from instinct confirms the image of a creature that creates its own world from a position of nearly absolute sovereignty. The most central concern of Gehlen's anthropology is this: how the human mechanism must be designed to enable him, as an active animal, to transform the deficiencies of his constitution — which under natural conditions are an extreme obstacle to his vitality — into an active means of his existence (p. 37). The main premise here is that the actions, by way of which the constructive achievements are accomplished, are detached from needs, dissociated from elementary drives (pp. 54ff.). According to Gehlen, only by means of a subordination of drives is it possible to achieve an impartial relationship to the objects of the real world. Under the impact of an anthropological constitution that assures man's access to the real object, epistemological problems become less important and the consciousness of convergence is neutralized. For if knowledge is acquired without being burdened by drives, the question about specific human conditions becomes obsolete. Even for Gehlen humans can only understand things by incorporating them into their manifold activities. But this hardly implies more than to manipulate the given data and to make them usable for intellectual purposes.

It is not the conditionality (*Bedingtheit*) of human life but its nonconditionality (*Unbedingtheit*). that is the central problem for Gehlen. That is precisely what causes worry. Once humans are dissociated from most drives and needs, it becomes extremely doubtful that they will ever be able to find peace in a world in which they could enjoy the opportunities of the spiritual and cultural mode of existence (*Daseinsweise*).

Gehlen responds with a thesis that is a curious mixture of empirical analysis and moral incantation: human actions are not the result of needs but rather needs follow from actions. It is only by way of actions that needs and interests have the opportunity to crystallize and become concrete. What then develops into human needs are always the subjective correlates of actions previously objectivated in institutions. This is precisely why every criticism of contemporary social conditions is seen as an "assault upon the foundations of this system," which must be prevented (p. 335). It is seen as nothing less than an assault upon humanity itself.

It is evident that what began as a schematic outline of a being characterized by openness toward the world, becomes reified as second nature by means of the compensatory institutions of the social world. Strictly speaking, history can only take place counterfactually. However, it does exist. Gehlen even adopts the concept of progress: by creating their own world, humans become the object of their own inquiry in a way that leads them beyond themselves (p. 348). Only heaven knows why this is so and why humans should need to reach beyond themselves if the institutions of the world, as they actually are, provide stability for their needs, and if their needs in fact develop from these institutions in the first place.

Rome, it is said, was not built in one day. Cognitive progress, which is always an advance in human self-consciousness, is a much more difficult business. It needs to be achieved by precisely that logic and by those conceptions that are supposed to be overcome. If one does not right away insist upon the complete solution, one thing is beyond doubt: the strategy of explanation of philosophical anthropology starts precisely with, and brings to conclusion, the problematics we encountered with Marx and Engels, which they did not systematically address. It is here that the modern consciousness which declares that humans make their own circumstances ultimately receives its anthropological foundation. A new stage in the development of epistemology is thereby reached. This is significant at first for the level of epistemological argumentation, which henceforth cannot be circumvented. Plessner and Gehlen demonstrate that man's biological design already points toward a spiritual-cultural mode of existence. Can there by any doubt about the fundamental meaning of this way of reasoning? The biological design reflects the limitations of a nature that banishes every spirit modeled after the human spirit, every thinking in terms of human categories. If the biological design "tends toward" a spiritual-cultural form of life, without already containing it, then this form of life, with all the knowledge and thinking that has entered it, must prove to be an acquired product of history. This is precisely how Plessner and Gehlen present it. But what is no longer presupposed here is precisely what has always been presupposed in philosophy in the two millennia of its existence: an absolute spirit within an absolute subject. Philosophical anthropology never intended to promote a materialist epistemology. It rather attended to its own affairs.[10]

In the meantime, philosophical anthropology has nearly become history. What it was primarily concerned about — to show that the biological design is the foundation of every form of cultural life — has now been substantiated by argumentation in natural science. Already Plessner had presented the design in terms of an inner logic of natural development. The knowledge about the actual process of evolution remained present in the background here as well, even if this was concealed by its use of the phenomenological method. It is more than merely useful to acquaint oneself with this natural-history foundation (*naturgeschichtlichen Grundlage*). Indeed, in this context it is even possible to reformulate the central epistemological question as follows: how was it possible to develop spiritual-cultural forms of life and knowledge from this biological starting point? What preconditions entered into this undertaking? In what way do these determine the result?

The Direction of Evolution: Autonomy

Humans are part of a long evolution of life. Their biological design is the result of a process whose mechanism may be in need of further clarification, but whose general validity can no longer be doubted. This proposition implies a consequence of greatest interest to epistemology, which already became manifest in our previous discussion of the epistemological advances in philosophical anthropology. If indeed human beings are in their very biological design predisposed toward a spiritual-cultural mode of life, then this mode of life must reveal itself as a quasi-natural consequence of their history, in particular of their natural history; and this is indeed the case. I am condensing the developmental perspective that culminates in man's spiritual-cultural mode of existence in a manner that would hardly be permissible if we hoped to determine the particular steps of this process. Yet such a condensation highlights the structural consequences of the entire process all the more impressively.

Evolution and Autonomy

Living beings are self-regulating, open systems. The characteristic of self-regulation implies that the duration and integrity of the body is regulated by means of a dynamic system located within the boundaries of the body itself. Openness implies that the life-sustaining interaction with the external world, metabolism in particular, is controlled as well through the internal organization. It is therefore possible to characterize the structural principle of self-regulation as the principle of autonomy. The structure of living beings, explains J. Monod, "points toward a definite, unrestricted self-determination which encompasses a quasi-total 'freedom' vis-à-vis external forces and conditions."[11] Such a principle can only be realized if the internal organization and the relationship to the external world are bound to one other in a system-specific manner. And indeed, the strategy to connect internal organization and the environment in a system-specific manner already applies to organic evolution. The process of the development of the organism is codetermined by its external relations. This is particularly true for the modes of conduct (*Verhaltensweise*), which become meaningful only in terms of the relationship of external and internal factors. Organism and external world, in terms of their conduct, are linked to each other in a functionally significant way. This is why the forms of life of living beings must be explained by way of the relation of the organism to its species-specific environment.

The structural principle of organization of every living being, i.e. self-regulation or autonomy, is at the same time the principle of evolution. Evolution in nature represents a genuine advance insofar as it increases the self-organization, that is, the autonomy which is structurally rooted in the very design of every living being.[12] This assertion is not altogether surprising, for two reasons: (1) Once established, structures only allow a development within the limits of the structures themselves. This causes a tendency to reinforce a development in the direction of the structure. (2) An increase in autonomy, however, also leads to an increase in the survival chances of a population. It makes possible a more adequate, more realistic reaction to the environment.

We are aware of the means by which autonomy has been increased, i.e. by expansion of learning at the expense of instinctual determination.[13] Of course, learning already exists at the earliest evolutionary stages, though embedded within instinctive modes of behavior. It has been possible to increasingly expand its significance at the expense of instinctive rigidities. It is hardly necessary to discuss explicitly why learning is the means for increasing autonomy; learning is an activity by way of which concrete experiences are processed in such a manner that they become usable in future situations. In terms of the human design, learning is an absolute necessity, one which has been pushed to the extreme. What has been called human openness toward the world is a willingness to gain knowledge of the world by one's own experience and insight.

A first epistemological conclusion, which is of strategic significance, must be drawn: the replacement of instinctual behavioral determinations by learned modes of behavior not only does not change the relationship between internal and external factors that is so important for the understanding of every life form, but rather accentuates it. This is precisely why it is also important for human beings. The inner logic of evolution — the increase in autonomy — demonstrates this. That is why cognitive categorical forms must be understood as a human means that permits coming to terms with an already present reality.[14] To know why these cognitive forms are the way they are, one needs to pay particular attention to those experiences that are incorporated into them and reconstruct the process by which the former comes to terms with the latter.

However important it consequently is to adopt the natural-history perspective in decoding the forms of human knowledge, this perspective leads into a trap. We have seen that Gehlen walked right into it when he assumed that humans create their world, relieved of drives and needs, in a sort of unmediated matter-of-factness (*unmittelbare Sachlichheit*). But this is not exactly how things are. Human cognition derives from a unique situation, which is social in its very origins. This determines the very structure of the constructs. Their genesis is built into them. To explain how this happens, it is necessary to briefly sketch the significance of community (*Sozietät*) in the development of cognitive constructs.

The Social Situation

Learning, to the extent to which it is vital for the organism, is precarious. This holds all the more because learning must take place in that realm which, while vitally important, remains unknown. Measures must inevitably be taken to assure that the next generation does not need to lick the dust. The appropriate means is the formation of communities. The strategic significance of communities within the evolutionary process consists of having created a protected area within which living beings such as the primates, who are greatly dependent upon learning, have been able to evolve.[15] There can be no human social existence without prior animal social existence.

Our observation that it is the evolutionary function of society to provide protected areas that make learning possible, presupposes a particular concern with protection and care during the period of early socialization. As a rule, one of the members of society, in most cases the mother, carries the main burden of socialization. This is particularly so in the area of cognitive development, and it especially applies to human beings. For the newborn, the mother or her surrogate is that particular object vis-à-vis which all primary experiences are made, and in engagement with which all categorical forms are developed. For the newborn, to speak with Erikson, the mother is nature.[16]

Only in connection with the sociological perspective does the natural-history perspective provide a foundation for epistemology. The reverse also holds true: the point of a sociological epistemology is not to shift to society the responsibility for the whole process of the development of cognitive constructs. This would not lead us one single step beyond philosophical doubt (*Aporien*). The point of a sociological epistemology is to approach the process of the development of social forms in such a manner that cognitive forms — knowledge in general — emerge as a product of experience in association with an already pregiven world of objects. But it must be taken into account that in this process the primary object is a competent adult other. The categorical formation of a framework for objects and events is as dependent upon this as the formation of space and time. Only within this perspective is it possible to understand how humans could have taken the step out of human ontogenesis from the level of natural history to the development of spiritual-cultural life-worlds.

The role of the mother or the significant other and of the wider society for the development of the child has always been recognized. Nevertheless it has been misinterpreted until this very day. It has always appeared as if the child must be motivated by adults to take over from them something which the adults already possess. Within the context of such a traditional epistemology it is unclear how a child can ever accomplish this achievement. The child, after all, understands nothing at first. It also remains unclear just how the transmitted forms come into existence in the first place. Such a traditional interpretation leads inevitably to an infinite regress. This process can be understood only when a new perspective is adopted and when it is realized that the organizational competence is to be found within the maturing individual himself.

Genetic Naturalism

The evolutionary logic that contributed to the development of episte-mology has now been taken up. Once again it has become evident that the history of thought harbors consequences. Piaget has opted for a genetic cognitive strategy, which he has translated into numerous investigations. This strategy, after everything we have discussed so far, is precisely what epistemology must be today — a naturalistic and materialist epistemol-ogy. And Piaget's theory is exact precisely in that sense in which natural-istic thinking can be conceived of today: not as a reduction of thinking to the laws of the motion of matter but as an evolutionary product whose origin does not yet reveal its results. In reviewing his work Piaget has ex-plicated these particular characteristics of his theory by declaring it to be naturalistic without being positivist.[17] In our present context only the strategy itself is of interest, i.e. the structure of the argumentation and its consequences.

The Naturalistic Starting Point

A naturalistic epistemology, as much as any other, has certain presuppositions. Nothing leads to nothing. What is decisive, however, is the starting point. In this respect Piaget is without ambivalence. He begins with an organism whose principles of organization are sufficiently efficient to set in motion the process of constructing cognitive forms. The biological principles of organization reach deep into phylogeny. They are encapsulated within the structural principle of all life — self-regulation. Piaget thus very consciously adopts the natural-history perspective we presented above.[18] To the extent to which living beings are constituted by way of the structural principles of self-regulation, the more concrete forms of life can and indeed must simultaneously be seen as a means and a result of these principles: as a means insofar as the organism is made vi-able by them and can realize its autonomy only through them; as a result insofar as autonomy becomes manifest in them in the first place, in the form of structural principles. It should be noted that this already applies at the organic level and continues at the cognitive level.

Every living organization, at every level of evaluation, contains autoregulations, and the same thing applies, a fortiori, I would say, in the field of behavior. It would follow that cognitive functions, seen in this light, are specialized organs of autoregulation controlling the exchanges underlying all behavior.[19]

The functional continuity between the organic and cognitive forms of or-ganization allows for an approach to the disclosure of the latter which cannot be justified at the epistemological level in any other way. The development of cognitive forms can be construed as a simple continuation of a strategy already begun at the organic level.

But the essential point about the statements which have just been made is that such cognitive schemata imply no absolute beginning but are built up by a progression of equilibrations and autoregulations. If they have no absolute beginning, as, for instance, by the intervention of a cause exterior to the system and emanating from the environment, it is because such formative interventions are assimilated into an already existing schematic which they simply serve to differentiate: thus, cognitive schemata are derived step by step, each from the preceding one, and in the last analysis they always depend upon coordination of the nervous system and the organic system, in such a way that knowledge is necessarily interdependent with the living organism as a whole.[20]

The negation of any absolute beginning implies something that was perhaps not evident at first sight — the radical negation of every metaphysical theory of knowledge. This can most easily be shown by the attempt to comprehend this strategy metaphysically. It could be argued that if thinking and spirit do not have their roots in the thinking of the empirical person, then they must exist prior to it, that is, be built into the material principle of organization, even if in a different form. Were we to read Piaget in this manner, this formulation would have to be seen as containing the exact opposite epistemological content: thinking has an absolute beginning which, however, is beyond the grasp of empirical experience. Once again it would be necessary to call upon a transcendental, or even transcendent, subjectivity. Yet what is actually meant — and this ought to be taken into account prior to every metatheoretical subversion — is something quite different. If thinking is to be conceptualized, in both its individual forms and in its entire mode of operation, as the continuation of strategies originating at the organic level, then the explanation of thinking does not already involve thinking. If cognitive modes of development are associated with natural forms of organization, then it is necessary to see these natural forms as tied to the modern (i.e. scientific) concept of nature. According to this concept, the specifically sociocultural human life forms, thinking included, cannot be encountered in the subhuman structures of either physics or biology. We also need to take into account a concept of process that is not conceptualized as a substance category, according to which every processual development is derived from something given from the start. In other words, the evolutionary process generates organizational forms whose specific structures are not preprogrammed from the beginning within the evolutionary context.[21] Piaget's epistemology is therefore naturalistic in a precise manner: the prerequisite for the explanation of thinking is not prior thinking but rather matter, to which thinking is not immanent. It would consequently be useful to stress the continuity of cognitive forms with natural modes of existence in a manner emphasizing the principle of evolution. What holds for the spiritual and cultural life-world of humans in general, holds for the cognitive forms in particular — they continue evolution and development, even if this continuation must now bridge a hiatus.

Constructive Realism

The strategy of genetic naturalism solves in a rather surprising manner the central problem of all modern epistemology — the relationship of subject and object. As we have seen above, the aporia of this relationship consists in the fact that all reflections on the conditions of thinking must presuppose thinking. The subject always precedes the object, especially in regard to the subject's own knowledge achievements. Marxism had proclaimed a counter strategy: if one starts with the biological organization, the point of departure is a material form of organization, and not thinking or intellect.[22] As we have seen, this claim was not redeemed, and it did not even become clear how this could have occurred. It became possible only after the biological revolution in the natural sciences in the nineteenth century: the cognitive forms must be understood as resulting from a coming-to-terms with experience. Even as categorical forms they are not prior to experience, and thus do not point to a preexisting transcendental or transcending subject. At first, this process appears to be a continuation of the Kantian critique, that is, the postulate of the convergence of all knowledge onto humans seems to become radicalized since it now includes even the categories. But if this is indeed a radicalization, it consists precisely in the elimination of all remnants of the metaphysical theory of knowledge still contained in transcendental epistemology. This is most apparent in what Kant presupposes and in what is presupposed here. The presupposition of genetic constructivism, with which we are concerned here, is fundamentally distinguished from the presuppositions of transcendental epistemology. Presupposed are certain organizational capacities of the organism, in particular a powerful sensory mechanism with the remarkable capacity of the brain. Not presupposed are those cognitive forms of reality perception that belong to a later encultured stage. They must first be developed.

On what grounds is the claim justified that the accursed subject-object problem can be put aside if the process of the acquisition of cognitive forms is the starting point? The answer is quite simple: if cognitive forms, including the categories, are the result of experience, then the very question — whether apprehending the object is possible in the first place and why it is possible to accomplish something in the real world by way of the cognitive forms — has become obsolete. The categorical forms — the object-schema, the schema of events, the schemata of space, time, etc. —

record the repeated experiences of a preexisting reality. They are not forms to which content is added but rather have their origin in content, because the experience of interaction with the outer world is integrated into them. They are, in short, realistic forms. And it is realism that must be attested to in this type of constructivism.

A genetic constructivism to which realism can be attested also solves the most subtle problem that was part of the subject-object aporia: the problem of interest and objectivity. It goes without saying that the process of construction is determined by those interests that get the whole process going. The opportunity that arose for human beings when the external world, which until then had been organized by instincts, was deconstructed, consists precisely in the fact that it has become possible to organize the world according to criteria that are relevant to action. Cognitive forms are indeed constructs; they do not simply mirror the object. However, this does not prevent their incorporating real data from the external world. On the contrary, the cognitive interest that initially predominates wants to make available to a foreign external world the minor and major action-oriented interests of everyday life. But this is only possible if in the pursuit of this interest any aspect of reality relevant to them is made comprehensible. The process appears more complex in its abstract description than it actually is. The development of categorical forms — the schemata of object and event, of space and time, etc. — are guided by a commitment to come to terms with the resistance of the pregiven real world of objects. The fact that certain relations are fixed within those forms is as much an expression of the experience that such recurring relations can be grasped as of the interest in stabilizing such experiences, because otherwise it would not be possible to deal with reality at all. Similarly, the conceptual manner of determining objects by way of particular attributes is dominated by the actual physical situation of human beings and their action-interests. *Up* and *down*, *sweet* and *sour*, *hard* and *soft*, are classifications that refer to a life situation which is indicated by bodily experiences. This does not in the least interfere with the incorporation of the external world's data into these constructs. Moreover, a living being that is not governed by nature in its interaction with the environment, and that therefore lacks an appropriately organized natural environment, is forced in the direction of a realistic, i.e. practical, appropriation of the external world in order to realize the elementary interests of life. In short, constructive realism becomes a human epistemological strategy. Constructivism and realism are insolubly intertwined.

To guard against misunderstanding: that the modern epistemological aporia has been resolved by way of genetic and constructive realism does not imply that the epistemological problems have been settled once and for all. On the contrary, as is always the case, the real work only begins once a new theory is gaining legitimacy. We merely claim that the formerly troublesome situation of the relation of subject to object has now been solved. The new start that needs to be made in determining the constitutive elements of a theory of knowledge must also, as was mentioned above, include the role of society.

The Role of Society in the Construction of Knowledge

The development of social life can in the first instance be construed as a process by means of which the survival chances of the population — in the face of ecological pressures — are increased. A more effective defense against enemies, a greater capacity for assertion in the competition for food, an increased ability to utilize food resources fully, together with a number of additional advantages, make social life one of the "prime movers" of evolution.[23] Yet we have already identified another and altogether different meaning: societies create the conditions that make it possible to incorporate an increased learning capacity into the organizational plan. It is precisely through this that they influence the directionality of evolution.

The significance of learning changes in the transition from the subhuman to the human stage of evolution. In other words, learning itself is an evolutionary phenomenon. While learning at the subhuman level consists essentially in concretizing genetically prestructured behavioral patterns, especially in play, the problem at the human level consists in developing these patterns of behavior into possible future forms of the life-process in the first place. This requires that cognitive forms adequate to the interaction with the world are developed simultaneously.

The changed situation creates an entirely new situation even for the process of knowledge acquisition: if it is no longer a matter of making concrete the more or less prestructured forms of behavior and social environments, then the process of knowledge acquisition must indeed originate "via the object" itself. All categorical forms must be developed in direct contact with the object. The dominant object that is the source of experience is the socializing agent, usually the mother. This has two significant consequences: if the child were constrained to develop its understanding of the environment by means of natural objects, then it could hardly be explained how the child manages to cope with the extraordinary frustration-potential that results from the condition of nearly complete incompetence. However, the significant other is always socially more competent than the child. The mother arranges her actions in such a manner that the growing child, by way of the means at its disposal, can have a chance to make experiences in the first place, thereby increasing its competence. A number of techniques are available for this, which can be observed in each interaction of a caring mother with her child. Some of these have in the meantime become the object of research.[24] In addition, the mother paralyzes the many frustrations that inevitably occur in the learning process.

From a naturalistic point of view, especially that which emphasizes the processual character of natural history, society achieves a vastly greater significance for the enculturation of human beings than earlier theories had granted. Earlier theories had merely asserted that cognitive constructs, that the spiritual and cultural forms of life in general, must somehow originate in society.[25] They could not derive from the competence of an individual conceived in his pure singularity. Precisely in this manner society has achieved the status of a subject sui generis, or, as it is sometimes called, a "nonliteral" subject. It is this sort of substantialization of society into a subject that has made sociology so ineffective in epistemology and that has also provoked the accusation of sociologism. And this is quite justified, since all talk of society as "nonliteral" subject undoubtedly merely mystifies the process. One simply cannot thereby understand how "society" manages to develop spiritual and cultural forms. This is very different with the naturalistic perspective we have pursued here: society is constitutive for the development of the spiritual and cultural life-world, because the child develops its ability of acquiring the essential categorical forms only in interaction with a more competent other. Once the categorical forms have been developed, the process of knowledge acquisition can be continued at the adult level.

The naturalistic constellation as presented here is reflected in the categorical forms themselves. In other words, the genesis enters the result, i.e. the elaborated cognitive constructs. This can be demonstrated most impressively by way of the development of the early world-view of the child.

The Child's World-View

Were we to determine the situation in which a newly born child finds itself from the only point of view that interests us here — the development of cognitive competence — and were we to do so in as simple a manner as possible, then we would have to conclude that the child must subject itself to one task in particular: to develop schemata of objects and events which permit a more effective intercourse with the (social and natural) external world. The acquisition of the entire range of competences is propelled by the necessity of accomplishing this task. In this accomplishment all the other competences are implicated. The question arises, of course, how this can occur. We have already mentioned two strategically important conditions: (1) the developmental process is inexorably tied to the object (this constitutes the naturalistic moment); and (2) the object is a social object, i.e. an "alter" (this represents the specifically sociological moment). It is precisely these two conditions that conspicuously determine the result. And it is exactly because categorical forms must be construed by way of experiences with the object that the very specific experiences the child encounters in the interaction with the social object are incorporated into them. The result is unequivocal: The schemata of object and event are clearly stigmatized by their having been developed in interaction with a behavior-oriented or action-competent subject. All objects are construed as if they were determined by a central power that causes them to act and to present themselves in just the way they do. All events are saturated with motivation.[26] Elsewhere I have illustrated this structuration by the precise formula that the basic categorical schema of object and event is a subjective one.

Categorical forms are operant mechanisms. Once they have been developed, they structure the perception of reality. This is why the primordial world of the child is in its basic elements thoroughly subjective. Of course, that children perceive things and events under the impact of the subjective schema has been known for a long time. But this fact has always been misinterpreted.

Projections

The subjective interpretation of the emerging life-world has frequently been merely taken for granted, sometimes, as in Feuerbach, with a tinge of philosophical profundity, or, as in Dilthey, with a touch of hermeneutic imagination.

If an explanation is offered at all, the most likely interpretation of the subjective world-view of the child rests on the assumption that it results from a projection of the "self" onto the total reality surrounding it.[27] This explanation, however, is open to misunderstanding and, even more annoying, it covers up all further problems. First, the self that is to be projected does not even exist. Second, the external world, into which the self is to be projected, does not exist either. Third, the theorem of projection does not adequately clarify why this projection should even occur. The truth is that the self and the external world must first be constructed, and in this process the subjective schema is developed as the basic structure. Although Piaget took notice of the inadequacy of the theory of projection and provided an excellent critique,[28] he was unable to transcend it systematically. The systematic deficiency in the explanation of a subjectively established world is closely tied to the ill-starred concept of "egocentricity."

Piagetian Egocentricity

Piaget describes the point of departure in the construction of the world as "egocentric." This concept appears to signal that the child allows the world to converge on itself as an already developed ego, and then to interpret the world as an always recurring ego. But this is precisely in opposition to what Piaget has in mind. A fundamental aspect of his developmental psychology has focused attention on the fact that for the newborn child the dualism between itself and the external world does not exist. The child possesses a downright protoplasmatic consciousness, which does not differentiate between the self and things (p. 235). This is why objects in the environment are integrated into the course of action without this difference rising to consciousness. Whenever Piaget refers to "egocentricity," he is guided by the idea that the child's intentions extend beyond the boundary of its body, regardless of their motoric sources. Precisely because there is a confusion between thought and body does the unreflected motoric self continue into infinity, so to speak (pp. 134ff.). The subjectivisms of the external world are extensions of the feelings and motoric drives of the self. According to this schema, the child does not carry its subjectivism into a world that exists apart from it; there is no such world. The child has simply not yet disengaged this opposing, external world from itself. This is why the world appears as subjectivistic and animistic as the self's own actions. Piaget emphasizes this by declaring that animism must be conceived as affective animism, that is, as a sympathetic animism under the sway of which the self has not withdrawn into itself. Egocentricity consists, if one follows Piaget, of a "confusion between one's own thought and that of others and [of a] confusion between the self and the external world" (p. 168). Animism and artificialism are expressions of this absence of differentiation between the self and the external world. They result from the participation of the self in the external world and the external world's participation in the self. These are not kept distinct (p. 221).

With these explanations Piaget apparently remains within the confines of projection theories, for what the protagonists of the theory of projection say essentially amounts to this: the boundaries of the self are not observed; the self is transposed to the outside and into a reality that is different for us, but not for the self. On occasion, Piaget makes use of the concept of projection, even if he firmly opposes its crude version, which involves a hypostatization of the self. The systematic deficiency can be traced all the way to linguistic usage, which, by the way, Piaget himself has recognized (pp. 228ff.). Piaget rejects the notion of translatability. "It is wrong to say," he writes, that "the child attributes consciousness to things or at any rate such an expression must only be regarded as meta-phorical" (p. 177). On the other hand, he reverts again and again to simi-lar formulations and even speaks without hesitation of the translation into the physical world of the ideas invoked in the child's mind (p. 150). If we follow Piaget, the child experiences a reorientation in his second year. It learns to direct its own actions and to coordinate different actions. Through this ability, the child also makes itself the subject of its own actions. In a systematic connection with these developments, the objects become substantiated. They achieve permanence and independence. All of these intellectual achievements remain bound to actual actions as long as they have not undergone a conceptual representation.

This process of internalization of actions into conceptual representa-tions begins at the stage of the so-called preoperational thinking, between the ages of 2 and 4. It is achieved by way of an improved interaction com-petence. As a result, the self is continually strengthened and the external world continually organized. Yet even this phase remains tied to the schema of interaction and, more concretely, to those modes of interaction which the child has mastered. In other words, the child is not yet capable of operating freely and sovereignly enough in the sphere of mental repre-sentations as is the case in the development of actual concepts and con-ceptual systems. And it is exactly this "semiconceptualization," to which Piaget attributes the psychomorphic mode of conceptualization, which is what we here call the conceptualization along the lines of the subjective schema, or simply the subjectivistic conceptualization. It is maintained in the subsequent stages of cognitive development. Until the age of 6 or 7, everything possesses consciousness. Egocentricity is animistic by defini-tion. Then the decline of egocentricity sets in. In the second animistic stage (6 1/2 - 8 1/2 years) consciousness is conferred only to moveable objects. After a transitional stage — the third animistic stage, between the ages of 8 1/2 and 11 1/2 — animism is finally expunged from the child's thinking, according to Piaget (pp. 171-93).

Nearly the entire progress that has been made in the past decades in cognitive developmental psychology is the result of the breakthrough achieved by Piaget's genetic epistemology. However, at that point the breakthrough became stuck.

The Internal Contradiction in Egocentricity. Piaget's strategic program is correct. The hiatus between organism and object-world is not present at the beginning. Closely tied to this is that on both sides the actual signifi-cant referents — subject and object — are missing. Yet if and as long as this is the case, it is inconceivable why distinctly formed subject-structures can be found on the object side. As long as they have not been formed on the subject side they cannot appear on the object side. If Piaget's explanation is to become plausible, we must assume that the child is equipped with its own forms of action. Only then can the child make use of it as cognitive forms. Otherwise it remains as inexplicable — as in the case of each of the previously discussed theories of projection — why the child puts a subjective construction upon objects that are already clearly recognized as divorced from the self and foreign to it. To the degree to which the child lacks distance from the external world, it also lacks distance from its own actions. And vice versa, to the degree to which the child gains distance from its own actions, it becomes aware of the external world as a world of objects separate from the self. The logic of Piaget's explanation would demand that from the very beginning the child's subjective world can only be recognized as a process of differentiation. The more the object-world would appear as opposed to the simultaneously developed subjectivity of the child, the more all subjective interpretations of the object-world would recede. But this is not the case. All subjective interpretations of the external world are developed and fostered during the whole period of childhood. They come much too late to permit an explanation in terms of the lack of dissociation between subject and object.

The Differentiation of the Social World. It is easy to locate this deficiency from a sociology of knowledge perspective: Piaget fails to provide what is decisively important for a genetic theory of development, namely, to make the developmental process of the child's conception of the world explicit. This requires an explanation of the child's interpretation of objects and events as a process in which interpretive schemata are conceived as realistic incorporations of the experiences gained in the encounter with the dominant object and the dominant social events in the child's environment. Piaget himself never tired of interpreting the developmental process as an assimilation to an already existing reality. Consequently it would have been necessary merely to conceptualize this reality more concretely. To emphasize the deficiency in Piaget's analysis: for Piaget, the child's conception of the world, in particular in its highly significant traits of animistic, artificial, and magical interpretations, remains self-interpretation. Piaget's terminology with its central concept of egocentricity does not emerge by chance. Even what he identifies as the child's realism is the realism of a world of conceptualizations that transfers the child's internal world to the outside. The egocentric schemata are, as Piaget argues, derived from inner experiences (p. 113). But this is precisely the opposite of how things are. To repeat, the child's conception of the world is in its interpretations an expression of actual experiences with an external world which are incorporated into a highly realistic interpretive schema.

Our emendation also reverses the interpretation of the concept of socialization as it occasionally surfaces in Piaget. For Piaget, egocentricity is inborn (p. 39); the originality of the child's thinking resists socialization and opposes it, but ultimately the coercion by adults gains the upper hand (p. 34). However, the reverse is true. The child encounters adults, including their cultural forms of life. Of course it is not the child's own world: it cannot even comprehend it. The child assimilates the world as best as it can. Cognitive schemata are a result, indeed an enduring result, of these efforts. They are formal schemata, but schemata that retain contents.[29]

The critique of Piaget's derivation of the subjective interpretive schema intends to point above all, through reference to contesting interpretations, to the origin of the well-known and elsewhere well-established subjective conceptualizations of the world. Let us summarize the result from the perspective of "constructive realism": (1) Cognitive forms must first be developed by humans. (2) The development of the schema of object-event is of paramount significance. This development, like the development of any other categorical schema, can only take place in the context of an already existing reality. (3) The dominant object in the child's environment is the caring significant other. The object-event schema is therefore developed in interaction with it. Hence the development of the subjective schema is a process involving the realistic incorporation of actual experiences.

Consequences:
The Species-History of Intellectual and Cultural Development

The reflection upon the social preconditions for the development of intellectual constructs has clearly demonstrated, in a discreet yet striking manner, how access to its understanding can be achieved through an analysis of its development in the early phase of ontogenesis. This approach has consequences that cannot be ignored. The process of constructing the spiritual and cultural life-world, and of *cognitive forms* in particular, has in all periods of human history been the result of the same anthropological condition. This development has, insofar as the original categorical forms are concerned, occurred in all periods under the same conditions. And this process has in all periods been advanced at the level of the adults. How far it was able to advance, however, was contingent upon the specific historical developments. Because this is so, the species-history of intellectual and cultural development must and can be reconstructed by way of the evolution of ontogenetic structures. The particular life-worlds in the different stages of history are nothing but the differentially developed constructs that arise in early childhood.

Caution is in order here. For the time being we do not know to what extent those adult life-worlds still accessible to us, in their evolution from hunters and gatherers up to industrial societies, have in fact been able to develop basic cognitive structures. Nor do we understand, beyond the broadest outlines, the connection between basic operational cognitive structures and the semantic level, that is, the level of fully articulated world-views. The evolutionary direction, however, cannot be doubted, and it must determine future inquiries.

Summary

Human beings are part of the process of natural evolution. Their biological plan of organization represents a peak in the evolutionary process. The structural principle in the organization of living beings — autonomy — is pushed to an extreme. Humans must first create their own world. They must develop the cognitive forms under which they can live. The convergence of the world onto humans, which came to consciousness at the beginning of the modern era, is thus a genuine discovery. The roots of this convergence lie in the principles of anthropological organization.

The naturalistic perspective compels a conceptualization of the structure of the world as a learning process by way of interaction with an already existing reality. The resistance of the world of objects presses humans to develop the cognitive forms, the categorical form in particular. Every future epistemology that attempts to be scientific must therefore begin as a naturalistic or materialist theory. It must start not with thinking and knowledge but with nature and with the natural organization the human being, which is thereby conceptualized strictly within the limits of an interpretation in terms of natural science.

This epistemological strategy was already formulated in a programmatic manner in the nineteenth century, after the collapse of metaphysics. It could be substantiated only after the scientific revolution in biology had laid bare the process-character of nature, that is, after it had created by way of evolutionary theory at least a basis for the understanding of the development of human beings. The epistemological problematic readily linked up with the analysis of the naturalistic plan of organization. The task is to show how, under conditions of this anthropological plan of organization, the cultural life-forms, cognitive forms in particular, could develop. It is precisely this program that was taken up by Piaget's genetic epistemology. Piaget looked for a naturalistic epistemology, and that is why he was so extraordinarily successful.

Unfortunately, Piaget did not convincingly manage to integrate the conditions of social life into the process of construction. His early writings in particular fail to show how the evolution of cognitive forms is necessitated by the concrete experiences of the object.[30] This renders his interpretations rather speculative. Only one thing would have been required in order to avoid this: to emphasize the naturalistic perspective and at the same time to consider that human beings create the categorical forms out of their social mode of existence. From this perspective it would have been easy to demonstrate something that is also decisively important to Piaget that categorical forms are neither brought along by nature nor simply adopted from the already existing life-world, but are actually created by the emerging social being. Piaget's genetic epistemology would have been in a better position than any other theory to integrate the experience of society. Society first comes into play by way of the caring significant other as an actual object which, however, is always already distinguished by a greater ability than the child still being socialized.

If we adopt this perspective, the child's conception of the world becomes surprisingly easy to explain: it is subjectivistic in its basic cognitive structure because it models itself after more advanced subjects. This perspective applies with equal stringency to the analysis of the intellectual history of the species. The worlds of adults, regardless of where and under what historical conditions they have emerged, are and can be nothing other than the more advanced cognitive structures encountered in early ontogenesis.

Notes

Translated from German by Günther Dux, Volker Meja, and Detmar H. Tschofen

1. René Descartes, *Oeuvres* (Paris: Charles Adam and Paul Tannery, 1964). The following quotation refers to the English translation in Elizabeth S. Haldane, ed., *The Philosophical Works of Descartes*, two volumes (Cambridge: Cambridge University Press, 1973).

2. On the role of God in Descartes's epistemology see Günter Dux, *Strukturwandel der Legitimation* (Freiburg: Alber, 1976), pp. 153ff.

3. Werner Heisenberg, *Das Naturbild der heutigen Physik* (Hamburg: Rowohlt, 1955), p.19.

4. Winch, who subscribes to this constructive idealism, appears to ignore this consequence, or at least fails to resolve the issue. See Peter Winch, "Understanding a primitive society," *American Philosophical Quarterly* 4 (1964): 307ff. See also Bryan R. Wilson, ed., *Rationality* (New York: Harper & Row, 1970).

5. For a substantiation of this assertion, I refer the reader to a thorough discussion in my *Die Logik der Weltbilder* (Frankfurt: Suhrkamp, 1981).

6. K. Marx and F. Engels, *The German Ideology*, in *Marx-Engels Werke*, vol. 3 (Berlin: Dietz, 1969), pp. 9ff. English edition used Marx-Engels, *Collected Works* (New York:

International, 1975), vol. 5, pp. 19ff. All quotes which follow refer to these two editions.

7. Helmut Plessner, *Die Stufen des Organischen und der Mensch*, 2nd ed. (Berlin: de Gruyter, 1965).

8. It is precisely this "tendency toward history" which Plessner has so skillfully worked out. See in particular his *Conditio Humana* (Pfullingen: Neske, 1964).

9. The following quotes refer to Arnold Gehlen, *Der Mensch* (Frankfurt: Klostermann, 1966), pp. 31ff.

10. I have previously tried to work out this historical threshold of philosophical anthropology. See H. Plessner's "Philosophische Anthropologie im Prospekt," in H. Plessner, *Philosophische Anthropologie* (Frankfurt: Fischer, 1970), pp. 255-329.

11. Jacques Monod, *Zufall und Notwendigkeit* (Munich: Deutscher Taschenbuchverlag, 1975), p. 28.

12. See Bernhard Rensch, *Neuere Probleme der Abstammungslehre* (Stuttgart: Enke, 1972), p. 304, and the literature that is cited there.

13. See H.F. Harlow, "Die Evolution des Lernens," in Ann Roe and George Gaylord Simpson, eds., *Evolution und Verhalten* (Frankfurt: Suhrkamp, 1969), pp. 70-99.

14. See Conrad Hal Waddington, *The Ethical Animal* (London: Allen & Unwin, 1960).

15. Hugh Miller has pointed out this function of societies. See Hugh Miller, *Progress and Decline: The Group in Evolution* (Oxford: Pergamon, 1964).

16. Erik H. Erikson, *Einsicht und Verantwortung: Die Rolle des Ethischen in der Psychoanalyse* (Frankfurt: Fischer, 1971), p. 102. English edition, *Insight and Responsibility* (New York: Norton, 1964).

17. Jean Piaget, *The Principles of Genetic Epistemology* (New York: Basic Books, 1972), p. 17.

18. Jean Piaget, *Biology and Knowledge* (Chicago: University of Chicago Press, 1971), p. 26. French: *Biologie et connaissance* (Paris: Gallimard, 1967).

19. Ibid., p. 34.

20. Ibid., p. 13.

21. Monod already suggested that it is necessary to relinquish the category of derivation. See Monod, op. cit., p. 53. Also see Piaget, *Biology and Knowledge*, loc. cit., pp. 14ff.

22. Piaget has taken notice of this program. See *Biology and Knowledge*, loc. cit., p. 56, n. 5; p. 100, n. 18.

23. Edward O. Wilson, *Sociobiology* (Cambridge, Mass.: Cambridge University Press, 1978), pp. 32ff.

24. Cf. the frequently discussed example of rule-learning within the context of interaction competence in the Peekaboo-game. See J.S. Bruner and V. Sherwood, "Peekaboo and the Learning of Role Structures," in *Play — Its Role in Development and Evolution*, ed. Jerome S. Bruner, Alison Jolly and Kathy Sylva (Harmondsworth: Penguin, 1976), pp. 277-85.

25. See particularly Emile Durkheim, *The Elementary Forms of Religious Life* (New York: Free Press, 1965). Original edition: *Les formes élémentaires de la vie religieuse* (Paris: Alcan, 1912).

26. Jean Piaget, *The Child's Conception of the World* (London: Kegan, Trench, Trubner, 1929), p. 188.

27. Ludwig Feuerbach, *Sämtliche Werke*, vol. 2 (Stuttgart: Frommann, 1959), p. 296.

28. Piaget, *The Child's Conception of the World*, loc. cit., p. 235. All quotes and references which follow refer to this book.

29. It should be emphasized that socialization theory and, within it, the role of adults and of the coercion exercised by adults are in need of revision, or at least in need of further refinement, also in regard to inquiries into the development of moral judgment. See *The Moral Judgment of the Child* (New York: Harcourt, Brace & World, 1932).

30. The opposition of form and content, as found though not sustained in Piaget's *The Child's Conception of the World* disappears. See, for example, pp. 171ff.

7

The Conventional Component in Knowledge and Cognition

Barry Barnes

The sociology of knowledge has had a chequered history. At one point, soon after the war, it appeared about to expire completely, and sociologists and epistemologists, concurring in the Pelagian misconceptions of the time, were tempted into premature obsequies. How premature is now all too clearly apparent. Over the last decade the subject has enjoyed a widespread and vigorous revival, so that its continuing existence and significance is no longer in doubt.

In its current form, the sociology of knowledge is less restrictively conceived than heretofore. Traditional scruples about addressing what is true, valid, or rationally justified, have been overcome. Our own natural science is now a prominent focus for research. Whereas earlier work in the sociology of knowledge was inspired by the need to account for erroneous or distorted cognition, today the basis of our own routine, "rational" cognitive processes is the predominant concern: we have grown more authentically curious about ourselves.[1]

Current trends in the sociology of knowledge will only be justified if knowledge generally proves to have an inalienable social dimension. The concern of the present essay is to show that this is indeed the case, and to display in a reasonably concrete fashion precisely what that social dimension consists of. There are of course many forms of knowledge, and it is difficult to propose arguments and offer illustrations which encompass all of them: any general account of knowledge faces problems in establishing

Acknowledgment: Many colleagues, both in my department at Edinburgh and elsewhere, have offered valuable commentary and criticism related to earlier versions of this paper.

its proper scope. Fortunately, the severity of this problem has been much alleviated by the demonstration that no absolute distinction can be drawn between theoretical and observational knowledge. This finding, carefully considered and justified by Mary Hesse in her study *The Structure of Scientific Inference*, suggests a general analogy between a great range of concepts and forms of knowledge, including empirical common sense and esoteric scientific theory. It indicates that conclusions of general significance can be derived from the study of specific, everyday, readily intelligible concepts.[2] In what follows, animal kinds and their properties form the basis for discussion, but the conclusions to be derived will be offered as conjectures concerning concepts and beliefs generally. Those who would restrict their scope or make exceptions should accept that the need for justification lies on their side, even though the argument for full generality is only touched upon briefly here.[3]

The Context of Learning

Let us start by asking how knowledge is acquired. For simplicity, let us at first be even more restrictive and merely consider how people learn to apply concepts[4] — that is, how they learn to classify. I shall postulate two basic features of any context of learning. First, people learn as they move around in an indefinitely complex physical environment of which they are aware; learning takes place in the course of the reception of complex inputs of information from "experience," or "the world," or "reality," or whatever term one favors. Second, learning always initially occurs within a social context; to learn to classify is to learn to employ the classifications of some community or culture, and this involves interaction with competent members of the culture.

These two postulates are of such importance to the argument that it is worthwhile to incorporate them into a rudimentary image or symbol of the learning context. Imagine a neophyte solely concerned with mastering the ways of classifying the physical environment currently accepted by his culture. Let us characterize him as an incompetent learner, *L*, interacting with a competent member or teacher, *T*, in a particular environment. Our concern must be with the processes whereby the learner acquires and the teacher transmits competence in the use of concepts. Two types of processes can be employed: ostension and generalization.

Ostension

Any attempt to make a direct association between a term, and an object, event, or process evident in the environment, I shall treat as an act of ostension. In the case of animal kinds, the image of pointing and saying is the best symbol for such an act. Imagine T conveying the usage of term x by repeatedly pointing to some particular and simultaneously saying x. As a result, L acquires a series of memories of particulars, all associated with x: in practice, he remembers so many particular x's. For example, T might point to a succession of particular birds, and on each occasion say "bird." As a result, L would become familiar with a number of accepted instances of "bird" and would himself take those instances simply as birds.[5] Ostension is an essential element in all verbally mediated learning. It is the ingredient which knots terms to the environment itself.

Generalization

Generalizations connect terms together and indicate associations between their instances. Thus, the generalizations attested by T provide L with standard expectations as to whether an instance of one term is also, or may become, or is in some way related to, an instance of another: "birds are egg layers," "birds can fly," "birds have feathers," are obvious examples. Like ostension, generalization is an essential ingredient in all verbally mediated learning. Generalizations provide expectations of experience. They are what make us regard a form of culture as a body of knowledge rather than a mere taxonomy.

The form of a generalization is variable, and can be used to convey the manner or intensity of the association of the instances of its terms. With animal kind terms, indicators of probability (p) are typically an important component of generalizations. The frequency of a relation may be indicated: "birds can usually fly"; or its reliability: "we think all birds have beaks"; or its analyticity, where an assertion is simply not allowed to be other than certain: "birds just are feathered bipeds." In what follows, the probability of a generalization has to be taken into account, but only in the most rudimentary and schematic way.

The Hesse Net

Let us assume that ostension and generalization are the only processes involved in the transmission of kind terms. If this is so, then L acquires all his information about the kinds recognized in his community via these two processes. And, since any T was once an L, it follows that all competent members of a community have built up their knowledge via such process. This suggests that the knowledge of any competent member can be modelled by the scheme in Figure 1, which I shall call a "Hesse net."[6]

In Figure 1 a number of concepts, C, are shown, tied together by generalizations (the lines), each having a "probability," p. The net should

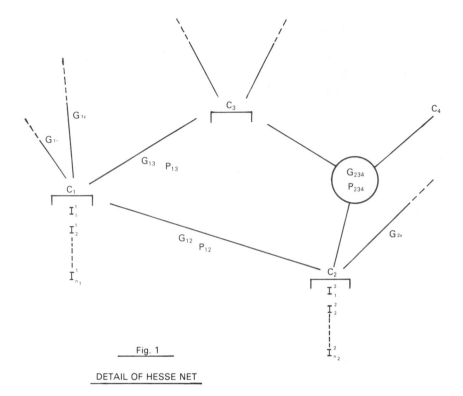

Fig. 1

DETAIL OF HESSE NET

be imagined extending out of the figure, involving more and more terms, until the entire conceptual resources possessed by the individual are included within it to comprise a connected whole. (Many of the concepts in a net will accordingly not be natural kind terms, but will stand for processes or for properties. But no additional problems are thereby created. Such concepts function in generalizations as readily as do kind terms. And to associate a term with a behavior or a property by ostension is no more difficult than to associate it with an object.) Finally, it will be seen that under every concept stands a number of specific instances, thereof. These instances I call the "tension" of the associated concept.[7] A tension may be constructed entirely by acts of ostension. But it may also be synthesized verbally, using particularly strong forms of generalization. For example, a tension for "animal" can be constructed, via statements like "cows are animals" or "pigs are animals," from the tensions of "cow," "pig," and the like. Note that there are not inherently different kinds of term, some with tensions given by ostension, and some purely verbally. Rather, there are tensions directly constructed by ostension; and other tensions so constructed indirectly, which incorporate into themselves the results of previous ostensive activity. Thus the tensions of a net stand in a formal equivalence to each other: they are all fundamentally of one kind. And one at each junction, they provide the connections which attach the net to the physical environment. The Hesse net is a useful reification derived from acts of linguistic usage. The structure of the net, once under the control of the imagination, is an invaluable resource in understanding the character of concept application.

Concept Application

The net has been presented as a model of the conceptual resources acquired by an individual as he becomes a competent member of his community. It summarizes everything that can be taught concerning proper usage of a term. The important thing now is to see that the acquisition of all that the culture can provide still leaves future concept application underdetermined and open-ended.

Imagine that L has fully acquired the concept "dog." How does he identify the next dog? Imagine first of all that a new particular has to be labelled as "dog" or "not dog" purely by reference to the tension of the concept "dog." In this case everything rests on the degree of resemblance between the particular and the instances in the tension of "dog." But the notion of "degree of resemblance" is problematic. L's perceptual and cognitive apparatus will indubitably be able to make out many relations of similarity and difference between the new particular and the existing instances. The next case will be discernibly similar to, yet different from, what has gone before.

An assertion of resemblance therefore, which is what the application of a concept amounts to in this case, involves asserting that similarities outweigh differences. But there is no scale for the weighting of similarity against difference given in the nature of external reality or inherent in the nature of the mind. An agent could as well assert insufficient resemblance and withhold application of the concept as far as reality or reason are concerned. It follows that the tension of a term such as "dog" is an insufficient determinant of its subsequent usage. All applications of "dog" involve the contingent judgment that similarity outweighs difference in that case. This is true even where the agent experiences the overwhelming psychological conviction that resemblance is extremely strong. Such conviction does not arise from the meaning of a concept but from the routine operation of the agent's own perception and cognition — something which is contingent and revisable.

If concept application depends only on the tension of a term, it is sociologically interesting in a profound sense. Not only is it the case that the instances within the tension are part of received culture;[8] the very processes whereby instances are one by one added to the tension are processes involving socially situated judgment. Put another way: concept application is not a social activity in the sense that it is determined by a culturally given classification of reality, but a social activity which gives rise to and develops the patterns of that very classification. The pattern does not account for the activity, but vice versa.

It is true that a concept is always part of a net, and that its application involves reference not just to one but to many resemblance relations. If an instance is held to be a dog it will be thought to resemble existing instances of "dog" more than it resembles instances of "wolf" or any comparable term. It will be the greatest perceived resemblance in a series of comparisons which matters (cf. the next section). But this merely increases the extent to which weightings of similarity and difference have to be made, and thus merely serves to reinforce the impact of what has already been said.

What, however, of the verbal generalizations (including perhaps definitions) in which a concept is included? Certainly such generalizations may have an important bearing on how a concept is applied, but they do not solve the difficulty of the underdetermination of concept application. All they can do is effect a sideways shift in the location of the problem of resemblance. For example, the generalization "dogs always have hair," can only take us across to another term, "hair," where the problem of resemblance recurs. Whatever in the appearance of O is taken as a candidate for being hair will be perceptibly similar and different to the instances in the tension of "hair."

"Defining one's terms" is not a strategy which can provide a sufficient basis for their subsequent use. Our inclination to apply a term in a given instance may be strengthened by taking heed of verbal definitions and the tensions of the terms to which it is thereby linked. But no strategy of definition can replace a problematic overall resemblance with an unproblematic "actual" measure of resemblance in some particular defined respect.

Past usage of a term could only provide a sufficient basis for future usage if the relation of resemblance were replaced with one of perfect identity. This implies the existence of terms only applicable to identical instances, between which no discrimination is possible. The application of such terms would be unproblematic, and their involvement in verbal generalizations could be used to render the application of other terms unproblematic. "All dogs and only dogs manifest dogginess," it might be held, whereupon the application of "dog" would become unproblematic, given the existence of a tension of "dogginess" containing only perfectly identical instances. (In such a case the tension need only contain one instance, which would embody or indeed *be* the very idea of dogginess.) Such an essentialist account of concept application would, if established, amount to a refutation of the claims of this essay. There is, however, no empirical evidence to indicate that essences act as magnets for our concepts. Actual processes of concept application do not involve identity: we get by without it. The open-ended use of natural kind terms proceeds on the basis of nothing stronger than the resemblance of instances

The outlines of the required account of concept application have now been set out. The key points are few: concepts are learned from authoritative sources within particular physical environments; the learning processes, ostension and generalization, build up a pattern of associations that can be imaged as a Hesse net; the development of the pattern proceeds on the basis of resemblance and not identity; and the existing configuration of the pattern is an insufficient determinant of how further particulars are added to it. We can now move on to consider a number of points suggested by the account.

The Effects of Learning are Delocalized

Consider a case where T and L are concerned to classify what is for both a new particular, O. L, being L, has not yet acquired all the terms current in his community. This can be conveniently symbolized in terms of a culture of three mutually exclusive terms, all available to T, but with one term remaining to be acquired by L (Figure 2). L, deciding that O resembles the instances of $C/2$ more than those of $C/1$ calls O a $C/2$. However, T, who might well argue with L's assessment of resemblance, finds a still greater resemblance between O and the instance of $C/3$. Accordingly, L is informed that O is actually a $C/3$ and finds himself learning a new term through a process of ostension. Because and only because of ignorance of $C/3$, L is less competent than T in the use of $C/2$.

A hypothetical example with the form of Figure 3 has been discussed by T.S. Kuhn.[9] A boy, familiar with the terms "duck" and "goose" and appropriate instances, calls a large white bird a goose, only to be corrected by his father, who offers the proper designation "swan." As the boy's experience of swans increases, so his use of the term "goose" becomes more competent. Moreover, it is difficult to see how this increase in competence could have been brought about either purely verbally or through further ostensive indications of accepted instances of "goose." Knowing what a

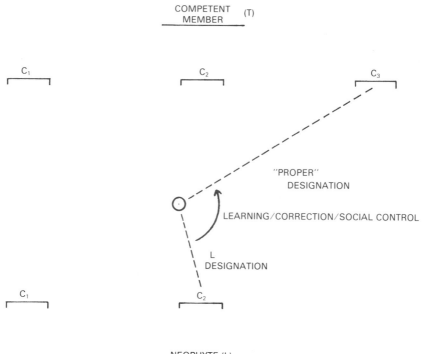

COMPETENT MEMBER (T)

c_1

c_2

c_3

"PROPER" DESIGNATION

LEARNING/CORRECTION/SOCIAL CONTROL

L DESIGNATION

c_1

c_2

NEOPHYTE (L)

Fig. 2

goose is involves knowing what a swan is. Proper application of the term "goose" involves familiarity with accepted instances of "swan." By generalizing this point, we arrive at the interesting conclusion that competent usage of a term ideally requires command of all the terms in the associated net. Atomistic theories of concept application (and hence of meaning), which consider solely the relationship between a single isolated concept and that to which it applies, are inadequate. Delocalized accounts, which deal with connected sets of concepts as organized wholes, are required.

Classifications Are Judgments

When an individual refers to previous usage to ascertain what a new particular should properly be called, he is confronted by a complex array

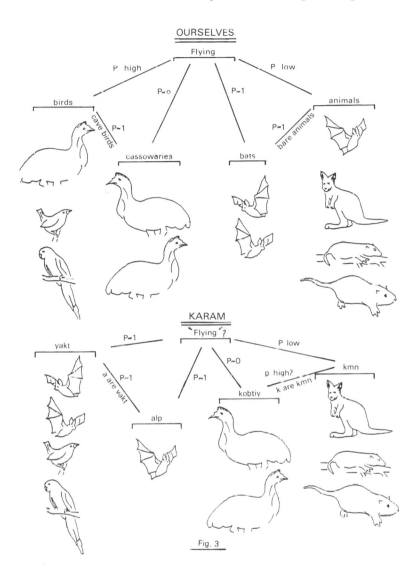

Fig. 3

of similarities and differences. No indefeasible justification can be drawn from such an array for selecting one term rather than another, or even for asserting "C" rather than "not C." There are grounds to be found in previous usage for *any* selection: *whatever* a new particular is called can be made out as in accordance with previous usage. Therefore, what the particular is *actually* called must be understood *formally* as a contingent judgment of the agent(s) involved.

Concepts do not come with labels attached, carrying instructions which tell us how they are to be used. We ourselves determine usage, taking previous usage as precedent. Moreover, such precedent is corrigible, since it is itself the product of judgments. It can always be said that previous usage was wrong, that it weighted similarity and difference incorrectly, and that it must be revised. Kinds of thing can be reclassified so that even previously paradigmatic examples of the proper usage of one term come to fall under another.

Usage develops as a sequence of on-the-spot judgments, each of which adds a particular to the tension of a term (or, where previous usage is revised, removes one). It is false to assume that usage is determined in advance, by meanings, rules, norms, logic, or similar entities. Usage requires detailed empirical study at every point: agents develop usage in ways which at all times relate to their full complexity as social actors and biological organisms. To understand concept application we must understand ourselves.[10]

Proper Classification Is Agreed Classification

Most of the time individuals apply classifications without hesitation, confident that their designations are correct and will be verified as such by fellow members of their community. And, for the most part, such suggestions are so verified. Suppose, however, that two individuals in a community were to differ over what they took to be a routine act of concept application. For the first, a creature was obviously and indubitably a dog; for the second, it was a cat. No amount of discussion altered matters.

In circumstances such as these, the members of the relevant community will typically pronounce which of the two individuals has made the "correct" designation. They will specify "proper" perception in terms of what members generally say they perceive, and "proper" analogy in terms of the weightings of similarity against difference members generally say they are moved by. Two points can be made about this judgment of correctness made by the local community. First, there is no fundamentally superior method of appraising correctness available than that of looking to this local judgment. Second, it is the only shared judgment with actual consequences in the local situation: it is, the only shared judgment of empirical and thus of sociological interest. From the usual sociological perspective, proper usage is specified in terms of the practice of the relevant community.[11] External evaluations of proper usage, such as, for example, an epistemologist might be tempted to apply to the discourse of an alien culture, have no sociological significance.

It is an empirical matter whether, and how far, a sense of proper concept application can be sustained in a collectivity. To the extent that members of a community differ on the proper application of a term, an eventual consensual usage, if one is to be achieved at all, must emerge from social negotiation. Members must seek to come to an agreement about usage in that particular case, perhaps hoping that, following from that precedent, future open-ended usage will be rendered less problematic.

All Nets Are Formally Equivalent

To the extent that a classification, or a body of knowledge, can be modelled by a Hesse net, an equivalence is implied with all others that can be so modelled. Consider first the different tensions in any two nets. These represent different ways of clustering particulars together. But the clustering is something which we do to the particulars, not something which is already done in "reality." "Reality" does not mind how we cluster it; "reality" is simply the massively complex array of unverbalized information we cluster. This suggests that different nets stand equivalently in relation to "reality" or to the physical environment. Consider next the cognitive processes involved in acquiring, developing, and revising networks. These reasoning processes are involved whichever network is considered, so they do not provide a basis for choosing between networks. This suggests that different nets are all equally "rationally held."

If neither reality nor pure reason can discriminate different networks, it is a plausible hypothesis that their incidence reflects local social contingencies which sustain them in their different contexts. Different existing nets are alternative conventional orderings of nature: they sit in their host societies as institutions.

The argument is that different classifications or bodies of knowledge must all separately be socially sustained *because* they are all rationally held and compatible with reality or experience. This contrasts with the widely held view where socially sustained beliefs are contrasted with those arising from rational appraisal of experience or reality. If something is analyzed as a convention or institution, it is often conceived of as some sort of fantasy, with no connection with the real world (or perhaps an inverted or spurious connection). But it is not that classifications are conventions *as opposed to* good representations of the world. Rather they are precisely conventional representations *of* the world.

The false contrast between the rational and the social, or between nature and culture, dies hard. It even lingers in the writings of those who have made major contributions to the emergence of a properly impartial sociology of knowledge. I cite an example from social anthropology, where a number of admirable studies of animal classification exist, and where the movement to a properly relativist treatment of knowledge and culture is well developed. Consider Bulmer's discussion of Karam animal taxonomy.[12] This work attempts to explain why, for the Karam, the cassowary occupies a special taxonomic status, being placed in the special taxon *kobtiy*, set apart from the taxon *yakt* of birds and bats. As Bulmer formulates the problem: "Why, to the Karam, is the cassowary not a bird?" The answer is allegedly that cassowaries perform a special role in Karam culture as representations of cross-cousins. Men's relations with cassowaries are structured in isomorphism to their relations with cross-cousins; and the special activities which thereby become appropriate with regard to the cassowary justify its being given a special taxonomic status.

For the moment, the details of this explanation can be set aside. Let us accept it as plausible and assume that the fieldwork on which it is based is reliable. What is of immediate interest is the framework within which the explanation is set. It is assumed that nature and culture have separate effects upon Karam knowledge. Hence, the extent to which their knowledge properly reflects nature is first discussed as a method of setting limits on the role of culture. It is only because nature cannot account for the taxonomic status of the cassowary that culture is given the opportunity to do so. Culture can explain only what nature does not.

How does Bulmer ascertain the extent to which Karam taxonomy corresponds with nature? This is done by comparing their taxonomy with our own, or, more precisely, with the taxonomy of our specialists in zoology and natural history. Our natural kinds, it is assumed, are the ones which correspond to real divisions in the nature of things. To the extent that Karam taxonomy corresponds to ours it is intelligible by reference to nature, and to the extent that it does not it is intelligible by reference to culture.

At (the level of terminal taxa) Karam show an enormous, detailed and on the whole highly accurate knowledge of natural history, and . . . though, even with vertebrate animals, their terminal taxa only correspond well in about 60 per cent of cases with the species recognised by the scientific zoologist, they are nevertheless in general well aware of species differences among larger and more familiar creatures.

At the upper level of Karam taxonomy, however, objective biological facts no longer dominate the scene. They are still important, but they allow a far greater, almost infinitely varied, set of possibilities to the taxonomist. This is the level at which culture takes over and determines the selection of taxonomically significant characters.[13]

A similar contrast between nature and culture is apparent in the work of Mary Douglas, for all that it has been so significant in stimulating a relativist approach to classification. Reviewing a range of work on the classification of physical nature, including Bulmer's 1967 paper, Douglas writes: "Physical nature is masticated and driven through the cognitive meshes to satisfy social demands for clarity which *compete* with logical demands for consistency" [italics added].[14]

This idea of competition between what is logical and natural on the one hand, and what derives from culture and society on the other, is deeply entrenched. Classifications may conform to the objective facts of nature *or* to cultural requirements. They may be logical or social. But this is the very opposite of what careful examination reveals: we need to think in terms of symbiosis, not competition.

Bulmer's work indicates that the alternative zoological texonomies of the Karam and ourselves can be modelled as alternative Hesse nets (Figure 3). Both nets can be satisfactorily read on to reality (in the sense of the physical environment). It is not that one net distorts reality more or less than the other. How can the pattern of either net distort reality? Rather, reality provides the information incorporated in both nets: it has no preference for the one or the other. Reality confers no privilege on our methods of classification; they have no special anthropological significance. So too for logic. The equivalence of the alternative nets indicates a lack of any formal differences in the two related patterns of cognition, theirs and ours.

By assuming a privileged status for our own taxonomy, Bulmer was led into organizing his admirable paper around the wrong question. It is misleading to inquire why, in Karam taxonomy, the cassowary is not a bird. This is analogous to asking: "Why to the British are kobtiy yakt?" which could readily lead on to pseudoproblems concerning the logical incompetence of the Western mind.[15] The most that one should seek to ask is: "Why, to the Karam, arc kobtiy not yakt?" and "why, to the British, arc cassowaries birds?"[16]

Induction

So far the various generalizations on a network and the associated probabilities have scarcely been considered. Yet they constitute what is actually believed of the world. To talk of the equivalence of networks without proper consideration of generalizations and probabilities was premature and requires immediate remedy. It will transpire, however, that nothing already asserted needs to be modified as a consequence.

The probabilities of generalizations were initially introduced as givens, transmitted on the basis of authority to new members of a community. But direct awareness and ongoing investigation of a particular environment must surely have some bearing on how probable this or that generalization is taken to be; so the problem arises of how the probabilities supplied by the ancestors relate to the information supplied by the world.

Universally, the processes of inference involved here are associative or inductive in style.[17] People derive or legitimize expected future associations by reference to the strength of such associations in the past: the more strongly particulars are thought to have been associated in the past, the more they are expected to be associated in the future. This inductive or associative characteristic of cognition is evident at many levels. General associative tendencies underlie simple, unconscious nonverbal learning, such as we continually automatically engage in as organisms moving through a physical environment. Similarly, there is experimental evidence of basic inductive propensities operative in conscious, but primarily nonverbal problem-solving situations.[18] With regard to verbal culture, messages can only transmit information if their component terms retain some of the associations acquired in earlier usage; an inductive presupposition is built into the way such messages are decoded. More generally, an inductive idiom is presumed whenever we engage in verbal discourse. Counterinductive assertions are unintelligible as they stand. In all the many existing styles of discourse and inference, accepted instances of a generalization tend to increase its p, and accepted counterinstances to decrease it. The opposite style produces bafflement.[19]

It is difficult to argue that basic inductive propensities are learned, or conventional or optional in character. Induction is a propensity we possess prior to learning, which is necessary for learning. Even the most heavily socialized kinds of learning depend on prior inductive propensities, which structure the form of the operations whereby verbal messages are decoded and their information extracted. We should not shrink from admitting that cognitively we operate as inductive learning machines.[20] This crude formulation stresses that basic inductive propensities are inherent in our characteristics as organisms. They are the form of our cognitive apparatus, not conventions learned by that apparatus. We are congenitally inductive.

How then do our inductive propensities relate to the given probabilities of our accepted generalizations? It is plausible but nonetheless misconceived to set the two factors in opposition, and make induction from experience a continuing threat to the prior probabilities given by authority. Just as with concept application there is no inherent conflict between external nature and culture, so with the probability of generalizations there is no inherent conflict between our inner nature and culture. The argument in each case is the same: the way we apply terms and the degree to which we accept generalizations are different sides of the same coin. It is true that when we accept something as confirming or disconfirming a generalization we tend to modify its probability appropriately. But just as classifying something as this or that is, in the last analysis, a contingent judgment, so, as a consequence, is taking something as a confirmation of a particular generalization. And just as the application of a term involves consideration of all the terms in a network, so confirmation of a generalization involves, as a consequence, consideration of all the generalizations and associated probabilities. Simply by reminding ourselves of the open-ended character of concept application, we can see at once that a given system of generalizations and prior probabilities can never be unproblematically revealed as incompatible with experience. The different generalizations, and/or different associated probabilities, maintained in different cultures all stand on a par with each other. Certainly, consideration of the Karam natural history previously discussed supports this point (Figure 3). For the Karam, the generalizations in which their animal kind terms function appear to provide an adequate system of instrumentally applicable knowledge. Karam generalizations about *kobtiy* appear as reliable and compatible with inductive propensities as our generalizations about cassowaries. Neither external nor internal nature threatens either system.

It is important to note the limits of this form of argument, lest it be taken as an assertion that beliefs and convictions can be voluntarily, even whimsically, picked up and set down again. The argument does show that an object can be *asserted* to be anything at all, and thus a confirmation of anything at all, without *formal* difficulties of any kind arising. But this is not to say that a given agent, in a given situation, is capable of *believing* anything at all. To assert something is one thing; to believe it another. The point of the argument is not to show that agents can believe any random thing they wish of experience, but to indicate that the generalizations and associated probabilities on *actual, existing* networks never in themselves stand opposed to experience. In actual situations, the application of terms and the confirmation of generalizations are alternative abstractions from the same cognitive processes, which are themselves a part of an ongoing overall pattern of activity. In stable situations, the linguistic acts which place particulars under the tensions of concepts thereby sustain the probabilities of the generalizations wherein the concepts are employed. In a network model of the verbal component of the culture of a stable collectivity, the probabilities on the network are what the cognitive operations of the collectivity bring them to. The probabilities are compatible with some mode of interaction with and experience of the environment, since they are sustained by a community with that mode of interaction and experience. In a stable culture, the preferred modes of concept application and inductive inference, carried out in the given environment of the culture, both use and sustain the probabilities on the Hesse net. Conversely, in a changing culture any clash between present inductive inference and previously given probabilities is merely a clash between present inductive strategy and that of the ancestors.

It might be accepted that, in a stable environment, inductive propensities, far from threatening a particular, communally accepted scheme of things, actually become organized into the very pattern which is the scheme. But questions might still be raised concerning a changing environment. If physical surroundings change, does this not force inductive inference into conflict with accepted authority? An immediate "no" can be given to this question simply by referring back to the earlier discussion of resemblances: any "new" particular will have similarities and differences with the instances in the tensions of a net, and will thus not differ fundamentally from a routinely expected particular. No additional formal insights into the general properties of networks, or rather of the processes which networks represent, can be produced by consideration of oddities or unexpected events.[21]

Coherence

At any point in the history of a culture, however stable, there are innumerable ways of assimilating information from the environment along inductive lines. If such developments were the consequence of totally independent individual decisions, involving even just a part of the range of associative possibilities, then it would soon be impossible any longer to talk to a shared verbal culture. A massive breakdown of communication would soon ensue, and exchange of information would become impossible. There is no a priori reason why this should not happen, but there are known cases where it does not. Among them can be counted the Karam and ourselves, as well as practically anything we are inclined to call a culture. In all cultures inferences show pattern, and hence are in some way restricted. The restrictions, however, are required neither by reality nor by our basic individual inductive propensities. They stand, just as the accepted forms of concept application stand, as the practices of some community, as institutions. Just as concept application is institutionalized so is inductive inference. It has been shown that these are little more than alternative ways of talking of the same processes. Such processes, within a stable culture, display a coherent pattern.

One way of talking of such a pattern is to say that the members of a culture share a theory. For example, it can be said that we ourselves have accepted from ancestors a species theory. This is a convenient and economical way of referring to the pattern in our modes of inference concerning animal kinds: our strong inclination to make out all the instances we encounter as belonging to a fixed list of kinds; our organization of instances in life cycles; our assertions of between-species relationships; our references to sports, hybrids, teratogens, and the like.

There can be no objection to presenting an economical description of our beliefs and inferences involving animal kinds as an account of our theory of species. But it is but a little way from here to a major error, manifested again and again in sociology, history, and philosophy, as idealist explanation. The error consists in citing the theory imputed to agents as the *explanation* of the details of their belief and cognition. For example, in the present context, it consists in accounting for our beliefs and inferences about animal kinds as derived from and determined by our theory of species.

Such a position is absurd. It has been held that no inherent restrictions bear on the use of a concept or the particular conclusions which may be drawn from a generalization. But a theory is itself commonly understood to be a set of concepts and generalizations. Since there are no inherent restrictions on concept application and modes of inference, and hence upon what a theory can be taken to imply, any attempt to invoke a theory as an explanation must be spurious. Yet there is no denying the popularity of this idealist mode of explanation, nor the temptation to explain cognition, in actual situations, as the consequence of holding to a theory.

A theory is not the explanation of restricted cognition in a culture; it simply *is* that restricted cognition.[22] To *describe* the coherent character of a mode of cognition in terms of restrictions in the range of observed cognitive strategies is a tolerable idiom of representation, but then to make out the restrictions as the *explanations* of coherence is to complete a vicious circle. Coherent restricted communal cognitions are institutions. To describe the specific characteristics of our representations of natural kinds, in contrast, say, to those of the Karam, is to describe alternative institutions. The explanatory problem is standard throughout sociology: "why this institution, in this context?" Just as elsewhere in sociology it is absurd to explain a given pattern of action as determined by the very pattern it displays, so too with a given pattern of cognition. (Or, to be more precise, so as a consequence with a given pattern of cognition; for cognition is not independent of action but a feature of it.)

Networks, Goals, and Interests

The foregoing argument shows that knowledge is institutionalized cognition. It reveals something of how cognition is institutionalized, and thus of the precise ways in which knowledge is a social phenomenon. These were the explicit objectives of the essay. The further question — "why this institution, in this context?" is a general problem in sociological theory. This is the point where the sociology of knowledge has to proceed in step with the overall research front in sociology. I shall continue a little further, and sketch the beginnings of an answer to the question.[23]

In looking at the linguistic routines of a stable culture we are looking at institutions sustained by authority and an apparatus of control. Such institutions will have specific advantages for the culture or for some sector of it: they will serve specific interests or further specific goals. There is also a diffuse general advantage derived from *any* form of coordination and routinization of behavior, and which discourages any massive breakdown in it, once established. Any institution, in coming into being, creates a vested interest in its own continuation. For example, any system of animal kinds may serve as a basis for communication, the transmission of information, and thus prediction, contingent only on the general maintenance of routines of usage. If someone shouts to us "cassowaries are coming," or, among the Karam, if someone shouts something like "*kobtiy* are coming," predictions can be made on the basis of transmitted information. But in both cases information is only successfully transmitted if both sender and receiver operate in terms of routinized habituated cognitive processes, if message encoding and decoding operates on a principle of maximum cognitive laziness. In any context where information is flowing there must be some tendency to make routine habituated cognitive operations the initial basis for decoding messages. Without some such tendency to cognitive laziness, inumerable alternative versions of a message would be equally plausible.

In the idealized case of a fully stable culture, routine patterns of concept application are sustained by some combination of specific interests or objectives and diffused vested interests. Changes in such a set of routines may arise, analogously, from changes in associated interests, or from the changed ability of some subsection of a community to further its interests at the expense of another. The processes wherein knowledge is evaluated, changed, and reevaluated will involve continuing reference to shared goals and interests. Note, however, that among such goals are specific, socially situated, predictive, and technical requirements: it is not that agents operate by reference to goals and interests instead of to considerations to technical and empirical adequacy; rather it is that the sense of technical and empirical adequacy is itself intelligible only in terms of contingent goals and interests.

The role of interests is best described in terms of an example. Although appropriate historical case studies exist involving straightforward natural kind terms,[24] they do require a more extended and involved presentation than is appropriate here. I shall use a hypothetical example involving the human gender terms *male* and *female*. Imagine a stable subculture wherein these terms are used of humans much as we ourselves use them. Instances of both kinds are routinely recognized and agreed upon; generalizations about both kinds are accepted as having so much strength and reliability. Both kinds occupy typical positions in a net, with tensions lying under them and generalizations radiating from them. And since the subculture is stable, the institution of gender thus represented can be assumed to be in equilibrium with the existing interests and goals running through the subculture.

Now let us introduce a new interest or goal into the system. Imagine that the subculture becomes concerned to use generalizations about males more effectively for predicting internal conditions in the human body. Present knowledge of males, routinely and unthinkingly interpreted, leads to perceived successful predictions only some of the time in the context in question; the requirement is to obtain such predictions more frequently. It is easy to imagine this new goal leading to the empirical investigation of the characteristics of males, to attempts to perceive as yet unperceived similarities among them, and to verbalize as yet unverbalized similarities. It could also lead to tentative reorderings of particulars, to revisions of the tension of "male," made with a mind to increasing predictive power. There are any number of ways in which such changes might proceed. Let us follow just one possibility.

Imagine that in the course of this activity recognition of an XY chromosome complement occurs for the first time. And imagine that several generalizations are then found to be more predictively useful, better to guess with when routinely and unreflectively applied to persons with the XY complement. Since nearly all persons with this complement are in the tension of male, a revision of this tension is favored. By inserting XYs and ejecting non-XYs, many generalizations, like "males secrete testosterone" or "males grow beards," acquire an increased predictive utility.

Thus a development in the tension of the term *male* might be made intelligible by reference to specific, newly introduced predictive goals. Note, however, that the entire preexisting constellation of goals and interests in the context would count as necessary conditions of the development, and would also affect the way in which it was conceptualized. At one extreme, the revision of the tension could be effected piecemeal, without conscious awareness, through a series of specific acts of concept application: "meaning change" could go unnoticed as a result. At the other extreme, revisions could be carried out explicitly, employing the language of realism. It could be said that males were "really" individuals with the XY characteristic; that errors existed in past usage; that those individuals in the tension of "male" who are not "real" males, and therefore never were, should be removed. Yet another alternative could involve self-conscious revision of the tension to form a new concept existing in parallel with its "parent." Thus a revised tension of "male" could be held to belong to a new concept "XY" or "XY male," usable alongside the initial unmodified original "male." "XY" would enter those generalizations where the replacement of "male" proved predictively profitable, but otherwise the old concept would continue in use. (This would involve a change in the sense of "male," which could in itself be commemorated as a change of concept, and symbolized by a new verbal sign, e.g. "male actor" or "common-sense male.")

The precise way in which a community assimilates a cultural change into its own self-understanding depends on its overall system of goals and interests and the distribution of power. To claim that males really are XYs is usually to invite conflict with other subcultures with other interests, and also to claim priority over common-sense knowledge in a society such as ours. The claim challenges others who might hold "male personality" or "male status" to be revisions of "male" with every bit as much predictive utility. Likewise, in implying that the common-sense term *male* is ontologically inadequate, it sets the expertise of a subculture above the common-sense knowledge available to the lay person. Conversely, peaceful coexistence of "XY male" and "male" usually implies peaceful coexistence between a subculture and the wider community, with the former either having no wish or no power to challenge the latter. Although there is no necessary connection here, realism does tend to be the language of cognitive colonialism, and instrumentalism the language of compromise and toleration.

In the above example a specified goal was taken to condition processes of learning and the reconstruction of knowledge. The presence of the goal contributed to the development of knowledge from an earlier to a later state. The development of knowledge generally, as a historical phenomenon, can be conceptualized analogously; although it is a dauntingly complex process involving the simultaneous operation of many interests and many kinds of interest.

As a scheme of things changes over time, it is in response to whatever goals and interests bear upon its evaluation, and are referred to in its development. At any point in time it is the basis and product of usage. Such is the present state of our own knowledge and classification, and of any other. We can now abandon the expedient assumption of stability with which the discussion started. Stability is a special case of the normal dynamic character of culture, wherein an ongoing usage advancing a diversity of shared goals and interests tends to reconstitute and reproduce the pattern of associations from which it initially developed.

Conclusion

The previous section developed a sociological, conventionalist account of knowledge and classification into an instrumentalist one. It is important to be clear about the characteristics of that instrumentalism. First, the goals and interests referred to are those sustained in the public domain, and they account for changes to a public phenomenon.[25] Changes in linguistic usage and associated changes in knowledge must relate to specific collective goals and interests. Even technical, predictive goals and interests vary from one context to another and are socially sustained. Insofar as a particular predictive goal structures the evaluation of knowledge, its very particularity must be understood by relating it to its social context, the existing knowledge therein, and the whole associated system of goals and interests.

This leads directly to a second point. In suggesting that specific, context-bound interests or goals feed back into and structure the evaluation of knowledge, the emphasis is on the terms *specific* and *context-bound*. I do not speak, as Habermas for example has done, of evaluation in terms of transcendental interests, since I cannot conceive of knowledge being rationally evaluated in relation to every possible kind of prediction and control.[26] This would require the simultaneous management of every probability on an entire Hesse network and the simultaneous evaluation of innumerable cognitive strategies. There is no method for such management and no criterion for such evaluation. Contingent restrictions in cognition are essential to coherent learning and anything one might be inclined to call the growth of knowledge.

Third, in no sense are classifications or beliefs *for* this or that. Still less are there different *kinds* of knowledge: "science" "for" technical-predictive interests; "ideology" "for" socio-political interests. Bodies of knowledge lack intrinsic features which would permit them to be described as of this or that kind. Such language is merely an unsatisfactory way of referring to how a body of knowledge is predominantly used at a given time. Its deficiencies become apparent when people change the way they use their knowledge and culture, and the "ideology" of one period bafflingly transforms itself into the science of another, or vice versa.

It is not even necessarily the case that alternative modes of use of a body of knowledge must interfere or conflict with each other. Karam animal taxonomy, for example, gives no sign of having been developed as a symbolic representation of an aspect of the social order *rather than* as an instrumentally applicable set of terms and generalizations. Bulmer's paper makes clear the instrumental adequacy of Karam knowledge.

Karam possess practical knowledge of *kobtiy* — their appearance, habits, behavior, and so on. Nor are there grounds for assuming that they have lost technical information or been encumbered with misleading or unreliable generalizations by making a contrast between "yakt" and "kobtiy." Karam culture, we might loosely say, is multifunctional, as a consequence of its development in a long historical process wherein many interests have borne in upon its users.

That such multifunctional development is *always* possible is easy to show by a general argument. Imagine a network with a structure which constitutes an adequate response to some specific interest or objective. Such a structure can then be adapted to a second interest, without losing any of its relevance to the first, simply by a differentiation of terminology. Imagine, for example, that the part of a network surrounding the natural kind term *man* has developed and stabilized in relation to technical-instrumental interests. It is always possible, at any time, to replace "man" with alternative concepts in a way which takes account of additional interests. "Noble/commoner," or "saved/damned," or any number of analogous substitutions may be made, with all existing relevant network generalizations being linked to the new terms separately so that nothing of the existing communal knowledge is lost.

This last point is merely a variant of the general argument of the essay. The analysis of the conventional character of knowledge and cognition pivoted around one central, all-important theme: conventions are open-ended; their future development is not determined by their earlier development or their intrinsic features, but remains a matter for those employing them. Since concepts are conventional orderings, it follows that concept application must be studied as the contingent linguistic activity of those using the concepts. The sociology of knowledge is just like any other brand of sociology in that its basic concern is the study of human action. And from this it can derive a useful touchstone for the general merit of its theories and hypotheses. If something is possible at the level of action, whether it be a conflict of goals and interests, a specialization and differentiation of tasks in relation to them, or the development of a multifunctional practice, it is also possible at the level of knowledge and ideas.

Notes

1. For a recent review of this field see B. Barnes and D. Edge, eds., *Science in Context* (Milton Keynes: Open University Press, 1982).

2. M. Hesse, *The Structure of Scientific Inference* (London: Macmillan, 1974).

3. Animal kind terms are not well suited to the illustration of the instrumental character of schemes of classification. Much better would be terms like *catalyst, reagent, fertilizer,*

antibiotic, enzyme, and the like. Nor is the way our knowledge deals with temporal sequence, process, and narrative well illustrated by the use of natural kind terms. But this merely makes animal kinds hard cases for the discussion which follows, and hence adds to the force of the argument.

4. In this discussion "term" and "concept" will be used interchangeably, and neither should be interpreted with undue precision.

5. The process of ostension is complex, and an endless source of problems. For an extended discussion of the difficulty of understanding ostensive learning cf. D. Campbell, *Descriptive Epistemology* (Cambridge: Harvard University Press, 1979).

6. For all its isomorphism with Hesse's "network model of universals," the network actually constructed here is different. There is, in the present instance, no question of the network's being constructed, as is Hesse's, out of true or false propositions.

7. I use the term "tension" in deliberate allusion to "extension" as used in philosophical semantics. In the extension of a term are thought to be included all the entities to which it properly applies or of which it is true. In the tension of a term are included only past instances of use — a finite number of instances. To talk merely of the tension of a term is to accept that its future proper usage is indeterminate. To talk of an extension is to imply that future proper usage is determined already.

8. Because concepts are employed open-endedly, any state of identity between the nets of individuals would be unstable, and would immediately deteriorate as those individuals cited different specific instances of concepts in using or passing on their knowledge. Hence only the overall morphology of a net is capable of becoming the common property of all the individuals of a community. This implies that the culture of a community is a highly problematic notion, and that even the most routine interpersonal communication is a very complex process demanding extended empirical study if its accomplishment is to be understood.

9. T.S. Kuhn, "Second Thoughts on Paradigms," in *The Essential Tension* (Chicago: University of Chicago Press, 1977).

10. The need for such an understanding is greatest not in order to make sense of the creative extension of usage but to properly appreciate what is involved in the most mundane routine examples of concept application. An adequate characterization of routine is perhaps the central problem of the human sciences. For present purposes three points about routine deserve to be taken into account. First, unthinking, unreflective identifications of particulars *are* made; it is a fact about ourselves, our perceptual and cognitive apparatus, that such identifications suggest themselves. Second, the formal analysis of resemblance above nonetheless remains applicable, even in the most routine cases of concept application. Third, these two points together suggest that unthinking identifications are therefore actual, but contingent and corrigible: to accept them as definitive is itself, formally speaking, a judgment — a decision not to override automatic tendencies socialized into cognition and perception.

11. Cf. L. Wittgenstein, *Philosophical Investigations* (Oxford: Blackwell, 1953).

12. R. Bulmer, "Why is the cassowary not a bird?" *Man* 2(1967):5-25.

13. R. Bulmer, p.6.

14. M. Douglas, ed., *Rules and Meanings* (London: Routledge & Kegan Paul, 1973), p.113.

15. *Yakt,* it might be said, are by definition flying animals, yet the British persist in calling *kobtiy* "yakt" without being disturbed by the contradiction; perhaps they have a prelogical mentality. All this is nonsense of course, but analogous nonsense continues to appear in the

literature.

16. The discussion implies that the languages of the Karam and ourselves are not directly intertranslatable in these instances. The emptiness of the notion of perfect translation is a general implication of the network model of concept application as developed here.

17. Those with an interest in inductive logic will find the term *induction* employed in what follows in an eccentric fashion, with little regard for what should count as a *good* inductive inference.

18. Cf. J.S. Bruner, J.J. Goodnow, and G.A. Austin, *A Study of Thinking* (New York: 1956).

19. Consider the problems which would be experienced on being told: "I no longer believe that ducks have webbed feet since all the ducks I have seen have had webbed feet."

20. See Hesse.

21. There are a number of treatments of this problem in the literature. I myself discuss it at some length in B. Barnes, *T.S. Kuhn and Social Science* (London: Macmillan, 1982). See also D. Bloor in this volume.

22. Note how difficult it is to state precisely what a theory *is*, and how questionable any particular answer always turns out to be. This is precisely because we wrongly assume the independence of cognitive processes and the thing they are determined by — the theory.

23. My answer suggests that linguistic and cultural change is intelligible in terms of goals and interests in much the same way as social change generally: it makes a bet, as it were, on that general explanatory approach within the social science which relies on interests and ends rather than values or functions (in the sense usually accepted in sociology). This general approach is carried forward by a wide range of fields and cannot be assessed simply within the perspective of the sociology of knowledge. There is no point here in reviewing the well-known general problems it faces or present indications of its overall promise. Its relevance in the present context is explained in B. Barnes, *Interests and the Growth of Knowledge* (London: Routledge & Kegan Paul, 1977), and its utility in empirical studies of scientific knowledge is apparent in D. MacKenzie, *Statistics in Britain, 1865-1930* (Edinburgh: Edinburgh University Press, 1981) and B. Barnes and S. Shapin eds., *Natural Order* (London: Sage, 1979).

24. See for example J. Dean, "Controversy over Classification," in Barnes and Shapin, n. 23.

25. What a pity that Quine chose to put his most beautiful formation of his pragmatist viewpoint in the singular: "Each man is given a scientific heritage plus a continuing barrage of sensory stimulation; and the considerations which guide him in warping his scientific heritage to fit his continuing sensory promptings are, where rational, pragmatic." W.V.O. Quine, *From a Logical Point of View* (Cambridge: Harvard University Press, 1953), p.43.

26. J. Habermas, *Knowledge and Human Interests* (London: Heinemann, 1972).

8

The Triple Legitimation:
A Model for a Sociology of Knowledge

Gérard Namer

Hypothesis

The sociology of knowledge is only conceivable as a study of the social legitimation of communicable representations. This implies that it must be based on both a sociology of legitimation and a sociology of the mass media.[1] It is advisable to separate the sociology of knowledge from the sociology of ideology, and treat the latter as a special case of the sociology of social imagination. Conversely, it is equally advisable to integrate the sociologies of science and of knowledge. The sociology of science should serve as a model for the sociology of knowledge, and the latter in turn be considered as a sociology of epistemological legitimation. The proper domain of the sociology of knowledge is consequently the "social construction of reality," to use the title of Berger and Luckmann's splendid book.[2] *I therefore call knowledge everything that passes for knowledge, i.e., that is legitimated as such by a particular authority in a particular society.*

I am indebted to Ziman's[3] notion of a social itinerary of knowledge. Ziman describes the process through which scientific knowledge acquires its legitimation: initially the work is presented as a typed text, then as a conference presentation, later as a journal article, and eventually it attains its final status of social recognition. Once the work becomes a chapter of a textbook, an item in an encyclopedia, or is even awarded a Nobel prize, the itinerary is completed.

The social itinerary of knowledge — in this case the itinerary of scientific knowledge — is thus the process by means of which social significance is added to the epistemological significance. The significance increases in relation to the social distance covered and the speed with which it is covered. This particular model of a social itinerary of knowledge is not derived from a physical theory of communication. Even if its idea is useful, we depart from it for the following reasons: the scientific and, more generally, the scholarly creator attempts to achieve recognition for his discovery by convincing others, arguing, or negotiating, thus leading the discovery on an itinerary from significant people to other significant people, from institution to institution. In contrast to the physical theory of communication, there is no sender, no message, and no receiver; there is instead a sender who relentlessly accompanies his message to the gates of the scholarly community (*cité savante*) and takes it, if possible, to the mass media.

The general idea I am suggesting here is that the social itinerary undergoes a triple legitimation: *by the scholarly community, by the mass media, and through acknowledgement by a social group.* This triple legitimation satisfies my definition of the sociology of knowledge. Historical knowledge, for example, is a totality comprising scientific history (e.g., a thesis on the Catharists), the historical event as constructed by the mass media (e.g., a "drama" or debate on a subject), and the historical event as received and conserved in social memory (*mémoire sociale*).

Apart from the itinerary I have described, which begins with scientific knowledge, I hypothesize that there are other possible itineraries actualized in the form of feedback by taking their point of departure from individual, serial, or collective creations. These other itineraries attempt to break the monopoly of the scholarly establishment. Collective creation depends on the particular type of knowledge and the structural context of the larger society. We may point to serial creation in the technical field, collective creation in the spheres of politics and mores, collective or serial creation in cooking or magic, pharmacopeia, chiropractic, and techniques for body relaxation. This scheme of a triple legitimation takes on a specific form depending on the type of knowledge. The itinerary is not always complete, and if there is no correspondence between the type of collective knowledge and the type of scholarly knowledge then there is no feedback.

Scholarly Knowledge

Scientific knowledge is produced in a social setting, for instance in the laboratory. It is brought into being by an experimental procedure involving specialized equipment, material techniques, and logical mathematical reasoning. We take scientific knowledge as a model of scholarly knowledge, by reference to the legitimation and institutionalization process. Knowledge is whatever passes for knowledge in an institution that guards the rules of legitimation. In 2000 B.C., for example, scholarly knowledge was divination. It was scholarly knowledge insofar as the rules for dissecting the liver or reading the signs were codified and the men entrusted with these operations were subjected to political controls regulating their number and defining their monopoly on knowledge.[4] This implies that a particular type of knowledge can emerge or vanish following the fate of society. Just as divination was once considered knowledge by virtue of institutional legitimation, so religion was considered knowledge by virtue of its control and dissemination by the church. An institution — the Holy Office, for example — was endowed with the power of legitimation through intuitive, affective thought procedures. This is neither science nor always truth, but it does involve an evaluation. In both cases legitimation procedures are operative. We may also speak of scholarly knowledge in the case of a school of painting which theorizes about its production, judges a piece of work in terms of its originality and its conformity vis-à-vis the school's techniques and outlook. Here the consensus on aesthetic taste is as important as judgment on techniques and theoretical perspective.

Whether it is the nature of Jesus, of the atom, or of perspective that is at stake, the scholarly community confers degrees of truth or value to the new work and establishes the category of knowledge and the school to which it belongs. Each scholarly community ensures the recognition of a work as new and acceptable, thus providing a memory, an accumulation of acquired knowledge.

The legitimation rules of this scholarly knowledge ensure the *relative autonomy* of knowledge in relation to global society. This autonomy is only relative, because the global society controls the knowledge community and its power of legitimation. The very existence of the scholarly community depends on certain legal ground rules: the teaching of a particular type of knowledge may be prohibited (e.g. psychoanalysis in the Soviet Union) or merely tolerated but not institutionalized (e.g. chiropractic in France). The first act of regulation on the part of the global society is the granting of professional status to a group of knowers. Further regulations encourage or discourage the accumulation and distribution of knowledge by controlling financial resources, granting access to the mass media, by the possibility of communicating knowledge to others in particular institutions. Scholarly legitimation is made possible by the different religious, ideological, economic, administrative, and political powers; it is also made possible by the powers of the previously established communities of scholars.

Once the power of legitimation is accorded, the autonomy of the scholarly community is established. A social need for scholarly legitimation appears. Even as powerful a figure as Stalin, who was able to physically eliminate any scholar, needed scholarly legitimations to support his views on linguistics. The autonomy of a scholarly community is itself a power base. The autonomy of the scholarly community cannot be reduced to its conflicts with global society. Once the scholarly community has acquired its right to exist and to elaborate and disseminate knowledge, its relative

autonomy becomes a complex internal process. The dual tradition —
Marxist and American — of the sociology of knowledge has had the merit
of emphasizing the regulatory action of needs, ideologies, and social
models of global society on the establishment of a system and a method of
scholarly legitimation. However, if there is in fact a constitutive action between the needs of a society and the birth of a science, it is an *indirect
constitutive* action. Merton has demonstrated the gap as well as the interplay during the seventeenth and eighteenth centuries between the needs in
navigation and the appearance of scientific theories that led to Newton's
achievement.[5] Technical findings corresponding to economic needs rise to
a theoretical plane (Newton) only by reusing and formalizing the empirical data supplied by technique. Similarly, between ideologies and social
imagination on the one hand and method on the other, there are as many
gaps as continuities.

Scholarly creativity plays a decisive role in filling the gaps and sustaining formalization. It is quite justified to establish a correspondence
between the use of statistics in sociology and the ideology of a world consisting of independent and interchangeable individuals. We can even
admit that a dominant social structure — e.g., the capitalist market or the
captive citizenry of a state bureaucracy — may find their reflection in sociological models. We may well suppose that such models become
crystallized into a method; however, it is evident that this formalization is
an invention, a new system which takes into account both the
logical-mathematical knowledge previously accumulated and the exact
nature of the social phenomenon studied, in this case mass society, where
isolated men herded together collide with each other like gas particles.
The increase in the number and frequency of dissemination can in the
same way become such an important phenomenon that it may be used as a
model for the new biological or microphysical theories. But there, too, the
essential part in invention is played by the matrix of formalization: the
epistemological gap between imagination, social models and method ensures the relative autonomy of the scholarly community and its
legitimation power.

The Social Itinerary of Scholarship

Scientific knowledge not only differs from nonscientific knowledge,
but varies according to the type or degree of scientificity. Given the
frequent phenomenon of schools competing within the scholarly community, a general model may be proposed and illustrated with examples
drawn from the historical sciences. The establishment of scholarly
legitimation takes place in three phases which are at once phases of episte-

mological and social legitimation. These three phases may be called: *admissibility*, *validity*, and *significance*. In the case of historiography, with the exception of totalitarian societies, several schools are in competition. In France, for example, there are at least three such schools: positivist, Marxist, and Annales.

The phase of admissibility is that in which at least a minimal recognition takes place, permitting the competing schools to coexist in the scholarly community or at an international congress. Explicit rules of consensus appear: rules to date facts, external and internal criticism of documents. These are rules established by the nineteenth-century positivist school. In this phase there is also at least a minimal recognition of the method of each school and of still usable past work. When historians of different schools agree to approve a thesis, there appears, at first implicit, a consensus of legitimation between the schools. This agreement grants a university degree to the author and epistemological recognition to his work. It recognizes the work as original, as well as in conformity with epistemological legitimation: the scholarly creation thus becomes socially *admissible*. At this level the scholarly community determines scholarly knowledge.

The second phase of scholarly legitimation transforms the new knowledge now considered admissible into *valid* knowledge. This is the phase where the work moves from recognition by a particular school to recognition by the entire scholarly community. This is also the phase where Ziman's schema of the itinerary of scholarly legitimation belongs, which passes from the typed text to the laboratory and from there to the fringe of the scholarly community into textbooks and encyclopedias. Here we must distinguish between the operation of the media and the impact of significant figures within the scholarly community. The significant figures of each school attempt to establish a journal for at least two reasons: to make the works of the school known and to give the school and its journal a legitimating power.

A hierarchy of learned journals is thus established and the strategy of the author and his research team consists in achieving the publication of their text in the journal with the highest standing. The significant figures of the minority schools enter into negotiation with the editors of the main journals of the dominant school. This occurs not only by way of the usual process of exchange of favors and temporary alliances, but also because the dominant journal cannot maintain its role unless it includes at least a minimum of articles from the minority schools, generally those most compatible with the journal's orientation.

A similar process takes place in regard to quoting and referencing. The speed at which admissible knowledge is diffused, reviews in the media, publication in specialized journals, as well as the number of citations, all contribute to granting to scholarly knowledge the status of valid knowledge. Valid knowledge is established by way of both epistemological and sociological ratification.

In the third phase of scholarly legitimation this admissible and valid knowledge achieves the status of a knowledge which is both epistemologically and socially *significant*. In this third phase the first two legitimations — scholarly legitimation and legitimation by the media — become manifest. This phase varies according to the type of knowledge. Generally, knowledge is considered epistemologically significant for the scholarly community if it gives a new direction to theory and opens new research perspectives. If it accomplishes both, it is selected by the scholarly community for general diffusion to a wider audience. In the human sciences, this encourages its dissemination by the scholarly media, for example in weeklies read by intellectuals and in specialized radio programs. In this manner the scholarly community, through eminent scientists, encourages the legitimation of significant work.

Legitimation by the Media

Legitimation of knowledge by the media varies from society to society, from one medium to another, and from one type of knowledge to another. While I propose a model here, only empirical analysis will be able to establish the concrete itinerary of a particular piece of scholarly knowledge. To once again take up the example of historical knowledge, history is everything that passes for history in a given society. History includes not only the intellectual history legitimated by the community of scholarly historians, but also the history consecrated in a thousand ways by the media and, beyond this, the history received, conserved, and elaborated by different publics. Legitimation by the media suggests that the relative autonomy of the community of scholars does not preclude a continuity of a social itinerary of scholarly knowledge. The second legitimation consists in the constitutive and regulating effect of the media on the knowledge legitimated by the scholarly community.

The Regulating Effect of the Mass Media

Each medium — paperback, radio, cinema, television — brings with it a certain prestige as well as a capacity to reach audiences which varies in extent, duration, and speed. Each medium provides different emotional and dramatizing qualities. The first type legitimates knowledge by making it a matter of public interest and discussion and thereby provides at least the possibility of consensus. This phenomenon was already apparent in the first newspapers of the seventeenth and eighteenth centuries, where in the intellectual world and in the world of the court there was a new fear of being mentioned in the newspaper as well as an obsession with having read it. As a place of social ratification, the media owe their power to their ability to create specialized aesthetic knowledge, which permits scholarly knowledge to be known differently, establishing a new cognitive structure. We are beginning to see here a particular linking of time and space, the imaginary and the real, the serious and the entertaining. The media sometimes derive secondary powers of legitimation from other domains: their official character in relation to political power (television) or cultural power (radio).

This first type of link between scholarly legitimation and the mass media is characterized by the hegemony of the former over the latter: the seventeenth-century newspaper gained prestige once it became a source of prestigious news from the republic of letters. The natural sciences during the seventeenth and eighteenth centuries used the semipublic letter and the newspaper in this way. History in the nineteenth century became diffused through the feuilleton, the popular novel, the opera. The scholarly history legitimated by the scholarly community pursued a didactic course, not only through popularization but also by finding expression in different genres: romantic fiction, round table discussions or debates among historians on the occasion of the publication of a new book, radio quiz shows, historical allusions during a political program or interview.

The media have a regulating effect on historical knowledge by making scholarly knowledge more prestigious, more accessible, and more widely distributed. At the same time, it also fragments knowledge, for example the historical knowledge previously unified by scholarly knowledge. The social construction of historical knowledge produced by each medium (cinema, press, radio, television) and the different genres within each medium (didactics, fiction, news, games) in which this knowledge is elaborated result in a construction and diversification of this historical knowledge.

The regulating effect of the media on scholarly historical knowledge tends to transform this knowledge and legitimate new historical knowledge which is from the beginning a media creation. The regulating effect is transformed into a constitutive effect.

The Constitutive Effect of the Media on Historical Knowledge

If the trajectory of books and the scholarly community which uses them provide one model of coordination between scholarly and media legitimation, another model appears with growing force in the challenge which media legitimation sometimes poses to the hegemony of scholarly legitimation. The media have an autonomous constitutive effect on historical knowledge: they create other facts, other logics, other historical proofs, and another quasi-historical scholarly community.

While during the past fifty years scholarly knowledge has favored economic, social, and cultural history, or the history of manners, the media have shown a preference for the history of events, which had been expelled from scholarly history. A historical fact is no longer selected in accordance with the logic or the premises of the historian, but according to a consensus between journalists as to which are the important events of the day, month, or year.

Therefore spectacular events lend themselves to being understood and received with intense interest by a broad public and constitute the historical facts of contemporary history, being presented as "immediate history." Already between the two world wars, totalitarian societies transformed radio speeches into historical events. Today this tendency has become general; political events — the taking of hostages, the hijacking of planes — are designed for the media. Conversely, the media create political events. They are not merely present at press conferences but their leading figures invent original situations: meetings, debates, unusual interviews.

This selection or creation of historical facts by the media brings the media's own analysis into competition with scholarly proof. In the media, rules other than those associated with scholarly proof determine the verification of historical hypotheses. The first of these rules dominates the disputes between historians, politicians, or witnesses of a past. This rule, established by the referee, is the rule of consensus: the discussion is geared toward a conclusion in which differences have been reduced to a minimum. The logic of the proof and of the scientific polemic between the opponents is limited by the norm of fair play which stipulates that each participant should speak alternately and for an equal length of time. Since all participants must be allowed to speak and since the debate must conclude with a formula which satisfies the common-sense understanding of even the average listener, these aesthetic requirements and those of a synthesis eradicate the epistemological differences between historians of different schools, as well as those between amateur historians, authors of memoirs, journalist-historians, and scholarly historians.

The second rule of legitimation substitutes proof by means of perception for scholarly proof by means of calculation or reasoning. Television is the best example, since it transforms the ordinary techniques of persuasion and spectacularization into rules of historical proof. Thus a proof is created and legitimized in a medium which consists of moving from commentary to audio-visual image and back again. Proof comes to mean the art of rendering the rationality of the discourse perceptible or, on the contrary, giving a rational coherence to the proposed audio-visual image. The authority of the film specialist or moderator takes the place of scholarly proof. This is how specialist journalists come to constitute a quasi-scholarly community: they claim to render coherent the immediate history consecrated by the media from day to day. Scholarly history is thus challenged by those who have power over the facts, which are organized in terms of a logic derived from the prestige of mass communication media.

Conflict between Legitimations and Media Feedback

The media both regulate knowledge legitimized by the scholarly community and simultaneously regulate and constitute a specific form of historical knowledge. Before a social itinerary of scholarly knowledge linking both forms of legitimation can be constructed, coordination or a hierarchy must be established between them. This itinerary does not occur without conflict, without negotiations between the leading authorities of the legitimation process. The initiative comes from the scholarly community which attempts to ensure the recognition of the import of a book, exhibition, or play, by securing several reviews through networks of contact. The importance and number of reviews in the special sections of daily newspapers and weeklies, and the intensity of personal contact with the leading media people potentially determine access to media of even wider impact: radio and television.

In the human sciences, legitimation by the mass media thus eclipses the importance of canons of epistemological legitimation. Within the university an author acquires his reputation and importance without regard to a clear distinction between the epistemological and social domains. The legitimation of an author's importance by the scholarly community is thus short-circuited. This very possibility of short-circuiting threatens the status of leading authorities in the scholarly community, who seek to maintain their power by securing positions as critics, series editors, and media specialists. Conversely, this short-circuiting also affects the eminent media figures who, originally without weight in the scholarly community, nevertheless manage to enter it owing to the power of the media.

Sometimes the short-circuit assumes the form of a bond between two eminent people: the scholarly authority knows which media person to contact when rapid dissemination is needed. Conversely, a historical specialist in the media knows that he can, if needed, rely on the scholarly authority for an urgent television program.

The conflict of legitimation varies with the media. It increases from the press via the radio to television. The scholarly community's penetration of the major publishing houses and high-culture journals leads to a situation where the legitimation conflict merely consists in the opposition of one particular section of the leading scholars and representatives of the dominant schools of criticism found in the publishing houses to those historians who do not partake in these established currents. In the sphere of radio, legitimation conflicts depend on the schools and publishing companies. We need only recall Sartre, who never taught at a university but nevertheless was able to establish himself in the university milieu through paperbacks, theatre, and radio. To become important in the scholarly community by means of radio, a historian must already possess certain scholarly credentials.

In the case of television the legitimation conflict is total. It is not merely restricted to the legitimation of significance but often affects the credentials of the historian himself, or even his very admissibility. Sometimes television imposes mundane historians without scholarly credentials or journalist-historians who use their credentials as journalists to play the part of contemporary historians.

The Third Legitimation: Variations in Public Reception

Public reception and the use of knowledge endorsed by the media at the end of the scholarly itinerary make up the third and final stage of legitimation. The reception of scholarly knowledge is determined by varying degrees of confidence in the media; it is organized by the cultural filters of different groups; and it finally is influenced by ideological apriority and social preconceptions. Specialized knowledge, the media, and the public are linked, and each social group grants a different hierarchy of general prestige to the media. For example, fishermen who receive information at sea about the market price of fish, information which changes their fishing behavior, have at least in the sphere of economic knowledge greater confidence in the radio than in television or newspapers. The conditions of reception of a particular kind of knowledge depend on the medium used.

We might want to inquire about the respective general hierarchy of influence granted to the media by each particular group and ask whether this hierarchy derives from professional practice, cultural tradition, or dominant political opinions. It is probable that the general hierarchy of media specific to each group changes in accordance with the particular type of knowledge: for the same fisherman the parish newspaper may be first in the media hierarchy in matters of religious knowledge. The reception of historical knowledge by fishermen does not only depend on the hierarchy of media, even if the latter can refer to an authentic cultural history: resistance of the oral tradition or of dialect to literacy, for example, will lead to a preference for the oral rather than the written media. On the other hand, in the old Protestant regions of the Cevennes, where the oral Protestant tradition was strengthened by secular school attendance, books and newspapers are preferred.

As long as the traditional community culture of an ethnic, religious, or ideological group, or the culture of a minority or of a group of partisan followers survives, the group is structured by cultural filters. Those who culturally control the group tend to continually update and confirm the group's hierarchy of types of knowledge, and this hierarchy constitutes a first cultural filter. This is the lesson to be learned from Gurvitch.[6] We can also use Berger and Luckmann's notion of the "social stock of knowledge" by asking how each individual ensures the hierarchy of his roles and each group the hierarchy of its functions. We can finally distinguish in each profession a body of functional knowledge and a body of knowledge perspectives used as points of orientation.

The second cultural filter which either encourages or discourages the recognition of knowledge is characterized by cognitive mechanisms already present: language, a logical system of demonstration, cultural familiarity. The historical romance could thus be related to the oral tradition of folk tales, scholarly history to the history reported in text books or to the collective memory of a specific group.

The recognition of history is determined by each group's own imaginary expectation of the historical narration: such a group may be based on age or sex as much as on partisanship or profession. A favorable attitude toward history can be associated with nationality (the French love history) as much as with age: history teachers know from experience that twelve-year-olds love history while teenagers no longer do. Later on, old people like history more than the middle-aged, and men more than women. Thus, for reasons associated with social and cultural conflicts, there may be either a positive attitude toward a media's historical program or irritation instead, or even its a priori rejection.

Conclusion

Legitimation Feedback

The itinerary of social knowledge — legitimation by scholars, by the media, and by the public — is not the only possible itinerary. It is the dominant one. Other itineraries based on the collective memory or oral tradition have competed with the scholarly itinerary for a long time. This competition of itineraries and their relative autonomy is gradually disappearing in Europe due to the processes of cultural unification brought about by literacy in a national language and later continued by the mass media.

During the nineteenth century industrialization and urbanization destroyed the forms through which oral tradition was transmitted in such a way that the collective memories were deformed. Since the 1960s, a reverse movement has begun to take place, with the mass media inspiring a renewal of collective memories. Everywhere regional memories are increasing: the memories of minorities, of forgotten generations, of long-lost professions. These published memories concern no longer only prestigious political actors, but often also simple people. We are confronted with a social need: different groups want to establish a particular memory and make it public through the media. This need is a new factor and tends to reset the itinerary of legitimations.

We now proceed from the social memory of a group toward the collective memory, thanks to paperbacks, radio, or television which eagerly embrace all forms of oral transmission. The problem of a contradictory multiplicity of memories is posed by the media and must be resolved by the scholarly community. The scholarly community must make coherent both these earlier contradictory memories and the immediate history written by journalists. Historical legitimation now tends to originate in a reverse itinerary of legitimation: the historian who participates in a regional or minority memory is motivated both by the desire to actualize his own memory and to bring order into the contradictory memories.

History, Physics, Religion, and Aesthetics

This model of a triple legitimation which I have described for the historical sciences is here proposed as a model for a sociology of knowledge. If it is kept flexible, this model may help account for both strictly scientific knowledge, such as physics, and nonscientific knowledge, such as religion or aesthetics.

Unlike the human sciences, the physical sciences look to the media mainly for a legitimation of their social rather than their scholarly significance. Where the media are able to short-circuit the legitimation of scholarly significance we find a few exceptions, for example in the case of spectacular themes which capture the imagination of the public and which are usually associated either with an emerging or still unsettled science (vulcanology, the big bang theory of astronomy, cancer research). Public debates concerning epistemological conflicts are similarly discredited by the natural scientific scholarly community, whereas scholars in the human sciences tend to approve of them. The scholarly community nevertheless creates internal institutions of confrontation and dissemination which it controls. These fields are receptive to feedback from the collective memory (pharmacopea, vulcanology). There is also indirect feedback in the forms of legitimation of significance by the media and legitimation by public reception: this feedback determines the politics of the reputation accorded to science as well as its social prestige.

In the sphere of religious knowledge, this model works only if we distinguish within the church between the levels of the scholarly community (Holy Office) and mass media; here the church plays the role of medium with its own authorities of transmission. Modes of feedback differ from epoch to epoch: new currents attempt to win publics, create new distribution networks, use particular media to achieve recognition and legitimation by the scholarly community. We may recall the intense conflicts between the mystics and the church. The hegemony of scholarly legitimation is always assured: either the individual or collective work is rejected or it experiences a scholarly reelaboration.

This scientific model can be applied to aesthetic knowledge only in totalitarian societies and in periods during which academicism dominates. In liberal societies the very plurality of schools provides an analogy to the schools of historical science. A fundamental difference is that the process of legitimating validity and importance follows different routes: a school of painting which can ensure that a work becomes acceptable possesses both an informal network of distribution (exhibition halls) and an official one (connections with municipal or state officials responsible for art purchases).

Scholarly legitimation thus occurs by way of success both in the hierarchy of critics and in that of exhibition halls. It is equally possible to receive a good review as a result of exhibiting in a good hall as it is to exhibit in a good hall as a result of receiving a good review. These different scientific, religious, and aesthetic examples suggest that the triple legitimation model can assume abridged or inverted forms. It should also be pointed out that this triple legitimation often tends to constitute collective memories.

There is throughout society a shared body of a priori assumptions: on the one hand both a collective and a group-specific common sense, on the other hand an a priori sentiment of creativity characteristic of a particular society. The eighteenth century, for example, with its fantasies of America and its utopias, permitted the mind free reign in its search of the Idea. Our century hopes to discover the new in the very nature of the destructuration of knowledge or the collapse of established values.

This sentiment of creativity is to a greater or lesser extent shared by such typical creators as scholars or painters, and it conditions from the beginning the different scholarly communities by the evidence of their creation. This, along with common sense and the collective memory, is another example of feedback from legitimated scholarly knowledge foreshadowing the knowledge of the future.

Notes

Translated from the French by Judith Adler and Volker Meja

1. I have discussed some of the notions developed here in greater detail in the following books: Gérard Namer, *Machiavel ou Les origines de la sociologie de la connaissance* (Paris: PUF, 1979), and Gérard Namer, *Rousseau: sociologue de la connaissance* (Paris: Klincksieck, 1978).

2. Peter L. Berger and Thomas Luckmann, *The Social Construction of Reality* (London: Allen Lane, Penguin Press, 1967).

3. J.M. Ziman *Public Knowledge: An Essay Concerning the Social Dimension of Science* (Cambridge: Cambridge University Press, 1968).

4. J.P. Vernant , L. Van der Meersch, J. Gernet, et al., *Divination et rationalité* (Paris: Seuil, 1974).

5. Robert K. Merton, "Eléments de théories et méthodes sociologiques," in *Science et économie dans l'Angleterre du 17e siècle* (Paris: Plon, 1970), pp. 404ff., ch. 13.

6. Georges Gurvitch, *Les cadres sociaux de la connaissance* (Paris: PUF, 1966).

9

The Fabrication of Facts:
Toward a Microsociology of Scientific Knowledge

Karin Knorr-Cetina

My lord, facts are like cows. If you look them in the face
hard enough, they generally run away.

— Dorothy L. Sayers

Facts and Fabrication

Dorothy Sayers's analogy between cows and facts hides both a philosophical and a methodological point. Since both will guide us throughout
this essay, I will begin by discussing each at some length. The philosophical point is that facts are not something we can take for granted or think
of as the solid rock upon which knowledge is built. Their nature is problematic — so much so that confrontation often scares them off. The
methodological point is that the confrontation has to be long, hard, and direct. Like cows, facts have become sufficiently domesticated to deal with
run-of-the-mill events.

That facts are problematic has been known to philosophers for some
time. The quest for the nature of facts — the core of the quest for the nature of knowledge — is a major reason for the proliferation of epistemological theories. The key dispute is where to locate the problem and how to
approach it. Kant, for example, saw the quest as a search for the conditions of possibility of pure science, and found his answer in the categorical
make-up of the human mind.

Recent theories of knowledge have tended to transfer the problem
from a knowing subject's constitution of the factual to a variety of other
locations. Most influential, perhaps, is the shift toward the logic of scientific inference advocated by what some have called objectivism.[1] To the
objectivist, the world is composed of facts and the goal of knowledge is to
provide a literal account of what the world is like. The empirical laws and
theoretical propositions of science are designed to provide those literal descriptions.[2] If the knowledge of scientific accounts is reality represented by
science, an inquiry into the nature of the real becomes an investigation of

how the logic of scientific accounts preserves the lawlike structure of the real.[3]

Can we say, then, that the problem of facticity is to be located in the correspondence between the products of science and the external world, and that the solution is to be found in the descriptive adequacy of scientific procedure? There is more than one negative answer to such a proposal. To begin with, while objectivism (in accordance with Marx) stresses the constraints (here identified with nature) which limit the products of science, it is itself oblivious to the constituted character of these products. Peirce has made it the point of his work to argue that the process of scientific inquiry ignored by objectivism (its "context of discovery") is itself the system of reference which makes the objectification of reality possible.[4] The problem of facticity is as much a problem of the constitution of the world through the logic of scientific procedure as it is one of explanation and validation. While the work of Bohm, Hanson, Kuhn, and Feyerabend may not have resulted in a satisfactory model of scientific success, it is generally credited with pointing to the meaning variance or theory dependence of scientific observation.[5]

Objectivism has been criticized within its own ranks for assuming a factual world structured in a lawlike manner by the constant conjunction of events. According to this critique, constant conjunctions of events result from laboratory work which creates closed systems in which unambiguous results are possible and repeatable. In practice, such constant conjunctions are exceptions — as is predictive success.[6] The laws proposed by science are transfactual and rulelike, rather than descriptively adequate. The practical success of science depends more on the scientist's ability to analyze a situation as a whole, to think on several different levels at once, recognize clues, and piece together separate bits of information, than on the laws themselves.

Equally relevant is that models of success which do not require the basic assumptions of objectivism are both thinkable and plausible, and have been proposed within the sciences themselves. Psychiatrists, for example, have often used behavioral therapy to successfully treat both major and minor psychic disorders for which they claim not to have nor need any descriptively adequate explanation. A better illustration, perhaps, is the mouse that runs from the cat.[7] Must we assume that the mouse runs because it has in its mind a correct representation of the natural enmity inherent in the cat? Is it not more plausible to say that any species which fails to run from its natural enemies will cease to exist, which leaves us only with those that did run? Like the progress of evolution itself, the progress of science can be linked to mechanisms which do not assume that knowledge mimics nature.

The critique of empirical realism adds another aspect to the constitutive role which both pragmatism and skepticism attribute to scientific investigation — that the experimenter is a causal agent of the sequence of events created and that conjunctions of events are not provided for us but created by us. The purpose of the present study is to explore how those constant conjunctions are created in the laboratory (suspending for the moment any assumptions about the vocabulary of nature). Rather than view empirical observation as questions put to nature in a language it "understands," we will take all references to the "constitutive" role of science seriously and regard scientific inquiry as a process of production. Rather than consider scientific products as somehow capturing what is, we will consider them as selectively carved out, transformed and constructed from whatever is. And rather than examine the external relations between science and the "nature" we are told it describes, we will look at those internal affairs of the scientific enterprise which we take to be constructive.

The etymology of the word *fact* reveals it as "that which has been made," in accord with its root in the Latin *facere*, to make.[8] Yet we tend to think of scientific facts as given entities, not fabrications. In the present study, the problem of facticity is seen as a problem of (laboratory) fabrications. This means that knowledge is understood in terms of the social process of production which leads to knowledge claims, a process which can be empirically analyzed and specified. Clearly, then, we step beyond philosophical theories of knowledge and their objectivist (or antiobjectivist) concerns. But I would argue that once we see scientific products as first and foremost the result of a process of construction, we can begin to substitute for those concerns, as some have suggested, an empirical theory of knowledge.[9]

The Constructivist Interpretation: Nature and the Laboratory

How do we defend the contention that scientific inquiry ought to be viewed as constructive rather than descriptive? And what exactly do we mean by this particular qualification? The first question can be answered simply. Even the briefest participation in the world of scientific investigation suggests that the language of truth and hypothesis testing (and with it, the descriptivist model of inquiry) is ill-equipped to deal with laboratory work. Where in the laboratory, for example, do we find the "nature" or "reality" so critical to the descriptivist interpretation? Most of the reality with which scientists deal is highly preconstructed, if not wholly artificial.

What is a laboratory? A local accumulation of instruments and devices within a working space composed of chairs and tables. Drawers full of minor utensils, shelves loaded with chemicals and glassware. Refrigerators and freezers stuffed with carefully labelled samples and source materials: buffer solutions and finely ground alfa-alfa leaves, single cell proteins, blood samples from the assay rats and lysozymes. All source materials have been specially grown and selectively bred. Most of the substances and chemicals are purified and have been obtained from the industry which serves science or from other laboratories. But whether bought or prepared by the scientists themselves, these substances are no less the product of human effort than the measurement devices or the papers on the desks. Nature is not to be found in the laboratory, unless it is defined as the product of scientific work.

Nor do we find in the laboratory the quest for truth which is customarily ascribed to science. To be sure, the language of scientists contains innumerable references to what is or is not true. But their usage in no way differs from our own everyday use of the term in a variety of pragmatic and rhetoric functions which do not have much to do with the epistemological concept of truth. If there is a principle which seems to govern laboratory action, it is the scientists' concern with making things "work," which points to a principle of success rather than one of truth. To make things work — to produce results — is not identical with attempting their falsification. Nor is it the concern of the laboratory to produce results irrespective of potential criticism. Scientists guard against later attacks by anticipating and countering critical questions before publication. Scientists' vocabulary of how things work, of why they do or do not work, of steps to take to make them work, does not reflect some form of naive verificationism, but is a discourse appropriate to the instrumental manufacture of knowledge in the workshop called a "lab." Success in making things work is a much more mundane pursuit than truth, and one which is constantly turned into credits in scientific everyday life via publication. Thus, success in making things work is reinforced as a concrete and feasible goal of scientific action, not the distant ideal of truth never quite attained.

"Truth" and "nature" are not the only casualties of the laboratory; the observer would find it equally difficult to locate those "theories" which are so often associated with science. Theories adopt a peculiarly "atheoretical" character in the laboratory. They hide behind partial interpretations of "what happens" and "what is the case," and disguise themselves as temporary answers to "how-to-make-sense-of-it" questions. What makes laboratory theories so atheoretical is the lack of any divorce from instrumental manipulation. They confront us as discursively crystallized experimental operations, and are in turn woven into the process of performing experimentation.

In place of the familiar alienation between theory and practice, we find an action-cognition mesh to which the received notion of a theory can no longer be adequately applied. According to the scientists themselves, theories in research are more akin to policies than creeds.[10] Such policies blend interpretation with strategic and tactical calculations, and are sustained by methodological "how-to-do-it" projections. Like the concern with making things work, policies are necessarily tied to an interest structure. Pure theory can be called an illusion the sciences have retained from philosophy.[11]

The Constructivist Interpretation II: The "Decision Ladenness" of Fact Fabrication

The inadequacy of those concepts associated with the descriptive interpretation of scientific inquiry is not surprising, given the framework in which they developed. It is no less surprising that a shift in the framework of analysis to the process of research brings new conceptions into being. We have said that this process should be seen as constructive rather than descriptive. Let us be more specific. The thesis under consideration is that the products of science are contextually specific constructions which bear the mark of the situational contingency and interest structure of the process by which they are generated, and which cannot be adequately understood without an analysis of their construction. This means that what happens in the process of construction is not irrelevant to the products we obtain. It also means that the products of science have to be seen as highly internally structured through the process of production, independent of the question of their external structuring through some match or mismatch with reality.

How can we conceive of this internal structuring of scientific products? Scientific results, including empirical data, have been characterized as first and foremost the result of a process of fabrication. Processes of fabrication involve chains of decisions and negotiations through which their outcomes are derived. Phrased differently, they require that selections be made. Selections, in turn, can only be made on the basis of previous selections: they are based on translations into further selections.

Consider a scientist sitting at an electronic table calculator and running a regression program on texture measurement data. The machine automatically selects a function along which it plots the data. But to choose among the eight functions at its disposal, it needs a criterion. Such criteria are nothing more than second order selections: they represent a choice among other potential criteria into which a first order selection can be translated. In our case, the program actually offered a choice between two criteria, maximum R^2 and minimum maximum absolute residuum. The scientist had opted for a combination of the two.

He obtains an exponential function for his data, which he says he does not like. He reruns the program, asking for a linear function, which he finds to be "not much worse" (than the exponential one). The idea, he says, is to get one type of equation, and eventually one size Beta coefficient for all runs of the problem, because it would be totally confusing to have different functions in every single case.

From observing the scientist, we might also conclude that the goal must have been to get a linear function. To reach a decision, the original task of the program was to select a function translated into the selection between one of two forms of the statistical fit of the curves. In a stepwise procedure, the scientist added translations into other criteria, such as uniformity over comparable data and linearity. He eventually chose the latter because it offered greater ease of interpretation and presentation.

In the present case, this kind of translation is seen as an inherent feature of decision making, or — to borrow an expression from Luhmann — of selectivity in general.[12] It allows us to see scientific products as internally constructed, not only with respect to the composite laboratory selections which give rise to the product, but also with respect to the translations incorporated within those selections.[13]

The scientific product can be seen as structured in terms of several orders or levels of selectivity. This complexity of scientific constructions with regard to the selections they incorporate is interesting because it suggests that scientific products are unlikely to be reproduced in the same way under different circumstances. If a scientific product is characterized by several levels of selection (or constellations of selections), it seems highly improbable that the process could be repeated, unless most of the selections are either fixed or made in a similar fashion.

Given that scientists working on a problem are related through communication, competition, and cooperation, and often share similar educations, instruments, and interest structures, the latter situation is not unusual. But this translation of selections not only points to scientific products as complex constructions incorporating layers of selectivity, but also (as we shall see) provides the threads with which laboratory selections and the products they compose are woven into the relevant contexts of research.

To reach some form of closure, selections are translated into other selections. To break up that closure, selections can be challenged on their own grounds. Selections can be called into question *because* they are selections, *because* they involve the possibility of alternative selections. If scientific objects are selectively carved from reality, they can be deconstructed by challenging the selections they incorporate. If scientific facts are fabricated in the sense that they are derived from decisions, they can be defabricated by imposing alternative decisions. In scientific inquiry the selectivity of what is incorporated into previous scientific work is itself a topic for scientific investigation. Previous selections constitute a resource which enables scientific inquiry to proceed: they supply the tools, methods, and interpretations upon which a scientist may draw in the process of research.

The "artificial" character of the scientist's most important tool, the laboratory, lies in that it is nothing more than a local accumulation of materializations from previous selections. The selections of previous investigations also affect subsequent selections by influencing the conditions of further decision making. The products of science are not only decision-impregnated, they are also decision-impregnating, in the sense that they point to new problems and predispose their solutions.

A scientist's work consists of realizing selectivity within a space constituted by previous selections, and one which is overdetermined. In more economic terms, we could say that scientific work requires the reinvestment of previous work in a cycle in which the selections generated by scientific work and their material equivalents are themselves the content and capital of the work. What is reproduced in this cycle is selectivity per se. This form of autocapitalization in regard to selectivity appears as a precondition for the accumulation of scientific results. It can be multiplied by increasing the number of scientists and financial resources. The conversion of scientific products into research money as described in recent economic models refers to this aspect.[14] We can also say it refers to scientific productivity rather than to scientific production.

The Laboratory: Context of Discovery or Validation?

To view scientific investigation as constructive rather than descriptive is to see scientific products as highly internally constructed in terms of the selectivity they incorporate. To study scientific investigation is to study the process by which the respective selections are made. Does such a study simply shift the focus of analysis from the philosophers' context of justification to that of the generation of ideas? Or from sociologists' realm of consensus formation to the origin of the discoveries about which an opinion is formed? I think not.

Let us begin with the philosopher's contention that validation is in practice a process of rational consensus formation within the scientific community.[15] Since the validators who form this community are presumably independent of the producers of knowledge, their critical judgment constitutes an objective basis of validation. However, if we look at the process of knowledge production in sufficient detail, it turns out that scientists constantly relate their decisions and selections to the expected response of specific members of this community of "validators" or to the dictates of the journal in which they wish to publish. Decisions are based on what is "hot" and what is "out," on what one "can" or "cannot" do, on whom they will come up against and with whom they will have to associate by making a specific point. The discoveries of the laboratory are made, as part and parcel of their substance, with a view toward potential criticism or acceptance (as well as with respect to potential allies and enemies).

Validations are made with an eye toward the genesis of the results being validated. Whether a proposed knowledge claim is judged plausible, interesting, unbelievable, or nonsensical, may depend on who proposed the result, where the work was done, and how it was accomplished. Scientists speak about the motives and interests[16] which presumably gave rise to the "finding," about the material resources available to those who did the research, and about "who stands behind" the results. They virtually identify the results with the circumstances of their generation. The scientific community lends crucial weight to the context of discovery in response to a knowledge claim.

On a more general level, both the producers and evaluators of knowledge claims are, according to those who favor the distinction between discovery and validation, generally members of the same "community." They are held to share a common stock of knowledge and procedures, and presumably common standards of evaluation, professional preferences, and ways of making a judgment. The validators of a knowledge claim are clients who potentially need a scientific result to promote their own investigations. The selections of previous research become a resource for continuing scientific operations, as well as being a topic of problematization in further research. The validators of a knowledge claim are often the most "dangerous" competitors and antagonists a scientist has in the struggle for credit and scientific authority.

The producers and validators who share methods and approaches, the producers and clients who need each other's services, and the competitors engaged in a struggle for credit or money cannot at the same time be assumed to be independent and, in that sense, objectively critical. Any separation between discovery and validation along these lines is not borne out if we look at scientific practice.

There is a second critique of the separation which should be made clear. We have heard that validation or acceptance, in practice, is seen as a process of consensus formation qualified as "rational" by some philosophers, and "social" by sociologists of science. But whether rational or social, the process appears to be one of opinion formation, and as such, located outside of scientific investigation. Hence, the usual classification of studies of investigation as inquiries into the context of discovery, with little or no concern for problems of validation, leading to the well-known thesis that studies of the production of knowledge in the laboratory are irrelevant to questions of acceptance.

But where do we find the process of validation if not in the laboratory itself?[17] If not in the process of laboratory decision making by which a previous result, a method or a proposed interpretation, comes to be preferred over others and incorporated into new results? What is the process of acceptance if not one of selective incorporation of previous results into the ongoing process of research production? To call it a process of opinion formation seems to provoke a host of erroneous connotations.

We do not as yet have science courts for official opinion formation with legislative power in the conduct of future research. To view consensus as the aggregate of individual scientific opinions is misleading, since (1) short of regular opinion polls we have no access to the predominant, general, or average opinions of relevant scientists, and (2) it is a commonplace in sociology that opinions have a complex and largely unknown relationship to action. So even if we knew what scientists' opinions were, we would not know which results would be consistently preferred in actual research. What we have, then, is not a process of opinion formation, but one in which certain results are solidified through continued incorporation into ongoing research.[18] This means that the locus of solidification is the process of scientific investigation, or in the terms introduced earlier, the selections through which research results are constructed in the laboratory.

The Contextuality of Laboratory Construction

Let us dwell for a moment on the idea that to study the process of production of research in the laboratory is to study part of the context of justification, or acceptance. The incorporation of an earlier result into the ongoing process of investigation is seen as a potential step toward solidification. The selection of an available method or interpretation extends its presence (for example, into one more publication) and prolongs its duration. It thereby increases the chances of its further selection and incorporation. An important question, then, is how these selections are made.

Let us first consider what the scientists themselves say when asked such a question. Much as in the case where one scientist evaluates another's work, we are referred to the specific situation in which the decision was made. When we ask, for example, why a particular instrument was chosen for a certain purpose, the response may range from "because it is expensive and rare, and I want to get to know it," to "it is more economical in terms of energy"; from "John suggested it and showed me how to use it," to "it happened to be around, so it was the easiest thing to do"; from "what I had in mind did not work, so I tried something new," to "they asked me to use this because it has just been bought and we have to show that we needed it"; from "it always works, according to my experience," to an astonished stare and the question — "well, what else could you do?"

The few examples above show that these factors have different roots and implications, that they arise from different points in the scientists' problematization preceding a decision, and that they correspond to different levels of generality. Taken together, they refer us to the varying situations scientists recall as grounds for their decisions. The existence of an energy crisis, or of the presence of a friend with a suggestion; a failure which triggers a variation in procedure, or a purchase which needs to be justified; a personal "experience" composed of the particulars of a scientific career, or official practice at a given point in time. We cannot hope to reduce these situations to a small number of criteria, much less a principle of rationality, which will allow us henceforth to predict a scientist's laboratory selections. Rather, we will have to take these selections as the product of cooccurrence and interaction of factors whose impact and relevance they happen to constitute at a given time and place, i.e., the circumstances within which the scientists operate.

Historians have long portrayed scientists' decisions as contingent upon the historical context in which they are situated, and some recent arguments in the philosophy of science also point in this direction.[19] If we take the idea of contextual contingency one step further to suggest that acceptance is a form of environmental selection analogous to the model of biological evolution, we have a plausible alternative to the model of (rational) opinion formation. Like adaptation, acceptance can be seen as the result of contextual pressures which come to bear on scientists' selections in the environmental niches provided by laboratories. If such an interpretation is taken for granted in biological evolution — why is it not an equally plausible characterization of the process of selective "survival" of scientific results? It has the advantage of specifying as potentially relevant the larger social context in which science is embedded and of which scientists' decisions form a part.

But it also has a disadvantage. If we cannot name, once and for all, the criteria according to which scientific results are chosen or eliminated, we are unable to say which selections scientists are most likely to make.[20] If the context of selection varies over time and place and as a function of previous selections, the rationale for scientific selections will likewise vary. If we add to these variable contextures the chance interactions of circumstantial variables from which selections crystallize, we cannot hope to arrive at generally valid observations about these crystallizations. We are left with the disheartening picture of an indeterminate contextual variation and a social scientist who cannot provide any definite specification of it. Those who have advocated this direction in the recent past have been accused of handing science over to the reign of irrationality, and ruling out the idea of directed or progressive scientific change.[21]

Contextual Contingency as a Principle of Change

Yet this indeterminacy need not have such disquieting implications for the social scientist, let alone implications of irrationality in regard to the selections of science. Recent developments in the theory of self-regulating systems (as well as in thermodynamics) suggest the opposite interpretation — that such indeterminacy is a necessary prerequisite for progressive, organized adaptation, and thus for survival and reconstructive change.[22] The effect of indeterminacy is no longer viewed as purely disruptive as is the "noise" of information theory which prevents correct transmittance of a signal, the "errors" in the genetic code which prevent normal biological replication, or the "perturbations" in a thermodynamic system. Rather, it is seen as the sine qua non for a progressive organization of the system toward increasing complexity, in spite of local error or loss of information.

To expound this thesis, let us look at the example of biological reproduction. We know that an "error" in the transcription of the genetic code is thought to be the cause of mutations. Yet this random event on the (strictly repetitive) genetic plane can benefit the species by creating a variation better adapted to changing environmental conditions than the original population. The species "reorganizes" itself by integrating a random mutation which has disrupted the orderly pattern of straightforward reduplication.[23]

In the language of communication theory (better suited to questions of social organization), the issue can be reformulated following Atlan.[24] Suppose we have a communicative link between two subsystems A and B. If there is no error in a message transmitted from A to B, then B will be an exact copy of A and the total information of both will be identical to that of A. If the number of errors is such that the ambiguity is identical to the amount of information A transmits, this information will be lost to such a degree that we cannot even talk about transmittance. This means that the structure of B is completely independent of that of A, and that the total information of both corresponds to that of *A* plus that of *B*. To the degree that the system depends on the communicative link between these subsystems, this total independence will amount to a destruction of the global system. With regard to the amount of information of the global system, the optimum is to have a nonzero transmission of information between *A* and *B* and a certain amount of error in this transmission.[25]

What does the claim that a certain amount of indeterminacy is constitutive for progressive self-organization suggest in the case of science? A minimal definition of scientific development seen as directed change would assume that scientific knowledge is progressively reconstructed knowledge based on the integration or elimination of earlier results, and that this reconstruction is a process of complexification. Complexification here means that the system is able to construct and reconstruct itself in new ways.

In common terminology, there are two correlates of this process. On the one hand, there is the ability of science to construct "new" information; that is, to produce innovation. On the other hand, science is apparently increasingly able to construct and reconstruct itself in response to challenges by providing solutions to the problem[26] — which is what we mean when we talk about the success of science. Both abilities are aspects of the process of complexification, which in Shannon's sense corresponds to an increase of information.[27] But without indeterminacy there could be no such increase of information. This indeterminacy seems to be nothing more than the degrees of freedom used by the system for a problem-absorbing reconstruction of itself. It becomes manifest in the observer's inability to specify in detail a small set of criteria or a principle of rationality according to which this reconstruction proceeds.

How does the idea of such a complexity-increasing reconstruction relate to the notion of contextual selection? Systems theory cannot conceive of self-organizing systems without assuming an environment to which a system responds.[28] Deprived of this notion of context, the argument introduced here makes no sense. It is the context which orients, through the selections it promotes, the process of reconstruction and development. We have introduced the notion of context here to refer to the fabric of situated variables on which the scientists base their decisions. These variables appear as the constraints upon which the scientists hold their selections to be contingent, and as the constraints they impose through decision-translations in order to reach closure in an essentially open and expanding sequence of events. Without indeterminacy with respect to these constraints, there would be no problem of closure. And without indeterminacy there would be no new constellations of selections.

The Constructivist Interpretation III: Innovation and Selection

I have drawn upon the analogies of systems theory and biological evolution to argue that the constructivist interpretation of scientific inquiry can be plausibly extended into a contextual model of scientific change in which indeterminacy (or contextual contingency and openness of selections) does not run counter to the idea of scientific success. Let us now examine the negative side of those analogies.

The idea of laboratory selections was introduced here as the link between what is normally separated into the process of acceptance and the process of investigation. I have defined investigation as constructive to emphasize the selectivity embodied in scientific results. But the notion of constructiveness not only points to the decision-laden fabrication of scientific products, but also alludes to the products of fabrication as purposefully "new" products. We have said that selectivity is itself instituted in scientific investigation. Previous scientific selections become a resource for further selections, and thus give rise to both a selective solidification and a diversification of scientific products. In biological evolution, the origin of diversification is clearly identified as a mutation. The first difficulty we face is to find the equivalent of such mutations in the process of scientific construction and reconstruction.

Toulmin's model of scientific change is the closest application of the analogy of biological evolution to the process of knowledge production of which I am aware, and he asks us to take it as a literal description.[29] According to Toulmin, at any given time we have a pool of scientific innovations and an ongoing process of natural selection among those innovations. The former rests with the creative individual scientist, the latter with the community of experts who judge the innovations.[30] Mutations are the variants produced by individual innovation, and their number depends on the degree of freedom of design at a particular time. The decisive factor in biological mutations is that they produce chance variations. With Toulmin, the element of chance is located in the freedom and creativity of the individual scientist.

This location of chance creates a major problem when the biological model is carried over to scientific (or more generally societal) development. In Toulmin's adaptation of the model, special parts of this development — the individual and innovation — are carved out and given over to chance operations. Left unaffected by chance are the actions of the scientific group and the process of selection of innovation. We recognize in this separation the classic distinction between discovery and validation. What is highly questionable is the rationale for such a separation. Why should the individual suffer (or profit) from chance while the group does not? Or why is the selection of innovation a process which makes sense and has direction while innovation itself is not?

Moreover, what do we count as innovation? In Toulmin's model, the published but not yet accepted products of scientific work constitute the pool of variations. As we have seen, however, these products are themselves the result of a complex process of selection in the laboratory. More specifically, they are the result of a directional process oriented toward the production of the new, or of innovation. This is implied when we say that the diversification of scientific products (or selectivity) is itself instituted in scientific investigation. From the point of view of the individual scientist as well, innovations are the result of intentional, directed work, and not merely chance happenings. It is the scientists' knowledge of what is a problem and what counts as a solution, educated guesses about where to look and what to ignore, and highly selective, expectation-based tinkering with the material that guides them toward an "innovative" result.

Once a result has been obtained, the careful selection of a publisher (and therefore an audience), as well as various marketing strategies, can turn a laboratory product into something which may be widely accepted as new. Nor should we forget that scientists select areas of work which have not been covered by previous research; thus their results are almost guaranteed to pass as new. Scientists constantly strive to secure personal access to resources not readily available to others (e.g., highly expensive or otherwise scarce technical instruments), thereby improving their own chances for being "first" with an innovation. In short, there is nothing nondirectional or purely random about the individual scientist's efforts toward innovation.

One consequence of the directed and constructed character of scientific "mutations" is that the scientist's socially defined being can be seen as the result of a process of individuation which consists of the identification of a person with the differential particularities of the work associated with the person's name.[31] In this way, the solidification of previous results through continued laboratory selections can be seen as leading at the same time to an accelerated diversification of scientific knowledge. Note that reference to the resource-character of selections within this accelerated diversification yields a purely formal specification: it says nothing about the substantial properties or degree of usefulness of the results. The substantial translations from which selections emerge will depend on the context in which they are taken. In this sense, "natural selection" becomes contextual reconstruction.

Apart from the purposive, directed character of scientific "mutations" and their consequences (which point more to Lamarck than to Darwin), another aspect of the present conception of research calls such analogies into question. Here laboratory selections are not linked to individual decision making but are seen as the outcome of social interaction and negotiation. Consequently, we must reject such equations as that between the individual and innovation on one hand and between the social group and validation on the other. In a trivial sense, we know that most laboratory work in the natural and technological sciences is conducted by groups, not individuals. The far less trivial implication is that both the products (including those considered innovative) and the ideas of the laboratory are social occurrences which emerge from interaction and negotiation with others. Scientific operations can only make sense within a discourse whose crystallization is found in the scriptures (the authoritative writings) of an area, but which is also constituted by the exegeses and symbolic manipulations in the laboratory.

Science has often been tied to the possibility of a special form of discourse, i.e. written communication. For example, Husserl considers writing to be the condition for the possibility of ideal objects, and therefore of scientific concepts.[32] Peirce argues that manifestation does not reveal the presence of an object but the presence of a sign, and reduces the logic of science to semiology. Derrida reminds us that the very idea of science was born in a certain epoch of writing.[33] Latour and Woolgar have recently illustrated the importance of writing in the laboratory,[34] and the sociology of science has long focused on specific aspects of scientists' written communication.

To say that without writing (in Derrida's wide sense of the word), science could not continue to exist is a commonplace. The point is that the communicative foundation of science constitutes the scientists' operations as a form of discursive interaction directed at and sustained by the arguments of others.[35] The indeterminacy which the analogy of biological evolution seeks to locate in the individual origin of innovation is rooted in the interpretive basis and social dynamics of such interaction. This social and symbolic foundation becomes most visible in the concrete negotiations of the laboratory, in the bargaining which marks the highly selective construction and deconstruction of scientific findings and leads to the continuous reconstruction of knowledge.

The social character of such discursive interaction cannot be limited to some separate context of acceptance through group consensus formation, nor can indeterminacy be isolated in individualized innovation. Innovation and acceptance are temporary stabilizations within a process of reconstruction of knowledge that is at base a social process. The origin of indeterminacy lies within the social, with its symbolic and interactional qualities, and not, as Toulmin appears to suggest, outside. The decisions which mark scientific products are locally achieved closures of this indeterminacy. It is within their social location that scientific facts can be seen as selectively constructed and reconstructed.

Internal and External Sources of Reconstruction

The lack of any simple equivalent to chance mutations throws up an analogical stumbling-block when we consider scientific development as a process of reconstruction of knowledge. The distinction between system and environment also raises difficulties when we consider the rationale for such a progressive reconstruction. For systems theory, progressive reconstruction (or an increase in complexity) is the system's response to a hypercomplex environment to which it adapts by increasing its own degree of complexity. More specifically, the internal reconstruction of a system results from a difference in complexity between system and environment.

But in scientific investigation, the accelerated reconstruction of scientific products is itself the issue of work — it is endogenous to scientific production. As we have seen, it results from the purposive and directional effort of scientists oriented toward the production of new information as defined relative to discursive problematizations.

The difficulty remains even if we switch from the notion of environmental adaptation to that of environmental selection, as required by the biological analogy. In Toulmin's model, the distinction between system and environment seems to correspond to the distinction between the internal world of science and the external affairs of a wider social context. Yet the logic of events is reversed: we do not get, first, a science-internal production of variants (innovations) and then a societal selection of those variants best adapted to the social context. According to Toulmin, the production of innovations is influenced by external factors through various channels, whereas their selective survival is regulated by the internal decisions of the scientific community (at least under normal and ideal conditions).

It is absurd, of course, to assume an opposite division of labor in which innovations are internally produced by scientists and externally selected by the nonscientific members of a society. Yet it is not clear why the former distinction, in which selective power is limited to scientists while external influences are limited to the process of research production, should necessarily be more compelling — if for no other reason than that the locus of selection is itself in the laboratory where it cannot be separated from the process of production. Thus, factors which influence the production of new information will also influence the selective solidification of previous information from which the new, to a significant degree, is derived. If the model of an evolutionary development of science emphasizes (correctly, I think) that the content of a pool of cognitive variants at a given point in science is the product of "internal" and "external" factors, it cannot claim simultaneously that the selection of these variants — which occurs largely during the production of the variants themselves — is an exclusively internal matter.

The traditional divide between the internal and external does not adequately distinguish between contexts which are relevant and irrelevant to knowledge production.[36] Neither systems theory nor theories of evolution offer immediate solutions to the problem. The difficulty is not new: we know that social systems do not have unequivocal boundaries, unlike biological organisms. To be sure, institutional and professional criteria of boundary maintenance exist, but their relevance varies with practical questions. For example, legal rules may effectively regulate access to a particular profession by means of criteria like a university degree, but do not suffice to specify the practical procedures of the respective practitioners. Boundary maintenance is itself at stake in social systems; they are at the center of continual debates and redefinitions. Along with individual scientists' everyday distinctions between "we" and "they," or between matters of "science" and matters of something else, there are degrees of freedom involved in these disputes, just as there are in the social scientist's various regenerations of the distinction. Yet I see no reason to assume a priori that the degrees of freedom between one disciplinary speciality and another are necessarily less than the degrees of freedom between scientists who work in a field and nonscientists who represent a social (or political or economic) interest in the field. If we counted their respective interactions and communications and considered the interests invoked in laboratory selections, we would most likely get the opposite impression.

Degrees of freedom as manifest in perceived borderlines must be seen as a function and not a presupposition of the self-organizing process. We cannot start from a particular division between systems like the one between the scientific community and the rest of the social context and then determine their interaction. As direct observation studies of scientific work indicate, the social context of scientific work is both more restricted and extended than the notion of a specialty community suggests. It is more restricted (more local) in that researchers draw upon a variety of variables that are situationally contingent. For example, their decisions may be influenced by measurement instruments which happen to stand around in the laboratory, or by arguments which come up in a technical discussion. The context of scientific work must be defined more broadly than previously suggested in that these variables and arguments are not, in principle, limited to (bounded by) the scientific community. Direct observation of scientific work suggests that laboratory operations are embedded within *transscientific fields* of interaction and discourse. Not only scientists, but also administrators, grant agencies, publishers, participate in these fields of discursive interaction. Transscientific fields are not logical classes whose members share specific characteristics. They are constituted by what is transmitted between agents; they come about through actual or potential (discursive) interaction and communication relevant to what happens in the laboratory.

To conclude: I submit that scientists' transscientific involvements are the locus in which the decision criteria invoked by laboratory selections are defined, revised, and negotiated. In other words, the constraints into which laboratory selections translate and the relationships which nourish these constraints refer us to the above-mentioned transscientific fields of symbolic transactions rather than to a scientific field of communities of specialists. To postulate a relationship between scientists' contextual involvements and laboratory selections mediated by decision criteria is not to suggest that we can read off these criteria from specific contextual involvements. Scientists' concrete decision translations are simply marked by the same kind of indeterminacy characteristic of practical action in general. However, the transscientific connection of inquiry, and, as a consequence, the social relativity of knowledge can be illustrated by means of concrete examples, as some of the microscopic studies of scientific work show.[37] Work within the framework of a newly emerging sociology of scientific knowledge has only just begun. It is the goal of this work to elaborate the notion of the constructive character of scientific work and of its transscientific connection persuasively and in empirical detail.

Notes

1. Critical discussion from different perspectives (leading to different conclusions) can be found in Roy Bhaskar, *A Realist Theory of Science* (Sussex, England: Harvester Press, 1978) and in Jürgen Habermas, *Knowledge and Human Interests* (Boston: Beacon Press, 1971), pp. 67ff.

2. This is not a naive statement of the empirical realist's position, although it may sound like one. The naive position would hold that the picture which science gives us of the world is a true one. In contrast, the above statement emphasizes an epistemic attitude rather than the correspondence of actual results. For a further discussion of this see B. van Fraasen, *The Argument Concerning Scientific Realism* (Los Angeles: University of Southern California, 1977), ch. 2, pp. 2ff. Suppe's formulation is that the results of scientific enquiry are generalized descriptions of reality which must be true in order for the theory to be adequate. Cf. Frederik Suppe, ed. *The Structure of Scientific Theories* (Urbana: University of Illinois Press, 1974), p. 211.

3. Cf. Habermas, p. 69.

4. See "The Logic of 1873" for a formulation of Peirce's program. Charles S. Peirce, *Collected Papers*, ed. Charles Hartshorne and Paul Weiss (Cambridge, Mass.: Harvard University Press, 1931-35).

5. For example, see the symposium edited by Suppe on the question of the meaning variance of observation sentences, in particular the introductory chapter by Suppe, pp. 3-241.

6. Cf. Bhaskar, particularly ch. 2:118 ff. for an exposition of this critique.

7. The example is taken from van Fraasen, p. 45.

8. This has been pointed out to me by Bruno Latour.

9. The observations upon which the present work is based were conducted in 1976-77 at a government financed research center in Berkeley, Calif. The center does basic and applied research in chemical, physical, microbiological, toxicological, engineering, and economic areas. My observations focused on a research group working on protein generation and recovery and on the purification, particle structure, texture, assessment of biological value, and application of plant protein research in the area of human nutrition. For a more detailed description of the work and empirical data involved see Karin D. Knorr-Cetina, *The Manufacture of Knowledge: An Essay on the Constructivist and Contextual Nature of Science* (Oxford: Pergamon Press, 1981). See also Karin D. Knorr, "Producing and reproducing knowledge: descriptive or constructive?" *Social Science Information* 16(1977):669-96; id., "Tinkering toward success: prelude to a theory of scientific practice," *Theory and Society* 8(1979):347-76. For a second study relevant here, one of the first based on participant observation of scientists at work, see Bruno Latour and Steve Woolgar, *Laboratory Life: The Social Construction of Scientific Facts* (Beverly Hills: Sage, 1979). See also the articles collected in the *Sociology of Science Yearbook* 4 (Knorr, Krohn, and Whitley, 1980), most of which are not based on direct observation. Observation studies similar to the above are currently in progress in various areas of science. See Michael Lynch, "Technical work and critical inquiry: investigations in a scientific laboratory," in *Social Studies of Science*. Special Issue on the Ethnography of Scientific Work (1982); Doug McKegney, "Inquiry into Inquiry: Local Action and Public Discourse in Wildlife Ecology," Ph.D. dissertation (Burnaby: Simon Fraser University, 1982); Michael Zenzen and Sal Restivo, "The mysterious morphology of inmiscible liquids: a study of scientific practice," *Social Science Information*, 21 (1982):447-73. These studies can be seen as "empirical epistemologies" of science. See Leo Apostel et al., "An empirical investigation of scientific observation," *Communication and Cognition* 6(1979):3-36. They also point toward a microsociology of knowledge interested in analyzing the social process of scientific investigation from a microscopic — instead of a cultural history or philosophical — perspective. It is the goal of these studies to address afresh the hoary old puzzles of the social conditioning of thought (Mannheim) within the domain of our most authoritative and esoteric system of ideas, scientific knowledge.

10. In 1907, the eminent physicist Joseph John Thomson said, "From the point of view of the physicist, a theory of matter is a policy rather than a creed; its object is to connect or coordinate apparently diverse phenomena, and above all to suggest, stimulate, and direct experiment." Joseph John Thomson, *The Corpuscular Theory of Matter* (London: Archibald Constable, 1907).

11. This is a paraphrase of Habermas, (1971, p. 315), whose meaning differs somewhat from what is intended here.

12. For a comprehensive exposition of Luhmann's systems theory approach, see Niklas Luhmann, *Soziologische Aufklärung: Aufsätze zur Theorie sozialer Systeme* (Opladen:

Westdeutscher Verlag, 1971); Niklas Luhmann, *Soziologische Aufklärung, Bd. 2. Aufsätze zur Theorie der Gesellschaft* (Opladen: Westdeutscher Verlag, 1975).

13. For the concept of translation see Michel Serres, *Hermes III: La traduction* (Paris: Minuit, 1974); and the illustrations by Michel Callon, "L'opération de traduction comme relation symbolique," in *Les incidences des rapports sociaux sur la science*, ed. Michel Roqueplo (Paris: CORDES, 1975), pp. 87-105.

14. See the quasi-economic model of Pierre Bourdieu, "The specificity of the scientific field and the social conditions of the progress of reason," *Social Science Information* 14(1975):19-47; and the revised version by Latour and Woolgar.

15. Cf. Karl Popper, *Conjectures and Refutations* (London: Routledge & Kegan Paul, 1963), pp. 216ff.

16. See also Derek Phillips, "Epistemology and the sociology of knowledge: the contributions of Mannheim, Mills, and Merton," *Theory and Society* 1(1974):82ff. Phillips has pointed out that, as a consequence, we have to assume, in opposition to Mills and Merton, that the motives and social position of an inquirer are indeed relevant for the evaluation s/he gets from fellow scientists.

17. Other areas relevant here are journals and publishers, or contexts in which decisions about the publication of results are made. Results which are not published or otherwise circulated effectively have a much smaller chance to even enter the process of general validation.

18. It is tempting to quote Wittgenstein here: "So sagst Du also, dass die Übereinstimmung der Menschen entscheide, was richtig und was falsch ist? — Richtig und falsch ist, was Menschen sagen; und in der Sprache stimmen die Menschen überein. Dies ist keine Übereinstimmung der Meinungen, sondern der Lebensform." ("So you are saying that human agreement decides what is true and false? It is what human beings *say* that is true and false; and they agree in the *language* they use. That is not agreement in opinions, but in form of life." See paragraph 241 of the *Philosophical Investigations* (trans. G.E.M. Anscombe).

19. I am referring here to Feyerabend's contention that the interpretations which scientists choose are relative to a cultural and historical context and can only be understood if we look at these contexts. The thesis rules out the possibility of specifying a set of context-independent criteria according to which consensus formation proceeds. In contrast, Kuhn does not rule out the possibility of such criteria. Paul Feyerabend, *Against Method* (London: New Left Books, 1975); and Thomas S. Kuhn, *The Structure of Scientific Revolutions* (Chicago: University of Chicago Press, 1970), 2nd enlarged ed. (first published 1962), particularly the discussion in the postscript.

20. Note that Toulmin's model of scientific evolution (the closest adaptation of the biological model) goes to some length to avoid such consequences. First, as we shall see later, Toulmin restricts the idea of environmental selection to a form of scientific selection. Second, as Lakatos points out in his critique of Toulmin, he invokes a "Cunning of Reason" in history which somehow secures the final validity of selections. For these and other reasons which will become clear later, Toulmin's model is not a contextual model as proposed here. Stephen Toulmin, *Human Understanding* (Oxford: Clarendon, 1972); Imre Lakatos, "Understanding Toulmin," *Minerva* 14(1976):126-43.

21. For a summary presentation of the whole discussion, see Imre Lakatos and Alan Musgrave, eds., *Criticism and the Growth of Knowledge* (Cambridge, England: Cambridge University Press, 1970).

22. In stochastic processes on the molecular level, in which the smaller the number of interacting molecules the greater the role of fluctuation, it has been shown that the absence of "errors" or indeterminacy corresponds not only to an absence of innovation and hence of an increase of information, but to an actual loss of information. Without chance fluctuations, the system cannot maintain itself in a stationary state. This means that without the intervention of "error," chance, or indeterminacy in biological evolution, for example, all species would disappear without being replaced. Cf. Henri Atlan, *Entre le cristal et la fumée: Essai sur l'organisation du vivant* (Paris: Seuil, 1979), p.545. For a propagation of the idea as a principle of order relevant to science see Latour and Woolgar.

23. Atlan's reinterpretation of the problem is crucial because it suggests that the point is not the construction of "order" out of disorder (indeterminacy, chance), but the emergence of organization as defined by an increase in complexity or system differentiation. The original definition envisioned an increase of repetition or redundancy with which the notion of order is associated in information theory.

24. See Atlan, p. 47.

25. As a simple example, consider the leak in the communicative network of the Nixon administration with regard to the bombing of Cambodia (kept secret by the administration). While the leak was disruptive for some core members of the administration, it may well have benefited the more global system of American democracy. The implication is that we have to take into account different *levels* of organization to distinguish between the disruptive and integrative (or organizing) effects of noise.

26. Of course, science produces new problems at the same time, which is part of the process of reconstruction.

27. The quantity of information within a system is taken to be a measure of the improbability that the combination of the different constituents of the system is the result of chance. This is why the quantity of information could have been proposed as a measure of complexity. Strictly speaking, there are three different versions of writing the quantity of information (see Atlan, pp. 79ff.).

28. According to Ashby, it is logically impossible that a self-organizing system be closed, i.e. a system which does not interact with an environment. If the system could change its organization solely as a function of its internal states, this change would be governed by a constant. True change has to be induced either through a program of change injected from the outside or through external chance interferences. See W. Ross Ashby, "Principles of the Self-Organizing System," in *Principles of Self-Organization* ed. H. von Foerster and G.W. Zopf (New York: Pergamon, 1962), pp. 225-78.

29. See Stephen Toulmin, "The evolutionary development of natural science," *American Scientist* 57(1967):470, for a short presentation of his model and of the nonmetaphoric reading intended (pp. 470ff.).

30. Toulmin seems to suggest that this is normally and ideally the case. Cf. esp. par. 4.

31. Since change and particularization are built into scientific products, we can also say that scientific work allows for differentiation effects, and these can be appropriated by scientists. The individuation provided by scientific work need not necessarily go to individual persons. Many would argue that the increasing socialization of science means that we have

an increasing appropriation of differentiation effects by groups, and more importantly, by institutions.

32. See Edmund Husserl, "Die Frage nach dem Ursprung der Geometrie als intentional-historisches Problem," in *Husserliana*, vol. 6 (The Hague: Nijhoff, 1962).

33. For a short presentation, see the chapter on "Logic as Semiotic" in the Dover edition of Peirce's selected writings. Charles S. Peirce, *Philosophical Writings of Peirce*, ed. Justus Buchler (New York: Dover, 1955), pp. 98ff. I am referring to Jacques Derrida, *Of Grammatology* (Baltimore: Johns Hopkins University Press, 1976), p. 27.

34. Latour and Woolgar.

35. Böhme has concluded that a concept of the scientific community within a theory of scientific action needs to be based on a theory of the process of argumentation in science. See Gernot Böhme, "The Social Function of Cognitve Structures: A Concept of the Scientific Community within a Theory of Action," in *Determinants and Controls of Scientific Development*, ed. Karin D. Knorr, Hermann Strasser, and Hans G. Zilian (Dordrecht, Holland: D. Reidel, 1975), pp. 205-26.

36. Cf. Ron Johnston, "Contextual knowledge: a model for the overthrow of the internal/external dichotomy in science," *Australia and New Zealand Journal of Sociology* 12(1976):193-203. Johnston summarizes some of the uses of the internal/external distinction which he traces back to assumptions enshrined in the history and philosophy of science that have been unquestioningly adopted by subsequent analyses of science.

37. See the studies cited in note 9 which have begun to document this constructivity and contextuality.

Part III
Knowledge and Power

Introduction

In this section, Norbert Elias, Juan E. Corradi, and Johannes Weiss discuss the relationship between knowledge and power. They agree that this relation must be viewed as a dynamic social process, and assign to the intelligentsia a significant role in the reevaluation and interpretation of the new modes of discourse. It is the intellectuals, they argue, who are potentially able to lead the way in freeing us from an evermore technologically efficient but also more routine existence. Corradi and Weiss characterize the present era as discontinuous with the past and no longer capable of satisfying basic human needs. We are, they suggest, facing a new situation that requires a radical reorientation. Weiss advises that we learn from past political and revolutionary struggles. Corradi proposes that the work of Foucault may be helpful in thinking more clearly about the current impasse. Elias, in an interview with Peter Ludes, tries out a "thought experiment" and tells us a utopian tale about the "great struggle of the intellectuals." In quite different ways, all three authors shed new light on the problem of the relation of knowledge and power.

Elias begins with the observation that some people are in a position to withhold or monopolize what most other people need. The more the latter need what has been withheld or monopolized, the greater is the power ratio of the former. It is more difficult to withhold knowledge (that is, means of communication and orientation) than capital or weaponry. Elias argues that the increasing power in the last two centuries of large national populations has been accompanied by compulsory education, which has been an indispensable adjunct not only of advanced industrialization but also of the increasing mechanization of warfare. Elias observes that in earlier historical periods, in which nature was less controllable and humans were less self-controlled, more in need of being controlled from without, priests had traditionally been the guardians of knowledge. To understand ourselves, it is important that we grasp the human experiences in those earlier periods, in which knowledge of the world of spirits was still dominant.

Even in our own time, Elias suggests, we can find a kind of academic knowledge that resists being tested, a new deductionism, as it were, whose most authoritative contemporary spokesman is Karl Popper. Nevertheless, those sciences concerned with both the empirical and the theoretical spheres can no longer adhere to the rules of formal logic, but must rely on factual observations that have taken the place of "wishful thinking." The role of knowledge in modern societies, and its potential role in future developments, Elias insists, can be brought out more clearly by thought experiments. What would happen in the Soviet Union if state control of physical force as well as control of the means of production were in fact maintained, while at the same time the monopolistic control of the means of orientation and communication were abolished? Or what would be the result of a "detached understanding" of long-term social processes if it managed to take the place of a form of argumentation which has in the past and until now tended to be distorted in order to serve private interests? What would happen if knowledge were made accessible to nonspecialists?

Here Elias agrees with Corradi. Power and knowledge are dynamic processes that occur in diverse settings and affect each other in ways that must be charted and understood. We only need to consider the new breed of knowledge/power brokers, the new managers of uncertainty who are involved in the "production" of the continuously changing realities. Corradi raises a series of poignant questions regarding these new managers, their cultural technology, and its detrimental effect on knowledge and culture. These uncertainties are symptomatic of a society that has come to a crossroads: we can now see the light at the end of the tunnel, but let us hope it is not a train!

Corradi examines the relationship between power and intellectual life and traces the origins of the new uncertainty back to Hegel and Marx. Ever since Marx located the origins of culture in the social relations of production, a new theoretical approach began to emerge, which resulted in a cultural crisis and a loss of status of the intelligentsia. We are no longer capable of comprehending culture in its totality nor able to locate it in a subjective consciousness or in an objective reality. How can one make sense of this maze of uncertainties? Are we doomed to chaos? Corradi does not think so. He believes that the present situation offers opportunities for examining culture and knowledge from a new and different perspective. Foucault's work, he argues, provides the foundation for a new sociology of knowledge which not only might dispel old illusions about knowledge but also advance the discipline itself.

The process which has occurred, Corradi observes, can be characterized as one of rationalization and expropriation of intellectual functions. He considers the first as the field of interaction of intellectuals, seen as a field of status competition — as a pitched battle for recognition. The second refers to the "totalizing function" traditionally fulfilled by intellectuals. Regardless of specialization and technical expertise, intellectuals have defined themselves by their ability to interpret, to place ideas in context, by producing meaning for others. More recently, some have abandoned that totalizing ambition and have come to see their work as part of a complex discursive web, as more impersonal. In other words, the totalizing and hermeneutic function has become more of a semiotic consciousness. All of these functions and activities formerly exercised by in tellectuals now seem to be undergoing a process of rationalization and expropriation.

The interpretation of cultural meanings, the total "gaze" and surveillance of culture so dear to intellectuals, the linkages and networks between ideas and practices, their struggles against each other, their tragicomic quest for power and recognition, are being quietly integrated into rational organizations, into a new type of "flexible," "postindustrial" bureaucracy, whose job it is to promote, direct, steer, and manipulate cultural and scientific production. The "new intellectual" is therefore a collective, impersonal, bureaucratic subject. Corradi discusses an exemplar of this type: the philanthropic foundation. It is a new and powerful actor in the field of culture. The problem is not, as it has been so often formulated, the obsolescence of the "traditional" or "general" intellectual in favor of specialized intellectual workers (although this trend is undeniable), but the bureaucratization of the totality. The whole is (still) the truth, and the whole is a machinery that processes statuses, proposals, ideas, and turns out "projects," reports, results, recommendations. What Sartre did in his room is now done (and perverted) by committees, program officers, foundation staffs, and boards of trustees.

Intellectuals cannot continue utilizing the old modes of discourse and still hope to attain a general level of significance and meaning. Corradi suggests that a change in perspective and methodology is required in order to explicate the new trends of a discontinuous history.

Weiss, in raising the question of the possible power of ideas, reverses one of the traditional and perhaps even constitutive assertions of the sociology of knowledge, that power necessarily represents salient elements of the structural rather than the intellectual realm of society. He asserts that the ideas of the different groups vying for domination can have considerable influence in the struggles for political power and that the significance of ideas increases in such contexts in direct relation to their radicalness.

The radicalness of ideas does not refer, as one might assume, to their capacity for innovation; on the contrary, the concept of radicalness refers to nearly irreducible insights into historical reality and ideas that have the potential for inducing political action. Weiss elaborates on and illustrates these notions by way of historical materials. He draws particular attention to the dynamics of revolutionary movements in modern Europe: both in the French and the Russian Revolutions, groups aspiring to dominate were able to achieve power once they relied on ideas more radical than their opposition. Ideas not only operate as ideologies or rationalizations but represent an intellectual force which may well be of decisive influence in determining the outcome of political struggles.

In his reflections on a unique aspect of the relation between power and knowledge, Weiss also examines the intelligentsia's role in struggles of this kind. According to him, intellectuals are characterized above all by the tendency to push ideas to radical conclusions; such radicalness is in turn constitutive for the mobilizing effect of ideas. Yet, while radical ideas have been instrumental in elevating certain groups to power, the dynamics of the interrelation between knowledge and power continue and tend to transform the ideas themselves, and, in some instances, lead to attempts to implement them, once power has been achieved, even against the resistance of the citizens. The establishment of dictatorial power and bureaucratic authority are the direct outcome of efforts to realize radical ideas. Weiss observes that such radicalness of ideas often is associated with the willingness to employ physical force. He concludes that the radicalization of ideas is by no means automatic but is itself linked to specific sociohistorical conditions.

10

Knowledge and Power:

An Interview by Peter Ludes

Norbert Elias

Ludes: The concept of power plays an important part in your sociological theory. I think it might be helpful if you explained why that is the case.

Elias: To put my understanding of the nature of power in a nutshell, I would first point out that the word *power* is somewhat misleading. It suggests an object which can be put in a pocket or which can be otherwise possessed, like the piece of soap in the bathroom of a sahib which his Indian servant believed to be the magical source of the White man's power. In fact, what we call "power" is an aspect of a relationship, of *every* human relationship. It has something to do with the fact that people as groups or as individuals can withhold or monopolize what others need — food, love, meaning, protection from attack (i.e. security), as well as knowledge and some other things. The more the latter need it, the greater the power ratio of the former. Usually groups or individuals from whom means of satisfaction are withheld, have something else needed by those who withhold means of satisfaction from them. Marginal cases apart, one always encounters power balances and different or equal power rates. The whole sociological and political discussion on power is marred by the fact that the dialogue is not consistently focused on power balances and power rates, that is, on aspects of relationships, but rather on power as if it were a thing. In this context this preliminary clarification is all the more needed because knowledge, too, is not a thing that one can put in one's pocket like a key.

Ludes: You have given us your definition of power. Could you add briefly your definition of knowledge?

Elias: It seems to be more difficult to withhold knowledge from others,

251

who like to have it, than capital or weapons. How, then, can knowledge become monopolized, thus endowing a group or person with a higher power ratio in relation to others?

Does this look as if I were trying to evade your question regarding the nature of knowledge? I hope not. I am on my way toward answering it. But a word or two must be said about the prevailing tendency to blur the distinction between the sociology of knowledge and its predecessor, philosophical epistemology. The latter could largely manage without a clear answer to the question "what is knowledge?"; the former cannot. But the answer has to unfold gradually. In a preliminary way I suggest that what we call knowledge is the social meaning of human-made symbols, such as words or figures, in its capacity as means of orientation. In contrast to most nonhuman creatures, humans have no inborn or, as it is often called, instinctive means of orientation. When growing up, humans have to acquire through learning sets of social symbols with their meaning and thus parts of a social fund of knowledge from their elders. Specific sets of meaningful social symbols have at the same time the function of a means of communication and of a means of orientation. Without learning social symbols with this double function they do not become human. Let me briefly add a few words about some of the astonishing properties of symbols with knowledge functions — they are changeable. At a given time their network can be made to fit that which they are intended to symbolize better than before. They can grow and decay. Their network can be made to cover areas of objects or connections previously not covered by them, therefore unimaginable for humans and unknown to them. They can shrink and regress so that these areas can again become unknown and unimaginable.

Ludes: That gives us a preview of what you mean by power and knowledge. Could you show us how they are interconnected?

Elias: The contemporary situation shows some remarkable trends that throw light on your question. As in so many other cases, these trends are contradictory. On the one hand, illiteracy has more or less disappeared in most developed countries and, although still widespread in others, it is diminishing there too. Cheaper books, a relatively inexpensive press, in conjunction with radio and television services have to some extent broken down barriers to the diffusion of knowledge, barriers that even in the nineteenth century were much higher and prior to that were often impenetrable for the masses. This is one trend of the knowledge explosion of the twentieth century. It is part of a process of functional democratization, a growing power potential of the masses. This change can be observed in one-party states and multiparty states. Compulsory education and the attendant higher educational level of the masses compared with previous centuries are an indispensable adjunct of advancing industrialization and mechanization of warfare.

State-societies, where for one reason or another the educational level of the masses is comparatively low and oriented toward prescientific models, are at a disadvantage in their competitive struggles, whether peaceful or military, with others where the masses have attained a higher rate of participation in the knowledge advances of our age. The population in countries of the latter type consists to a larger extent of individuals who in their own thinking are not too bound by authority, who up to a point are better able to think and judge for themselves. Even in the more advanced countries this expansion and democratization of knowledge to the urban masses is still in the early stages, for there are many countercurrents. But even the present expansion of knowledge, the rise of educational standards reached so far, has been enough to increase very noticeably the power potential of a country's population.

The literate urban masses of industrial nation-states cannot be governed in the same manner as the largely illiterate agrarian masses which up to the nineteenth and twentieth centuries formed the majority of a country's population almost anywhere in the world. Access to wider knowledge, to better and more comprehensive means of orientation increases the power potential of human groups. Together with other factors which can help to increase the power potential of a nation's population — such as the closely connected capacity for effectively organizing itself — the pronounced rise in the standard of knowledge has been one of the main levers of the process of functional democratization mentioned before. With a rise in a population's standard of knowledge its power potential is apt to rise not only in states with the formal institutions of democracy, not only in multiparty states, but also in states with the formal institutions of a dictatorship, in one-party states. So closely linked is the economic development of a country to its population's standard of knowledge, that a country with relatively high educational standards, governed by military force contrary to the wishes of its population, is likely to stagnate or run down economically. The process of industrial development tends to lose its impetus if the support of those who work for it cannot be enlisted by a country's regime.

Ludes: Did you mention countercurrents to the democratization of knowledge?

Elias: The knowledge explosion of the twentieth century shows certain trends that, in terms of the distribution of power, have exactly the opposite effect from that which I have just mentioned. There is, for example, the staggering growth of humanity's fund of knowledge as a whole, which consists to a considerable extent of highly specialized technical and scientific knowledge, usually accessible only to limited groups of experts, to the oligarchs of knowledge, who thus have a kind of monopolistic grip on it.

While the knowledge explosion has begun to affect and in some cases change the masses all over the earth, it has also created new means of countering, of controlling and channeling the rising power potential of a country's population. Because there are so many of them, and so many divided from, as well as tied to, each other by a still growing number of interdependent specialized occupations, the mass of a country's population is greatly dependent on organizers, coordinators, decision makers on a variety of levels, the highest of which is the governmental level. There are a number of fields where only state governments or, in the United States, the federal government, and perhaps some top groups in business enterprises can decide or refuse to finance research needed for advances in knowledge. As projects become more expensive, their results become, at least for a time, the well-guarded property of those who have advanced money for them. Yet over time, it is never very easy to make a close secret of scientific advances. In the long run scientific advances in knowledge cannot be monopolized effectively, in contrast to prescientific knowledge, which can be monopolized. But in the short run, attempts at keeping scientific advances secret can certainly succeed. Tendencies toward monopolization of scientific knowledge are therefore on the increase. In a number of cases, especially the exploration of space, they obviously help to increase the power potential of governments in relation to those they govern.

Ludes: Could you give an example showing how these contradictory trends affect the practice of our social life?

Elias: A great number of contemporary states, perhaps the majority, are either multiparty or one-party states ruled by politicians who have got there through, or with the help of, a party organization. Those countries that are not ruled through one or several parties mostly represent regressions to or survivals from the condition of autocratic dictatorship, hereditary or not; they are ruled by undisguised military force. The question is: why party states? That they are a novelty of the nineteenth and twentieth centuries is easy to see. No doubt, they have antecedents in previous centuries. You might think of the Guelphs and Ghibellines or the Whigs and Tories. I do not want to bore you with an analysis of the differences or with an account of the stages in the development of parties, e.g. in France or in the United States. It must be enough to say that in the twentieth century party organizations have become a normal feature of the political life of all the more advanced and of many of the less advanced countries, either in the form of a parliamentary or in that of a dictatorial regime. One may not have given enough attention to the question of why party organizations led by professional politicians, who, in many cases, have risen to the top through the career ladder of a party organization or with its help, have become an integral structural characteristic of many state-societies of our age. The extreme compartmentalization of the social sciences may have something to do with this neglect. To answer this question the sociology of political institutions, especially of the state, the sociology of economic institutions, and the sociology of knowledge have to work hand in hand.

Political mass parties, now often state institutions, are, in the first instance, the functional corollary of the rising educational levels of a country's population. These on their part are functionally related to the steadily advancing scientization and technization of societies which in turn, particularly in their military and economic aspects, are spurred on by interstate competition as the lever of last resort within the many-levered dynamics of state-societies. Altogether the pattern of interdependence between state population and state government during the nineteenth and twentieth centuries acquired some new structural characteristics, especially in the more developed countries. Advancing industrialization, often considered today as an autonomous process, formed part and parcel of a process of power rivalries between states. It was preceded by, and can, moreover, be considered as a later phase of a long process of commercialization. Both are relatively late stages of a much longer and more comprehensive process of increasing differentiation of social functions, traditionally called "division of labor." In the later phases of this process, this growing specialization increased the dependence of a society's population on high level coordinating agencies, on party establishments, and governments. An increment of dependence of the ruled on the ruling groups, however, is identical with an increment of the latter's power ratio. Hence with advancing industrialization, the range of the functions of governments became wider and their power potential correspondingly greater.

Yet, at the same time, the dependence of governments on a country's population increased, thanks, among other things, to its higher standards of knowledge, self-control, and consequent capacity for organizing itself more effectively. The web of interdependencies binding governing and governed groups, established and outsiders, to each other, became more closely knit and the balance of power between them, at least in multiparty states, somewhat less uneven compared with those between princes and their subjects in the long preceding era.

In the present era, continuous centralized governmental attempts at controlling and directing the opinions and attitudes of the state population are, as one can see, counterbalanced by often more diffuse and intermittent attempts on the part of the various sections of a state's population at controlling and directing governments. Political parties are one of the principal organizational channels for these attempts on the part of both governments and governed at controlling and directing each other. They show clearly the degree of unevenness in the balance of power between them. In multiparty states the balance of power, though still uneven, is less uneven than in one-party states because controlled and nonviolent competition between parties, changes of governments according to enforceable public rules, as well as the possibility of extraparliamentary pressure on governments, help to increase substantially the power potential of the state population. Even this short survey indicates that a sociological synthesis giving due attention to changes in the distribution of power enables one to perceive more clearly the changes in the structure of society of which the rise of political parties and party governments forms part.

Within the figuration of levers responsible for this change, the rise in the standards of knowledge available to the state population through better schooling, the media, and in many other ways, plays a significant part as a factor of its power ratio. Knowledge is taken for granted in these societies. One can often see only its insufficiencies, not its factual function and public growth. They can probably stand out in fuller relief only if one compares present conditions more systematically with those of the past.

Ludes: As it is your view that one cannot understand one's own time unless one compares its condition with those of other ages, could you perhaps tell us a little more of your understanding of the development of knowledge and power?

Elias: With the exception of short periods such as the development of city-states in Athens and Florence, state-societies in past ages were ruled almost everywhere more or less autocratically, without *institutional reciprocity* of control. Estate assemblies, in some cases, offered small privileged groups chances of controlling their hereditary princes who in turn tried to control them. The mass of the population had only one means of expressing discontent or despair — they could riot and revolt. In the great majority of cases these revolts did not change the balance of power. That only happened when an unplanned process of functional democratization played larger resources of power into the hands of larger and larger sections of a state population. Successful revolutions were usually directed against autocrats claiming a power surplus which they in fact no longer commanded. The rulers of France, England and Russia had lost their power superiority already before the successful revolutions started. By comparison with the old-type autocracies even the new-type autocracies, the communist party dictatorships of our age, heirs of a successful revolution, can be seen as spurts of functional democratization. If standards of knowledge and living in state-societies of this type are allowed to rise further, as they must be, if further advances in industrialization and the chances of economic or military competition with the commonwealth of multiparty states are not to be blocked, the pressure for greater reciprocity of control is likely to increase in these dictational countries too.

Most people living in one of the more developed multiparty nation-states find it difficult to imagine what it felt like to live in one of the old-type monarchical autocracies of which the ancient pharaohs were just as much an example as the emperors of Russia, China, or Ethiopia. I should like to give you an example from ancient Egypt. That may seem a long way off. But the picture that emerges is not so different from that which one might discover in some European countries of the eighteenth century, except perhaps for the explicitness and the complete unconcern of its brutality, indicative of an earlier stage of a civilizing process. In ancient Egypt one also encountered the first reactions against this unconcern and unrestraint of more powerful groups vis-à-vis groups with a lower power potential. The American egyptologist Breasted, in his book *The Dawn of Conscience*, was perhaps the first to point out that one encountered in ancient Egypt what were probably the earliest reactions against the unconcerned exploitation of power inequalities. Pharaohs and their gods, in some cases, admonished powerful people not to misuse their power superiority. The gods of the netherworld weighed the heart even of great and mighty people to see whether they had been just — the term *justice* or its equivalent apparently was at that particular stage in the development a symbol of the incipient conscience formation indicating its close connection with the state. The experiences of our own time may make us a little weary of the assumption that a conscience is a natural part of human beings. It is formed as part of a civilizing process in connection with specific forms of external social constraint. There are many examples from ancient Mesopotamia and ancient Egypt indicating that the sense of identity with human beings outside one's own group can be completely lacking, a reminder that under specific conditions, wherever it already exists, it can always shrink and shrivel. The example I am going to quote shows a condition of almost unlimited power inequality which was once the normal condition of humans in state-societies everywhere and which is still encountered in some countries in our time, although one would probably try to conceal it from public scrutiny and not present it as an example in a school text.

The art of reading and writing was in ancient Egypt the preserve of a privileged caste of state and temple functionaries ranging from high-placed court officials to tax collectors. Documents probably used at a writing school where the latter were trained tell pupils about the good life they will have when they go through the country collecting taxes with the help of the Nubian soldiers:[1]

The scribe has moored at the river-bank. He reckons the tax, with the attendants bearing staffs and the Nubians rods of palm. They say: Give the grain! There is none. They beat him vigorously. He is bound and cast into the well. They beat him, drowning him head first, while his wife is bound in his presence. His children are manacled; his neighbors have abandoned them and fled. Their grain is gathered. But a scribe, he is the taskmaster of everyone. There is no taxing of the work of the scribe. He does not have dues. So take note of this.

It is a familiar picture: illiterate peasant masses ruled with the help of small literate and privileged minorities aided by soldiers fed with the tax-grain. Similar figurations can be found in the development of many state-societies prior to the expanding development of science and industry in the nineteenth and twentieth centuries.[2] The singularity of the twentieth century, when illiteracy virtually disappeared in some countries and rapidly diminished in others, stands out more clearly when seen against this background.

One also has to consider why in almost all traditional state-societies, next to the warriors represented by princes as their commander-in-chief, priests formed the most powerful and high-ranking group. Priests were the traditional guardians of a society's fund of knowledge. They provided what human beings, together with some other basic requirements such as physical security and food, needed most — additional means of orientation. That the knowledge which priests guarded and produced did not have the character of scientific knowledge should not obscure the fact that this, the provision of knowledge and its translation into social practices, was their primary social function. In former ages human beings were exposed even more helplessly than they are today to the vagaries of nature, the accidents of illnesses and physical insecurity, and numerous other misfortunes. They died at a much earlier age. Priests "knew" why all that happened to people. They knew how to communicate with the unseen powers and ward off their ill-will, securing their blessing through ritual, prayer, and sacrifice. They also knew what happened to people after death and how to allay the fear of punishment after death for one's misdeeds in life.

Magic-mythical knowledge of this type could be acquired, directly or indirectly, only through a revelation from the spirit world. It had the character of a mystery, partly or wholly known to priests. Hence it was easy to monopolize this type of knowledge; it was easy to use its possession as legitimization of an exclusive social cadre, a means of securing a high power ratio in relation to those who needed this knowledge, who had to know the ways of the spirit world to find their own way through life. From the time of ancient Sumer and Egypt to the end of the European Middle Ages and beyond, possession of this nonscientific type of knowledge assumed the form of a priestly monopoly and of a highly centralized knowledge monopoly at that, when its representatives formed a closely knit, monarchically ruled church.

It is useful to have this centralized monopoly of knowledge in mind when looking at the various ways in which scientific knowledge can become monopolized. The difference is illuminating. The road for the ascent of a scientific type of knowledge was opened when the church's monopoly of the basic means of orientation and its power to punish deviants broke down. On its own the break-up of the knowledge monopoly of the old church does not explain the rise of science. But it was a *conditio sine qua non*. Cases such as those of Giordano Bruno and Galileo show the church's means of guarding its knowledge monopoly in its vigilant struggle against deviant and dangerous knowledge.

The breakdown of the church's monopoly of knowledge, which for a long time included that of Latin reading and writing, was no accident. At first sight it may appear solely as the outcome of a conflict between a mother church and dissident daughter churches and sects. In fact, dissident or heretic movements, open or disguised, occurred unsuccessfully throughout the Middle Ages. The success of breakaway churches and sects in the Renaissance was in the last resort due to the changing balance of power between popes and princes, between the Christian church and the Christian states in favor of the latter. The widely known maxim *cuius regio eius religio* said as much. The long drawn-out struggle for supremacy between priests and warriors, which within the realm of the Roman Church had culminated in the struggle for dominance between pope and emperor, in its unplanned course finally played into the hands of princes superior resources of power compared with those available to the popes as the guardians of revealed knowledge. It became clear that the power resources of princes, military as well as financial, surpassed those of the popes. There was nothing the church could do against the expropriation of its property in countries such as France and England. Its representatives had to resign themselves to the fact that in some cases rulers demanded a considerable degree of control over the church organization in their dominions and that in others they defected altogether in favor of a church organization of their own which they could control. The popes could maintain a precarious independence among the warring princes only by becoming themselves secular rulers of a territorial state. It is significant that in the period which saw the end of the church's monopoly of the fundamental means of orientation and the renaissance of secular knowledge, a new term gained currency for the dominions of princes and rulers of all kinds. It indicated the ascent to a new level of conceptual synthesis and surpassed in its generality and precision such conventional terms as *kingdom*, *civitas*, or *res publica*. I refer to the term *il stato* which appears to have been used first in its present sense at the time of Machiavelli in the political and historical literature of Italy, and quickly took root in many other European languages. It transformed itself at the time into the English term *the state*. As church organizations in more and more European countries came under the de facto control of secular rulers, control of knowledge also passed increasingly to the state. Ultimately it was the alignment of competing princes or, in some cases, of self-ruling cities which decided victory or defeat of the reformation in any particular country or city-state.

Ludes: Does this view not differ from Max Weber's view of Protestantism?

Elias: Perhaps. Max Weber had a marvelous intuitive understanding of power relations, especially with regard to his own country. There is for instance his analysis of the situation of landowners and land workers in East Prussia, or his private view of the German bureaucracy. He saw more clearly than anybody else before that a monopoly of physical force played a key role in the constitution of a state. But he did not pursue this line beyond the bare statement. For some reason, which one can only guess, Weber, like most other theorists in the field of sociology, failed to work out a concise, empirically testable model of power in his theoretical writings. Even in his own time he saw how dependent church organizations and other religious bodies were on governmental decisions or, to be more exact, on the wholly secular power relations within a state. He knew the close association of the German Protestant Church with the imperial regime, of the Anglican Church with the royal regime in England. He knew of the French republican legislation separating church and state, of the suppression of the Eastern Church by the new Soviet state. But in his writings Weber often gives the impression that he regarded churches or sects as autonomous social organizations. He ignored the obvious fact that the fortunes of Puritan sects in countries with an absolutist regime were different from their fortunes in countries without such a regime, such as England or America. In the German states ruled by autocratic princes the equivalent of Dutch or English Puritan sects had to keep very quiet if they wanted to be tolerated at all. Unlike their English or Dutch counterparts they had no chance of gaining political power. It is significant that the German Pietists were called "quiet people" (*die Stillen im Lande*). Nor did he refer to the fact that the flowering of Protestant sects in England and America was made possible by the exceptional character of the English state formation process. In the sixteenth and seventeenth centuries England became a sea power. The navy became the country's main instrument of defense and attack. Hence the Stuart kings, lacking a standing army to support them, did not succeed in establishing what in England is still called a despotic regime. It was in the struggle against the kings that the English Puritans came into their own until they were curbed once more by the rising power of a Protestant aristocracy and gentry equally opposed to royal absolutism and to Puritan nonconformism. This constellation drove a number of Puritan groups from their English homeland and made them seek refuge in the North American colonies. Their flowering was intimately connected with the singularity of North American state formation. But we are straying a little.

If one tries to understand the relationship between power and knowledge, one has to start on the ground floor, not the fiftieth. One has to take into account that the scientific or purely secular type of knowledge which today dominates in more differentiated countries the thought and action of people over a wide sector of their life represents a late phase in the development of knowledge. One cannot omit the high power surplus in relation to other groups which a highly centralized church organization could derive from its monopolistic administration of nonscientific or revealed knowledge. It enabled church authorities to exclude a large part of the population from direct access to the literary sources of revealed knowledge. For a time, the church was the sole guardian of the fund of knowledge. It is unlikely that the breakthrough to a scientific production of knowledge could have been achieved if the continuity of the development of knowledge linking antiquity to modern times had lapsed completely with the disintegration of the Roman Empire. For a time after the collapse of the state, members of the Roman Church were the sole possessors of the art of reading and writing in the Western world. Whether the new ascent would have been possible without that link with antiquity, is a question that needs to be raised, though perhaps it cannot be answered. In this context the reference to the medieval church can serve as a reminder of the high power potential which monopolization of revealed knowledge can convey to its representatives.

It is useful to keep in mind two trends, complementary and ambivalent in their relationship, which were already on the move under the umbrella of the old church, but which came fully into their own only with the break-up of the church's monopoly of knowledge. These two trends were the rise of state governments, instead of church governments, to the position of main controllers of knowledge, and the rise of a new type of knowledge, of secular or scientific knowledge which was more difficult to control. The two trends were in many ways connected, sometimes as allies, sometimes as opponents. One could speak of a two-pronged process of secularization.

Let me say a few words about the distinguishing properties of scientific knowledge. In contrast to revealed knowledge — of an imaginary spirit world with its built-in authoritarian tendencies — scientific knowledge had strong built-in antiauthoritarian tendencies. Heirs of a revelation from largely invisible spirits and of channels of communication with them could easily exclude others from access to the knowledge they possessed. They could keep it to themselves and, in a variety of ways, make others pay for the services they could give on account of their knowledge. Intentions and aims, good will or ill will of spirits could not be ascertained by means of a systematic study of the observable course of events. These could only be known to humans if a spirit itself declared to some human beings its plans, wishes, or intentions. The church saw itself as the heir and guardian of such a revelation from the spirit world. Compared with the authoritative knowledge based on it, knowledge gained through individual observation and reflection, though in some cases useful, could only appear to men and women of the church as knowledge of subordinate and inferior cognitive value. It did not provide information about the all-powerful spirit world of God and his son, of saints and angels and, of course, of devils, about the world of good spirits in the midst of which, according to people's experience, they themselves lived.

Ludes: It is odd to hear you talk about what today would usually be called religion. But you do not use the word. Instead you speak of a specific type of knowledge.

Elias: But is that not what it is? People *knew* that there were saints and angels which could help them, and bad spirits and devils which could tempt them to do forbidden things for which they would later be punished in hell. If I used the term *religion*, people would immediately associate it with the emotionally shallow kind of belief which today, if at all, comes to life only on a Sunday and plays little part in their everyday life. I am speaking of human beings for whom knowledge of the invisible spirit world represented by visible symbols was far more important as a means of orientation than knowledge accessible to human senses.

Millions of human beings regard knowledge of a spirit world as the lynchpin of their whole orientation in this world. What right have I to disregard them? Would I not be a very bad scientist indeed if I considered in my exploration of human knowledge only what I myself regard as correct knowledge and disregard other forms of knowledge? It is a grave mistake to confine a theory of knowledge to the consideration of what we call scientific knowledge, disregarding other forms of knowledge.

If a long-term inquiry into the development of knowledge conclusively shows that scientific knowledge in its two spurts — in Greco-Roman Antiquity and Renaissance and post-Renaissance Europe — was late in becoming the dominant type of knowledge, I have to inquire what other types of knowledge were dominant before. I have to explain why they were dominant before as principal means of orientation, why, after the abortive attempt in Antiquity and undoubtedly with its help, the takeoff into science finally succeeded, at least in the field of nonhuman nature, and why then a process of scientization, often inadquately called "rationalization," helped to induce increasingly rapid changes in society at large. If one considers the process of scientization, with its manifold ramifications and applications on its own without reference to the long antecedent dominance of another nonscientific type of knowledge, one is neither able to see in proper perspective the rise to dominance of a scientific type of knowledge, at least with regard to nature, nor the distinguishing structural characteristics of scientific compared with nonscientific knowledge. One is for instance unable to understand in that case how immensely difficult it was for human beings to gain confidence in themselves, in their own ability to acquire worthwhile knowledge through what we now call systematic scientific research. We must compare the latter kind of knowledge with that acquired through the observation of omens, the flights or intestines of birds, or of oracles, such as that of the Delphian priestess, of miracles such as the healing powers of Lourdes, that the transition from the dominance of the nonscientific to the scientific type of knowledge, which now appears obvious, if not simply rational, was slow and late in coming into its own. People preoccupied with their own insecurities may not understand how much greater, all-pervasive, direct, and continuous the threat to people's security was and still is at earlier stages in the development of human societies when nature was less controllable and humans themselves less self-controlled, more in need of being controlled from without.

Under these conditions, the need for enlisting the help or warding off the wrath of powerful spirits was overwhelmingly strong. One cannot ignore these needs and means of orientation, the collective knowledge devised to satisfy these needs. We do not sufficiently reconstitute and explain for our own understanding the human situation and experience in which the need for knowledge of the spirit world was dominant. And because we do not understand them, we cannot understand ourselves. Today, in a period when the results of research in sciences such as physics and biology have thoroughly changed almost all aspects of people's life, the cognitive value of the blending of antecedent learning, theoretical synthesis, and empirical observation of detail as a road to advances in knowledge, is well understood. It seems almost self-evident. Every rational human being, it seems, can recognize its value for himself. And as every human being is widely held to be rational by nature, people cannot easily understand that their ancestors, being their equals by nature and therefore by definition rational, could not see the cognitive value of this mode of procedure as well as they themselves do. They tacitly dismiss from their mind the inconvenient question of why the scientific mode of acquiring new knowledge has been so late in coming and why, before that time, the human quest for knowledge about the spirit world was so dominant and powerful. People often seem to imagine that scientific knowledge, being "true," being the right kind of knowledge, necessarily *had* to come. The long struggle for recognition of its cognitive value is often forgotten or represented as if scientific "truth" was bound to win. An episode from the life of Galileo throws light on a time when the cognitive value of what we call scientific knowledge and particularly of empirical evidence was not yet obvious. Let me tell you about it.

Galileo had heard of the invention of the telescope in the Netherlands and had produced a better one for himself. One of the first things he did was look through it at the moon. Now, at that time, according to the received knowledge, the moon, like other heavenly bodies, was believed to be perfect. It was thought to be perfectly round and smooth. When Galileo looked at it through his telescope, he saw immediately that this was incorrect. There were apparently mountains on the moon. From a distance, some areas of the moon's surface did not look so very different from what one might expect the earth to look like when seen through a distant telescope. That was heresy. The heavens could not possibly look like the earth. But Galileo insisted. He wrote a little account of it which was praised by some of his acquaintances and attacked by others. When he invited one of the latter to look through his telescope and see for himself, he declined. Mere observation by human beings with their imperfect senses obviously could not refute the accepted and authoritative teaching about the moon which was logical and consistent with the main body of belief — the teaching according to which the earth and the whole sublunar world were imperfect, while moon, sun, and stars, being nearer to the heavens, were perfect.

That was a difference one cannot forget: revealed knowledge and axiomatic or deductive knowledge were not open to empirical tests; sciences such as physics or biology are. Theories in these fields can and must be checked again and again. As every scientific advance and discovery, however convincing and authoritative, can be checked against relevant evidence, it is always open to revision or rejection. The discoveries of pioneering scientists provided a paradigmatic model showing that and how it was possible by a blend of individual learning, observation, and reflection to produce new knowledge and orient oneself in one's actions accordingly, often in contradiction to established authority. Sciences, natural and social, were one of the most powerful levers liberating humanity from its strong tendency to find contentment in submission to authority.

Ludes: Could one not argue that there are very strong tendencies in the opposite direction — toward monopolization of knowledge by scientists? You yourself in your essay "Scientific Establishments" have forcefully argued in that sense.

Elias: You are right. There are in our time strong tendencies toward the production of a kind of academic knowledge which cannot be tested by means of experiments, case studies, statistical measurements, or in any other way. Particularly in the human sciences one frequently comes across abstract intellectual constructions which are presented as theories, though they defy any attempt at empirical testing. Perhaps one could speak of a new deductionism or of neoscholasticism. The difference is that the old scholastic philosophy was bound to a common body of revealed knowledge and a number of authoritative writings interpreting it. From this axiomatic knowledge learned men could draw their conclusions, for instance about the nature of concepts. But the new deductionism is much more individualized. In this case a scholar can think out his or her own axioms individually. One can start from whatever belief, whatever set of political values one cares to adopt. It is not even necessary to state one's axioms. Most representatives of the new deductionism prefer not to be too explicit about their own axioms. Hidden behind a veil of words, they have often the character of social beliefs or political ideals which defy examination in the light of empirical evidence. So far, outside the communist countries, this kind of dogmatism has not been centralized. But although still diffuse, it is probably the strongest single factor hampering discovery in the social sciences and arresting their advance. Their representatives are often tolerant of each others' bias even if it is antagonistic to their own, because others' fixation on the preconceived axioms, the others' axioms and deductions justifies their own. The assumption is that even research claiming to be scientific starts from axiomatic beliefs extraneous to scientific procedure. The tendency to conceal the nonscientific values and beliefs at the root of these intellectual constructions may indicate some awareness of their flaws; but conscience, evidently, is not yet strong enough. So far, deductionists in philosophy, sociology, economics, or whatever, pursue their journeys of nondiscovery unconcerned about their futility, comforted by the well-known excuse: everybody does it. Thus committed to extrascientific values and beliefs, they can draw from them long chains of conclusions to their hearts' content.

The prescription is simple: invent sets of concepts and a vocabulary of your own in accordance with your preconceived belief; use this vocabulary according to convenience in order to define or disguise your axioms. The main point is that some axioms for basic concepts and the conclusions drawn from them must be consistent and form a coherent system of arguments. However, be careful to maneuver concepts in such a way that they can sometimes be linked to empirical evidence, however peripheral and opaque, and to factual experiences which everyone can understand. That gives your readers an opportunity to come up for air from the ocean of arcane abstractions and to think they can follow you. Do not do it too often, though. They will think you serious and profound if they cannot quite understand what you are saying, and you will be free to argue in your own idiosyncratic way. Also, it will be appreciated if you offer from time to time a typology of the Linnaean type, a static classificatory scheme consisting of conceptual boxes you have invented. Unlike that of Linnaeus, which was based on a comprehensive and diligent inquiry into details and consisted of testable conceptual symbols well fitted to the observable evidence, your typology will consist of highly abstract conceptual boxes of your own invention conforming to your hidden axioms, and therefore not easily testable by means of empirical research, if at all. That is how one can make knowledge a mystery and by arguing in a highly intelligent and sophisticated, though as highly idiosyncratic manner, gain from its production a measure of power and authority. If you are very clever it is not difficult to do that sort of thing. It is like building sandcastles at low tide. That is the problem of producing knowledge generally. Symbols are elusive. You sit at your desk with a white sheet waiting for your composition of symbols to fill it, but patterning symbols can be like replacing a matrix. They dissolve easily.

The difficulty is that theories based on fixed axioms and developed from them deductively are of little use in scientific fields which require empirical and theoretical research. There are of course others. Sciences such as pure mathematics or formal logic proceed from axioms deductively. In these fields tests of consistency are enough to show whether conclusions drawn deductively through chains of intermediaries from a given set of axioms are correct. But in the field of natural and social sciences, systems of arguments deduced from freely chosen axioms, however consistent in themselves, do not deserve to be called theories. In these fields, theories have to legitimize themselves through their ability to stimulate and guide empirical research and, in turn, be testable by means of research of this kind. In contrast to one-level sciences such as pure mathematics, two-level sciences require not only consistency tests but empirical tests as well. There is no need to make a mystery of the nature of theories in these two-level sciences. Theories, in this case, are models of synthesis at a variety of levels. They are, at a given stage of a scientific process, symbolic representations of connections between observable details where no connections were known before. An intellectual construct deduced from untestable axioms and as a whole, therefore, equally untestable, cannot fulfill the cognitive functions of a scientific theory. In some respects a symbolic representation of the kind we call theory has cognitive functions akin to those of a geographic map. A wanderer through an unknown region who arrives at a particular spot may not know with certainty how this spot fits into the wider layout of the region through which he is passing. A map could show it to him. But there are no maps of undiscovered regions. There are no theories of undiscovered connections. There may be provisional hypotheses indicating possible connections which for the time being cannot be confirmed, cannot be securely fitted into the main body of symbolic representations serving human groups as means of orientation. Intellectual syntheses deduced from axiomatic ideals and beliefs cannot fulfil this cognitive function. Like maps drawn up according to freely chosen assumptions and without cross-references to the layout of the land itself, they are gravely misleading, useless as means of orientation. There is a lot of useless knowledge produced these days.

Ludes: You mean scientists can produce knowledge of no cognitive value, even a bit of deception? But surely not in the natural sciences?

Elias: No, not so much in the natural sciences. There, scientific establishments of each discipline have ways and means of critically examining claims to innovation, to advances in knowledge, and of arriving at a consensus about the cognitive value of theory proposals. Collective control of innovations, the examination of their cognitive value through an autonomous body of colleagues in many natural sciences is rather impressive. It deserves the closer attention of sociologists all the more, as nothing like it exists in their own field. In the natural sciences, one of the best remembered exceptions is the case of Lysenko. This was an example of state power trying to destroy the relative autonomy of the production of scientific knowledge. It was an example, too, of a wish to please a powerful ruler overwhelming that autonomy of deduction from an axiomatic belief destroying the continuous dialectic movement between deduction and deduction.

Ludes: Is that what you mean by deductionism? Could you perhaps give an example from outside the natural sciences?

Elias: Deductive forms of research starting from hidden or half-hidden wishes or beliefs are not only widely practiced and often presented with authority, they have also found a persuasive advocate in a well-known philosopher of great intellectual power. Karl Popper is, in our time, probably the most authoritative spokesman of the new deductionism. What is more, he follows his own prescriptions; he practices what he preaches. He presents a theory of science clearly deduced from his own preconceived image of an ideal science. Hence in his presentation the description of how science de facto proceeds is never clearly distinguishable from his view of how science ought to proceed. It is not difficult to see what is the ideal science that serves him as point of departure for his deductions about science and its method in general. The title of one of his books, *The Logic of Scientific Discovery*, indicates which science serves him as model. It is logic and, presumably, mathematics which in its pure form is not clearly distinguishable from formal logic. These one-level sciences do proceed from clearly defined axioms deductively. What Popper implies is that all sciences ought to proceed in this manner. The difficulty is that two-level sciences, sometimes called by Popper "empirical sciences," cannot follow this prescription because, in contrast to formal logic and pure mathematics, they operate at both the empirical and theoretical levels at the same time or, in the old language, deductively as well as inductively. Recurrent cross-fertilization is indispensable — the development of theory stimulating empirical research and vice versa. Some of the obscurity in Popper's writing is due to the fact that he ignores or tries to blur the difference between one-level and two-level sciences. As a result, while two-level sciences proceed by deduction as well as induction, Popper remains firmly wedded to the old quarrel between theories of science advocating either a purely deductive or purely inductive scientific method of research or asserting that scientific research de facto proceeds either in one or the other way. One can only guess that, in his theory of science, he has set himself an impossible task. Having set his heart on deductive disciplines, on mathematics and logic as the ideal prototype of science generally, he constructs a theoretical model of a science which makes it appear that two-level sciences can, should, or do proceed more or less in the same way as these one-level sciences. Hence he does not allow for the possibility that results of empirical research, though dependent on theory, can also confirm or destroy it. While stressing the need for testing theories, he blurs the difference between empirical tests and tests of logical consistency. That agrees with the whole tenor of his philosophy. Although he pays lip-service to experience, observation, and experiment, he firmly stands in the line of tradition of those philosophers for whom, as for Descartes and Kant, in the last resort their own reasoning is the sheet-anchor of certainty.

The difference between the old deductionism of the church and the new deductionism widespread within and without the groves of academe, among Marxists as much as among conservatives, among philosophers, sociologists, historians, and many others, is quite striking. It points to one of the reasons why in our time professional participants in the possession of existing or in the production of new knowledge do not command nearly as large resources of power in relation to other groups as did the old church. Representatives of the latter, the old deductionists, could gain certainty from a large body of traditional authorities as the communal depository of revealed knowledge and its interpretation. No one but they had access to it. Moreover, their knowledge was buttressed by a large, reasonably well-integrated hierarchical organization comprising thousands of people. They were bound to each other not only by a common belief, but also by a centralized hierarchical control, at times not very efficient, but putting some constraint on individual members. In contrast, the new deductionists are hardly bound to each other. Mostly, in adopting axioms, beliefs, ideals, they can fall back, individually, on their own resources. In many though not in all cases, the adoption of a deductionist creed is the expression of an extreme individualism: I am my own master; I can choose my own assumptions; I will not allow mere facts to divert me from my beliefs or from what I believe to be the demands of reason. Often the extreme individualism of a deductionist creed shows itself in pangs of solipsistic despair, the negative complement of the rewarding belief in the omnipotence of pure reasoning. The rational deductionist is a secularized relative of the man who did not need to look through Galileo's telescope. He too knows that what one perceives if one looks at the moon through a telescope or, for that matter, if one arrives there in person, is determined by what one has known or thought before. But he does not think that what one has known or thought before, can also be changed as a result of new observations of details about the moon. He does not allow for a world existing independently of the knower's almighty intellect and his axiomatic belief. He does not consider that there is an unknown world yet to be discovered, and that the advanced knowledge of this world may convey to those who acquire it and are in a position to fight for it, power chances which may enable them to confirm or overthrow existing theories, established axioms, values, or beliefs.

Ludes: Are you not in danger of overrating a little the power of scientists?

Elias: I am trying not to. I am trying to bring into the open the paradox of the scientist's case: the dependence of all more advanced and differentiated industrial state-societies on further scientific advances, in all fields, social as well as natural, has become greater than ever. In former days scientific discovery used to be haphazard, accidental, an often anonymous and unplanned social process, or intermittent, the work of an exceptional genius, of an unusually gifted great person here and there. Scientific discovery has now become, to a much higher extent, an institutionalized routine, a planned social process. Thanks to the scientization of knowledge, its advance has become steady and continuous in a great number of fields. There are thousands, perhaps millions of people at work in search of new discoveries, and human knowledge, on low as well as on high levels of synthesis, is expanding at an unprecedented rate. Modern societies thrive on research. Production of new knowledge, or in other words research, has become one of the greatest industries. Discoveries, innovations in knowledge, fuel the development of societies and are fueled in turn by their national and social rivalries and conflicts.

Yet in spite of the central part played by the production of new knowledge and its applications to social requirements, the power ratio of the professional producers of new knowledge, who are often also the guardians and teachers of a society's existing fund of knowledge, is not particularly high compared with that of two groups of economic specialists, entrepreneurs and trade unionists, and particularly compared with politicians.

Ludes: But is that not what one would expect? Politicians are after all especially concerned with problems of power.

Elias: I know, there is a strong tendency to equate power with political power. But is that right?

Ludes: No, of course not. But many people would agree that politicians are more concerned with problems of power than any other group. It is a simplification, but could one not say that power is what politics is about?

Elias: A special kind of power, yes. But not power in general. That is a little difficult, I know. We have a traditional classificatory scheme according to which human societies are divided into an economic and a political sphere which is sometimes called "social" and sometimes "societal," probably because it is confusing to call the third box for the leftovers "social." Whatever is classified as political or economic is social as well. This conceptual scheme, moreover, is sanctified and removed from critical examination by academic institutions. There it is fairly normal to divide social sciences into political science, economics, and sociology. This greatly strengthens the response that power is the proper concern of politicians and accordingly of political scientists. Economists are not greatly interested in problems of power. Nor, oddly enough, were sociologists for a long time interested in power relations outside of the immediate political realm. Yet power struggles play a very large and basic part in all relationships between and within economic enterprises. They play a large part too in the movement of prices and wages, in determining rates of investment and productivity, of inflation and unemployment. That economics has never quite lost the character of the "dismal science," is partly due to the almost complete neglect of problems of power by academic economists, perhaps as a one-sided overreaction in the opposite direction to the one-sidedness of the Marxian theory, with its fixation on one particular type of power struggle, which is better than nothing.

As for sociologists, I do not want to expand on that subject. Let me only mention the famous theory of the so-called nuclear family. Not a word about the changing balance of power between the sexes or between parents and children, which plays so central a part in shaping family relations. I know what I am saying because at an earlier stage in my life I studied the changing balance of power between the sexes in European societies very thoroughly and I know how different the sociological approach to family relations would be if sociologists were no longer afraid to touch this aspect. Experiences such as this have contributed to the certainty with which I can say that power balances are an aspect of all human relationships.

Ludes: But why have you not published that so far?

Elias: One of those accidents. After I had finished the two volumes on the civilizing process and a small book, not yet published, called *The Society of Individuals*, I wrote *The Changing Balance of Power Between the Sexes*. At that time I typed everything myself. Carelessly I had made no carbon copy of the manuscript left in my office at Leicester University. Many years later, at my request, a colleague took it from the shelves and put it on my desk to forward it to me. Perhaps it fell down. In any case, the cleaners put it in the incinerator with the garbage.

Ludes: What a pity. But why do you think is it today a fairly well-established and popular idea that power is mainly associated with politics?

Elias: There are two interconnected reasons. First, power is a bit of a dirty word. Many people seem to feel that power should not exist. They mean of course power inequalities. One shrinks from the idea of associating something valued negatively with something valued positively, such as the family or personal relationships generally. Second, political power is a special kind of power. It is even today perhaps the most conspicuous form of a hierarchic power relationship. Most people would probably be ready to say that a head of government, especially a dictator such as Stalin or Mussolini, is a powerful man. They might say that a British prime minister or the presidents of France and the United States have great power, and victory in a war or even in a state election will still be widely acclaimed as the apogee of power. The centralized control of military and police forces still endows generals, party leaders, heads of state, with a high power potential compared with other resources of power. In many situations it still is, even if it remains in the wings, the decisive factor in power struggles between and within states, though the revulsion against the use of violence is growing. Compared with politicians who in more developed societies have become the main contenders for control of the twin monopolies of physical force and taxation, people who as private persons participate in the monopolistic control of the means of production are not only less conspicuous, they are ultimately also dependent on the controllers of state monopolies, particularly in their capacity as controllers of military and police forces and of taxation. They are dependent on them not only because the nonviolent character of the relations of production, of economic relationships generally can be maintained in the long run, even in an age of general education, only if the integrated state monopolies and especially that of violence function smoothly and effectively, but also because the private monopolization of the means of production, by its very nature as a private monopoly, is never as highly centralized as state monopolies, is segmental compared with the monolithic character of state monopolies. That Marx in his budding theory of power treated the power potential derived from the monopolistic control of military and police forces purely as a derivative of the monopolistic control of capital was certainly one of the major weaknesses of his theory. But then he never made the attempt to develop a unitary theory of the power aspects of human relationships.

Ludes: You are saying that there are different sources of power. Do you mean to say that one is inclined to associate power particularly with state power, with the political sphere of society in general, because this is the most conspicuous or because it is the strongest form of power? Could you tell us a little more about what constitutes state power and how it relates to the power to be derived from knowledge?

Elias: I shall try, but I know you would not wish me to expand too much in that direction. Take the most elementary aspects. Think of absolute princes or dictators. How do they manage to keep control over their country? First of all by controlling a well-organized military or police force which alone is entitled to use violence within their country, which can more or less effectively prevent all other people from using violence by threatening them with violence or using it against them.

Ludes: Yes, I know. The monopoly of physical force. You have shown how it originates.

Elias: And the monopoly of taxation. It is not the use of physical force alone, but its monopolization, the effective exclusion of all other groups or individuals from using physical force, which accounts for the normally superior power rate of governments and particularly of dictatorial governments in relation to the governed. The effective monopolies of physical force and taxation endow governments with a higher power potential than the governed, enable the few to control and constrain the many. Many dictators of the twentieth century have learned to use their monopolized agencies of physical force, their military and police forces, to monopolize control over many other resources — they have often learned to do that very effectively, although their task is more difficult than it was for the autocratic princes of former days.

I shall confine myself to naming a few social requirements over which totalitarian dictators of the twentieth century usually try to maintain a monopolistic control. The Soviet Union is probably at present the most accomplished regime of this type. There the government combines with the monopolies of physical force and taxation a monopoly of the means of production — the whole processes of capital formation and investment are controlled by the state — a monopolistic control of all associations, such as parties, trade unions, or any other attempts of people to organize or assemble. With these monopolies, the Soviet government further combines a monopoly of the means of orientation, a knowledge monopoly. Many other contemporary dictatorial regimes also try to establish a centralized control of the means of orientation. But the Soviet attempt, after the breakdown of the knowledge monopoly of the medieval church, is probably the most successful of its kind. It greatly adds to the high power potential which the Soviet government derives from its comprehensive accumulation of monopolistic controls and without which the centrifugal forces of the Soviet Union's many nationalities exerting pressure against Soviet Russia's centralizing supremacy, could perhaps not be kept in check quite as firmly. The dictatorial autocracy of the Soviet Union differs in a number of respects very markedly from the monarchical autocracy of the Russian Empire of which it is the heir. The unification of belief throughout the vast empire in terms of an inner-worldly social doctrine, Marxism-Leninism, is an example of that difference.

Perhaps the example helps to answer your question regarding state power and knowledge. One may doubt whether a vast industrializing empire requiring for its advance a relatively high standard of secular knowledge could be kept together by the threat of physical force alone, aided perhaps, as in the days of the Czar, by unifying means of orientation provided by a church. A secular social doctrine whose interpretation and development can be centrally controlled probably serves better than a supernatural belief the requirements of a dictatorial government whose principal task, in conjunction with the defense of the realm, is industrialization, machinization, increasing productivity, or improving the standard of living. It is odd to think that many of the virtues ascribed by Max Weber, under the name of "inner-worldly asceticism," to the preaching of Puritan sects, such as application to work and traditional sexual morality, can now be rediscovered as part of an official doctrine in industrializing countries, especially under Communist Party rule.

Ludes: You have pointed to a number of monopolies controlled by governments as the source of their power. You say that in the case of the Soviet Union a monopoly of knowledge is one of them. Do you then think that the various monopolies you have mentioned have equal weight as sources of governmental power?

Elias: That is a difficult question. But I can at least say why it is difficult. To establish reliable military and police forces as executive organs of a governmental monopoly of physical force has, in the twentieth century, become fairly easy. It is far more difficult to establish and maintain throughout a vast empire a watertight control of the means of production and perhaps even of association than of knowledge. The control of deviant means of orientation is more difficult than the control of unlicensed means of violence. That said, I must add that the main reason I find your question difficult is lack of knowledge. Let me suggest a thought experiment. What would happen in the Soviet Union, if the other monopolies I have mentioned were fully maintained with the same severity as now, but monopolistic control of the means of orientation and communication were abolished? People could express in books, newspapers, magazines, and through other media views critical of, or even directly opposed to official doctrine. If you inquire into the power potential of knowledge you have to envisage situations such as this.

Ludes: But are there not in Western countries, too, tendencies toward a monopolistic control of knowledge?

Elias: There most certainly are. Soviet control may be stricter, more monolithic and efficient because the competition between parties in Western contries or that of the media greatly enlarges the scope for the expression of divergent views. Nevertheless, the complete dependence on public finance and state control of most of the schools in many Western countries, for instance, where children may spend as many as eight or ten of the most impressionable years of their lives, can give governments an almost monopolistic influence on the knowledge of history, religion, biology, and many other fields selected for transmission from one generation to another.

There are many other examples of monopolies in the field of knowledge and its transmission in Western societies. In a number of academic fields, intellectual constructs presented as theories are couched in a particularly difficult language, not because the subject demands it — in fact, the teaching of the subject itself might greatly benefit from a simpler, less forbidding language — but because of the academic prestige attached to theories which are difficult to understand and which can exclude the noninitiated from access to the field. Councils of medical men and jurists can limit the number of university places in their field to limit competition. The editors of periodicals specializing in book reviews, for reasons of their own, can decide to block the sale of a book by sending it to a reviewer from a different field, as happened with one of my books on sociological theory. Reviewed by a historian, it was presented as a lot of nonsense. There are many other ways and degrees of monopolizing knowledge.

In Eastern societies there is a state monopoly of the basic means of orientation which is particularly inflexible in the social sciences where one particular doctrine, Marxism-Leninism, holds a monopolistic position excluding other theories and thus innovations of thought. In Western countries there is instead a great variety of knowledge monopolies, large and small, but no centralized state monopoly of the basic means of orientation, either in the field of nonhuman nature or in that of human societies. In all these fields, consensus may or may not arise from discussions between competing views.

Ludes: But are there not in Western countries, too, certain types of knowledge completely monopolized by the state, not only knowledge concerning advanced types of weaponry but also a wide range of technical and scientific knowledge which, in the standard phrase, might be useful to any enemy?

Elias: Yes. In this sphere monopolization of knowledge does not simply mean that knowledge is selectively and ideologically distributed to others. It means total secrecy. No one outside a selected circle of initiates is admitted to this kind of knowledge. In many cases the gain to be expected from this kind of secrecy is temporary rather than permanent. This is part of an arms race. The development of new weapons, new chemicals, new types of sophisticated machinery generally is a very time-consuming business. Spies who steal from another country the results of experiments made in the course of ten or fifteen years may save the country for which they are spying a lot of money and time which can be of vital importance in an arms race. I mention this because it allows me to refer once more to one of the distinguishing characteristics of scientific knowledge crucial to the monopolization of knowledge. It is extremely difficult, if not impossible, to keep an advance in scientific knowledge and its practical applications secret indefinitely. If one group of people has made such an advance, it is a question of time and money when a competing group will make it too. This is an important factor in the relationship between power and knowledge. And not even with regard to knowledge alone. Think once more of the monopoly of physical violence. Its maintenance depends today in part on a knowledge monopoly. One of the principal characteristics of the twentieth century is the difficulty in preventing a determined opposition group within a state from gaining access to, or even from making at home, some extremely destructive weapons, thus breaking at least for a time a state's monopoly on violence. In the Middle Ages it was extremely difficult for peasants to gain access to the costly equipment of horse, armor, sword, or lance which gave a group of knights ravaging the countryside an irresistible military superiority. Today militant opposition groups can violate the state's monopoly on physical force for many years provided they have sufficient support from the population. That support is crucial.

Ludes: In your writings you have demonstrated how and why state organizations emerge. You have stressed that over time the techniques of control and supervision at the disposal of state authorities, and especially the control of violence, have become increasingly effective. Now you appear to stress the opposite view. You point to the fact that armed opposition in defiance of the state's monopoly on physical force may under certain conditions also become more effective.

Elias: Yes. The two views are not incompatible. Scientific advances and those in social organization are helping to make the state's supervisory techniques in controlling both violence and tax evasion more effective and stringent. As is usual in the development of societies, the same advances may also benefit trends in the opposite direction. The nature of scientific research does not always enable one to bring into focus at once all the aspects of a discovery one tries to present. At the time I started research in this field, I jumped as it were into the knowledge stream. The investigation of long-term processes in general and particularly of state formation

processes was not fashionable. It was important to show that social processes have a structure, and I was fortunate enough to discover that in
France the state formation process leading from a condition of almost
complete disintegration of the power resources of the nominal central
authority to a highly effective centralization based on the twin monopolies
of physical force and taxation, had a fairly straight and continuous social
progress in that direction (of course, with regression and
countermovements). I tried to point out that the process in that direction
was the outcome of a series of struggles on a variety of levels which resulted in the emergence of a full-fledged monopolization of physical force
and taxes. But the concept representing the static result of the long sequence of a knock-out competition, the concept of a monopoly on physical
force, impressed itself more strongly on the mind of readers than the concept of a monopolization *process*. Many readers must have received the
impression that the social institutions emerging from a long process have
the same character as natural organs resulting from a process of biological
evolution. But states that have evolved in connection with a long series of
struggles between centrifugal and centripetal forces, as a result of victories of the latter, can also partly or wholly disintegrate as a result of victories of the former or of lost wars with rivals — although the lessening of
inequalities within a state and the heightened national consciousness of a
literate population makes the complete disintegration of industrial
nation-states more difficult.

My theoretical model of the formation of a state can be wrongly interpreted as model of a natural process: once a monopoly of physical force
has come into being, one may think that it is there forever. That is a
misinterpretation. Complete or partial disintegration of states are
frequent occurrences. Hitler's bid for European hegemony resulted in a
partition of the former German Reich. Intrastate and interstate conflicts
can result in the splitting, or partition, or fragmentation of states. There is
no contradiction between strong trends toward strengthening the central
control of states in our time and countertrends which may be directed
toward the break-up of the central monopolies but which may also be directed simply toward checking the controllers of these central monopolies
more effectively and stringently.

Ludes: Is that what you mean by functional democratization?

Elias: Yes, partly. The increasing power potential of the state population
connected with such factors as higher educational levels and greater dependence of governments on the governed, who need to be highly motivated if a complex state-society is to function well, does not become fully
effective if the organizational and institutional means at the disposal of

the state population for curbing the controllers are not fully developed. But even if the pressure is diffuse, if the control is not highly organized, the sentiment of the mass of the population, technically often called "public opinion," is today a stronger factor in the fluctuating power balances of a state-society than ever before. That is why manipulating public opinion on the part of governments and, in multiparty states, of political parties, has in our day become a fine art. That is a point to remember in any discussion of the relationship between power and knowledge. Knowledge, in the twentieth century more than ever before, has become a cheap commodity. A vast network of educational institutions from elementary schools to universities which in continental Europe is mostly financed by the state, has the function of transmitting specific sections of a country's social fund of knowledge to the younger generation. The fund of knowledge of the more developed industrial nation-states of our age has become so vast and the acquisition of large funds of it so indispensable for anyone wishing to lead a normal adult life in these societies, that it has been determined not only to allow but to compel every child to acquire the fundamentals of social knowledge in a dozen different fields or so.

I cannot make here more than passing reference to another function of compulsory education closely connected with that of transmitting knowledge and equally indispensable for a normal adult life. Next to the family, the school is the most important civilizing agency of children in our society. That is not, of course, on the program. It is as a by-product of the transmission of knowledge that schools perform their civilizing function, that they help children to master their more impetuous urges and to channel them into the acquisition of knowledge, skills, and the growth of conscience. To show in greater detail when and why princes or other governing agents felt it necessary and were able to finance schools and special institutions for the training of teachers, is a task which for the greater part still lies ahead of us. But the fact itself, the fact that governments felt impelled to finance, partly or wholly, a steadily expanding set of institutions for the compulsory education of their country's youth and the rising educational standards of the population, was certainly an important factor enhancing the power potential of the state-population. But the pendulum swung back and forth. Because a rise in educational standards helped to increase the power potential of the governed, governments were often weary of it and their support for the country's educational institutions was often lukewarm. This ambivalent attitude toward the spread of knowledge showed itself even more strongly in the attitude of many governments and, indeed, of professional politicians toward a social group, a large section of which was specifically concerned with the handling, diffusion, and production of knowledge. I am referring to the group of people rather vaguely called "intellectuals."

Ludes: I was wondering whether we would come to them. In the political and sociological discussion of our time intellectuals are frequently mentioned. For some groups they are a perpetual feature of their political demonology. But who are they, these intellectuals? We know where we stand when we speak of industrial workers and industrial entrepreneurs as social groups or of professional politicians. Compared with them, however, the intellectuals as a social group seem elusive. You suggest that they have a special affinity to knowledge. Yet it is difficult to imagine intellectuals as a group comparable to these others.

Elias: Yes, I agree. As a social group intellectuals are elusive. Since Mannheim the term *free-floating* has gained currency in connection with them, or perhaps I should say with us. One of the reasons they are elusive is the fact that, as a group, they are much more highly individualized and diverse than any comparable groups you have mentioned. They have no single representative organization. Politicians have their parties, workers their trade unions, employers their federations.

Ludes: Yes, there is no federation of intellectuals, who are rather individualistic, although there is a tendency among them to join professional associations. But there must be some common characteristics, some specific functions which mark people out as intellectuals and give them the appearance of a group.

Elias: I have often wondered about that. Could one perhaps say that intellectuals are specifically concerned with the production, distribution, and handling of social symbols? I know it sounds odd. But human beings live after all in a symbolic universe of their own making. At a much earlier stage of social development, people were often producers of food, tools, and weapons, builders of huts and houses, and producers of symbols at the same time. As societies became wealthier and more differentiated, the occupation with symbols became a social specialty. Of course, symbols with the social function of knowledge are only one class of symbols among others. Sculptors, composers, film makers, playwrights, and the mimetic intellectuals are producers of symbols too. School teachers are transmitting symbols from one generation to another. As I said, symbols which possess the social function of means of orientation are only one class of symbols, and people who are specialists in the transmission and production of knowledge are only one class of intellectuals. There is a close affinity between the specialized occupation with symbols and the specialized occupation with culture.

Ludes: That is helpful. It explains the diversification of intellectuals. But is it enough?

Elias: Perhaps not. As you say, it gives one a closer grip on their social function and distinguishing characteristics as a particularly individualized and diversified group with little organizational cohesion.

Ludes: And yet apparently with sufficient common characteristics to make them appear as a coherent group?

Elias: Well, although most intellectuals have an occupation and are in that sense specialists, they are at the same time nonspecialists. They are people with knowledge, understanding, and sensitivity beyond their own occupational specialism. They usually have broad cultural interests and a tendency to think for themselves, to form what they see as an independent opinion and develop a well-thought-out set of critical arguments about a wide field of topics. This highbrow stance, this competence and interest beyond their occupational specialism, and most particularly the tendency to take a well-argued critical view of things is regarded, according to taste, as the great task and virtue of intellectuals or as their unforgivable sin. Because they hold so many positions devoted to the production, transmission, and management of new knowledge, their power potential is fairly high. Because of their tendency toward independent individual judgment and the low cohesion of any grouping they form with each other, their factual power ratio compared with that of more firmly organized social groups is low. Although *intellectual* is often used as a derogatory term by political groups on both the Right and Left, the severest critics of intellectuals are usually intellectuals themselves.

Ludes: But is mutual criticism enough? Is it not also necessary that knowledge producers — in this case especially social scientists — work out alternatives, possibly realizable, to predominant patterns of social life?

Elias: Yes, that is important. Perhaps I can tell you a little utopian tale with which I have played around for some time. It is called "The Great Struggle of the Intellectuals." Utopias, imaginary tales of state-societies as they could, should, or should not be, are very useful for clearing one's mind. They are also often enjoyable. I do not think I can tell you the whole story, but some parts of it have a bearing on our topic.

Ludes: Fine, do go ahead.

Elias: For reasons I will tell you about in a moment, two groups of intellectuals played a central part in the great debates of the country. They were known as Traditionalists and Innovators. It was a wealthy society. Within it inequalities in living standards and the power ratios of the various groups had shrunk, though they had not completely disappeared. But memories of the time when they had been much greater lingered on. In their wake, some innovators fought for further equalization of both. The main focus of conflicts and tensions, in the period of which I am speaking, had shifted from within the state to between states. That was presumably one of the reasons why within the country dissensions between two camps of intellectuals and the influence they had on government policy now played a much larger part than before.

Inequalities in the wealth and power rates of different countries were still great. Conflicts in the form of cold and hot wars were frequent. Shooting wars were extremely destructive and affected everyone on earth. The country of the Traditionalists and Innovators had managed to keep out of the wars. Some districts had suffered severely from hostilities between neighboring countries. The financial compensation the country had received did not help very much those who had been killed, crippled, or damaged by radiation. The whole issue was very alive and influenced both the battles between the political groupings and the leading politicians in the country at large as well as those between the two camps of intellectuals, the "Trads" and "Inns," as they were called. But before I go on, I have to explain one of the curious institutions of this country and tell you briefly about its history.

One of the central institutions of the state was public debates about fundamental issues between at least two representatives each of the Traditionalists and Innovators. They took place in one of the enormous halls they had in this country, seating many thousands of people or, if the weather was fine, in an equally large stadium. These debates served the clarification of basic issues and between 60 and 90 percent of the country's population listened to them at home and watched them on their screens. The debate itself usually lasted two hours. There were set rules, an umpire who summed up — I will not bother you with details. After two hours, five additional questions which had come in from the country at large during the debate, were chosen by an umpire and read out to the debating teams, who were expected to answer them briefly, but could also refuse to answer. The main point was that, when all this was over, an immediate vote was taken throughout the country, in which all watchers and listeners, who by a previous signal had made themselves known as participants, could take part. They all had at home and also at their seats in the hall or stadium a number of buttons. By pressing one or several of them voters could immediately make known fairly differentiated responses to the debate. They could for instance express the view that the information and arguments presented by one team were irrefutable and definitely more convincing than those of the opposite side. Pressing another button could indicate qualified consent with one view, agreement with part of it, though not with the whole. A more recent technique allowed people to say that, although one side had convinced them, they thought a few points of the other side were valid. Another button allowed the public to say that in their view the issue of the debate was inconclusive but that they saw no point in pursuing the matter further. Yet another button, finally, allowed them to say that, although inconclusive, the matter deserved to be discussed once more; therefore plans for another debate should be made. There was a discussion in the country at large about allowing voters an even more differentiated response, but we need not go into that.

These debates and the views about them expressed by the public at large had a strong impact on governmental decisions. But to understand that one must know two things. First, the educational level of the population was much higher than it is today. There was a widespread conviction buttressed by public debates that a desirable and enjoyable society was possible if all its members had knowledge, competence, and sensitivity of judgment far beyond the requirements of his or her occupational specialization. Fossilized and corrupted knowledge had been weeded out from schools, universities, and educational institutions generally.

Ludes: Do you remember one or two examples from your utopian country which might help us understand better what its citizens regarded as corruption of knowledge?

Elias: Certainly. There was the case of a leading theoretical physicist, a mathematical genius who was all the more famous as his body was atrophied by an incurable illness. He moved in a wheelchair. He could not speak clearly. His wife and a close circle of friends had to translate to others what he said. But his intellect was clear and powerful. At that time some physicists still maintained that the universe had a beginning. He was one of them. In his mathematical calculations he had gone beyond the big explosion — the big bang — which was then believed to have been the beginning of our universe, and had found that the exploding entity might have had the character of a singularity. Asked in an interview why he laid so much stress on the concept of a "beginning" which was disputed by other almost equally famous theoretical physicists, he replied that quite apart from his mathematical calculations, which pointed toward an entity of enormous density as the origin of the universe, he also believed that people would feel happier if they thought that the universe had a definite beginning. This statement was taken up by some of his opponents as an example of the corruption of knowledge.

Those engaged in research, in extending discovery of the natural and social world, could not allow themselves to be influenced in their findings by what they thought made people happy. It was absolutely certain, they insisted, that the blind natural processes of the physical universe ran in many respects counter to human wishes, to what would give humans satisfaction and enjoyment. The same, they pointed out, was true of the social universe. Largely resulting from unplanned social process, it did in many respects not agree with human needs, with the desire for contentment. To think that the world was made to please humans, they said, was a child's dream and dangerous — it blocked recognition of the fact that the unplanned natural and social processes could not be expected to comply with human needs, except as a result of the concerted exertions, knowledge, and wisdom of human beings themselves. The good world, they insisted, had not been given to human beings as a present; humans themselves had to create it. Efforts in that direction, they claimed, were bound to become paralyzed if theoretical physicists or, for that matter, social scientists preferred one theoretical model to another because it would make people happier or better fitted their own ideals. That was corrupted knowledge. Of course, I only repeat what I have learned about the early discussions in that country. But perhaps it makes the problem a little clearer.

Ludes: Yes, it does. I suppose there was some literature.

Elias: Yes, there was. When I heard about this country, the whole struggle which I have just mentioned was already a thing of the past. I should have mentioned that the event which brought the whole issue in the open and which acted as catalyst for the reform movement that followed, was the publication of a book written by two great people, husband and wife, now long dead, but known to every child in that country. It was a book in two volumes called *The Pollution of Knowledge*. The first volume demonstrated how and why politicians corrupted knowledge. It brought into focus some of the problems I have mentioned before. It demonstrated the constraints in the situation of politicians which, given the then existing institutions, were conducive to the corrosion of knowledge by partisanship and dogmatic beliefs. It demonstrated how political struggles compelled participants to twist their arguments to suit sectional interests, which were not always identical with their country's best interests.

As the authors pointed out, for a long time everyone had been accustomed to this corruption of knowledge; it seemed impossible to do anything about it. Case studies demonstrated in detail the harm done by the continuous spread of misleading knowledge, by this pollution of a country's culture. The second volume was concerned with the pollution of knowledge by specialists for the production of new knowledge and for the diffusion, management, and intergenerational transmission of knowledge.

In their case, as the authors pointed out, the ideological distortion of knowledge was often less obvious; it was usually more disguised, partly because the overt aim of knowledge specialists was the presentation of unbiased research results, partly because knowledge specialists were less powerful than other, better organized groups such as professional politicians or the two principal groups of economic specialists. As a result, knowledge specialists were in many respects dependent on more powerful groups. They tended, knowingly or not, to drive along ideologically in their slipstream. There was some uneasiness about the pollution of supposedly unbiased knowledge prior to the publication of the book. The book itself demonstrated that this pollution of knowledge and the misorientation resulting from it went far deeper, was more widespread and dangerous than anyone had known before. That set the reform movement going.

Ludes: And the great public debates between two teams of knowledge specialists were the result of that movement?

Elias: I am coming to that. They were part of the story. There were apparently related things which had to be done. It was their experience that the problems confronting them could not be solved unless several interdependent conditions were gradually changed. A series of disastrous wars and other calamities lay behind them. All these disasters, they now saw, were partly due to the faulty judgment and lack of adequate knowledge of those in government and their advisors. At least in some cases these people had been elected to their high offices by the greater part of the population. So the disasters were also due, in part, to the faulty judgment of the population itself. Their educational level, and perhaps the spectrum of knowledge offered to the younger generation, did not prepare them sufficiently for the task of selecting the most suitable people for governmental offices or of asserting their potential power when they felt they were being misled. People were easily swayed in their judgment by emotional rhetoric and ideological distortion of knowledge. One of the tasks, members of the reform movement recognized, was developing high schools and teacher training establishments to allow all men and women a clearer, wider, more certain and factual orientation about the internal and external affairs of their country and indeed of humanity. They believed that this would also enhance their capacity for enjoyment. The enormous success of the public debates I mentioned before confirmed that view. Great public debating contests became almost as popular as soccer games. Already at school, debating contests at various levels were a regular feature. They greatly helped children in their acquisition of knowledge and were widely enjoyed.

The difficulty was that one could not introduce in schools the kind of knowledge that could serve as the basis for a vivid, solid, and differentiated understanding of this world, unless one improved simultaneously the flow of communication between knowledge specialists and the mass of the population. That required a firm determination by the knowledge producers themselves to present as much as possible of the knowledge produced in a form accessible to interested nonspecialists, to the public at large. There was a prolonged debate within the circles of specialists about ways and means of lessening the esoteric presentation of their research results, of widening the flow of communication with the public at large. How much technical language closed to all but the specialists in a particular knowledge field was indispensable for a clear statement of the research process and its results? How much of it was merely a means of enhancing the status of a group of knowledge producers in the eyes of the general public or in its status struggles with other groups? It was found that the use of highly specialized verbal and nonverbal symbols was indispensable in some cases. In others, it appeared, the use of a complicated, precious, and arcane language was merely a conceit used on the assumption that it added to the prestige of a discipline, and often enough as a means of disguising basic flaws of the knowledge produced. The internal debates showed that a considerable improvement in the flow of communication to the outside world was possible in all fields, but that the scope for improvement differed from field to field. Finally the internal discussion widened into a broader public discussion culminating in one of the great public debates between a team of Traditionalists and a team of Innovators. Although it ended in a draw, it proved to be an important stepping stone in the gradual reform of the way in which new means of orientation, discoveries in all fields were normally presented and integrated into the curricula of schools and universities. Gradually the preference for the presentation of knowledge in a clear, simple, and vivid literary form gained the upper hand; and as the high esteem of obscurity and ideological distortion diminished, one could see how much pseudo-knowledge had been hidden behind it. Greater accessibility of the specialists' knowledge, particularly of their advances and discoveries, opened new sources of interest and enjoyment for the public at large and made it easier to raise the educational standard of the whole population.

The new information that flowed through the wider channels helped to enhance people's capacity for orientation in their social and natural worlds. It gave them a firmer grasp not only of their own country's internal affairs, but also of its global interdependencies and of their long-term, as distinct from momentary interests. It also raised, beyond all expectations, the country's peaceful competitive capacity in the economic, technological, and cultural spheres and, generally, its standing in world affairs. One should remember that although, at the time I am speaking of, power differentials between states were still great, and interstate relations still disturbed and disturbing, intrastate differences of power chances and living standards in the country itself were small. People were educated and civilized enough to enjoy discussions, small and large, on a great variety of topics, to take sides intensely but without venom, without much need to show off, and to judge arguments on their merit. They were not as worried as people are today by the question: "is it good or bad for me or for us?"

Ludes: That was already the result of the struggle and the reform movement you have mentioned?

Elias: Yes, but I have to add one further link in the chain. I have already briefly referred to one of the most curious institutional arrangements that emerged from the movement of reform. On the one hand, their public debates on fundamental and long-term issues were, according to law, conducted exclusively by knowledge specialists. Professional politicians were not allowed to take part in them. On the other hand, also according to the law of the land, knowledge specialists were not allowed to enter governments and, although it was not wholly impossible, there were considerable barriers making it difficult for them to enter political parties. If one asked people the reason for this institutional arrangement, they would usually tell you that it represented a division of labor. Politicians immersed in governmental or party work were usually confronted with, and often overwhelmed by, short-term problems. Although at least some decisions they had to make required an unbiased understanding of long-term and fundamental issues, in many cases they did not have the time and in some cases the knowledge required for the consideration of issues which demanded a firm and factual long-term orientation. As some knowledge specialists pointed out, the qualities required for governing a country were not necessarily the same as those required for the rise in a party organization. If governing politicians, perhaps in conjunction with their military or economic advisors, pursued an arbitrary partisan policy or, as often happened, a policy positively harmful to their country and perhaps dangerous to humanity, there was no group of people in their country whose institutional position and professional competence endowed them with sufficient authority to be heard, if they stood up and advised caution or a revision of governmental policy. It had to be a body of individuals who were not only de facto sufficiently detached from the turmoil of short-term politics, but who were also *known* to be reasonably detached from the hurly-burly of these day-to-day battles, known above all to be without political ambition. The question was, how one could leave unimpaired the ultimate power of those who governed to decide all issues of state and at the same time create an independent institution whose members could publicly debate major policy issues with results which were purely consultative, not binding on governments, and yet sufficiently authoritative and backed by a wide public opinion to make governments think twice. That, as far as I could gather, was the basic idea.

Knowledge specialists in the service of governments or political parties had neither sufficient independence nor power to offer effective advice to governments or party leaders which fundamentally differed from the course dictated by sectional short-term interests, unrealizable ideals, and dogmatic beliefs. Moreover, sectional short-term interests pursued within a country were often at variance with that country's long-term interests. In politics, the former prevailed. There was no one to represent the latter publicly and with authority. Even if a voice of that kind had existed, no one would probably have been ready to listen to it.

Defects such as this were among the major institutional reasons for the grave errors of judgment on the part of governments and their advisors which, as one now recognized, were responsible for the dismal events of the past. Politicians, I was told, faded away, leaving behind a country which had to bear the burden of their errors. A judiciary counterweight to governments was not enough. There was a need for an independent court of knowledge debating not only behind closed doors, but also in public. In the past, knowledge specialists had been too fragmented, too divided among themselves, and too dependent on governments or public and private financing to make their voice heard, even if they clearly recognized the pitfalls and the long-term dangers of their government's policy and the tainted knowledge used there as a guide. With few exceptions, the power rate of scientists and knowledge specialists was small compared to that of political and economic specialists. The expert skill of knowledge specialists was certainly needed. Their discoveries were one of the main motors of social development. Specialization of knowledge had probably increased at a faster rate than ever before. There was a widening gap of understanding both between the public and experts and among the experts themselves. The media bravely tried to bridge the gap. But as time went on, it became clearer that new institutional means were needed to provide regular channels of communication between the guardians and producers of society's expanding fund of knowledge on the one hand and, on the other hand, the public at large and all kinds of institutions which were consumers of knowledge and which required the help of independent knowledge specialists. A growing trend had thrust more and more knowledge specialists into a role akin to that formerly held by courtiers in the service of powerful princes. That was one of the reasons for the widespread corruption of knowledge.

A relatively autonomous council of knowledge whose members could speak with integrity though not necessarily with one voice was the answer to problems of this kind. In matters of knowledge it was by no means always the majority that was right. The ultimate aim in the production of new knowledge was establishing consensus about the cognitive value of research results among those able to judge. But if at a given time attempts at establishing consensus failed, it was useful for those who needed expert information and for society at large, to know exactly what the differences between the experts were and why they could not come to an agreement. Public debates could demonstrate where experts differed and why.

In the preceding era the habit had grown, in some fields of knowledge more than in others, to allow different and perhaps antagonistic views to stand side-by-side in silence, without any communicating channels between their representatives and without debates. What remained was a landscape of ivory towers. The tradition of civilized controversy and the skills required by it had more or less disappeared. To revive that tradition and to cultivate these skills again was one of the reasons for the institution of debates between teams of experts. Many divergencies of view fitted into the mold of Trads and Inns; if they did not, one allowed for other labels. From the public point of view, the open discussions were an instructive way of bringing into focus the area of agreement among experts and the reasons why, for the time being, they could not agree beyond it. Open debates were also a useful way of discovering to what extent disagreement had a substantive reason, such as a real gap in the existing factual knowledge, and to what extent it was due to incompatible preconceptions of one or both sides.

Ludes: It would be a useful way to round off this account if you could give us one or two brief examples of the topics debated by the two teams.

Elias: I will do that in a moment. Allow me just one more concluding remark about the institutional setup. There were several interlocking problems that had to be solved. One of these was how to secure, for the information of governments and public alike, the best knowledge available for assessing a public issue — knowledge produced with a long-range perspective and thus not dominated by the political and social divisions of the day. That experts were divided into Traditionalists and Innovators was a convenient but elastic framework for a debate. Both sides were committed to the ethos of the institution, to the aim of providing fact-related, not doctrine-related knowledge and of seeking agreement with each other, of allowing oneself to be convinced by the views of one's opponents. The public tournaments were only one part of a more complex structure. The two teams engaged in a particular discussion, or some of their members, could sit as a council with or without the invitation of governments and make pronouncements or publish a report on a topic under discussion. In practice this was not done too often. If it was, their statement or report (in most cases critical of government policy) was usually received with respect and was rarely without influence on government decisions. One of the most famous of these reports was written in a tense international situation threatening war. The report was concerned with the problem of which long-term changes in the internal balance of power and thus in the political system of the belligerent countries were likely to be brought about by the threatening war. There was some agreement and some disagreement among the experts. They also made a distinction between the likely political consequences of a short and of a long war. Complete agreement had been reached about the likely changes in the political system brought about by a long war. The report outlined in detail that in the experts' view a long war leaving everywhere a greatly impoverished population diminished in size, was likely to lead to the disappearance of the existing political system in all belligerent countries. One could not be certain, they said, of the systems that would take their place. But it was not unlikely that they would have the form of a military dictatorship or even of a number of smaller dictatorships or a new kind of feudalism. As it happened, the war did not take place.

One of the best-remembered public debates had as its theme the question of whether human societies could exist without compulsion. It was won by the Traditionalists. They had started from the position that compulsion was indispensable. The Innovators, starting with a defense of human liberty, had gradually come to the admission that terms like *liberty* and *freedom* were too vague, that some form of constraint was simply due to the fact of human beings living together as families, as neighborhoods, towns, classes, or states. But then they raised the question: What kind of constraints? What safeguards were needed against self-interested compulsion on the part of more powerful groups? There followed a series of further public debates exploring in detail the problem of prisons and other formal types of compulsion as well as informal types. That produced considerable clarification of the whole issue and resulted in a series of reforms.

Another topic of public debate, the last I may mention, was centered on the question of whether industrial societies could exist without change. As one might expect, the Traditionalists started with an exploration of the possibility that even industrial societies could in principle continue to exist forever in their present form, either with regard to their structure values. This possibility was denied by the Innovators, who explained in some detail the unintended consequences of the driving forces of contemporary societies. Widely remembered and slightly ridiculed was the phrase of one of the speakers of their team: "Feeling under one's feet the throbbing pulse beat of the dynamics of a contemporary society — how can one be a Traditionalist?" Yet the Innovators persisted in following this track. Shunning rhetoric, they emphasized that using as a beacon, as a guiding principle of governmental and party politics, an idealized picture of an industrial society as it already existed, was no less a wish-dream than the use for the same end of an idealized picture of a future society with complete social equality of all its members. It was perfectly correct, they said, to maintain that under no imaginable circumstances could the present power hierarchy of states or the internal conditions of one of these states remain unchanged for any length of time. For that, they argued, the built-in, unplanned dynamics of the emerging global commonwealth of nation-states was far too strong. Any policy dictated by the wish that everything should stay as it was and, therefore, be designed to arrest the intrinsic impetus to change present societies was bound to founder — no less than any policy based on the assumption that, at a given moment, only one future condition of society was possible. Nor could one any longer take into account merely the internal development of a particular state, as if it existed in isolation, independently of the development of other states. One always had to reckon, they said, not only with one possible future, but with a whole spectrum of possible futures of the whole of humanity. The Innovators had developed a certain skill in designing possible futures. To design possible futures as a kind of thought experiment, they said, greatly helped them to clarify their own minds about present conditions. The Traditionalists, as was the habit in that more civilized age, admitted in the course of this debate that it was not realistic to try to arrest change, to attempt to preserve society as it was, given the enormously strong propensity toward change inherent in contemporary societies. What one had to do, they suggested, was steer the inevitable change into channels best suited to the continuation of the highly valued tradition. The Innovators were also concerned with the problem of how to steer the dynamics of society with the help of a clear understanding of its structure and motive force. But they were concerned with discovering *new* channels. They were very persuasive, and in terms of popular votes they gained a resounding victory in the debate. But even in the era of the Trads and Inns, a majority vote in a public debate, though a true test of public opinion at a given time, was not necessarily a reliable test of what we used to call the "truth" of a statement.

Ludes: And that, I believe, brings us to the end of this particular thought experiment?

Elias: Yes, it does. Don't you think that it has thrown a bit more light on the problems of knowledge and power?

Notes

1. W.K. Simpson ed., *The Literature of Ancient Egypt* (New Haven and London: Yale University Press, 1978), p. 344.

2. In England the corresponding development took a somewhat different course: as a social cadre with its own social identity and cultural traditions the English peasantry was virtually annihilated as a result of the enclosures. Its disappearance had far-reaching consequences for the development of the multipolar balance of power between the principal social strata and between the state population as a whole and the privileged oligarchies who had access to governmental positions. In the seventeenth and eighteenth centuries English tenant farmers differed considerably from continental peasants — a factor on the road to electoral parliamentarism.

11

On Culture and Power:
The Modern Husbandry of Knowledge

Juan E. Corradi

Culture as Comedy: The Torn Soul

In the preface to *The Philosophy of History* Hegel inscribed his famous dictum on the belatedness of philosophy. To philosophy he ascribed a capacity to take stock of the world, all the while remaining impotent to rejuvenate it. Perhaps never before had a crucial function of culture been stated so succinctly, as the ability to reconstruct a totality from disparate human experiences and to extract from them a sublime and sublimated surplus value. Hegel defined culture as an enterprise of translation, as work upon work, as the higher double of the common life. Yet, as we enter the ideal city of culture and contemplate the spectacle of its immense and artificial activity, we are tempted by derision. As in concrete cities here too there is much rubbing of shoulders, meeting of strangers, millions of ephemeral exchanges, the prevalence of paradox, the mixture of the retrograde with the advanced, a parade of novelties trailing old consequences. Like real cities, it is worldly and ghastly; unlike them, it is wordy and ghostly. Paul Valéry ventured a description of this imaginary place, which I shall quote at length:

Then, in an apocalyptic light, I adumbrated the disorder and the fermentation of an entire society of demons. Situated in a supernatural space, it seemed like a sort of comedy of what happens in History. Fights, factions, triumphs, solemn execrations, executions, riots, tragedies around power. . . . In this Republic every rumor spoke of scandals, of striking and stricken-down fortunes, of plots and criminal attempts. There were chamber plebiscites, insignificant coronations, many murders *by speech*. Not to mention larcenies. This entire "intellectual" nation was like any other. One found in it puritans, speculators, prostitutes, believers that seemed impious and the ungodly that feigned belief; there were false simpletons and true fools, and authorities, and anarchists, and even executioners whose blades dripped ink. Some thought themselves priests or pontiffs, others prophets, others Caesars, or else martyrs, or a little of each. Many took themselves in their very actions for children or for women. Most ridiculous were those who appointed themselves judges and hangmen for the tribe.

. . . Each of these demons often watched himself in a paper mirror; in it he considered himself

293

as the first or the last of beings. . . .

I vaguely searched for the laws of this empire. The necessity to amuse; the need to live; the desire to survive; the pleasure to astound, to shock, to chide, to teach, to despise; the pricks of jealousy led, irritated, heated, explained this Hell.[1]

That the sanctuary of culture should be a place for impious acts has been a topic of debate since the eighteenth century.[2] Diderot gave it dramatic force in *Le neveu de Rameau*.[3] It was this state of disintegration which Goethe rendered as "self-estranged spirit"[4] in his translation of the dialogue — a term later adopted by Hegel in a brilliant misreading of Diderot which he attached to *The Phenomenology of Mind*.[5] There culture appears as a discipline of dissonance "which renders and tears everything," as "the inversion and perversion of all conceptions and realities, as universal deception of itself and others." But Hegel saw in such a condition a movement of the spirit toward a higher stage of freedom and self-realization, beyond simple certainties and beyond morality itself.

We owe to Lionel Trilling an elegant book[6] that explores the modern repertoire of responses to culture. Our culture has become more complex, differentiated, diverse, and less attached to clear truth. We live in a world of radical immanence, of self-production and self-consumption, of self-referentiality and simulation.[7] Having erased the last vestiges of transcendent warrants we find ourselves, as Freud described us, like full prosthetic gods, creatures of our own making. We thus suffer from an ailment for which Hegel reserved the word *Zerrissenheit*. Like other cities, the cities of the mind have become more crowded and artificial, subject to greater pollution and faster tempos than, for instance, the Paris that caused Rousseau such deep spiritual trouble.[8] Likewise, our reactions to culture are more intense. The manner in which our spirit "pours scornful laughter on existence, on the confusion pervading the whole and on itself as well" (Hegel) betrays greater distress. The forms of social secession in which we indulge, our search for "authenticity," are concomitantly more radical. In short, our love/hate of culture is more frantic. As Trilling has shown, the situations and experiences upon which we bestow the epithets "authentic" and "inauthentic" — the diagnoses that we put forth for our cultural malaise and the cures we propose — have greatly changed and become more varied over the past two centuries.[9] Irony, poetic stasis, the detachment of grand synthesis, withdrawal into nature or oneself, the alternating faith in, and rejection of, technology, play, eroticism, *amor fati*, psychotherapy or else the praise of folly, are some of the responses to what different generations chose or rejected as culturally inauthentic.

With Hegel began a trend that has continued unabated down to these days and that we may characterize as a *distantiation* from a pious conception of culture — from that conception of culture "as the development of the self to perfection through its active experience of 'the best that is thought and said in the world.'"[10] In the *Phenomenology* Hegel used the term *Bildung* to discuss travesty, deceit, the pains of the torn consciousness, and the vicissitudes of the base self. Marx advanced the critical onslaught by making culture derive from and depend on the social relations of production. Classical sociologists like Simmel saw a widening gap between the objective achievements of culture and the capacity of the self to cope with them.[11] Freud maintained a relentless ambivalence toward culture to the end.[12] And modern anthropologists added to the dissolution of its unitary pretensions by a thoroughgoing relativism, thus completing the task of undermining begun by historians. Culture then appears as neither simple nor unitary; not a road to self-perfection but a source of deep wounds; a ceaseless activity of signification whose meaning remains elusive; a formidable reality that seems nonetheless "unreal"; an environment as inescapable as it is uncertain — intractable, it would appear, to old controls.

In the remarks that follow, I shall seek to reshape this rubble by articulating some of the dimensions of intellectual culture as we now perceive them. I will then put forth some hypotheses concerning the connection between culture and power. Finally, I shall speculate on what is new in that connection.

Culture as Totality: The Obsolescence of the Intellectual Gaze

Although specialized cultural endeavors may provide varying degrees of satisfaction and elicit varying degrees of commitment, modern culture as a whole is fraught with ambivalence and uncertainty.[13] Since so much ink has already been spent on the various "crises" that afflict the world, one is hesitant to use the term.[14] Nevertheless, it is possible to speak of a crisis of contemporary culture and to locate it on the level of totality. The crisis becomes evident in our inability to envisage an overall coherence and harmony in culture, to secure the grounds for its different components, to produce convincing explanations for the articulation of those components; in short, to make sense of the growing cultural conglomerate. Yet this "making sense," the search for general significance and meaning, the attentiveness toward totality, have been the self-appointed tasks of intellectuals. What has traditionally defined an intellectual has been a capacity in excess of his particular competence: the capacity to know for what and for whom that which he knows matters.[15] This surplus of reflectivity, this metacognitive and metacreative activity, this transcendent view identifies the "intellectual gaze."

The intellectual gaze is the secular heir to forsaken priestly functions.

This gaze betrays a will: to control the conditions of one's own activity, to direct its consequences, to articulate disparate practices, to determine their overall significance, and place oneself on the level of the whole to which the different parts contribute. It is a will to an essentially symbolic power that acts as a mediation in society. Like other social elements, the intellectual world possesses resources, contradictions, and fault-lines which give it potential either for streamlining oppression or for projecting emancipation. To speak of a cultural crisis, then, is to speak of the transformations of these functions, of changes in the intellectual gaze perhaps so fundamental that they endanger the species "intelligentsia."

The present crisis of culture is the result of successive and disparate attacks. Fifty years ago, the joint impact of historicism and Marxism rocked the self-confident autonomy of culture by arguing for the radical incommunicability of epochal experiences on the one hand and emphasizing, on the other, the social location of cultural producers as the external determinant of their work. Karl Mannheim tried all his life to cope with a sensibility that stressed the differences among knowers vis-à-vis the objects of knowledge and which thereby threatened to plunge culture into the morass of self-refuting relativism.[16] The sociologies of knowledge and culture emerged as byproducts of that quest, but they failed to provide satisfactory answers to the original dilemmas that called them into being.

A second preoccupation, this time with the very medium of culture, i.e. language, helped to further undermine certainty. As opposed to the uncertainty that comes from an external environment, however one might construe it: as the past, as a biological or economic infrastructure, or as the arbitrariness of the subject, this other doubt arose from the inner core of culture itself, from that without which it is not conceivable — from meaning as such. From late Wittgensteinian philosophy of language it was argued that meaning is both conventional and contextual.[17] This philosophy undermined the old premise of the scientific enterprise — the assumption that an objective, transsituational descriptive language is possible. Structuralism, for its part, later harped on the dissociation of language — and of all semiotic systems — from its system of references.[18] Such an approach placed a wedge between words and objects, and a connection that was once believed to be necessary now stood as arbitrary.[19] Language came to stand as a dense mediation; its opacity threw doubts on any claims to know. It is possible to bracket the issues raised by linguistic mediation and extrinsic determination, and in fact this is done in a large number of day-to-day endeavors, such as the pursuit of "normal science." Nevertheless, to seek security in a dubious "object as such," to beg for the return of the transparency of language, to remain tied, in short, to a positivistic faith as the only alternative to solipsism or relativism, no longer makes philosophical and sociological sense. The uncertainties to which we have pointed are not symptoms of a loss of nerve, nor do they lead to chaos. They announce a sort of maturity. They provide the occasion to conceive our activities in a new light — to treat the cultural world, its regularities, and its organization in a different manner.

Culture as Grid: The Discovery of Discursive Formations

The question is how to produce an account of culture that assumes rather than ignores the two problematic dimensions that its crisis has pressed upon us, namely, the inability to encompass it in a totalizing gaze and the incapacity to anchor it either in a subjective consciousness or in an objective reality. How to envisage a phenomenon that has become both weightless and dispersed. How to trace the contours of a system that is objective without the warrant of referentiality. How to approach an activity that does not have its source in the consciousness of a subject. How to discuss a process that is not embedded in continuous history.

The work of Michel Foucault attempts to answer such queries and to study culture and knowledge within a new conceptual space.[20] From Foucault's work we can glean a sociology of knowledge[21] that simultaneously encompasses three critical dimensions of culture: semiotic distance, structuration, and socio-historical location. By "semiotic distance" I point to the irreducible gap between language and its reference, to the impossibility of positing objects of knowledge that stand invariant to all and any knowers. Yet this impossibility need not lead to affirming the primacy of the subject and its consciousness, for while the initial relation between a word and a concept may be arbitrary, once established it is nevertheless binding. Objects of knowledge are not constituted in an act of intentional consciousness, as phenomenologists would have it, but in semiotic activity. Second, this semiotic activity tends to coalesce in knowledge systems with their own rules of operation that cannot be manipulated at will by the users. "Structuration" means that semiotic activity is systematic. It determines the relative position of subject and object of knowledge. In short, semiotic relations determine their own terms according to identifiable patterns. Finally, the socio-historical process is seen as a series of destructurations and restructurations, in which discontinuity, multiple causation, and even chance play a significant role. Such a view clearly entails a polemic against an evolutionary notion of process, against any idea of progress, accumulation, unfolding, or eventual "revelation." The conception of language embodied in this approach is not so unfamiliar: it is of Viconian pedigree. And the idea of history it displays is similar to that proposed by Max Weber in his *Wissenschaftslehre*.[22] In the eighteenth century, Vico anticipated problems that would occupy the human sciences two hundred years after his death. And he proposed solutions that remained ignored until quite recently.[23] For Vico, language was not a deliberate invention on the part of men who think thoughts and then look around for ways of articulating them. For him intelligence (*logos*) came after, not before, the use of symbols. Minds (*ingenia*) are formed by the character of language, not language by the minds of those who speak it.[24] This suggestion remained dormant until it was discovered anew in our century, especially in literary[25] practice and study.

We are born into traditions of speech and writing which form our minds as much as our minds form them. Vico denied the possibility of an unaltering, logically perfect(ible) language, constructed to reflect the basic structure of reality. For the Neapolitan philosopher there was no such structure — just a symbolic machinery instead, the history of which he sought to trace. Language was considered a social device through which civilization was produced. Vico noted that utterances not only attract attention to something outside, but may themselves be acts or intrinsic elements of action.

If words can be a form of action, then language has to be approached not solely in terms of meaning but also in terms of usage. The return to this Viconian view has shifted the manner in which we deal with symbolic structures.[26] These can be seen as machines in the sense that they are productive of forms of life. It is in this fashion that locutions, the use and structure of a language, have a "necessary" or "organic" connection with particular types of political and social structure, religion, law, economic life, morality, technology, military organization, and so on. Discourse appears as a practice inserted in a larger order of practices.

To break away from overall "pattern and meaning" in history was the intention of Max Weber. His famous answer to Marxism was not contrary to usual constructs to vindicate the primacy of ideal against material factors. Weber sought to represent history as a grid formed by independent lines of causation. He likened it to a giant railway network with crucial switching points.[27] For Weber there was no single logic in history, but a multiplicity of discernible trends constructed step by step, that could or could not combine or intersect, depending on still further contingencies. He thus assigned to events a power of irruption that had previously been denied by both idealistic and materialistic philosophies of history. From this vantage point, Weber considered such philosophies as more or less covert versions of an unacceptable theodicy.

To Vico we may trace the discovery of the poetic, performative, socially productive properties of discourse, and to Weber the saliency of discontinuity, of combinations, and of events in history. Foucault's work actualizes, develops, and articulates the twin notions of discursivity and discontinuity, turning them into vehicles for a series of studies on madness, medicine, imprisonment, sexuality, and governance.[28] In stressing irruption and discontinuity, Foucault not only dispels the illusions of the conventional historiography of ideas — tied to a gradual, revelatory model of historical process — but also rejects the scientific belief that knowledge progresses through an ever better approximation to posited invariant objects. Instead we witness shifting conceptions of the objects of discourse. In stressing the changing conception of objects as a result of shifting rules of discourse, Foucault draws our attention to the operations of, and the statements generated by, the discursive rules, both of which are constitutive of the objects themselves.

Objects are not external to discourse but are located and served up by the operations of discursive rules. The latter regulate the possibility of appearance of statements. For Foucault, objects are not defined with reference to invariant things "out there," but "by relating them to the body of rules that enable them to form as objects of a discourse and thus constitute the conditions of their historical appearance."[29] Such rules, constraining and enabling at the same time, determine the conditions of possibility of different discourses.[30] These conditions are the limits of discourse itself, its parameters. They offer it the objects about which it can speak, they determine "the range of linkages that discourse must accomplish in order to treat them, to name them, to analyze them, to classify them, to explain them."[31] Discourse is conceived as a practice we impose on things. "It is in this practice that the events of discourse find the principle of their regularity."[32] My purpose here is not to review Foucault's studies but to measure the distance that separates them from other theories of culture.

Culture has been hitherto primarily "understood" and "interpreted."[33] Now and then, sociologists attempt to "explain" it by reference to external social facts, but they are usually chided for it.[34] The most subtle among them argue that, properly understood, the sociology of knowledge is itself a variant of the interpretive method, in the hermeneutic, subjectivist tradition of inquiry.[35] Starting from the premise that texts and statements, cultural artifacts and social actions are laden with meaning, the sociology of knowledge endeavors to unravel the different layers of that meaning, supplementing the most immediate and apparent levels with a disclosure of underlying authorial intentions and overarching contextual presuppositions. The philosophy, history, and sociology of culture have been wedded in this way to a peculiar negantropic gesture. They represent attempts to embrace the multiplicity, dispersion, and inconsistency of cultural particulars, to exorcise the proliferation of senses and to find *the* sense. For the practitioners of these disciplines, cultural objects tend to form unified totalities, the origins of which are in either individual or collective subjects.[36] Their method seeks to locate in culture some central ideational structure. But the cultural field often resists coherence and totalization: it gives us objects that are diverse and decentered. For instance, in the same text, different discourses are braided, a plurality of voices is heard, styles and symbols clash.[37] The combination and intersection of these discourses produces an *éffet de trompe l'oeil* — the illusion of depth within which the scholar searches for hidden meanings,[38] authorial intentions, privileged origins, and the secret of epochal styles. Against all this, what Foucault has proposed is simple but devastating: to disassemble the mechanism that produces cultural effects rather than search within the confines of their imaginary space.

Discourses are not reducible to a single logic or unitary process. Their origins are tentative, their developments heterogeneous, and the irruption of events, even sheer chance, play an important role in their appearance and interplay. Discourses interact with each other and with nondiscursive practices; they overlap, displace, and subordinate one another; they form grids, and in the space thus produced their bearers hold determinate positions, trading statements about objects that are only conceivable within such grids. Cultural achievements and forms of knowledge are only possible in the territory established by these discursive formations. The operation of discursive rules provides for the coherence and regularity in each region of knowledge, and in each period asserts a determining effect across regions. The rationality and legitimacy of knowledge claims are warrantable only with reference to the conditions required by the discursive rules themselves.

From this vantage point culture looks like an intricate discursive web, and this formulation already suggests what other, traditional approaches to culture have failed to appreciate. To the question of how to apprehend culture there have been three answers. One has been to ignore its articulations altogether and engage single-mindedly in a particular activity. This is a pragmatic mode of apprehension. A second answer has been to map culture on some sort of base, variously construed as an economic platform, a social formation, or a civilizational process. This is the materialist approach. The third answer has been to transcend the cultural conglomerate by imputing to it a general theme, a conceptual system, a style, or set of nodal values, much like we bestow a personality upon a person. This is the idealist conception of culture. None of these approaches pays enough attention to the discursive tissues of a culture, its specific materiality, its constraining and enabling properties, its natural history. That is what some contemporary trends in discourse analysis have sought to do.[39] They have opened up a field of investigation centered on the formation and appearance of particular discourses. Another series of studies investigates the linkages of particular discourses to institutional arrangements that lend support to those discourses and are in turn modified by them. It is here that the sociological interest in discursive formations is secured. The interest is a concern to elucidate the demands that formal features of a discursive formation, a knowledge system, impose on the institutional arrangement to realize its program, and how the discursive formation provides the institutional arrangement with the support of knowledge for the latter's claim to legitimacy and the exercise of power.

Foucault's critical studies on the emergence of the clinic, psychiatry, prison, and sexuality illustrate a set of relationships between discourses and nondiscursive practices. They are all, however, historical investigations on "achieved" phenomena. In this regard, "archaeology" is tied to the belatedness of philosophical reflection. To study a discursive formation *in statu nascendi* is much more difficult. Beginnings are harder to detect, because we are more thoroughly immersed in the events that give them shape. This chapter has tried to show that, on the level of knowledge about knowledge, we have made some real progress, or that, at the very least, we have dispelled some illusions. The intellectual gaze has become keener with regard to the past. However, as we survey the present and look into the future, we sense that we have crossed a threshold. A qualitative change has taken place. It has less to do with the sharpening of our critical and reflective capacities than with their practical and effective expropriation. The intellectual gaze is becoming institutional, administered. Hitherto intellectuals could fancy themselves "functionaries of humanity"[40] by virtue of their ability to articulate, ground, and summarize culture. Today, other functionaries who do not claim the title of intellectuals are able to promote, contain, suppress, steer, and monitor culture by virtue of their organizational emplacement and equipment. Between the totalizing intellectual and the manager of knowledge there is no continuity but a gap — the consequence of a historic dislocation.

Culture as Resource: Toward the Husbandry of Knowledge

I have followed the vicissitudes of the intellectual gaze to the threshold of an important change. What on one side of the line can be described in terms of, first, a dual vision, a torn soul, a divided self, a metacognitive capacity, a reflexive consciousness; and then as a distinct mode of surveying gridlike configurations of culture, on the other side changes into a practical technology, advanced forms of management, processing procedures, transactions within and between complex organizations tending to their environments. We may further mark this change by juxtaposing metaphors. It has been said of cultural objects, be they works of art or products of knowledge, that while they speak the language of reference, they also emit a sort of lateral message about their own processes of formation. It is this lateral message that has allowed intellectuals to speak of cultural patterns, value, style, or alternatively, of discursive formations. Cultural activities generate out of their own movement a lateral aura accessible to critical and reflective minds. Consider the following reformulation: cultural activities produce lateral data that can be recycled on the level of monitoring and management. It is clear that the model of such epistemic regime is not to be found in philosophy but more likely in something like second-generation nuclear technology: breeder reactors produce power and generate new fuel at the same time. The soft technology to harness and recycle culture exists. It is to the assembly of such technology and its implications that I shall turn next.

It is time for a brief recapitulation of the foregoing thoughts. In the first section I dwelt on an aspect of culture as a social activity — the quest for recognition or status. The second section explored the self-monitoring function of culture, its reflectivity, its double nature as culture and metaculture. I argued that the exercise of such function has traditionally elevated a cultural worker to the level of an intellectual. I further maintained that the prime modes with which intellectuals have monitored culture and which together constitute their "gaze" — modes that are essentially holistic, hermeneutic, and retrospective — have reached an impasse, as the premises and assumptions on which they rest no longer hold. Those premises and assumptions have been replaced by a different methodology, a mode of analytical discourse wedded to semiotics and to a conception of discontinuous history. It is my present thesis that each of these three dimensions of culture — status, monitoring, and network — are being subjected to an ever-increasing control by processing organizations.[41] The existence of these organizations, their strategic situation, the processing technologies they develop have radically altered the cartography of culture, rendering some of the old functions obsolete, shifting the social position of intellectuals, and forcing upon us the need to reconceptualize the relationships between culture and power. We may therefore speak, echoing Weber, of a rationalization of culture, and most particularly of knowledge production, but only on the condition that we abandon the perceptions of culture and power to which the humanities and the social sciences have accustomed us over the years.

The culture/power duality is an obstacle to the proper understanding of present trends. We have grown used to associating rationalization with bureaucracy, to perceiving power as imposing limits on the free development of culture, as demanding of it practical applications and legitimizing symbols, as emanating from the state, as imposing rigid goals and imposing them repressively. We are thus sidetracked from alternative hypotheses; that power is not a property to be held or conquered but a function exercised from a multiplicity of strategic positions, the total effect of maneuvers, tactics, and techniques; that power is not located in a privileged site, like the state, but is produced in diverse settings; that power does not simply impede, repress, and pretend, but that it also solicits, promotes, and sets in motion; finally, that power and knowledge are not alien to each other but intertwined in circuits whose diagrams must be drawn.

The technology of knowledge processing has been assembled from heterogeneous sources and has developed in a social and institutional space that is neither fully private nor fully public, but somewhat intersticial, and as the total effect of strategies, programs, and intentions that do not stem from a coherent purpose, emanate from a central place, or serve a single interest. Its appearance and growth confirms the modern view of history as a multiple series of tentative beginnings. These commencements may or may not coalesce into coherent patterns. One of such many threads — but one that is paradigmatic — can be found in the development of American philanthropy.[42] The rationalization of philanthropy was a function of the advocacy of a basic attack on the causes of social problems rather than the amelioration of undesirable effects. Rationalized philanthropy began to seek knowledge of the fundamental causes underlying the problems of mankind and, as a result, focused on programs of research and experimentation designed to build up a fund of understanding that transcended mere symptoms. Related to this advocacy of basic knowledge was the establishment of foundations with wide discretionary mandates in different areas of social concern.[43] To implement philanthropic inquiry into causes and operationalize their broad mandates, managerially advanced foundations[44] developed programmatic strategies with which to implement their general goals. Such approaches serve to focus and systematize funding efforts, making it less likely that resources will be diverted to miscellaneous endeavors and merely supportive tasks. Such programmatic strategies came to represent a large diversity of fields of activity. Managerially advanced foundations vary in the number and diversity of the objectives they pursue and the geographic spread of their concern. Their inquisitive and operational "gaze" encompasses ever larger domains of culture, with national and international dimensions.

These foundations seek to achieve their goals through the funding of selected projects. The task involved in the project method is to develop those raw materials with which they review and evaluate, into projects capable of successfully achieving such ends. Such processing tasks are characterized, however, by a large measure of uncertainty and ambiguity on various levels.

First, the goals of managerially advanced foundations are so general as to make it difficult to determine the precise nature of the outcome sought. This condition leads to difficulties in selecting projects for support. The problem is compounded by lack of knowledge of the transformation process by which the goals are achieved. Second, to attain goals, foundations make attempts to convert the raw materials they solicit and gather into projects with a potential for success. These raw materials are none other than the basic elements of a living culture: persons, ideas, and institutions involved in knowing and creating. They are self-activating and interactive agents that make standardized assessment and prediction of their activities problematic. Finally, foundations, like other organizations, need to produce results which are satisfactory to the members of the social environment in which they operate. Foundations must legitimize their existence and operations by making difficult claims to effectiveness, since neither their goals nor the means pursued to attain them are very clear. In brief, managerially advanced foundations stand in a dimension altogether different from, and sometimes opposed to, the conventional model of rational bureaucracy, with its clear-cut hierarchy, determinate chains of command, and established objectives. Yet it is precisely the management of uncertainty, the persistence in rationalizing the ambiguous, which makes these organizations advanced, for they succeed in developing modes of control that are subtle and supple, in setting up delicate instruments for sensing the pulse of a culture, in mounting a machinery of observation to which little escapes, in building an apparatus that detects, monitors, and steers cultural creation and knowledge production by making possible decisions of the order of seeding, selective breeding, neutralization, conservation, and promotion of knowledge to full growth and use.

It is impossible to view managerially advanced foundations as monolithic, static, sovereign, or willful entities. They are the paradigmatic instance of novel organizational patterns and a different mode of power. Their structure is one in which organizational goals, hierarchies, and positions are emergent and fluid. They are produced, reproduced, and continuously altered by processes of negotiation, inquiry, and legitimization. The power these organizations exercise over knowledge is not a property held by a group or class, is not localized in a definite concrete space, is not subordinated to deep-seated interests or structures, and is not imposed from above over recalcitrant subjects. It is a technology that cuts across different activities, people, institutions; that links them, prolongs them, makes them converge and operate in a new mode: a productive mode in sites that are not explicitly economic, a political mode in sites that are not explicitly political. Organizational power points to a network of *strategic emplacements* in continuous redefinition and to a technology of "reality production." The reality processed by this technology consists of modifiable boundaries and hierarchies of cognitive areas; modifiable statuses of individuals, ideas, and institutions; modifiable articulations of culture with other social practices. "Streamlining," "normalization," and "husbandry," all capture the process to which culture is subjected.

To cope with the uncertainty within which they operate and the dynamics of the environment they inhabit, foundations develop grant-making processes through the use of certain information bases and procedures. The latter serve to protect them from the risks inherent in their work, enhance their credibility with the public, and promote an aura of objectivity about the performance of their work. The need to secure an information base on which to ground their operations requires a specialized staff which assists in the establishment of policy and in the selection of grants. This staff has both specific knowledge of various fields and a strong generalist orientation. Through this staff, the erstwhile totalizing intellectual gaze has become operational.

Foundation program officers engage in program development, proposal evaluation and investigation, recommendation of proposals, and monitoring and evaluation of grants. Each of these involves uncertainties, since there are neither codified bodies of knowledge nor clear guidelines for decision. To contend with that uncertainty they develop criteria and procedures for assessing the attributes of candidates and ideas, for transforming these into realizable projects, and for evaluating the progress of these projects once they are approved. Such criteria and processes are, in turn, the result of multiple negotiations with trustees, superiors, fellow program officers, and with an external task environment composed primarily of clients and consultants. The technology of knowledge husbandry then consists in the overall effect of transactions negotiated around strategic points of contact. The exercise of power consists in the organizational linkage of these points of contact where they already exist, and in their emplacement where they do not. Once established and managed, cultural activities tend to gravitate toward organizations and pass through them, as knowledge producers become applicants for grants, as their institutions, ideas, and *personae* enter the abstract machine on one end and come out with modified statuses on the other, as cultural developments are tended to *in ovo* and accompanied over their life cycle by a watchful gaze, as this watchful gaze monopolizes two types of competence — interdisciplinary and interactional — as new discursive rules are established for proposing,[45] projecting, and reviewing activities, and finally, as cultural surplus value is captured by the whole network. These organizations are gatekeepers to important resources and facilities in society.[46] According to such a view, the individuals in those organizations engage in evaluative processes in which raw materials are assessed and rewards allocated. Such organizations produce an output in the form of changed statuses or allocations in the external environment. Yet this characterization falls short of seizing the importance of innovation and creativity in the operations of managerially advanced foundations. Their creative rather than merely controlling capacity is determined by the ability to establish systematic points of contact with significant actors in the external and internal work environment. This allows them, first, to establish an effective information-gathering system with sensitivity toward changes in the environment; second, to develop and present effectively such informational inputs; and finally, to generate bases of support within the environment. Internally, foundation officers seek approval and funding for proposed projects against a backdrop of financial resources and competing programs and proposal needs. Externally, they rely on the efforts of grantees and the latter's institutions to carry out grant projects, and also on grant candidates to submit project ideas. They sometimes solicit the advice of external consultants. Within this context relations are characterized by balances of influence and dependency in which the parties seek to protect their autonomy. This is a research domain of extraordinary potential interest in which some inroads have already been made.[47] For instance, there are studies of foundation officer-client and -consultant relations[48] and other studies on the nature of programs officer dependency relations with peers, superiors, and trustees within the foundation, that have been projected or are in course.[49] By focusing in detail on particular nodal points within the network of foundation activities, these studies should provide a clearer understanding of relationships between knowledge and power in advanced industrial society. Inasmuch as foundations find themselves in a restive, critical environment,[50] claims and charges directed at them should provide an opportunity to investigate the management of legitimacy by such modern organizations and their potential or actual collusion or conflict with the state, social classes, other occupations, and their clientele. Of great significance in this context is the dual nature of foundations as public/private organizations. On the one hand, they are public trusts, employing funds which have been granted tax exemption on behalf of public purposes. On the other hand, they are private entities established through the contributions of private individuals and controlled internally by private boards. Thus private management combines with public purposes in a single organization. The issues of private interest and public control and accountability are of particular saliency in this domain, where research should proceed. My purpose here has been a different and preliminary one: to trace the formation of a novel and specific technology of power in the area of culture; gauge the distance that separates this technology from classical conceptions of culture; and present a diagram of this technology as a new field of social action. On closing these remarks, we may pose some questions concerning the general societal implications of the changes surveyed and risk some answers that may serve as working hypotheses.

Is the new technology of culture control socially neutral? No — and for two good reasons. First, at any given time this technology is subject to appropriation by a ruling group and to reappropriation by the collectivity. Second, this technology is not a toy — however sophisticated — in the hands of already established actors who may use it at will. On the contrary, its existence defines a new set of social relations, and hence new conflicts between different actors, and with different stakes. The point is to identify the exact nature of the social relations the new technology institutes, the potential struggles it entails, the main opponents in such conflict, and the issues over which conflicts develop.

Does the new technology imply a different model of society? Yes — one characterized by programming,[51] that is, by the capacity to act upon itself, to produce its own reality to an unprecedented degree.

Is the model of a programmed society a matter of choice? No, especially once the new technology of culture control has been established. The issue is not whether to choose between this type of society and other types, but to establish alternative projects of participation and accountability within it. In this regard, the analyst cannot prejudge the issue. His or her role is to analyze the mechanisms of control, display them, and clarify the dimensions of conflict around them.

Has the new technology of control important implications for the kind and the modes of knowledge developed in society? Many, but the most important is the disappearance of metasocietal warrants for the cultural order, such as transcendent truth or value, evolution, progress, or any mode of historical teleology.

Does the new technology have significant implications for the manner in which we may approach culture in relation to society? Yes. It renders obsolete the conventional issue of the humanities and the sociologies of culture and knowledge, by relegating further toward the periphery of concern such issues as the distinction between truth and ideology, such methods as hermeneutics, narrative historiography, or the imputation of consciousness to collective actors, such social types as the intelligentsia, such ancient critical concepts as alienation and repression.

Is this a final diagnosis? Only a hunch, and a beginning.

Notes

1. Paul Valéry, "Lettre d'un ami," in *Monsieur Teste* (Paris: Gallimard, 1946), pp. 91-92.

2. The most recent example is Régis Debray, *Le pouvoir intellectuel en France* (Paris: Ramsay, 1979). See also J. Leenhardt and B. Maj, *La force des mots* (Paris: Megrelis, 1982).

3. Cf. Denis Diderot, *Le neveu de Rameau* (Paris: Garnier-Flammarion, 1967).

4. "Der sich entfremdete Geist." Goethe's translation of the dialogue was published while Hegel was writing the *Phenomenology*. Hegel took the term — and the concept — to make it preside the section of his book entitled "Der sich entfremdete Geist; die Bildung."

5. I have followed the French translation by Jean Hyppolite, *La phénoménologie de l'esprit* (Paris: Aubier-Montaigne, 1941), vol. 2, pp. 50ff.

6. Lionel Trilling, *Sincerity and Authenticity* (Cambridge, Mass.: Harvard University Press, 1971), inspired these remarks.

7. Thus Herbert Marcuse's first title for his *One-Dimensional Man* (Boston: Beacon Press, 1964) was "The Technology of Self-Consumption." For a different and later statement cf. Jean Baudrillard, "L'ordre des simulacres," in his *L'échange symbolique et la mort* (Paris: Gallimard, 1976).

8. Cf. Bronislaw Baczko, *Rousseau: solitude et communauté* (Paris: Mouton & Maison des Sciences de l'Homme, 1974). See also Gérard Namer, *Rousseau: sociologue de la connaissance* (Paris: Klinksieck, 1978).

9. See Trilling, *Sincerity and Authenticity*, op. cit., chs. 5, 6.

10. Ibid., p. 43.

11. Cf. Georg Simmel, "Der Begriff und Tragödie der Kultur," in *Philosophische Kultur: Gesammelte Essays*, 2nd enlarged ed. (Leipzig: Kröner, 1919), pp. 223-53.

12. Sigmund Freud, *Civilization and Its Discontents* (*The Complete Psychological Works of Sigmund Freud*, Standard Edition, vol. 21) (London: Hogarth, 1961).

13. The classic statement of this predicament remains Max Weber, "Science as a Vocation," in *From Max Weber: Essays in Sociology*, ed. H.H. Gerth and C. Wright Mills (New York: Oxford University Press, 1958).

14. One exception to the trend is Norman Birnbaum et al., *Au delà de la crise* (Paris: Seuil, 1976).

15. Cf. Juan E. Corradi, "Over krities bewestzegn en hedendaagse macht," in *Intelectuelen tussen Macht en Wetenschaap*, ed. G. van Benthem van den Bergh and David Kettler (Amsterdam: Van Gennep, 1973).

16. Cf. Kurt H. Wolff, ed., *From Karl Mannheim* (New York: Oxford University Press, 1971).

17. See the discussion in Anthony Giddens, *New Rules of Sociological Method* (New York: Basic Books, 1976), ch. 1.

18. On structuralism cf. Fredric Jameson, *The Prison-House of Language* (Princeton: Princeton University Press, 1972).

19. For a brief summary cf. Terence Hawkes, *Structuralism and Semiotics* (London: Methuen, 1977).

20. Especially the following books by Foucault: *Folie et déraison* (Paris: Plon, 1961); *Naissance de la clinique* (Paris: PUF, 1963); *Raymond Roussel* (Paris: NRF, 1963); *Les mots et les choses* (Paris: NRF, 1966); *L'ordre du discours* (Paris: NRF, 1971); *Surveiller et punir* (Paris: NRF, 1975); *La volonté de savoir* (Paris: NRF, 1976).

21. Cf. Edith Kurzweil, "M. Foucault: The End of Man," *Theory and Society* 4:(1977):395-420; Beng-Huat Chua, "Michel Foucault and the Sociology of Knowledge," paper presented at the IX World Congress of Sociology, Uppsala, Sweden, 1978.

22. Max Weber, *Gesammelte Aufsätze zur Wissenschaftslehre* (Tübingen: Mohr, 1968).

23. Cf. *The New Science of Giambattista Vico*, trans. and ed. Th. Goddard Bergin and M.H. Fisch (Ithaca and London: Cornell University Press, 1970).

24. Recently, on this view, cf. Jacques Derrida, *De la grammatologie* (Paris: Éditions de Minuit, 1967).

25. Obviously James Joyce, *Finnegan's Wake* (London: Faber & Faber, 1939). See Norman O. Brown, *Closing Time* (New York: Random House, 1973).

26. As in Gilles Deleuze, *Proust et les signes* (Paris: PUF, 1964), ch. 8.

27. Cf. Max Weber, *Gesammelte Aufsätze*; Alexander von Schelting, *Max Webers Wissenschaftslehre* (Tübingen: Mohr, 1934).

28. For a discussion of some aspects of Foucault's work see *Critique* 343(1975):1207-66.

29. Foucault, *The Archaeology of Knowledge* (London: Tavistock, 1972), pp. 47-48.

30. As stated by Régine Robin in *Histoire et linguistique* (Paris: Colin, 1973), pp. 83ff.

31. Foucault, *Archaeology*, p. 63.

32. Foucault, "Orders of discourse," *Social Science Information* 10(1971), p.20.

33. Cf. Karl-Otto Apel, *Hermeneutik und Ideologiekritik* (Frankfurt: Suhrkamp, 1971).

34. Cf. George Henrik von Wright, *Explanation and Understanding* (London: Routledge & Kegan Paul, 1971).

35. E.g. Arthur P. Simonds, *Karl Mannheim's Sociology of Knowledge* (Oxford: Clarendon, 1978).

36. As in the work of Georg Lukács and Lucien Goldmann.

37. See Mikhail Bakhtine, *Esthétique et théorie du roman* (Paris: NRF, 1978).

38. A case in point is Karl-Otto Apel, "The prominence of the problem of understanding in modern philosophy of language, hermeneutic phenomenology, and in the philosophy of the 'Geisteswissenschaften,'" paper presented at the International Seminar on Meaning and Understanding, Cerisy-la-Salle, June 1979.

39. Cf. Régine Robin.

40. The term is Husserl's.

41. See Yeheshel Hasenfeld, "People Processing Organizations: An Exchange Approach," in *Human Service Organizations*, ed. Y. Hasenfeld and R. English (Ann Arbor: University of Michigan Press, 1974).

42. Cf. Joseph C. Kiger, *Operating Principles of the Larger Foundations* (New York: Russell Sage, 1954); Warren Weaver, *U.S. Philanthropic Foundations: Their History, Structure, Management, and Record* (New York: Harper & Row, 1967).

43. See Weaver for a description of the main trends in the development of foundations.

44. Cf. Arnold J. Zurcher, *The Management of American Foundations: Administration, Policies, and Social Role* (New York: New York University Press, 1972), esp. ch. 2.

45. The rhetoric, history, and general social implications of the discursive practice of proposals are largely unwritten. Some elements may be gleaned from Louis Marin, "Pouvoir du récit et récit du pouvoir," *Actes de la recherche* 25(1979):23-43; and more extensively from his *Le récit est un piège* (Paris: Éditions de Minuit, 1978); also from Foucault, *La volonté de savoir*; George Steiner, "The Distribution of Discourse," in *On Difficulty and Other Essays* (Oxford: Oxford University Press, 1978).

46. The classic references are Diana Crane, "The gatekeepers of science: some factors affecting the selection of articles for scientific journals," *American Sociologist* 2(1967):195-201; Harriet Zuckerman and Robert K. Merton, "Patterns of evaluation in science: institutionalization, structure, and functions of the referee system," *Minerva* 9(1971):66-100.

47. See Carol Kunzel, "Grant-Making in Major American Foundations: Program Officers and the Decision-Making Process," unpublished doctoral dissertation, New York University, October 1979.

48. Primarily Richard Colvard, "Foundations and professions: the organizational defense of autonomy," *Administrative Science Quarterly* 6(1961):167-84; "Foundations and their clients: why the project method?" *American Behaviorial Scientist* 5(1962):4-6.

49. See the notes and bibliography in Kunzel.

50. Cf. for instance Commission on Foundations and Private Philanthropy, *Foundations, Private Giving, and Public Policy: Report and Recommendations of the Commission on Foundations and Private Philanthropy* (Chicago: University of Chicago Press, 1970).

51. Cf. Alain Touraine, *La voix et le regard* (Paris: Seuil, 1978), pp. 15ff.

12

Radical Ideas and Power

Johannes Weiss

The observations which follow explore the assumption that under certain conditions the power of the ideas in operation are of decisive causal importance for the probability of certain individuals or groups to realize power in social struggles. This hypothesis appears to contradict the dominant, even constitutive assumption, particularly of the classical sociology of knowledge, that ideas and systems of ideas are either merely dependent variables or a function of the "real" conditions of societal power and interests, or — Max Scheler is an excellent example — that there is an ontological gulf between the spheres of the "ideal factors" and the "real factors." It is assumed that the former, while performing a necessary guiding function, can never be of causal importance in determining action. One of these two positions is invariably constitutive of the sociology of knowledge since, as an empirical science, it must accept the "reality" of society as final reference point for its explanatory efforts. However, it is possible that a residual idealism is concealed in the sociology of knowledge, which reveals itself in the separation of the world of ideas from the "true reality" of social and historical action.

The thesis which will be developed more fully here is that, under certain conditions, the relative importance or power of ideas is connected with the radicalness with which ideas are developed and advocated. I shall speculate on why and under what circumstances such a connection arises. The rather general title of this paper requires specification. Initially I am concerned with the role of the radicalness of ideas in the struggles for the opportunity of gaining and increasing power rather than with the role of ideas in preserving existing power constellations. More precisely, I am concerned with the struggles for political power chances (*Machtchancen*), and eventually with revolutionary power conflicts, i.e. those conflicts in which fundamental changes in the redistribution of political power are at

311

stake.

Following Max Weber, "power" will be defined in a broad and unspecific sense as "the probability that one actor within a social relationship will be in a position to carry out his own will despite resistance."[1] An individual's or a group's relative degree of power is thus expressed (1) in the range and attachment of a group of adherents and (2) in the ability to realize particular aims in competition with other individuals or groups. It shall remain open whether the term *power* is still useful when the likelihood to realize a particular will is largely based on the persuasive power of an ideology.

"Radicalness of ideas" shall pertain to the extent to which a system of ideas employed in power conflicts manages to rely on fundamental ideas or principles which are as few in number and as simple as possible. The system of ideas possessing the highest degree of radicalness is accordingly that system whose propositions are not further reducible in the eyes of the participants.

The systems of political ideas must meet two conditions:

First, this radicalization must appear as an increasing (and finally no longer surpassable) deepening of insight into the historical and societal reality and consequently into the ultimate causes of existing conditions. Marx's definition is useful here: being radical means to go to the root of things. This radicalness of ideas must be experienced as a return to the genuine and real causes of the historical (and particularly the "material") realities and not be removed from them by abstraction or mere speculation.[2]

Second, along with providing insight into reality, the system of ideas must determine the approaches and — above all — the aims of effective actions. Thus only those "guiding ideas" of political action which can simultaneously provide a final and absolute foundation for both knowledge and action are radical in an emphatic sense. Marx expressed this in the formula that new principles for the world must be developed out of the principles of the existing one. The connection between these two conditions (or dimensions) of radicalization is highly sensitive and precarious. Especially the satisfaction of the second condition can easily lead to a situation in which these guiding ideas are gradually emptied of concrete contents. As long as this process is subjectively perceived by the actors it will have a decisive influence on the persuasive and motivational power of the guiding ideas. This is the case for those social movements and social conflicts in which real societal power is at stake. Although Lenin attacked left-wing radicalism as "doctrinarianism" (and as "infantilism of the communist movement"),[3] it may nevertheless be argued that he represents in an ideal-typical manner the "radicalness of ideas" we have in mind —

precisely because he succeeded in meeting both the above conditions.

The following considerations will be presented in a very sketchy and preliminary form. They remain essentially theoretical, also in the "negative" sense of dealing with more or less plausible hypotheses and even speculations. Yet the impulse which has given rise to these considerations is not merely theoretical. It did not arise as the logical consequence of a general theoretical system but is the result of work on historical power conflicts, especially on the dynamics of revolutionary processes in modern Europe. In the course of this work it became apparent that there is not only a specific connection between the ability of revolutionary movements to assert themselves against an existing power and the radicalness of their guiding ideas; it also became evident that *within* the revolutionary camp the chances for success of competing factions (and individuals) vary with the radicalness of their ideas. This second point is crucial because it suggests that the "force of ideas"[4] has not only had the general effect of a driving force for these revolutionary efforts, as has frequently been argued, but that it has also determined the direction of the revolutionary microprocess. This is especially true in *those* phases which, in retrospect at least, appear as (causally) decisive. Perhaps the most important and striking examples of this are the French Revolution, which terminated in the authority of the Jacobins and Robespierre, and the Russian Revolution, which terminated in the rule of the Bolsheviks and Lenin. Even among professional historians there is a consensus that the greater radicalness of ideas was in these cases a deciding factor in the outcome of the power struggles between the revolutionary (and counterrevolutionary) groups and individuals. In both instances the group which prevailed against competing revolutionary groups was the one which was representative of the most radical guiding ideas (as defined above), i.e. the Jacobins and the Bolsheviks. In time this radicalness gained them extensive mass support, which they certainly did not command at the outset.[5] That Lenin and Robespierre (the "Robespierre who succeeded")[6] prevailed within their own factions was, in turn, less the result of certain "charismatic" qualities than of their ability to articulate, advocate, and see through this radicalness most clearly and most convincingly.[7] Specific intellectual abilities and character traits but also rhetorical and agitatorial skills account for this.

Similar observations could probably also be made about numerous other revolutionary power conflicts (primarily, though not exclusively, in the Europe since the French Revolution). For present purposes it is irrelevant whether the revolutionary movements or groups in question were able to long maintain the positions of power they had gained (which is indeed not the case for either the revolutions of 1848 and 1870, the German Revolution of 1918-19, the French Revolution, or even for the Russian Revolution). Finally, these observations can also be applied to the outcome of other power conflicts and to the success of political groups whose guiding principles were decidedly antireformist, antiliberal, and above all antisocialist. The success of fascist movements in general and of German National Socialism in particular comes to mind.[8]

I shall now attempt to formulate several hypotheses about possible explanations of the relationship between the radicalness of ideas and the political realization of societal power.

1. We must begin with an assertion which perhaps still belongs to the domain of definition and explication of the matter at hand. Our reflections were initially limited to revolutionary power conflicts, i.e. conflicts in which comprehensive changes involving the whole society are at stake and which involve fundamental transformations in the existing distribution of power. Such an interest in fundamental change, if perceived as such, does not merely require a general ideological justification but also a legitimation accepted as an ultimate authority, as final and intellectually irresistible. There is overwhelming evidence for the view that in the case of revolutionary upheavals such legitimations have by no means a merely rationalizing and therefore "ideological" character. In addition, they are constitutive in the development and maintenance of the revolutionary willingness to act. Such a demand for an ultimate and comprehensive spiritual meaning suggests that the degree of radicalness of competing revolutionary systems of ideas is a decisive factor in the success of the various revolutionary groups and individuals.

Here we might ask whether these considerations and assumptions are true. The availability to groups and individuals of a system of (explanatory and legitimizing) ideas of the most comprehensive and fundamental kind represents a constitutive condition of the emergence of a revolutionary willingness to act in a narrower sense. However, it is by no means the logical consequence of this assumption that the relative probability of success of competing groups and individuals is linked to the degree of radicalness of their respective "programs." This second assumption presupposes other assumptions, in particular that competing revolutionary conceptions can be arranged on a continuum of radicalness and that the nature and evolution of the revolutionary power conflict can provide sufficient opportunities and avenues for intellectual disputation about the respective conceptions, thus providing a basis for influence and for adjustments of influence on a large scale. The significance ascribed to the dispute (particularly between competing revolutionary groups) about the more radical conception during the revolutionary power conflict can be seen as an indication of the importance of a comprehensive and fundamental system of explanation and legitimation for the revolutionary movement as a whole.

2. The next assumption moves on an even more fundamental plane. It refers to the significance which can be attributed to the radicalization of the ideological apparatus in making possible decisive political and particularly revolutionary action. Political action will be decisive and successful in proportion to the actors' conviction that theirs is the only right way. This applies most of all when life and death are at stake in the power struggle, as is usually the case in revolutionary conflicts. References to other, more open possibilities are characteristic of philosophical, scientific, and political discourse. Yet the doubts which emerge in such discourse must, even in their mere theoretical form, be eradicated from the guiding ideas of an action which relies on the clarity, definitiveness, and the utmost certainty in the premises of its supporting ideas. This prerequisite is met by the process of radicalization as characterized above (which can take place on numerous planes, according to circumstances).

In the discussion about the effect of the *philosophes* of the eighteenth century (in particular Montesquieu and Rousseau) on the actors in the Revolution of 1789[9] it has frequently been argued that their influence did not result from the contents of their ideas, but rather from the motivating (emotional) vigor of these idea systems.[10] Their influence was achieved by way of a condensation and radicalization of their (heterogeneous, even contradictory and to a large extent "moderate") works of thought to certain basic ideas (liberty, equality, the sovereignty of the people, the goodness of man, and so on). The power of these basic ideas to determine action (and even their highly emotional contents), their achievements as *idées forces*,[11] may be largely explained by the fact that in this process of reduction, as seen *from the viewpoint of the actors*, these fundamental ideas experienced a progressive increase in "reasonableness" (*Vernünftigkeit*) and thus — in the traditional sense of the term — in their philosophical quality. The influence of another factor on the actors and events at the time ought to be mentioned in this connection. This was the view that these fundamental and guiding ideas in the works of the *philosophes* coincided with the most comprehensive and detailed historical (political, juridical etc.) knowledge, i.e. that they were by no means removed from the world as merely abstract principles.

These last remarks already refer to the following assumptions, which deal with the specific characteristics of the social carriers of revolutionary power struggles, i.e. the intellectuals and the masses.

3. There is broad consensus that in the revolutionary power conflicts discussed here the leading role was played by a social group which has been referred to as "intellectuals" (intelligentsia) or sometimes also

"ideologists."[12] Again according to widespread opinion, this group is characterized by the fact that its members are concerned with the intellectual and critical penetration of social and political conditions and developments. Furthermore, they are said to conduct their affairs as publicly as possible and aided by the media at their disposal. The specific role of intellectuals in the struggle between societal interests is attributed to the fact that they are less involved in pursuing their own (material) interests than in expressing and realizing their specific group interest in the intensive and critical intellectual work of discussion and publication. In view of this it is hardly natural or "logical" that intellectuals typically function as pioneers and leaders in revolutionary power struggles (even when these assume the character of mass movements). The question arises whether this observation is compatible with the general hypothesis advanced by Max Weber as well as Karl Marx, in the latter's case in direct reference to the French Revolution,[13] that the decisive factors in power struggles are not ideas but in the final analysis always interests.

A critical analysis of this scheme (which places ideas on one side and interests on the other) might well provide a solution to this problem. Even entirely "material" (i.e. physical or economic) interests can generally be translated into revolutionary political power (which challenges and overcomes existing conditions) only to the extent to which an ultimate and absolute legitimacy has been bestowed upon them by ideas. According to Mannheim,[14] it is the intellectuals who perform this process of transforming conflicts of interest into conflicts of ideas. Intellectuals are in a favorable position for this task because their own interests are less directly affected. The reverse assumption, that ideas can determine action only insofar as they are rooted in (largely material) interests, appears to be far less generally valid. In certain circumstances it is the ideas of those who believe themselves to be free from every egoistic group interest and to serve "reason" and history alone, which have a particularly strong motivating power.

Going beyond these general statements, we shall now formulate a specific hypothesis. The development of political ideas and conceptions and the disputations about them in intellectual circles are characterized by an inherent tendency toward increasing radicalness. The type of intellectual referred to here[15] provides an explanation and critique of the existing historical world. He consequently finds himself in a situation in which he can only advance, in his own terms and those of others like him, by progressively deepening and clarifying his ideas. This tendency toward a progressive radicalization of ideas and goals is typical for intellectuals and is greatly encouraged by their specific social forms of interaction and communication (e.g. salons, clubs, journals, treatises, etc.).[16] It is further intensified in situations where intellectuals are persecuted by a powerful state and find themselves involved in conspiratorial forms of organization.

It is indicative of the pervasiveness of the tendency toward increasing radicalization typical of intellectual circles that even members of such social groups as the aristocracy are affected by it. Whether consciously or not, such aristocrats thereby effectively rob themselves of the very basis of their material and social position.[17]

A further observation is of possible importance in this context. There is a special affinity between the prerevolutionary and revolutionary intelligentsia and the legal profession. This was especially so for the French Revolution but it is true beyond it as well (see Kerensky, Lenin, and Castro). More than half of the twelve members of the Committee of Public Welfare (according to Coser's classification this committee was constituted only by representatives of typically intellectual professions[18]) were lawyers. Even if this proportion should not have been significantly overrepresentative, it must be considered how much importance should be given to this fact for the process of ideological radicalization. A decidedly normative (and in tendency even doctrinaire) orientation is typical of the way of thinking of members of the legal profession. Moreover, they can be characterized by their need to force things to their extremes (*Konsequenzmacherei*, as Weber put it). Such an attempt to reduce the multitude of historical facts to a single transparent order based on as few, simple, and evident supreme assumptions as possible (and offering the highest degree of normative attraction) apparently has a strong affinity to the above-mentioned mentality characteristic of politically minded intellectuals. Their profession, which involves them in experience with juridical rhetoric, affords them the practice required to deal with the compelling logic of a normative order. This experience probably played a significant part in the implementation and realization (by publication and agitation) of the revolutionary ideology.[19] The juridical backgrounds of the leading representatives particularly of the French Revolution have been emphasized by many authors, though in a somewhat more general context. G.W.F. Hegel[20] speaks, for instance, of the "advocates, ideologists and men of principle" whom Napoleon finally chased away. Jakob Burckhardt[21] remarked of Robespierre that he "emerged as a jurist with a completely one-sided rhetorical imagination, a terrible man, immersed only in his juridical logic and seeking to accomplish its realization at all costs."

But finally it must also be pointed out that jurists (as practitioners of law) were that group of intellectuals with the most intimate experience of the misery of a broad population. This experience, apart from aiding their style of rhetoric and agitation, was also useful in the substantive elaboration of their political ideas.

4. These last remarks may be summarized as follows: specific characteristics of the mentality of intellectuals (of the type discussed here) and of the group dynamics which dominate in such intellectual circles explain why radicalness of ideas increases the likelihood of their realization of power. The question remains whether a similar assertion can be made with respect to the probability that power can be achieved among intellectuals as a whole or among certain other individuals outside these circles. This question pertains mainly to the masses, the second most important and, in relation to the power issue in its narrower sense, frequently decisive[22] carrier of revolutionary struggles.

Alexis de Tocqueville's thesis provides one possible way of arriving at an affirmative answer: "The writers not only provided the people, which carried out the Revolution, with their ideas; they also conveyed to it their temperament and their mood."[23] Such an assumption (which sees the revolutionary masses as a large club of ideologists) is perhaps exaggerated and unnecessary for our purposes. Tocqueville's remark about the religious character of the French Revolution — which represents a completely new type of revolution — may well point in the direction in which the answer can be found. Tocqueville argues that, as far as its form of execution is concerned, this political revolution spread even "to distant places by preaching and propaganda." Equally important, its religious character reveals itself openly in the contents of its guiding ideas: "It perceived the citizen abstractly, as removed from any particular community, just as religion sees man as a universal being. . . . It was able to make itself understood to everybody because it always referred to the conditions in society and government which were less distinct and, as it were, more natural."[24]

The same thought is evident in Emil Lederer's more general formulation: "Two things are essential for every genuine revolution: that it is an *idea* and that it can mobilize a *social* force. As an idea it must be comprehensive, it must be a truly universal idea in order to inspire this general emotion."[25]

Such statements not only assert a general connection between the availability and persuasive power of political (revolutionary) ideas and the capacity to mobilize the masses; they also imply that the attractiveness of these ideas to the masses and their mobilizing power is founded on their specific radicalness. According to this view, the effectiveness of radical ideas disseminated by ideologists does not lie primarily either in their simplicity or in a specific quality which would permit their simplification for the people. While this aspect cannot be ignored — there have been justified references to the "seductive simplicity" of *Lenin's* revolutionary theory[26] — the power-granting persuasiveness of these radical ideas for the masses is to be found elsewhere. First and foremost, it can be derived from the fact that the masses experience their own misery as one which can be explained in terms of more general or fundamental societal causes. (Marx insisted that the proletariat must move away from mere class-specific experience and, of necessity, move toward a universal human perspective.)

If there were not in the masses at least the beginnings of such an experience or of such an interpretation of their own situation, the mobilizing power of these radical ideas of the philosophers and ideologists would remain inexplicable. Conversely, it is plausible that once this process of exercising ideological influence on the masses has been started, a progressive radicalization takes place which can move quite far away from concrete experiences and interests.[27] Since the hoped-for fundamental improvements (especially of the material situation), are not immediately forthcoming after the removal of the traditional power, this is likely to generate a willingness to follow the spokesmen of the more radical conception.[28] The exhaustion or collapse of this willingness is just as likely after repeated disappointments. As soon as this occurs the ideologists lose their influence with the masses. It is not a necessary (nor typical) consequence that the ideologists thereby lose their inclination toward radicalness, which for them, in contrast to the masses, is a matter of "identity." If in the meantime they have been able to avail themselves of the appropriate means of power, they will be inclined to realize their radical conceptions even against the will of the masses: the execution, fortification, and extension of power may produce a tendency toward a system of dictatorial and centralized bureaucratic authority of a special kind, a system characterized by a specific relationship between bureaucratic violence and ideological rigor.

A few brief considerations about this latter type of system of authority will follow since here, too, a peculiar and constitutive interplay exists between the radicalness of ideas and political power, and because the connection to what has been discussed thus far is not merely logical but also typically genetic. A specific kind of radicalism is initially a decisive means for accomplishing and extending power. In the course of the change of its *modus operandi* it is unlikely, at least immediately and typically, to become the residue of a subsequent and perhaps cynical ideological justification of power based on physical force and perhaps even terror. The representatives of the type of authority discussed here are likely to retain their irrevocable faith in the superior, even absolute truth of the ideas they represent. In their view, neither the necessity to employ physical and terrorist force in reinforcing their authority nor the development of a centralized bureaucratic apparatus as a tool of authority are sufficient to discredit the fundamental ideas from which authority is derived, at least not in the short and medium term. The ideological radicalness discussed here embraces a positive relationship both to physical force (especially in its terrorist form), as a means of reinforcing authority, as well as to bureaucracy. A brief attempt to illustrate this assertion will follow below.

1. In political conflicts radicalism of ideas is associated with a willingness to employ extensive physical force. The reason could well be that human reality, particularly the mere physical life of the individual, possesses no independent legitimacy vis-à-vis the absolute right of the Idea. The indifference of ideological rulers toward their own (civic and physical) lives has often been stressed in this connection. It typically involves a union of the purest and most definite embodiment of their ideas with personal modesty and a willingness to die for those ideas. Such indifference is probably the best indicator of the existence of real (not just simulated) radicalism. Its motivation, persuasive powers, and success are also associated with an indifference toward the lives of *others*.[29]

Disrespect and contempt for the resistive realities in general and for human life in particular is thus a constitutive element of the kind of radicalness of ideas discussed here. In radical political movements it may occur that a group committed to the use of force and terror splits off from one which restricts itself to agitation and propaganda, e.g. in the English Chartist movement and in the case of the disintegration of the first socialist and revolutionary party in Russia (Zemlja i Volja) into the Narodnaja Volja and the Cornij Peredelj.[30] It is probable that this transition to physical force is increasingly determined by the more decisive (and abstract) ideological position. The general assumption that terror from below is the manifestation of a "desperado" mentality (i.e. a desperation about the hopelessness of the cause) is accordingly untenable. This is equally true for the assumption that terror from above is always the manifestation of an interest in the pure preservation of power. This causal connection between ideological radicalism and a willingness to employ force emerges, above all and for obvious reasons, where the ideological conception is doctrinaire, i.e. where the intellectual penetration of the sociohistorical reality is progressively suspended in favor of abstract moral and political ideals or postulates. Physical force is used as the functional equivalent of the ideology's missing or diminishing cognitive power of persuasion (and of the practical effectiveness closely connected with this cognitive aspect).

2. A similar diminution of the dominant ideas is also characteristic of the bureaucratic aspect of the authority of typical ideological rulers. Bureaucracy — defined by Weber as "authority through knowledge" — means in this context: central planning, regulation, and control of progressively larger areas of societal and individual life in accordance with a few highly abstract aims or principles. The reality of society is merely the sub-

stance which, for an "authority through knowledge" of *this* type,[31] must be formed in the image of a pure and true order. The ruling representatives of such authority have no other interest than to embody[32] and realize these principles and this order.

In this (early) form bureaucracy assumes the character of value rationality: the "spirit" has not yet left the "apparatus" to the devices of its endogeneous instrumental rationality and to the requirements of everyday life. It uses this apparatus to represent and realize ideals, which exist in a very tense relationship with the given reality, as a result of their great and especially of their one-sided normative radicalness. Thus, bureaucracy is here a tool in the fundamental *transformation* of societal conditions, and itself an exemplary representation of the essential traits of the desired transparent and reasonable social order.[33] With respect to the French Revolution and the authority of the Jacobins, Saint-Just (whose last speech before the convent, which was cut short, dealt with the necessity of institutions), more so than Robespierre, is perhaps the ideal-typical representative of this kind of ideological radicalness, which finds its adequate political expression in the thorough bureaucratization of all social relations.

Let me raise the issue as to whether the power conflicts used as examples, in particular the two great revolutions in modern European history, do not represent such unique developments that they are unsuitable evidence for even the most cautious theoretical generalizations. The unique nature of these power conflicts is evident in the specific and constitutive way in which they were subject to the authority of radical ideas. It has often been said of the French Revolution that in it, as Hegel stated, for the first (and perhaps last) time "man's existence centers in his head, i.e., thought, inspired by which he builds up the world of reality."[34] W. Grab emphasizes the entirely new radicalism of the French Revolution: "It was the first revolution which aimed at the complete dissolution of the old conditions, i.e. which was oriented toward the future, and which wanted to establish a new political and legal order. Its radical and consistent protagonists made a conscious break with tradition and the past in order to create a community based on liberty and social justice."[35]

Against such objections it can be argued that the persuasive power of the assumptions briefly sketched above cannot be made dependent on the number of cases that meet the presupposed conditions. Nor would a restricted applicability mean that these assumptions have no significant theoretical implications for sociology. Finally, there is the issue of whether these assumptions could not be useful even if the matters which need to be explained are not (in the historically modern sense) revolutionary or not even political power conflicts. It is plausible that this specific kind of

power conflict is only a particularly distinct, radical, and pure manifestation of the decisive characteristics.[36] If these assumptions were applied
generally, their ideal-typical character would have to be taken into consideration even more thoroughly than usual, also in regard to those exceptional political revolutions.

The positive relationship between the radicalization of ideas and political power does not arise for the first time in the French Revolution, which
is neither an inevitable archetype nor a prototype for it. Its emergence can
be expected in circumstances in which people strive to liberate their individual and societal lives from the shallowness, routine, and constraints of
traditional institutions and to reestablish their lives on a new, intellectually and morally more convincing foundation. The process of the
radicalization of ideas and corresponding shifts in power toward increasingly radical positions is set into operation by certain factors. It is less the
transition from traditional to rational forms of legitimation that is responsible for this than the rejection of both merely traditional *and* instrumentally rational forms of legitimation in favor of forms which primarily advocate value rationality. (This could well be because the search for spiritual
meaning is in principle inexhaustible.)

Tocqueville's remarks about the religious nature of the French Revolution indicate that similar processes have occurred in earlier periods,
even if their guiding ideas had typically been of a religious nature. It is
possible that the powers of legitimation and motivation of genuine political radicalism first became evident and were first realized in the course of
the French Revolution. (This remains true even if the "cult of the highest
being" is not interpreted as Robespierre's idiosyncracy but as the result of
the legitimation deficiencies of the Republic of Virtue.) The emergence
and success of this inner-worldly political radicalness had been readied in
the sphere of religious thought and religiously inspired political practice.
The puritan "revolution of the saints," which has been characterized as
the "earliest form of political radicalism,"[37] describes perhaps that phase
in European history in which religious radicalism encounters ideas and
principles increasingly interpreted in a purely inner-worldly sense. This
occurs in such a way that they aspire to even greater radicalness in the
course of this secularization. This reference to the religious origins and
character of radical political ideas[38] may help reveal the historical and
material significance of the assumptions which have been presented. This
does not suggest that these assumptions about the radicalness of ideas and
societal power are only applicable within the sphere of genuine religious
power struggles. In power conflicts, however, the processes of the progressively greater radicalness of ideas and ideologies (as well as the resulting
dynamics of power processes) can be set in motion and gain significance

only once certain factors are present: the struggles must be perceived as inner-worldly and the guiding ideas must no longer be seen as divine commandments pronounced by charismatic leaders and entailing absolute obligation. These ideas must be seen as achievements of human reason or as instruments of human interests.[39]

In conclusion, another perspective will be sketched all too briefly, which indicates that the hypotheses which have been presented point to the level of abstraction of a general sociological theory. Social relations in general and power and authority relations in particular derive their enduring intersubjective safeguards from justifications which provide meaning. Situations can arise in which traditional justifications become problematic, in which the sociocultural totality is materially affected. In such situations, both a successful transformation and preservation of the existing conditions require the formulation and persuasive advocacy of a formal justification which is more penetrating and/or more internally consistent. This would imply that a specific tendency toward radicalization inheres in the societal process, which becomes acute whenever the constitutive instability and contingency of societal arrangements become visible. In this regard, too, Marx's thesis (in the preface to the *Critique of Political Economy*), that mankind only sets itself tasks it can solve, does not apply. The desire for more radical, fundamental, or consistent meanings is not always accompanied by an ability to create such meanings and prevail with them. It could very well be that the present era is in this respect characterized by a wide and fundamental gulf between a need and the capacity to satisfy it. This is certainly true if the disenchantment of the world is taken seriously as a sign of the present. The multitude of radicalisms which emerge in rapid succession and which compete with one another as well as the manifold manifestations of ideological regression support this thesis.

Notes

Translated from German by Volker Meja and Robert Tonks

1. Max Weber, *Wirtschaft und Gesellschaft*, 5. Aufl., I. Halbband, (Cologne and Berlin: Kiepenheuer & Witsch, 1964), p. 38. English: *Economy and Society*, ed. Guenther Roth and Claus Wittich, vol. 1 (Berkeley, Los Angeles, and London: University of California Press, 1968), p. 53.

2. Henry Peyre's observation is important here: that the prerevolutionary philosophers played an essential part in the establishment of a historical consciousness and that their criticism of the aristocratic and royal aspirations to authority was based on historical research. "The Influence of Eighteenth Century Ideas on the French Revolution," in *Einführung in die Geschichte der französischen Revolution*, ed. E. Schmitt (Munich: Beck, 1976), pp. 124-51.

3. V.I. Lenin, "Der 'linke Radikalismus' als Kinderkrankheit des Kommunismus," in *Werke* (Berlin: Dietz, 1959), pp. 1-91.

4. Charlotte von Kalb, in a letter to Hölderlin's mother, on revolutionary endeavors at the University of Jena. Cit. P. Härtling, *Hölderlin* (Darmstadt: Luchterhand, 1978), p. 208.

5. Karl Marx, in the *18th Brumaire of Louis Bonaparte*, proclaims an "ascending line" in the French Revolution from the Constitutionals and Girondists to the Jacobins, and speaks of the victories of the "more daring allies" (cf. Schmitt, p. 69). See Dietrich Geyer, *Die Russische Revolution* (Göttingen: Vandenhoeck & Ruprecht, 1977), for a comparison with the dynamics of power in the Russian Revolution of 1917, as well as Roy Medwedew's *Oktober 1917* (Hamburg: Hoffmann & Campe, 1979), which contains interesting observations by other authors, e.g. Berdyaev (p. 14) and Trotsky (p. 91). Finally, Crane Brinton, *Anatomy of Revolution* (Englewood Cliffs, NJ: Prentice-Hall, 1963) believes that a generalizable pattern of revolutionary dynamics can be derived from the various phases of the French Revolution: 1. The Rule of the Moderates, 2. The Accession of the Extremists, 3. Reigns of Terror and Virtue, 4. Thermidor. Lenin himself (in "Zwei Taktiken der Sozialdemokratie in der demokratischen Revolution," *Werke*, vol. 9) called the Bolsheviks the "Jacobins of today's Social Democracy." See also his article (1917) "Kann man die Arbeiterklasse mit dem 'Jakobinertum' schrecken?" (Lenin, *Werke*, vol. 25).

6. A. Mathiez, *Le Bolchevisme et le Jacobinisme* (Paris: Librairie du Parti Socialiste, 1920), cited in E. Schmitt, p. 24; Mathiez saw a direct causal connection between Robespierre's lack of success and the absence of a "coherent doctrine comparable to Marxism."

7. A particularly good example is Lenin's famous "April Theses" (see Hellmann, *Die Russische Revolution* (Munich: Deutscher Taschenbuchverlag, 1975), p. 188. The Mensheviks called them a false document and a swindle and said that they were written "in complete abstraction from circumstances, time and place." Cit. Roy Medwedew from the newspaper *Jedinstvo* (9th April 1917): p. 88).

8. This assertion is illustrated by a quote from Joseph Goebbels: "When we are told: you are radical!, we can only reply: Have we ever claimed that we are *not radical*? . . . When we are told: you are too rigorous! You are too emphatic! You do not make any compromises! — we can only reply: we never left this in doubt even when we were in our time of opposition. And I believe that this is why the German people granted us their devotion. The people *want* it." H. Heiber, ed., *Goebbels-Reden* (Düsseldorf: Droste, 1971), vol. 1, p. 119. See also p. 234 (speech at a special meeting of the District Propaganda Leaders at the 7th *Reichsparteitag* of the NSDAP): "only extremes have a penetrating effect on the people." For interesting references to Italian Fascism see Emil Oesterreicher, "Facism and the intellectuals: the case of Italian futurism," *Social Research* 41(1974):515-38.

9. Similar statements have also been made about the influence of Marxism on the Russian Revolution.

10. Such an interpretation is proposed by Henri Peyre, p. 142, who is very receptive to the importance of ideas in history.

11. Fouillée, quoted by Peyre.

12. For a differentiated typology of revolutionary leaders see C. Leiden and K.M. Schmitt, *The Politics of Violence: Revolution in the Modern World* (London: Prentice-Hall, 1973), ch. 5 ("The Domination of Various Types of Leaders in the Various Phases of the Revolutions"); C. Brinton, ch. 4 ("Types of Revolutionists").

13. *Die heilige Familie*; see Schmitt, p. 28; Weber's corresponding observation can be found in the introduction to his *Wirtschaftsethik der Weltreligionen*.

14. Karl Mannheim, *Ideology and Utopia* (New York: Harcourt, Brace, 1936), p. 142.

15. The direct opposite of this type is the intellectual whose essential characteristic is an inability or unwillingness to act in a power-related context. This is because his system of arguments is inconclusive. Lewis Coser, *Men of Ideas* (New York: Free Press, 1965), provides a particularly good typology of the "men of ideas," especially with respect to the different attitudes of intellectuals to political power.

16. See Heinrich Cunow, *Die Parteien der grossen französischen Revolution* (Berlin: Vorwärts, 1912) for the role of the mass media (particularly the press) in the French Revolution; R. Pethybridge, *The Spread of the Russian Revolution* (London: Macmillan, 1972) for the Russian Revolution.

17. "So completely had our nobility forgotten that new political theories, once they are generally accepted, inevitably rouse popular passions and bear fruit in deeds, that they regarded even the doctrines most hostile to their prerogatives, and in fact to their very existence, as mere flights of fancy, entertaining *jeux d'ésprit*." Alexis de Tocqueville, *L'Ancien régime et la révolution* (Paris: Gallimard, 1952), vol. 2, p. 196.

18. Coser, pp. 145ff. See also the references to the overrepresentation of the jurists among the intellectuals in Walter Markov and Albert Soboul, *1789: Die grosse Revolution der Franzosen* (Berlin: Akademie, 1975), p. 24. Schmitt, p. 91, refers to M.J. Sydenham, *The Girondins* (London: Athlone, 1961), who ascertains the same social background of the Girondins and Jacobins and the predominance of the legal profession. See, finally, Max Weber's general observations in the passage on natural law in *Wirtschaft und Gesellschaft* (Cologne-Berlin: Kiepenheuer & Witsch, 1964), vol. 1, p. 643.

19. Geyer, *Die Russische Revolution*, p. 70, observes — with respect to the advocate Kerensky — that these were skills of particular importance in a time "in which history had become theatrical and the pathos of great agitators determined issues of power."

20. G.W.F. Hegel, *Vorlesungen über die Philosophie der Geschichte* (Stuttgart: Reclam, 1961), p. 598.

21. J. Burckhardt, *Vorlesungen über die Geschichte des Revolutionszeitalters: Rekonstruktion des gesprochenen Wortlautes von Ernst Ziegler* (Basel-Stuttgart: Schwabe, 1974), p. 215.

22. On this point, see Georg Rudé, *Die Volksmassen in der Geschichte: England und Frankreich, 1730-1848* (Frankfurt: Campus, 1977). Rudé's book is a general rejection of the conventional view that the (political) masses were generally an irrational mob, lacking ideas, "gens sans aveu."

23. Tocqueville, p. 200.

24. Ibid., p. 89.

25. Emil Lederer, *Einige Gedanken zur Soziologie der Revolution* (Leipzig: Neue Geist, 1918), p. 13.

26. Geyer, p. 81.

27. On this process in the French Revolution see Rudé, p. 202.

28. See Robespierre's criticism of the Encyclopaedists as "not on the level of the rights of the people." Quoted V.Pl. Volguine, "L'Idéologie révolutionaire en France au XVIIIe siècle," in Schmitt, p. 218).

29. "The defenders of liberty have never believed that a long life is awaiting them. Their existence is uncertain and fragile. I do not believe in the necessity to live but in virtue and providence." M. Robespierre quoted by Friedrich Sieburg, *Robespierre: Mensch und*

revolutionärer Diktator (Munich: Heyne, 1975), p. 300. K. Eisner is characterized by E. Toller not only as a "moralist" but also as the one minister among those in the Munich *Räterepublik* who distinguished himself by his "determination to act, by his extreme courage." Tankred Dorst, *Die Münchner Räterepublik: Zeugnisse und Kommentar* (Frankfurt: Suhrkamp, 1972), p. 82. Eisner's election address before the Independents (1919: 23-44) is also a good example of radical political thought.

30. See Boris Souvarine, *Stalin: Anmerkungen zur Geschichte des Bolschewismus* (Munich: Bernard & Graefe, 1980), p. 49.

31. See Jakob L. Talmon, *The Origins of Totalitarian Democracy* (New York/Washington: Praeger, 1960), pp. 132ff.

32. Billaud-Varene, one of the Thermidorians, saw the cause of Robespierre's authority over people in the fact "that he openly displayed the strictest of virtues, the most unlimited devotion and the purest of principles" (cit. Sieburg, p. 106).

33. See M. Walzer's hypothesis in *The Revolution of the Saints: A Study in the Origins of Radical Politics* (London: Weidenfeld & Nicolson, 1965), that the "ideological keenness" of puritanical radicalism was combined with a distinct interest in "discipline and order" and "control and self-control" (p. 310). Furthermore, it made a considerable contribution to the development of modern bureaucratic discipline. Once established, though, the latter can completely forego this "radical enthusiasm" (p. 306). In this respect Walzer refers specifically to the parallels between the Holy Commonwealth, the Jacobin Republic of Virtue, and the authority of the Bolsheviks, and compares also the particular disciplinary rigor of Cromwell and Lenin. Already H. Marcuse had discovered aspects of an internal world of asceticism in the postrevolutionary Soviet bureaucracy. Herbert Marcuse, *Soviet Marxism: A Critical Analysis* (New York: Columbia University Press, 1961).

34. Hegel, *Vorlesungen über die Philosophie der Geschichte*, p. 593.

35. Walter Grab, *Die Französische Revolution: Eine Dokumentation* (Munich: Nymphenburger, 1973), p. 11.

36. One of the characteristics of both great European revolutions is war with other nations. In both cases, though in different ways, it was probably decisive in supporting the radical tendency in the internal power struggles. See Talmon, (p. 97) on the validity of this connection in the French Revolution.

37. See Walzer's (p. 317) "Model of Radical Politics" for a general view of the "Revolution of the Saints," as well as his more detailed observations about the social carriers of this revolution (clerics and educated laymen) in chapters 4 and 5. Christopher Hill, *Puritanism and Revolution: Studies in Interpretation of the English Revolution of the 17th Century* (London: Secker & Warburg, 1958), p. 123, emphasizes the crucial importance of the universal aspirations of the guiding ideas of the English Revolution (brotherhood of men and not just brotherhood of Protestants).

38. See Talmon, pp. 8ff.

39. See Wolfgang Mommsen, *Max Weber: Gesellschaft, Politik und Geschichte* (Frankfurt: Suhrkamp, 1974), p. 112, for his observations about Weber's (not further developed) views. Mommsen concludes his discussion of Weber's considerations concerning the influence of Puritanism on the emergence and effectiveness of the "extreme rationalistic fanaticism" of human rights with the statement: "According to Weber, the real secret of success of the theory of natural law was its finality, the total absence of compromises with the reality of everyday life, which daily exhibited numerous examples of its actual inequality" (p. 116).

Part IV
Empirical Studies

Introduction

The objections which have occasionally been raised against the classical sociology of knowledge and some of its intellectual preoccupations have, especially in the English-speaking world, often focused on the relative absence of empirical investigations concerned with the interrelationship of knowledge and society. Yet a more comprehensive conception of the sociology of knowledge may well lead to the conclusion that many pieces of empirical social research do in fact deal with the question of the social context of knowledge. The *potential* empirical research program of the sociology of knowledge is considerable, ranging from investigations into highly technical and specialized forms of knowledge and their development to studies concerned with everyday knowledge. Such a broad conception of empirical issues is reflected in the concluding part of this book; the essays assembled here deal with issues ranging from quantum mechanics and mathematical ideas to the transformation of everyday knowledge into specialized forms of knowing as well as such mundane knowledge as that of the eater.

Paul Forman and W. Baldamus examine one of the most difficult issues in the sociology of knowledge, namely the possible link of social and sociocultural conditions outside the immediacy of the social organization of highly specialized knowledge producers, to what is for many a paradigmatic case of context-free knowledge, physics, mathematics, and logic. It is particularly with respect to this question that the contemporary sociology of knowledge is beginning to derive some of its own identity.

Karl Mannheim and other founders of the field had maintained that these forms of knowledge are outside the realm of sociological analysis because they develop according to an immanent logic. Although the taboo of a sociological examination of the ideas of physics, logic, and mathematics has been seriously challenged and to a great extent undermined, rigorous empirical investigations are scarce and prove to be most difficult.

Forman examines the character of quantum mechanics, the fundamental theory of atomic and subatomic physics, to probe the elective affinity of the culture of the Weimar Republic in the 1920s in Germany (where the theory originated), and certain aspects and features of quantum mechanics itself. The thrust of Forman's analysis is therefore neither a crude, mechanistic association between knowledge and society nor a simple materialist account of the origin and the nature of quantum mechanics. He rather asks why the theory itself, not reality, has certain characteristics which in turn it attributes to operations of nature.

Forman's intriguing examination of the notions of individuality, intuitive evidentiality and anticausality as "true" and "alleged" attributes of the theory and the disparity between them, leads him to the carefully explicated conclusion that the inflated interpretation and use of the theory were the result of, and a response to, the German-speaking culture of Central Europe. Forman asserts that the generally weak social and intellectual position of the German physicists in the post-World War I era made it impossible for them to effectively oppose the *Zeitgeist* of the period. They attempted to accommodate their work to these facets of Weimar culture. Consequently, the philosophical reconstruction of quantum mechanics and its narrower, "true" character deviated sharply under these social and political circumstances.

Baldamus is more interested in the origin of ideas. He analyzes an equally recalcitrant question in the sociology of knowledge and does so in a more radical fashion than Forman. Baldamus asks whether a sociology of mathematical ideas is possible. Mannheim, writing in the late 1920s, had excluded mathematical ideas from the subject matter of the sociology of knowledge, which undoubtedly reflected the spirit of his age. Baldamus points out that Mannheim should be credited with introducing into the discussion of the nature of knowledge an entirely new vocabulary of contextual concepts that were to replace existing formal concepts with the intention of examining the social determination of knowledge. Thereby Mannheim removed once-powerful barriers to the sociological study of cognition. Also of importance to philosophers of mathematics, as Baldamus shows, contextual definitions provide a means by which the study of the possible social roots of mathematical ideas may be fruitfully opened. Toward this end he analyzes the vocabulary of an essay by the philosopher of mathematics, Hilary Putnam, and demonstrates, especially with respect to the notion of rationality, the "indispensability of contextual definitions in philosophy." He concludes that the sociologically fascinating aspect of this kind of empirical work concerns the ways in which *new* knowledge is injected into existing contexts of received forms of knowledge. Intellectual transformation or innovations occur by way of terms taken almost directly from everyday language. The link Baldamus discovers is in some ways similar to the relationship Forman explores. However, Baldamus makes a far more general claim. In order to inject a new dimension into established, technical discourse communities, reference to everyday discourse and its social context is necessary. The transformation of the former as the result of such borrowing may at times have revolutionary consequences (cf. Thomas S. Kuhn).

The focus of Gernot Böhme's study into the scientization of midwifery is compatible with the investigations by Forman and Baldamus, since Böhme provides a detailed account of how and under what conditions everyday knowledge becomes transformed and the monopoly of medical specialists. The analysis of the transformation, demarcation, and interrelation of different forms of knowledge and their respective communities, based on a comprehensive conception of the sociology of knowledge, is a useful reminder that such a perspective invariably leads one to examine the potential conflict between different groups, strata or classes of knowledge carriers.

Böhme traces the emergence of (medical) experts on childbirth outside everyday life, that is, the scientization of childbirth by delegating to specially trained experts acts of daily life which were once an integral part of everyday experience.

He is not convinced, however, that such an intellectual and social transformation of knowledge is evidence of progress, and examines the possibility that different forms of knowledge perform distinct functions. He provides a detailed social history of midwifery including an examination of the incipient conflict between physicians and midwives. The midwife and her life-world knowledge clashes with the "scientific" knowledge of the physician. Clinical knowledge of childbirth not only separates the individual from knowledge but is also *new* knowledge. It assimilates and transforms everyday knowledge. Baldamus's observations appear to be confirmed in this instance as well.

The last essay in this section takes us back most directly to the world of everyday life and its knowledge, and further asserts its relative significance to the analysis of all forms of knowledge. Marie-Noël Stourdze-Plessis and Hélène Strohl present a magnificent array of research topics on and around what they call "the knowledge of the eater." They outline the contours of a sociology of cooking and eating which truly forms part of the sociology of knowledge inasmuch as it deals with the meanings of a whole series of social competences ("knowledge" understood in the French sense of *savoir faire* and *savoir vivre*). They start by questioning the present explosion of all sorts of hedonistic, medical, ecological, gastronomic, touristic, and even pseudoreligious discourses on food. It is as if our semiotically oriented culture had substituted words and images for tasty morsels. But if intellectuals are gourmands of concepts, their increasing interest in food also indicates that they are fast becoming true gourmets. The point is that cuisine is a form of *Bildung*. The authors suggest that the senses should become instruments of inquiry in a future ethnography of markets, cooking practices, eating habits, and table manners.

In addition, the authors claim that the processes of cooking and eating must be considered a "total social fact," and not a marginal occurrence or an index of more "basic" social processes. Through this elementary and alimentary social fact we learn how societies modulate the rhythms of work and leisure and the behavior of men and women, how they parse their private and public spheres, their past and present. Beyond this, eating is a form of communication — not only the occasion for the various intertwinings of food and speech, but also a sign system with its own "grammar." Finally, the sociology of the table — which is also a sociology of the body — may become a critical discipline by suggesting how the progressive rationalization of food preparation and eating practices in the West (such as the passage from the *table à la française* to the *table à la russe* toward the end of the *ancien régime*) has segregated and even deleted important areas of experience. Here too, the dialectic of dis- and re-enchantment is at work. In the end, the sociology of eating turns into the study of the vicissitudes of conviviality. The essay by Stourdze-Plessis and Strohl is an open invitation to sociologists of knowledge to bring their ingenuity and intellectual equipage to the kitchens and dining areas of the world.

13

Kausalität, Anschaulichkeit, and *Individualität,* or How Cultural Values Prescribed the Character and the Lessons Ascribed to Quantum Mechanics

Paul Forman

Quantum mechanics is the fundamental theory of atomic and subatomic physics. It is the basic set of rules held by the theorist whether he be calculating the electrical resistance of a new semiconductor to be built in an industrial laboratory or the mass of a new elementary particle to be produced by a high-energy accelerator. These rules were found in 1925-26 and elaborated in the following years in a scientific milieu whose language was German and whose center lay in Germany. Of course, Niels Bohr's institute was in Copenhagen. And P.A.M. Dirac, a young research student at Cambridge University, was among the earliest and most important contributors. Overwhelmingly, however, the creation of quantum mechanics was an enterprise of Germans and Austrians. Consequently, as a product of Germany it may appropriately be considered in relation to German culture.

The following discussion of the character of quantum mechanics is in the form of three probes. Each opens with a statement of the *true* bearing of the theory relative to one of three concepts or characteristics paraded in

This paper was originally presented at a workshop in Lecce, Italy, Sept. 3-6, 1979, organized by the Istituto di Fisica and the Istituto di Matematica of the Università di Lecce and by the Gruppo di Storia della Scienza dell' Istituto di Fisica 'G. Marconi' of the Università di Roma. It has been published in slightly different form in Italian in the proceedings of that workshop: M. De Maria, E. Donini et al., *Fisica e Società negli Anni '20* (Milan: CLUP/CLUED, 1980), pp. 15-34; and in German in Nico Stehr and Volker Meja, eds., *Wissenssoziologie,* Sonderheft 22 of the *Kölner Zeitschrift für Soziologie und Sozialpsychologie* (Opladen: Westdeutscher Verlag, 1981), pp. 393-406. Comparable endeavors to explain the origin and interpretation of quantum mechanics along cultural lines are: Lewis Feuer, *Einstein and the Generations of Science* (New York: Basic Books, 1974); S.G. Brush, "The chimerical cat: the philosophy of quantum mechanics in historical perspective," *Social Studies of Science* 10 (1980):393-447.

German in the title: causality, individuality, and intuitive evidentiality or visualizability. This is followed by a brief exposition of the *alleged* character of the theory regarding that concept — alleged first of all by the creators of the theory. These allegations are found to diverge markedly from what, a moment before, had been posited as warranted regarding these concepts. Each probe then concludes with an explanation of this disparity between the true and alleged character of quantum mechanics. The explanation given makes appeal to the role of that concept in German-speaking Central European culture in the era of the Weimar Republic, the culture of the region and period in which quantum mechanics was created.

I speak of the *true* character of quantum mechanics. I trust the reader will not therefore suppose that I believe in, or am logically obliged to believe in, a *transcendental* truth of any sort. What is at issue here is not whether quantum mechanics or any other scientific theory is True — whether it represents the world as it *really* is. At issue is merely whether the theory has certain specified characteristics: whether it represents the world in an *anschaulich* manner, whether it admits ascription of individuality to the subatomic entities with which it deals, and whether it warrants the denial of causality in the operations of nature. Granted that quantum mechanics, or any other representation of the world, can never be established as True, for we can never make a direct comparison of the representation with that which the representation claims to represent. Our case is essentially different. That which is represented — the theory — is presented to us directly as an intellectually apprehensible entity. It is quite reasonable here to ask for open-minded observers capable of being brought by reason and evidence to recognize "what is the case" (to use the expression of the early Wittgenstein).

I also speak of unwarranted interpretations of quantum mechanics as explicable by reference to the broader cultural milieu in which its creators lived and worked. I trust the reader will not suppose that I am oblivious to the internal culture of physics which creates and maintains an ample inventory of preconceptions about the explanatory models to be employed in the description of nature and the interpretations to be placed upon them. This internal culture, along with individual idiosyncrasy, can be held responsible for the greatest part of the ever-present misunderstanding and misinterpretation of scientific innovations — not least by the innovators themselves. It is characteristic of such scientific conservatism that the innovator himself, together with most of his contemporaries, fails to appreciate how wide and deep is his break with tradition.[1] But our case is just the opposite: all sorts of "lessons" of a thoroughly and intentionally revolutionary character are announced nearly simultaneously with the discovery of a theory which, properly understood, barely supports, or even flatly contradicts, the claims founded upon it. We are dealing here not with the commonplace misconstructions in which new wine is poured into the old bottles of scientific culture. We have, rather, the exceptional, but by no means unprecedented, circumstance that the concocting of a new wine is taken as an opportunity to cast away the old-fashioned bottles and blow new ones to a modish form.

My purpose is not to demonstrate this proposition, but merely to make it plausible. With respect to *Kausalität,* I have argued the point at length in an earlier publication.[2] With respect to *Anschaulichkeit* and *Individualität,* I present a hypothesis and a program of investigation. The apothegmatic form is chosen chiefly for concision and distinctness of expression.

Kausalität

Quantum Mechanics as Statistical Theory of Atomic Processes

An essentially statistical character was given matrix mechanics, the earliest form of the new quantum mechanics, as it developed along the Göttingen-Hamburg-Copenhagen axis in the summer and autumn of 1925. The "quantum mechanical variables" which Werner Heisenberg conceived, and which Max Born recognized as matrices, were probabilities of atomic transitions, or algebraic combinations and derivatives of such probabilities — more precisely, probability amplitudes. To be sure, the wave mechanics conceived by Erwin Schrödinger in the winter of 1925-26, as an antithesis to matrix mechanics, was intended to provide a continuous, space-time description of the behavior of individual particles. But the wave equation and its solution, the wave function, did not admit of such an interpretation compatible with the facts of atomic physics.

Schrödinger himself, by demonstrating the formal equivalence of matrix and wave mechanics in the spring of 1926, opened the way to Born's statistical interpretation of the wave function in the summer of that year. Thus wave mechanics too became what matrix mechanics had been all along, a statistical theory of atomic processes. And this latter expression permits only one minimal construction, which is natural and free of all unnecessary ontology: that the wave function describes an ensemble of identically prepared systems, and thus gives only the distribution of outcomes of a large number of sensibly identical experiments; the wave function does *not* describe an individual particle.[3]

Again from the very outset, the inventors of quantum mechanics were confronted with the puzzling circumstance that the quantum mechanical variables — whether represented by matrices, differential operators, or "q-numbers" — do not always commute with each other. As a consequence of this essential peculiarity of quantum mechanics, the statistical distributions of any pair of variables specifying the dynamical state of a particular degree of freedom of an atomic system are not independent. Rather, they are subject to a condition — the Heisenberg uncertainty principle — which places a lower limit on the extent to which the spreads of the statistical distributions of the values assumed by those two variables may be reduced simultaneously.

Quantum Mechanics Alleged to Demonstrate
the Failure of Causality

It was in conjunction with his first resort to wave mechanics — to treat the collision of an electron with an atom — that Born, in the summer of 1926, proposed the probabilistic (statistical) interpretation of Schrödinger's wave function. In his brief initial announcement of the results of this investigation, Born stressed that "from the standpoint of our quantum mechanics there is no quantity which causally determines the effect of a collision in the individual case." He then freely confessed that "I myself am inclined to abandon determinedness in the atomic world."[4] In the following months there were further declarations by German physicists that quantum mechanics shows that causality does not hold.[5] Their culmination was Heisenberg's famous paper setting out the uncertainty principle. "The true state of affairs," Heisenberg there declared, "can be characterized thus: because all experiments are subject to the laws of quantum mechanics . . . quantum mechanics establishes definitively the fact that the law of causality is not valid."[6]

Notice that Heisenberg's statement is categoric. Not only has he dropped Born's restriction, "in the atomic world," but his assertion is so general, so sweeping, that it could be supposed to apply even to the sphere of human will and action. Heisenberg intended nothing less. Clear allusions in that direction were already being made by Sommerfeld and others. Bohr — with whom Heisenberg was then in daily contact — would soon come forward with explicit parallels between the laws of quantum mechanics and the laws of human thought.[7] Derivations of freedom of the will from quantum mechanics became more common and more dogmatic in the following years, and were extended by Bohr in a vitalistic sense to preclude physical description of the processes of life.[8]

There is great disparity between quantum mechanics, per se, and the world-view implications immediately ascribed to it. Quantum mechanics is merely a statistical theory. As Einstein repeatedly but vainly emphasized, it cannot be regarded as a complete description of an independently subsisting microscopic world. Nor can it be regarded as an appropriate conceptual basis for describing our macroscopic world, where, unquestionably, we deal with individual objects and events, not statistical ensembles.[9] Thus even categoric statements about the invalidity of the law of causality in the *physical* world go much too far, not least because they slur over the fact that quantum mechanics is a deterministic theory of probabilities. As for the still farther-reaching world-view implications ascribed to quantum mechanics — that it ensures free will, or the impossibility of a physicochemical explanation of life — one must say that these are completely unwarranted.

Why This Misuse of Quantum Mechanics for Sweeping Epistemic Renunciations?

These immediate anticausal interpretations of quantum mechanics and inflations of its significance for the issue of determinism were limited to German-speaking Central Europe. British physicists, even those intimately involved with atomic physics and the nascent quantum mechanics, remained oblivious to the broader epistemic significance of the theory until their consciousness was raised by Central European colleagues. The same was largely true of American physicists.[10] French physicists were unhappy about the indeterminism of quantum mechanics, and drew few world-view implications from it.[11]

We are therefore led to look for special circumstances, unique, or largely unique, to the environment of German-speaking Central European physicists, which may have called forth their misuses of quantum mechanics. Briefly stated, the critical characteristics of this cultural milieu were:

1. Antiintellectualistic, romantic irrationalism, celebrating "life" and immediate, unanalyzed experience. "I maintain," said Richard Müller-Freienfels in the introduction to his *Philosophie der Individualität*, "and in this I am at one with many recent thinkers, that rational logic is the basis of only one kind of knowing, not of knowing generally. Life is more than rational *Wissenschaft*, and to me philosophy is not merely *Wissenschaft*, but knowing, knowing even also of that which does not enter into *Wissenschaft*. Indeed, philosophy is more even than knowing; philosophy is itself life."[12]

2. Antipathy toward causality. As is to be expected with such a widely diffused but highly confused *Lebensphilosophie*, its proponents defined the movement chiefly in negative terms, that is, by what they opposed. Most regularly and insistently that target was causality, "the mechanism and determinism of a causal explanation which calculates every-

thing in advance, makes everything comparable, dissolves everything into elements."[13]

3. Antagonism toward physical science, and more particularly toward the theoretical physicist. This arose, first, because the physicist's cognitive goals epitomized that which *Lebensphilosophie* rejected; second, because the physicist was held responsible for modern technology and industry, and thus for our alienation from nature, from our primitive roots, from the simple life, and so on.[14]

The German physicist, especially the theoretical physicist, who before and during World War I enjoyed so much esteem, now, in the Weimar period, found himself despised. Gone were those values and attitudes which had ensured him an honored place in German society and in the eyes of his university, displaced by others distinctly hostile to the theoretical physicist's enterprise. In an effort to realign their discipline with dominant cultural values, individual German physicists had been delivering manifestos against causality even before the discovery of quantum mechanics. Typically, they asserted that through wrestling with the problems of atomic physics their science would find the way to free itself from this odious axiom.[15] Thus we should not be surprised that once a nondeterministic theory of atomic processes was at hand, German physicists were disposed to view it and represent it in public as providing that liberation from causality so generally desired.

Anschaulichkeit

Quantum Mechanics as Abstract, Unpictorial Theory

When in the spring of 1925 Heisenberg began to work along those lines which led him to matrix mechanics, it was with an emphatic commitment to give up pictorial atomic models. Heisenberg sought to give concrete expression to Bohr's and Pauli's contention that a solution to the baffling problems facing atomic theorists would lie in a renunciation, for atomic processes, of causal description in space and time.[16] (Causality and space-time description, which in 1927 Bohr would find to be complementary, were in 1924-25 regarded by him and others as more or less equivalent.) Certainly the last epithet one could apply to the highly abstract theory created by Heisenberg, Born, Jordan, and Dirac is *anschaulich*, intuitive, pictorial.

Wave mechanics, on the contrary, was conceived by its creator as a highly *anschaulich* description of subatomic entities and atomic processes. However, the apparent *Anschaulichkeit* of this version of quantum mechanics proved to be largely illusory. First, the "waves" or "clouds" are not of mass or electric density as Schrödinger pictured them, but of probability density. Second, the waves are not in real space at all but in configuration space, a space with as many dimensions as there are degrees of freedom in the atomic system. Finally, the wave function does not describe the behavior of an individual particle (let alone the particle per se), but of a statistical ensemble of identical particles or systems.[17]

The Epithet Anschaulich
is Applied to Quantum Mechanics

The program behind matrix mechanics was to create an atomic dynamic free of any *anschaulich*, pictorial, elements. Yet within months of the discovery of this unpictorial calculus, Heisenberg was complaining to his friend Pauli that "I'm always infuriated whenever I hear the theory referred to only by the name matrix physics." What Heisenberg heard in his colleagues' words and tone, and reacted to so defensively, was an antipathy toward a theory so emphatically *unanschaulich*.[18]

Born, the less resolute character, saw in his probablistic interpretation of Schrödinger's wave function a *via media*. While enjoining renunciation of "the causal definiteness of the individual events," it nonetheless allowed "the retention of the familiar conceptions of space and time, in which the events take place in an entirely normal way."[19] Heisenberg was unhappy about Born's deviation from the quantum-mechanical creed, his compromise with the "populäre Anschaulichkeit" of wave mechanics.[20] At first Heisenberg tried to dismiss the problem by arguing that "the hypothesis of the atomistic structure of matter is, from the outset, *unanschaulich*."[21] He soon realized that the issue could not be ignored: the theory had to be cleared of the stigma of *Unanschaulichkeit*.

Heisenberg's preoccupation with this problem is evident in his essay presenting the program and achievements of *Quantenmechanik* to a wider scientific public in the autumn of 1926. Using *Anschauung, anschaulich*, etc., once in every 250 words, sixteen times in all, Heisenberg concluded that "thus far there is still some essential feature missing in our picture."[22] The result of Heisenberg's continuing struggle with the problem through the winter of 1926-27 was his uncertainty principle paper, which he titled "On the Intuitive [*anschaulich*] Content of the Quantum-Theoretic Kinematics and Mechanics."

There and thereafter Heisenberg sought to remove the stigma of *Unanschaulichkeit* by redefining the "intuitive" quality so as to make it predictable of his irremediably unpictorial quantum mechanics. This redefinition equated "intuitive" to "satisfactory" in a strictly positivist sense: "From an *anschaulich* theory in this sense one ought thus demand only that it be without contradiction with itself, and that it permit prediction, without ambiguity, of the results of all imaginable experiments in its domain."[24] Perhaps the best index of the wantonness of this solution is that in their colleagues' eyes Heisenberg and Born (who joined in this redefinition) had simply inverted the ordinary, accepted signification of the word. Thus we find Arnold Sommerfeld, Heisenberg's teacher, speaking of "the fuzziness or *Unanschaulichkeit* (in Heisenberg's mode of expression the *Anschaulichkeit*) of our contemporary world picture."[25]

Why This Dissimulation of the Unanschaulich Character of Quantum Mechanics?

The factors operating on the originators of quantum mechanics so as effectively to prescribe their representation of their theory as *anschaulich* were largely those presented above in the discussion of *Kausalität*. As regards *Anschaulichkeit*, the true character of the theory ran counter to the *Zeitgeist*, rather than, as with causality, offering physicists an opportunity to sail with the intellectual currents. Where *Kausalität* was the pejorative code word in the antiintellectualist "philosophy of life," *Anschauung*, *Anschaulichkeit*, etc. were among the principal shibboleths of this *Lebensphilosophie*. It is no mere coincidence that just at this time German mathematicians were enchanted by the program of L.E.J. Brouwer, a Dutch romantic antiintellectualist and anticausalist, who called for an intuitionistic mathematics. As with acausality among physicists, the attraction this program exerted on German mathematicians was not diminished but rather heightened by requiring a severe restriction of their epistemic ambitions.[25] Dissimulation of the *unanschaulich* character of quantum mechanics, the attempt to redefine *Anschaulichkeit* in order that the epithet could be applied to this unintuitive theory, was chiefly a result of the physicists' weak social-ideological position in post-World War I Germany; they simply had not the strength to oppose the *Zeitgeist*.[26]

Individualität

Quantum Mechanics Precludes Individuality

Attacking the "complex of catchwords" that was complementarity, Schrödinger observed in 1949 that "during these twenty years of empty talk, and because of this empty talk, the most important result of the 'new mechanics' has fallen from sight — the physically *and* philosophically most significant finding. Every physicist knows of it, but one does not speak of it, regards it as less important, veils the subject with a convenient but obscuring jargon. The *particle is not an identifiable individual.* There is no longer individuality in the absolute sense."[27]

This, the most direct and least arguable consequence of the new quantum mechanics for our world-view, has two bases. The first is in quantum mechanics per se, the uncertainty principle, which, it is commonly said, by placing limits on our capacity to follow the path of a particle, prevents us from knowing whether we have confused the particle with another identical particle. But this statement clearly begs the question. For if the particles had any individuality from the point of view of the quantum mechanics, there would be no danger of confusing them. Rather, one should simply say that the quantum theory has no place, no means, for ascribing individuality to subatomic particles of a given species, and that experimentation is found fully to confirm the consequences of this logical exigency.

The other basis for asserting that the elements of the physical world picture lack any individuality is quantum statistical mechanics, the so-called Bose-Einstein and Fermi-Dirac statistics. Introduced independently of, but coincidentally with, quantum mechanics, the new statistics result from new rules for determining the relative probability of the various possible states of a complex system. These new rules differ from the rules underlying classical statistical mechanics precisely in that the older rules assumed the distinguishability, hence individuality, of the particles comprised by the system. The new rules, by contrast, give emphatic expression to the assumption of the indistinguishability, the absence of any individuality, of the subatomic particles of a given species.

Although there had been from the middle of the nineteenth century general agreement that the atoms of a given element were "as alike as manufactured articles," that was scarcely ever taken to imply absolute indistinguishability. Nor did the classical physical theories permit any natural expression of such a notion.[28] It was only quantum mechanics *cum* quantum statistics which, *nolens volens,* deprived the elements of our physical world picture of individuality, as a matter of principle.

Quantum Mechanics is Alleged to Demonstrate Individuality

Among the lessons of quantum mechanics none is clearer or surer than the denial of individuality to subatomic particles. Nor was this most striking consequence of the theory completely overlooked. Heisenberg, in his autumn 1926 essay on "Quantenmechanik," noted as one of the principal results of the new quantum statistics that "the individuality of a particle can be lost."[29] But never again did this simple truth flow from Heisenberg's pen. Whether Bohr too saw this truth for even a brief moment, I do not know. But when, in the summer of 1927, he first pronounced on the issue, it was to advance the perverse thesis that the main bearing of quantum theory was to demonstrate not merely the individuality of atomic processes, but indeed the "indestructible individuality" of material particles. Then and later Bohr went farther to draw explicit analogies with the individuality of living organisms and human personalities.[30] No other physicists, not even Heisenberg and Rosenfeld who were Bohr's loyal disciples in philosophical matters, were prepared to go nearly so far as he in celebrating individuality as the main lesson of atomic physics.[31] Yet certainly none openly contradicted Bohr's contention, while many found it easy and natural to tip their hats, not only in Germany but throughout Western Europe and in the United States.[32]

Misrepresentation of the Ontologic Bearing of the Quantum Mechanics and Statistics

Individuality is traditionally one of the strongest cultural values among the educated elites of the West, and especially so in Germany, where the ideal of the autonomous individual personality compensated Germans for their tradition of authoritarianism in the social and political spheres.[33] As this ideal was central to romanticism, it had once again great appeal in Germany due to the strong romantic tradition of that linguistic and cultural region.[34] In his perceptive study of developments in German academic ideology around the turn of the century, Fritz Ringer noted "the amazingly frequent reappearance of certain themes and images in modern German academic literature." Ringer found that "the principle of individuality was one such theme," and emphasized that "it is impossible to imagine the mandarin creed without the concept of individuality."[35]

In the Weimar period, commonly seen by contemporary observers as a return to the romanticism of a century earlier, this cultural value was given even freer reign than in the decades before World War I when progressivist ideology was ascendant in Germany as elsewhere in Europe and the United States.[36] Although that progressivist ideology retained an important place for "individualism" — which in any case must be sharply distinguished from "individuality" — it placed the greatest emphasis on rational organization and coordination. The mode of research support characteristic of the prewar period was establishment of large, centralized research institutes to pursue tightly integrated research programs. In the Weimar period, on the contrary, the predominant and characteristic pattern of support was wide distribution of small grants to individuals to carry out their own independently conceived research projects.[37] Although there were many factors behind this striking reorientation, the romantic emphasis on the individuality of the researcher was important.

In Weimar Germany invocations of *Individualität* could be heard everywhere.[38] Books with *Individualität* in their title were just about as numerous as those with *Kausalität*.[39] The shibboleth answered perfectly to the irrationalist *Lebensphilosophie* of the period. This was stated straight out by Theodor Haering, professor of philosophy at Tübingen, in the opening sentence of one of those numerous books: "From the middle ages stems the expression *individuum est ineffabile,* individuality cannot be comprehended with words and concepts; our own irrationalism-happy age would perhaps best say instead: 'individuality is something irrational.' "[40]

This equation of individuality with irrationalism is fully explicit in Bohr's first presentation of the doctrine of atomic individuality in the summer of 1927: the quantum postulate implies on the one hand the individuality of atomic processes, and on the other expresses an "inherent irrationality."[41] Thus we should not be surprised to find irrationality and individuality linked with failure of causality. A biologist-philosopher, basing himself not on the new quantum mechanics, but on the anticausal manifestos by German physicists in the early 1920s, could write at this same time that "the causal world picture of the physicist is dissolving; into its place steps one which recognizes individuality, even for the molecular process."[42] Nor should we expect Bohr's to be the only attempt to introduce a "principle of individuality" into atomic physics. Arthur Korn, a German physicist who still clung to the mechanical tradition of the late nineteenth century, proposed in 1926 to make the bridge to quantum theory by modifying the deterministic character of classical mechanics through an *Individualitätsprinzip* whose effect makes itself felt in very high-frequency oscillatory processes.[43]

Recapitulation and Conclusion

The quantum mechanics introduced in 1925-26 proved to be an incompletely causal theory. It went some distance toward meeting the obligation which many German-speaking Central European physicists had assumed under pressure from their environment: to eliminate *Kausalität* from their science and world picture. These physicists sought to make the most of acausality in quantum mechanics, exaggerating and trumpeting it. The theory grossly violated the requirements of *Anschaulichkeit,* one of the strongest positive values of the cultural milieu. Far from making this intrinsic feature of quantum mechanics one of the epistemologically pertinent "lessons" of atomic physics, its originators sought to free their theory from the stigma of *Unanschaulichkeit*. This they did by redefining the meaning the word was to have in physics. Finally, the one inarguable "lesson" of quantum mechanics, and the statistics integral to it, is that individuality does not exist in the atomic world. This clear implication, so much at variance with the cultural values of Germany and the West, physicists either suppressed, or, flying unchallenged in the face of the facts, maintained the diametrically opposite proposition.

My conclusion is that there was little connection between quantum mechanics and the philosophic constructions placed on it, or the world-view implications drawn from it. The physicists allowed themselves, and were allowed by others, to make the theory out to be whatever they wanted it to be — better, whatever their cultural milieu obliged them to want it to be.

This conclusion is admittedly radical. But it does not touch the question of the social construction of reality so directly as one might at first be inclined to suppose. It is neither a statement about the physicists' practice in their laboratories nor about the physicists' theories as descriptions of reality. It is rather a meta-meta statement, a statement about the physicists' statements about their descriptions of reality.[44]

Notes

1. T.S. Kuhn has been steadily concerned with this social/epistemological phenomenon, most recently and directly in *Black-Body Theory and the Quantum Discontinuity, 1894-1912* (New York: Oxford University Press, 1978).

2. P. Forman, "Weimar culture, causality, and quantum theory: adaptation by German physicists and mathematicians to a hostile intellectual environment," *Historical Studies in the Physical Sciences* 3(1971):1-115.

3. A. Einstein, "Elementare Überlegungen zur Interpretation der Grundlagen der Quanten-Mechanik," in *Scientific Papers Presented to Max Born* (New York: Hafner, 1953), pp. 33-40, and reproduced in Einstein, *Collected Writings* (New York: Readex Microprint, 1960), item 266. It appears, however, that my interpretation of Einstein as well as quantum mechanics may be superficial: Arthur Fine "What is Einstein's statistical interpretation, or, is it Einstein for whom Bell's theorem tolls?" Forthcoming in *Topoi* (1984).

4. M. Born, "Zur Quantenmechanik der Stossvorgänge: vorläufige Mitteilung," *Zeitschrift für Physik* 37(1926):863-67.

5. E.g., A. Sommerfeld, "Zum gegenwärtigen Stande der Atomphysik," *Physikalische Zeits.* 28(1927):231-39; P. Jordan, "Kausalität und Statistik in der modernen Physik," *Naturwissenschaften* 15(1927):105-10.

6. W. Heisenberg, "Über den anschaulichen Inhalt der quantentheoretischen Kinematik und Mechanik," *Zeitschrift für Physik* 43(1927):172-98; also, "Über die Grundprinzipien der 'Quantenmechanik'," *Forschungen und Fortschritte* 3(1927):83.

7. N. Bohr, "The quantum postulate and the recent development of atomic theory," *Nature* 121(1928):580-90; Como Congress lecture, Sept. 16, 1927.

8. N. Bohr, *Atomtheorie und Naturbeschreibung* (Berlin: Springer, 1931), pp. 14-15, 66, 76; Forman, n. 3, pp. 108-9.

9. The one important exception was A.S. Eddington. See P. Forman, "Reception of an Acausal Quantum Mechanics in Germany and Britain," in *The Reception of Unconventional Science*, ed. S. Mauskopf, "AAAS selected Symposium, 25" (Washington, D.C.: AAAS, 1979), pp. 11-50.

10. J.R. Oppenheimer in Göttingen in the autumn of 1926 was probably already alert to these issues, for he was duly impressed by the "fantastically impregnable metaphysical disingenuousness" of the German physicists he met there. Quoted by A.K. Smith and C. Weiner, *Robert Oppenheimer: Letters and Recollections* (Cambridge, Mass.: Harvard University Press, 1980), p. 100. However, American physicists do not appear to have begun to draw sweeping indeterministic conclusions from quantum mechanics until 1929-30.

11. Some evidence on this point is given by R. Maiocchi, "Paul Langevin's epistemological considerations on quantum mechanics and the reactions to them in French culture before World War II," *Scientia* 110(1975):493-518. (In Italian with English translation.)

12. R. Müller-Freienfels, *Philosophie der Individualität*, 2nd ed. (Leipzig: Meiner, 1923), p. 4. The first edition appeared in 1921.

13. Theodor Litt, *Die Philosophie der Gegenwart und ihr Einfluss auf das Bildungsideal* (1925), as quoted in Forman, "Weimar culture, causality, and quantum theory," op. cit., n. 3, p. 18.

14. Forman, pp. 8-19.

15. E.g., H. Weyl, R. v. Mises, W. Nernst, pp. 76-86.

16. Daniel Serwer, "Unmechanischer Zwang: Pauli, Heisenberg, and the Rejection of the Mechanical Atom, 1923-1925," *Historical Studies in the Physical Sciences* 8(1977):189-256; Wolfgang Pauli, *Wissenschaftlicher Briefwechsel, vol. 1: 1919-1929*, ed. A. Hermann, K.v. Meyenn, V.F. Weisskopf (New York: Springer, 1979), p. 231 passim.

17. While almost all physicists, of whatever nationality, from 1927 until the present would, if pressed, acknowledge this fact, when left to themselves, and especially when popularizing their theory, they often pretend that the wave function describes not only the behavior of individual particles but indeed the particles themselves.

18. Heisenberg to Wolfgang Pauli, Nov. 16, 1925, in Pauli, *Briefwechsel* (1979), op. cit., p. 255; Heisenberg to Einstein, Nov. 16, 1925 [sic] (Einstein Archive, Princeton). For the following see also my "Reception of an Acausal Quantum mechanics," n. 10. A different view is taken by Arthur I. Miller, "Visualization lost and Regained: The Genesis of the Quantum Theory in the Period 1913-27," in *On Aesthetics in Science*, ed. J. Wechsler (Cambridge, Mass.: MIT, 1978), pp. 73-102.

19. M. Born, "Quantenmechanik der Stossvorgänge," *Zeitschrift für Physik* 38(1926):803-27, p. 826.

20. Heisenberg was so wrought up as to use this expression in a scientific publication, in which he claimed to reveal the genuine *Anschaulichkeit* of quantum mechanics. n. 7, p. 196.

21. W. Heisenberg, "Quantentheoretische Mechanik," Deutsche Mathematiker-Vereinigung,

Jahresbericht 36(1927):24-25; abstract of a lecture at the Naturforscherversammlung, Düsseldorf, Sept. 23, 1926.

22. W. Heisenberg, "Quantenmechanik," *Naturwissenschaften* 14(1926):989-94. This, the elaborated text of the lecture cited in the previous note, shows considerable difference from the abstract presumably prepared in advance of delivery.

23. M. Born and W. Heisenberg, "La mécanique des quanta," *Electrons et photons: rapports et discussions du cinquième conseil de physique [Instituts Solvay]...1927* (Paris: Gauthier-Villats, 1928), p. 144. The typescript of the original German text of this report is at the Humanities Research Center, University of Texas, Austin. The first page, with the passage in question, is reproduced in Albert C. Lewis, *Albert Einstein, 1879-1955. A Centenary Exhibit...*(Austin, Texas: University of Texas, Humanities Research Center, 1979), unpaginated. Heisenberg's initial redefinition of *Anschaulichkeit*, given in the opening lines of "Über den anschaulichen Inhalt," op. cit. n. 7, did not yet deviate quite so far from the accepted meaning of the word.

24. A. Sommerfeld, "Über Anschaulichkeit in der modernen Physik," *Unterrichtsblätter für Mathematik und Naturwissenschaft* 36(1930):161-67.

25. Forman, n. 3, pp. 60-61; L.E.J. Brouwer, *Collected Works*, vol. 1: *Philosophy and Foundations of Mathematics* (Amsterdam: North Holland, 1975), pp. 2-4, 481-87; T. Tonietti, "A research proposal to study the formalist and intuitionist mathematicians of the Weimar Republic," *Historia Matematica* 9(1982):61-64.

26. While none but the proponents of the matrix mechanics had any interest in dissimulating the character of this version of quantum mechanics, *Anschaulichkeit* was so general a cultural value, within physics as well as outside of it, that Schrödinger's wave mechanics had, as a seemingly *anschaulich* theory, a much greater appeal than did matrix mechanics, no less in Britain and the United States than in Germany. Recently M. Beller has used citation data to test, and confirm, the relative appeal and utilization of matrix and wave mechanics.

27. Schrödinger to Sommerfeld, Feb. 13, 1949, (Archive for History of Quantum Physics). Lewis Feuer put his finger on "individuality" in *Einstein and the Generations of Science* (New York: Basic Books, 1964), pp. 116-17, 198-99, in conjunction with a psychological characterization of Niels Bohr which is right on the mark. However, Feuer has not connected *Individualität* in the right way with the other two sides of the triangle — quantum mechanics and the cultural milieu.

28. Wilhelm Ostwald, *Individuality and Immortality* (Boston: Houghton Mifflin, 1906), p. 46, saw, from his monist viewpoint, that "individuality means limitations and unhappiness." Consequently he maintained that individuality was not to be found at the fundament of the scientific world picture, which, for him, was the basis of our personal, social, and ethical world picture. The more pertinent precedent is contained in the final chapter of Josiah Willard Gibbs, *Elementary Principles in Statistical Mechanics* (New York: Scribner's Sons, 1902). But there is no evidence that even the most acute of Gibbs' contemporaries and immediate successors were impressed by the logical lacuna which Gibbs was attempting to fill. See: M.J. Klein, *Paul Ehrenfest*, vol. 1 (Amsterdam: North Holland, 1970), p. 136.

29. W. Heisenberg, ibid., n. 23, p. 993.

30. N. Bohr, ibid., n. 9, pp. 14-15, 37, 43, 65.

31. Carl F. v. Weizsäcker, also a disciple of Bohr in lessons of atomic physics, is a puzzle *in re* individuality. His collected semipopular writings, *Zum Weltbild der Physik*, 7th ed. (Stuttgart: Hirzel, 1958), is full of complementarity but has not a word on individuality. Nonetheless there are various indirect indications that Weizsäcker promoted *Individualität* as a principal lesson of atomic physics. Thus in 1943 there appeared in Germany, under Weizsäcker's wing and under the title *Elementarteilchen, Individualität und Wechselwirkung*, a translation of Louis de Broglie, *Continu et discontinu en physique moderne* (Paris: Michel, 1941). Again, Weizsäcker's student, K.M. Meyer-Abich produced, with repeated citations of his mentor, an exceptionally acute and sympathetic study of Niels Bohr's physical thought, under the title *Korrespondenz, Individualität und Komplementarität* (Wiesbaden: Steiner, 1965), in which Bohr's claims regarding individuality in atomic physics are accepted in full.

32. For example, V.F. Lenzen, "Individuality in Atomism," in *The Problem of the Individual* (Berkeley: University of California Publications in Philosophy, vol. 20, 1937), pp. 31-52.

33. E.g. Leonard Krieger, *The German Idea of Freedom* (Boston: Beacon Press, 1957), p. 130 passim.

34. Peter Kapitza, *Die frühromantische Theorie der Mischung: Über den Zusammenhang von romantischer Dichtungstheorie und zeitgenössischer Chemie* (Munich: Fink, 1968), pp. 158-59, 176-78; Ludwig W. Kahn, *Social Ideals in German Literature, 1770-1830* (New York: Columbia University Press, 1938), pp. 6-7, 14-23, 91-95 passim. Reprinted: New York: AMS Press, 1969.

35. Fritz Ringer, *Decline of the German Mandarins* (Cambridge, Mass.: Harvard University Press, 1969), p. 108.

36. I know no study of this progressivist phase in Euro-American culture; I have pointed to a few characteristic phenomena in an unpublished (and still incomplete) study of the social institutions of the physicists at the turn of the century.

37. Forman, "Financial support and political alignment of physicists in Weimar Germany," *Minerva* 12 (1974):39-66.

38. A classical statement of the thesis of German individuality vis-à-vis the West is Ernst Troeltsch, "The idea of natural law and humanity in world politics," address to the Hochschule für Politik, Berlin, 1922, translated as an appendix to Otto von Gierke, *Natural Law and the Theory of Society, 1500 to 1800*, 2 vols. (Cambridge: Cambridge University Press, 1934), and also appended to the condensation published by Cambridge University Press in one volume in 1950. Troeltsch's affirmation of the value of *Individualität* is all the more significant because of his general opposition to the radical *Lebensphilosophie* of the period.

39. As listed in the subject index of *Deutsches Bücherverzeichnis*, vols. 7-16 (Leipzig: Börsenverein der deutschen Buchhändler, 1926-32), covering the years 1921-30.

40. Theodor Haering, *Über Individualität in Natur- und Geisteswelt* (Leipzig & Berlin: Teubner, 1926), p. 1.

41. N. Bohr, ibid., n. 8.

42. Ludwig Bertalanffy as quoted in Forman, ibid., n. 3, p. 111.

43. Arthur Korn, *Die Konstitution der chemischen Atome* Berlin: Siemens, 1926), pp. 118-19; *Physikalische Zeits* 27(1926):802.

44. Or a meta-meta-meta statement if one chooses to distinguish between the formalism of quantum mechanics and the ordinary language interpretation/explication of that formalism.

14
Epistemology and Mathematics

W. Baldamus

Like all other academic disciplines, sociology has become increasingly specialized, and there exist now roughly twenty-five specialties in Britain.[1] Not surprisingly, in North America the number of institutionalized areas of specialization is considerably larger, probably around thirty-five.[2] This chapter concerns the question: could there be yet another branch of sociological inquiry, a sociology of mathematical knowledge? It seems plausible that such a specialization would have to be (at least initially) a subdivision or perhaps a variant of the traditional sociology of knowledge founded by Lukács, Scheler, and Mannheim. In either case it would be necessary to make mathematical ideas, beliefs, and activities accessible to sociological concepts. This problem has nothing to do with what is sometimes called "mathematical sociology."[3] The explicit aim of mathematical sociologists is to *apply* conventional mathematical techniques to describe certain forms of social behavior, like networks of roles, interaction patterns in small groups, and so on. In this approach the cognitive relevance or effectiveness of mathematical expertise has to be taken for granted and there is no intention of making it an object of inquiry. Nor do these studies claim to contribute mathematical innovations. Outwardly this restriction can easily be seen from the fact that they are published in sociological and not in mathematical journals. That is worth mentioning because it provides us with a first clue of the direction in which a sociology of mathematical knowledge has to proceed: it will have to include advanced mathematical topics yet remain within the range of problems that are interesting to sociologists.

In view of the growth of all sorts of popular introductions to mathematics it may seem that the esoteric barrier surrounding the community of academic mathematicians is not entirely insurmountable. *Scientific American*, for example, publishes regularly contributions from leading mathematicians addressed to the general reader. However, most of this material is highly selective. It consists of fascinating puzzles, games, conundrums, tricks, paradoxes, conjectures presented in simple arithmetic, geometry, or algebra and interlaced, whenever possible, with historical anecdotes of one kind or another. Though for readers with a natural curiosity for insoluble puzzles it is edifying and entertaining to learn that Pierre de Fermat, the celebrated seventeenth-century French mathematician, wrote on the margin of a book a baffling theorem for which generations of mathematicians unsuccessfully sought the proof, no sociologist would find this interesting. Certainly not a specialist in the sociology of knowledge. After all, since countless mathematicians for three centuries have failed to discover a proof of "Fermat's last theorem," it was evidently not an important contribution to mathematical knowledge. And even if he were told by a historian of mathematics that the development of mathematics since (at least) the time of Pythagoras (c. 550 BC) simply abounds with such episodes, this information would reinforce rather than abate the deeply rooted sociological conviction that there is something conspicuously trivial about mathematical problems. And if it is true that throughout history generations after generations have been particularly fascinated by the recalcitrance of insoluble mind bogglers, this may even suggest an element of irrationality underlying the remarkable frequency and obduracy of such conduct. How else could we understand, sociologically, why Fermat's last theorem was short enough (i.e. $x^n + y^n = z^n$) and yet sufficiently intelligible to be described on the margin of a book? By what sort of reasoning was the challenge — this theorem is and will remain forever insoluble — received by the community of professional mathematicians?

Mannheim took great care to exclude mathematics and formal logic from the subject matter of the sociology of knowledge altogether. His crucial arguments on this matter in *Ideology and Utopia* are based on a single paradigmatic statement, 2 x 2 = 4. Being aware that he was addressing a singularly nonmathematical audience, he had to use a very simple example; at the same time it had to be one that would bring out dramatically the central epistemological issue.

Relativism is a product of the 1930s, the debate on relativism, absolute truth and historical knowledge of

the modern historical-sociological procedure which is based on the recognition that all historical thinking is bound up with the concrete position in life of the thinker (*Standortgebundenheit des Denkers*). But relativism combines this historical-sociological insight with an older theory of knowledge which was as yet unaware of the interplay between conditions of existence and modes of thought, and which modelled its knowledge after static prototypes such as might be exemplified by the proposition 2 x 2 = 4. . . . A modern theory of knowledge . . . must start with the assumption that there are spheres of thought in which it is impossible to conceive of absolute truth existing independently of the values and position of the subject and unrelated to the social context. Even a god could not formulate a proposition on historical subjects like 2 x 2 = 4.[4]

We can see here that it is not the triviality of abstract mathematics, but its sociological irrelevance which Mannheim wanted to expose. But he went further than that. He used the prototype 2 x 2 = 4 repeatedly in those passages in which he attacked "the orientation towards natural science as a model of thought."[5]

The spectacular success of *Ideologie und Utopie* was partly due to the restrictions Mannheim had imposed on the program of the sociology of knowledge. By 1929 the intelligentsia of the Weimar Republic was painfully aware of the political irrelevance of formal logic, mathematics, and natural science. In addition to nine political parties there existed numerous politically engaged religious, moral, and artistic movements. The most compelling impact of Mannheim's sociology was its astonishing extensiveness: his thesis of the "social determination of knowledge" covered all types of political, moral, and aesthetic commitments and convictions in all their manifestations, from sophisticated philosophical dogmas to political party programs and public opinion. Yet at that time he did not offer a synthesis or an explicitly formulated message; he offered a new *vocabulary*. This was not a system of formally defined explicative and stipulative definitions. It was made up entirely of familiar terms of everyday language: "knowledge," "thought," "experience," "reflection," "beliefs," "ideas," "meaning," "interpretations," "perspectives," "world-views," "standpoints," "insights," and so on. All these terms were used in the sense of what is nowadays called contextual definitions. A given notion like "knowledge," "thought," or "belief" acquires a tangible meaning from the particular political-historical context in which it is used existentially. The important thing was to identify such contexts by discovering the socially determined standpoint of the knower, the thinker, the believer. To do just that was the new procedure which Mannheim's program introduced to sociology.

The combined simplicity and extensiveness of the new sociological specialization was particularly captivating and persuasive to the new generation. Mannheim's lectures at Frankfurt from 1930 to 1932 were crowded with students from all departments. In the situation of a manifestly total collapse of the traditional German philosophical and intellectual heritage, along with mass unemployment and the rise of fascism, the charismatic force of his teaching was all the more effective, as his style of lecturing was unassuming, detached, and unrhetorical. Though none of us could really comprehend what he was driving at, everything he said was new and relevant to the current political and intellectual situation.

From today's point of view, the sociology of knowledge has to face a number of issues and topics which were not yet important in the 1930s nor would they have been accessible to the contextual definitions of the classical vocabulary. Both the restrictiveness and extensiveness of Mannheim's approach will have to undergo revision. But this demands first an adequate understanding of two of Mannheim's central concepts which are culturally and linguistically untranslatable into English: *Standortgebundenheit des Denkens* and *Weltanschauung*. The most widely accepted translation of the former is "socially determined modes (or styles and structures) of thought." Such translations are misleading because they cannot indicate that throughout Mannheim's work the notion of *Denken* (which is equivalent to thought, cognition, reason, rationality) is used synonymously with *Wissen* (knowledge). Correspondingly the term *Wissenschaft* is much wider than "science." As regards *Weltanschauung*, the literal translation, "world-view," fails to capture the normative-ethical connotations of the German term. Any revision must take into account that the classical sociology of knowledge was *ipso facto* a theory of knowledge which apprehended knowledge, thought, and world-views as a single epistemological issue.

As pointed out by Nico Stehr and Volker Meja,[6] the overly extended approach of Mannheim presents fewer difficulties to present-day sociologists than the restrictions of his program. Several sociological specializations have emerged which cover a number of problem areas more exhaustively than was possible five decades ago. This applies notably to political sociology, the sociology of religion, and sociological theory. In recent years many specialists in theory have ventured into social philosophy, political philosophy, and epistemology. Ironically the initial sociological achievements of Lukács, Scheler, and Mannheim had been brought about precisely by advancing in the opposite direction. This was accomplished by a long and hard struggle with the epistemological heritage of Kant, Hegel, and Nietzsche. To open up a sociological access to the social determination of knowledge, cognition, and world-views, it was necessary to remove one powerful obstacle, the deeply institutionalized epistemological ingredient of the Continental tradition in theoretical philosophy. In this tradition the German word *Epistemologie* is used (even today) synonymously with *Theorie der Erkenntnis*, the literal translation of which is "theory of cognition." The sole subject matter of the epistemological (cognitive-theoretical) ingredient within the specialization of professional theoretical philosophy was (and still is) the apprehension of what may or should constitute universally valid truths. The concrete political, social, and economic situation on the European Continent in the 1930s offered a vantage point (to use one of Mannheim's favorite terms) to see the irrelevance of universally valid truths and thereby shift the focus of attention to *socially* determined structures of knowledge and cognition (*Denken*). It is often overlooked by present-day philosophically informed theoretical sociologists and sociologists of knowledge alike, that it is no longer justifiable to ignore, bypass, or repress the problem of universally valid truths. The vantage point of the classical sociology of knowledge has vanished out of sight.

I do not have the space here to show in detail why we cannot continue to ignore the epistemological truth claims of the advances in mathematics and natural science. The only possible defense for such restrictions would be the argument that these advances are far too esoteric-technical to be accessible to contemporary sociologists of knowledge. As it stands, that argument is convincing enough, but the inevitable consequence would be to conceive the sociology of knowledge today as an extraordinarily narrow specialization compelled to survive on the childish assumption that mathematically based sciences are still modelled on the proposition $2 \times 2 = 4$. The scope for translating the esotericism of advanced mathematics and mathematically based natural science into everyday language is extremely limited. Nevertheless, if we remember that Mannheim's most characteristic procedure consisted in replacing formal concepts with contextually defined vocabularies of ordinary speech, that task is not entirely hopeless. The importance of contextual definitions (in contradistinction to explicative and stipulative definitions) had been recognized by philosophers of mathematics in the last decade of the nineteenth century, notably Frege and Husserl. By an apparently fortuitous coincidence, a new interest among philosophers of mathematics in the early works of Frege and Husserl has emerged since about 1975.[7] This is particularly remarkable as Husserl's pathbreaking *Philosophie der Arithmetik* of 1891 has never been translated into English.

At first sight these new debates appear to be too esoteric and uninteresting to sociologists because they are addressed to an audience of professional mathematicians, logicians, and theoretical philosophers. However, as epistemology is the most central topic in current theoretical philosophy, the problem of contextual definitions might at least be marginally interesting to sociologists of knowledge. With this in mind I will offer a brief nontechnical explication of the "context principle,"[8] wide enough to cover both its philosophical and sociological significance. To define an object or experience contextually means that a familiar term or symbol of everyday language is injected into the technical vocabulary of a particular scientific community by reiterating it, without an explicit definition, in various contexts of the received technical knowledge of that community. Sociologically the important thing is that this is done inconspicuously. Whether the inconspicuous reiteration of newly introduced contextual definitions occurs inadvertently, unconsciously, or surreptitiously must be left open at present. I have already mentioned as an example the way in which Mannheim introduced to a sociological community the proposition "2 x 2 = 4." By reiterating it in various epistemological contexts of socially determined knowledge and thought, his aim was to demonstrate that universally valid truths of mathematics, logic, and natural science have no sociological meaning. The German original edition of *Ideology and Utopia* was published in 1929. In 1979 Hilary Putnam, a philosopher of mathematics at Harvard University, published a paper entitled "Analyticity and apriority: beyond Wittgenstein and Quine."[9] Putnam points out in the introduction that the paper concerns "the nature of mathematical and logical 'necessity.'" The term *necessity* is in quotes because it refers critically to the way in which it has been used by Wittgenstein and Quine to denote truth. Throughout the paper Putnam speaks of "mathematics *and* logic" as a single subject of inquiry. He thereby indicates that he is aware of the fact that the earlier convention of calling that subject "mathematical logic" is somewhat redundant (initially through work of Quine, Davis, Benacceraf, and others in the 1950s and 1960s). The paper is very technical but short enough for a brief context analysis. In the space of eighteen pages Putnam reiterates the statement "2 x 2 = 4" as much as twenty times; (the seemingly trivial difference between "2 x 2" and "2 + 2" is not unimportant to mathematicians and logicians but need not deter us here). The high frequency of this statement is not accidental because it symbolizes paradigmatically the crucial importance of arithmetic and number theory, a large problem area which historically reaches back to seminal advances in mathematical logic made by Cantor, Frege, Weierstrass, Dedekind, Peano, Russell, and others between 1890 and 1910.

If a sociologist browses through Putnam's paper he will find many other reiterations of formally undefined terms. Quite a few of these will strike him as very technical and therefore puzzling, but there are also numerous common knowledge reiterations. The contrast between technical and nontechnical terms or topics may be dealt with by distinguishing between esoteric and exoteric vocabularies. As Putnam's paper covers two topics which are esoteric from the standpoint of a sociologist — epistemology on the one hand and mathematics plus logic on the other — we have to group all his reiterations into three types: (1) esoteric epistemology, (2) esoteric mathematics and logic and (3) exoteric common knowledge. What is to be called a reiterated term depends on the length of a given text. With a short paper of eighteen pages it will be sufficient to treat any term as reiterated which reoccurs five times or more. The next step is simply to order the reiterations in each group according to the relative frequency of their reoccurrence. The counting does not need to be pedantically accurate because it is only the relative frequency that matters. For the present purpose I shall confine myself to iterations with a frequency of at least eight for each group. The result is as follows:

Group 1		Group 2		Group 3	
a priori truths	44	Peano Arithmetic	27	rationality	58
conventions	21	$2 + 2 = 4$	20	explanation	33
acceptance	20	mathematical truths	16	beliefs	19
epistemology	10	mathematical proofs	15	interpretations	17
empirical fact	8	universal quantifier	11	understanding	11

Professional sociologists are likely to assume that Group 3, containing "rationality," "explanation," and so forth, would seem to reflect the legacy of Max Weber and Mannheim. This is not so. The tenets of Putnam's recent publications are clearly not concerned with sociology (or social philosophy). From his point of view this ingredient of his vocabulary represents exoteric common knowledge terms, defined contextually. This means that in addition to addressing an audience of professional theoretical philosophers, mathematicians, and logicians, his explications (particularly in the concluding sections of the paper) are also addressed to the wider audience of educated laymen.

There is nothing quantitative about a context analysis. Counting the frequency with which particular technical and ordinary terms reappear is only a means of making esoteric specializations more accessible to the sociology of knowledge. Nor has this method any resemblance with statistical procedures. The possibility of identifying a statistical universe which may account for the astonishing variations in the relative frequency of reiterations seems remote. But it is clearly an empirical method. In that it owes a lot to the early development of Lazarsfeld's and Berelson's content analysis.[10] Among its most innovative applications was the analysis of political propaganda, popular literature, radio, and films. Behind this was the idea that the stereotyped reoccurrence of characteristic phrases, themes, or topics could be sociologically investigated. However, these pioneering studies had to be confined to simple popular (exoteric) manifestations of politics and culture. The first scholarly application of content analysis to knowledge was undertaken in Paul Lazarsfeld's *Main Trends in Sociology* (1973), in which he explores for example the penetration of Western sociology into East German sociology.

Let us look for a moment at Putnam's concern with rationality. The first mention of it occurs on p. 431 in a section called "The 'Revisability' of Mathematics." The relevant paragraph begins like this:

> Although *all* mathematical truths are "metaphysically necessary," i.e. true in all possible worlds, *some* mathematical truths are "epistemically contingent." . . . For example, the only way to convince myself that it is possible to make *n* triangles with *m* rigid bars of equal length (for certain values of *n* and *m*) may be to actually produce the figure . . . . Now the statement that *these m* matches (or whatever) are arranged so as to form *n* triangles is certainly an *a posteriori* statement. It is even an *empirical* statement. Yet my rational confidence in the mathematically necessary statement "it is possible to form *n* triangles with *m* rigid bars" is *no greater* than my confidence in the empirical statement.

As this paragraph contains the first mention of "rational confidence," one might think a formal definition would be required. But as neither in that passage nor subsequently a formal definition is attempted, this is a good illustration of the curious indispensability of contextual definition in philosophy. Most sociologists would be inclined to take it for granted that professional epistemologists and mathematical logicians can dispense with the awkwardness, unclarity, and unsurveyability attached to contextual definitions. All the same they have one advantage over sociologists: the received contexts themselves into which they embed undefined terms are firmly grounded in a large and well established vocabulary of precise definitions. In the above quotation, the newly introduced notion of "rational confidence" is embedded simultaneously in two contexts of received knowledge, epistemological and mathematical truths. The immediately following paragraph is momentarily confined to mathematics only:

> If this point has not been very much appreciated in the past . . . it is because of the tendency to think that a fully rational ("ideally rational") being should be mathematically omniscient — should be able to "just know" all mathematical truths *without proof.* (Perhaps by surveying all the integers, all the real numbers, etc., in his head.) This is just forgetting, once again, that we *understand* mathematical language *through* being able to recognize *proofs* (plus, of course, certain empirical applications, e.g., *counting*). It is not irrational to need a *proof* before one believes, e.g., Fermat's Last Theorem — quite the contrary.

When I first noted the expression "ideally rational" — used with quotation marks — I thought: "he *does* know about Max Weber after all!" But when I read on and found that the words *rational* and *rationality* reoccurred three or four times on every page, always in contexts of the philosophy of mathematics, I changed my mind. It would have been too good to be true. Something was missing, something unmistakenly Weberian in the central sociological tradition: the important fact that Weber and practically the entire community of the *Verein für Sozialpolitik* were struggling with two contrasting manifestations of rationality: the mental rationality of knowing, believing, and understanding, and the physically observable rationality of hierarchically structured organizations in the realm of bureaucracies, governments, armies, churches, political parties, trade unions, scientific-academic communities, and the like. This has to be emphasized because, as we shall see later on, hierarchies are also a central topic in logical theory (mainly set theory, which roughly corresponds to what sociologists and anthropologists persist in calling "classification").

The next criterion from Putnam which once again is devoted to both epistemology and mathematics leaves no doubt that he is solely dealing with strictly nonphysical rationality:

> Of course, the status of "$2 + 2 = 4$" is quite different. We do not need a *proof* for this statement (barring epistemological catastrophe — e.g., coming to doubt *all* our past *counting*: but it is not clear what becomes of the concept of rationality itself when there is an epistemological catastrophe). Perhaps "$2 + 2 = 4$" is rationally unrevisable (or, at least, rationally unrevisable as long as "universal hallucination," "all my past memories are a delusion," and the like are not in the field). But, considering that "$2 + 2 = 4$" can sometimes be part of an *explanation*, is the fact (if it is a fact) that a rational being could not believe the denial of "$2 + 2 = 4$" (barring epistemological catastrophe) an explanation of the *truth* of "$2 + 2 = 4$"? Or is it rather a fact about *rationality*? [Quotation marks and emphasis in original]

This paragraph needs to be studied very carefully. Even though Putnam says at the beginning of the following paragraph: "Putting this question aside, like the hot potato it is," his vocabulary of rationality, explanation, beliefs, and truths continues to reoccur throughout the remaining ten pages of the paper. It is impossible that specialists in the sociology of knowledge are particularly worried about the sort of mental epistemological catastrophes and delusions to which Putnam refers. What *is* a serious problem to sociologists emerges from the phrase "coming to doubt all our past counting." For in our language the past means history. So to us the awkward fact lies in the *long* history of counting. Five millennia (or thereabouts) of arithmetic truth come dangerously close to universal validity. Dangerously, because to reflect on that fact would compel us to ask: what could possibly be sociological about it? Alternatively we might be driven into the (fascinating but entirely unsociological and unhistorical) field of the genetic epistemology of Piaget and his followers. Worse still, not far away from this epistemology there loom the neurosciences, computer sciences, and systems theory, all of which rely on mathematical and logical knowledge. The sociological importance of Putnam's work is to remind us that we do not need to resort to these specializations. The mental notion of rationality of the sociological tradition is irrevocably entrenched in the physical rationality of society which ordinary people come to know and experience in the context of organization, bureaucracy, and power. In that context catastrophes of a total or partial collapse of the collective memory of the human species are real enough.

If one reexamines Putnam's work in this perspective, its extensive concern with rationality, explanation, beliefs, interpretations, and understanding takes on a deeper significance for the sociology of knowledge. It shows how new knowledge is introduced into the established contexts of received knowledge. He achieves this entirely through recourse to undefined ordinary vocabulary. By profusely reiterating the familiar notions of rationality, explanation, etc. within the established technical contexts of professional epistemology, mathematics, and logic, he injects a radically new dimension into the existing technical contexts. That the new vocabulary is remarkably similar to the received vocabulary of sociology is probably accidental. If so, it is a fortunate coincidence. The manner in which sociologists, from Tönnies, Durkheim, and Weber to Parsons, Luhmann, and Habermas, have revised and extended received contexts by exploring and introducing new ones is quite similar. They too have always done it by transforming familiar expressions of ordinary speech into contextual definitions of sociology. The difference is that here the contrast between received esoteric and new exoteric vocabularies is bound to be less distinct and hence more difficult than in any other discipline. And within sociology as a whole it is most cumbersome in sociological theory.

Before I go on to the mathematical-logical counterpart of the sociological theory tradition, the epistemological ingredients of the connection between received esoteric and new esoteric knowledge have to be clarified. The conventional philosophical analysis of the long-term transition of new into received knowledge and thought goes back to the logical positivism of the Vienna Circle of the late 1920s and early 1930s. This movement emerged in the same historical and sociopolitical situation as Mannheim's sociology of knowledge. But as it was restricted to the natural sciences it was systematically disregarded, not only by Mannheim but by all classical sociologists. The antipositivistic tenets of classical (and some modern) sociology are well documented and need no elaboration. The legacy of the Vienna Circle reemerged around 1960 as a new epistemological specialization which called itself "philosophy of science." The dominant topic was the problem of "the growth of knowledge," i.e. the growth of natural science knowledge. In retrospect it has come to be recognized that this restriction was only possible by overlooking the decisive contribution of mathematics and logic to the growth of natural science knowledge. Today it may seem all too obvious that mathematics and logic are not merely a sort of auxiliary instrumentarium that helped along the expansion of modern science, but its very fundament. It is in that sense that we now speak of "the mathematics-based sciences." However, the recognition of the crucial impact of mathematics and logic was only won in the course of a long struggle in the philosophy of mathematics. This struggle evolved within the esoteric confines of a specialization, mathematical logic. The mathematical kernel of of this development was what is variously called "theory of classes," "theory of types," or "set theory." Epistemologically, the most innovative phase took place during the first three decades of this century. But it was only in the 1950s and early 1960s, largely owing to the works of Quine, Church, Benacceraf, and Putnam, that set theory finally established itself as an independent branch of mathematics. The development of mathematical logic is too esoteric and complex to extract the epistemological components relevant to contemporary sociology of knowledge. There is however one very characteristic feature which might be made accessible to nonmathematical sociologists: the conspicuous abundance of eponymous innovations. These are easily recognized in the standardized convention of attaching to a specific, datable, and relatively enduring innovation the name of its inventor, like for instance "the Cantor paradox," "the Russell paradox," "Russell's theory of types," "Zermelo's axiomatization of set theory," "Löwenheim's theorem," to mention a few of the most frequently cited eponyms. The most typical contexts of datable eponymous innovations include paradoxes, theorems, proofs, axiomatizations, type theories, and hierarchies. During the earlier phases of mathematical logic it was customary to call such innovations discoveries. That custom undoubtedly reflects the enormous, if latent influence of the cumulative discovery-like advances in natural science. To illustrate the spirit of this period one quotation among countless similar ones might be sufficient:

> It is easy and tempting to deprecate the importance of the paradoxes: to regard them as riddles or jokes that are puzzling and entertaining but without serious implications for logic of mathematics. But they do have the most serious implications. . . . The emergence of a contradiction shows that a mistake has been made. Now what kind of mistake — or kinds of mistakes — do the paradoxes reveal? At first Russell thought there was an obvious and easily rectified error in the Burali-Forti paradox, writing that the "... premise... that the series of all ordinal numbers is well-ordered ... must ... be rejected ... In the way ... the contradiction in question can be avoided."[11]

He thought the Cantor paradox showed simply that in Cantor's proof "there is no greatest number . . . the master has been guilty of a very subtle fallacy."[12] Indeed, the first paradoxes published arose so close to the frontier of transfinite arithmetic that they occasioned little general distress. But Russell's own paradoxes revealed contradictions in that part of set theory which underlies all other branches of mathematics, and in the notion of predication that is central to logic itself. Frege acknowledged that Russell's paradox "shook the foundations" of his carefully worked out logico-mathematical system. The shock of its publication was described vividly by Hilbert: "When it appeared in the mathematical world, it produced literally the effect of a catastrophe."[13] Gödel characterized Russell's work on the paradoxes as "the most important of Russell's investigations": "By analyzing the paradoxes to which Cantor's set theory had led, he freed them from all mathematical technicalities, thus bringing to light the amazing fact that our logical intuitions (i.e., intuitions concerning such notions as: truth, concept, being, class, etc.) are self-contradictory."[14]

Today philosophers of mathematics are more reserved in using the vocabulary of discoveries. But the reason for this is that from the 1950s onward the interdependence of mathematics, logic, and natural science became increasingly certain. Nevertheless, the datability and relative endurance of mathematical and logical innovations has remained a salient feature of the current literature.

For the mathematical layman it is unnecessary to comprehend what theorems, paradoxes, hierarchies mean. The unmistakable and remarkable historical fact that as eponyms they are precisely datable is sufficient to perceive the historical sequence of these innovations as a development of cumulative advances, no matter how amazing this is in its epistemological significance. In what follows I have extracted a selection of the most typical examples, arranged in chronological sequence.[15] The choice is inevitably arbitrary.

1826	Lobachevsky' geometry	1904	Zermelo's axiom of choice
1830	Peacock's algebra	1905	Richard paradox
1831	Galois' groups	1906	Peano paradox
1847	Boolean algebra	1907	Grelling paradox
1847	de Morgan's laws	1908	Brouwer's programme
1850	Cayley's matrix algebra	1908	Zermelo's axiomatization
1851	Bolzano's paradoxes		(of set theory)
1867	Peirce's function	1908	Whitehead-Russell's theory of types
1880	Peirce's disjunction	1911	Padoa's theorem
1874	Cantor's (two) diagonal methods	1912	Wiener's type theory
1884	Cantor's cardinals	1914	Hausdorff's proof
	Cantor's ordinals	1915	Cantor's general theorem
	Cantor's theorem	1915	Löwenheim's theorem
1878	McColl's logic	1916	Lésniewski's quantifiers
1879	Frege's Begriffsschrift	1917	Suslin trees
1884	Frege's cardinals	1917	(Löwenheim-) Skolem theorem
1882	Pash's axioms	1917	Mirimanoff paradox
1885	Weierstrass' infinite sets	1918	Weyl's continuum thesis
1888	Dedekind's paradoxes	1920	Löwenheim-Skolem theorem
1889	Peano's axiomatization	1920	Post's theorem
	(of arithmetic)	1922	Fraenkel's theory of types
1890	Schröder's duality theorem	1923	Skolem paradox
1894	Peano's notations	1923	von Neumann's (transfinite) numbers
	(of mathematical logic)	1924	Schönfinkel's theorem
1897	Burali-Forti paradox	1924	Ackermann's proof
1899	Hilbert's axiomatization	1925	Hilbert's hierarchy
	(of Euclidean geometry)	1926	Ramsey's (simplified) theory of types
1899	Cantor's paradox	1927	Bernay's theorem
1900	Hilbert's tenth problem	1927	Brouwer lattice
1902	Russell's paradox	1927	Skolem normal form

1930	Gödel's completeness theorem	1943	Kleene computability
1930	Gödel's incompleteness theorem	1943	Gentzen's theorem
1930	Gödel's numbering	1946	Markow chain
1933	Skolem's axiom system	1949	Tarski's axioms of geometry
1934	Gentzen calculus	1950	Davis hierarchy
1936	Tarski's truth tables	1950	Henkin's completeness theorem
1936	Kleene hierarchy	1951	Beth's completeness theorem
1936	Rosser's theorem	1952	Kleene hierarchy
1936	Stone's lattices	1954	Pap hierarchy
1936	Turing machine	1955	Beth's completeness theorem
1936	Post's algorithm	1956	Tarski hierarchy
1936	Quine's axiom (of reducibility)	1957	Craigh's lemma
1939	Stone's theorem	1958	Chang-Morel's theorem
1937	Bernay's axiom system	1959	Addison's theorem
1937	Turing computable numbers	1962	Hanf number
1940	Gödel continuum	1963	Cohen hierarchy
1940	Birkhoff's theorem		

The historical sequence of mathematical and set theoretical advances should help to extend and clarify the epistemological notion of received and new esoteric knowledge.[16] Unlike the sociological specializations where advances are brought about by incorporating common knowledge terms and experience into the technical contexts of sociology, in mathematical philosophy and logical theory this procedure is supplemented by adding strictly esoteric advances into the subject matter and vocabulary of received knowledge. This particular feature more than anything else has made it possible to ascertain the inseparable connection between mathematics and natural science. There is another aspect of this which should be taken into account: the (for the sociologist) odd phenomenon of accurately datable and (more or less) cumulative revisions and advances in the vastly esoteric and abtruse specializations of mathematics and logic in no way resembles the conventional use of eponyms for labelling discoveries and inventions in the physical, cosmological, and biological sciences. The deceptive similarity rests on the flimsy historical accident that mathematicians and scientists have found it equally convenient to incorporate the ordinary vocabulary of "discovery" and "invention" into their professional terminologies — without even remotely becoming aware of it. The most prolific use of eponymous discoveries and inventions emerged over the past hundred years in the medical sciences. Any medical dictionary exhibits an abundance of eponyms, from "Abrikosov's tumor" to "Zuckerkandl's bodies." A historian of medicine, neurology, or pharmacology would probably be able to provide a date for most of them. But in professional medical journals and textbooks dates are rarely mentioned. They are certainly not needed by medical practitioners.[17] Nothing can show better that scientific discoveries and inventions are not the same thing as mathematical and logical advances. This raises the difficult question of why mathematical and logical eponyms are so accurately datable. There are cases where the exact date of a specific mathematical discovery or invention has become known to posterity because it was announced in a letter which the discoverer/inventor sent to a colleague. Normally the date is the year in which he first published his new findings in a professional mathematical or philosophical journal.

Two precautions must be noted. First, the rate of occurrence of eponymous discoveries and inventions in a given period of time is inevitably understated. Since only the most interesting or useful ones tend to become attached to the name of the originator, the actual rate of all cognitive advances per unit of time (year, decade, generation, or whatever) is always larger. Second, the reception period varies considerably. In the case of eureka-like innovations, it can be as short as one year. The best-known examples of long delays are perhaps the reception of Cantor's, Frege's, and Gödel's contributions to arithmetic and set theory. The reception (and revision) of Frege is still going on today.[18] But whether the reception process is quick or slow, it always begins in the isolated, most esoteric confines of specific mathematical specializations and from there spreads to successively wider audiences.

To appreciate the sociological importance of the recent trend in the epistemology of mathematics and logic more fully it will be necessary to compare it with the latest development of sociological theory. This specialization is nowadays much involved with philosophy and therefore has a bearing on epistemology. I have in front of me Jürgen Habermas's *Theorie des kommunikativen Handelns*.[19] It is a two-volume monumental work of 1,170 pages. To penetrate an inquiry of such caliber and extensiveness in the space of a chapter is out of the question. For the specific epistemological issues of the sociology of knowledge it will suffice to point out briefly a few characteristic aspects of Habermas's conception of rationality. The key words of the subtitle of volume 1, translated into English, are "rationality of action" and "rationalization of society." The centerpiece of this volume is Weber's theory of rationalization. The subtitle of volume 2, "Zur Kritik der funktionalistischen Vernunft," is difficult to translate. The text shows that it is Talcott Parsons' functionalist theory of society which forms the main object of a critical revision, particularly his construction of a functionalist *system theory*. An important clue for the epistemological implications of these discussions is Parsons' use of the cybernetic concept of "hierarchies of controlling and conditioning factors." In the background of Habermas's reconstruction of Parsons it is evident that Luhmann's version of system theory has been of considerable influence.

Finally, the critical evaluation of the Parsonian tradition in sociological theory includes many complex classificatory schemata (vol. 2, pp. 193-414). All of them are derived — intuitively but nonetheless conspicuously — from set theoretical constructions. The most familiar type is of course Parsons' "2 x 2 table." Mathematical philosophers should be pleased that one of them[20] shows four small boxes inside one of four large ones. They will see at a glance that these boxes-within-boxes represent a paradigmatic exemplar of "Russell's paradox," otherwise called "Russell's vicious circle principle."

Notes

1. Cf. W. Baldamus, "The hidden values of the university grants committee: an inquiry by chain letter questionnaires," *Sociology* (forthcoming, 1984).

2. Cf. N. Stehr and L. Larson, "The rise and decline of areas of specialization," *American Sociologist* 7(1972): 3, 5-6.

3. Cf. e.g. H.C. White, A. Boorman, and R.L. Breiger, "Social structure from multiple networks: blockmodels of roles and positions," *American Journal of Sociology* 81(1976):630-781.

4. Karl Mannheim, *Ideology and Utopia* (London: Routledge & Kegan Paul, 1936), pp. 70ff.

5. E.g., ibid., pp. 261ff.

6. N. Stehr and V. Meja, "Wissen und Gesellschaft," *Wissenssoziologie*, ed Nico Stehr and Volker Meja (Opladen: Westdeutscher Verlag, 1981), pp. 9, 11, 15.

7. See e.g. M. Steiner, *Mathematical Knowledge* (Ithaca, N.Y.: Cornell University Press, 1975); H. Putnam, "Analyticity and apriority: beyond Wittgenstein and Quine," *Midwest Studies in Philosophy* 4 (Minnesota: University Minnesota Press, 1979) and M.D. Resnik, *Frege and the Philosophy of Mathematics* (Ithaca, N.Y.: Cornell University Press, 1980); for a nontechnical review of Resnik cp. C.W. Kilmister, "Logical inference," *The Times Higher Education Supplement* October 23, 1981.

8. Resnik, pp. 166-69.

9. Putnam, op. cit.

10. W. Baldamus, *The Structure of Sociological Inference* (London: Robertson, 1976), pp. 136-39.

11. Bertrand Russell, *The Principles of Mathematics* (Cambridge: Cambridge University Press, 1903), p. 323.

12. Bertrand Russell, "Recent work in the philosophy of mathematics," *International Monthly* 4 (1901), p. 95.

13. D. Hilbert, "Über das Unendliche," *Mathematische Annalen* 92 (1926): 161-90. p. 169.

14. K. Gödel, "Russell's mathematical logic," in *The Philosophy of Bertrand Russell*, ed. P.A. Schlipp (Evanston, Illinois: University of Illinois Press, 1944), pp. 123-53.

15. For a more comprehensive (though still selective) collection of mathematical and logical eponyms see the author's "Zur Soziologie der formalen Logik," in *Wissenssoziologie*, ed. Stehr and Meja, pp. 472-73. I am greatly indebted to Carmel Jones for typing, editing, correcting, and retyping successive drafts of this list.

16. What I can say here only briefly owes much to Niklas Luhmann, "Die Ausdifferenzierung von Erkenntnisgewinn," in *Wissenssoziologie*, ed. Stehr and Meja, which also appears in the present volume, ch. 5. In the perspective of knowledge reception processes, his analysis includes on a more sophisticated level the infusion of new into received contexts, in the sense that cognitive advances are cumulative because in the long run the rate of growth of new contexts is faster than the revision or withering away of received contexts.

17. I owe this information to an extensive correspondence with Rosanne Wrench, Wolfson College, Cambridge.

18. See Steiner; Resnik; Kilmister.

19. Jürgen Habermas, *Theorie des kommunikativen Handelns* (Frankfurt: Suhrkamp, 1981).

20. Ibid., p. 376.

15

Midwifery as Science:
An Essay on the Relation between Scientific and Everyday Knowledge

Gernot Böhme

Toward a Sociology of Knowledge Concept of Knowledge

The claims of the sociology of knowledge have been far too modest. "Sociology of knowledge": this sounds like sociology of youth, urban sociology, industrial sociology. "Knowledge": just one among many possible subjects of sociological interest. However, worse still than with the specialties mentioned above, which can at least define "youth," "city," "industry" sociologically, the sociology of knowledge has left the definition of "knowledge" to epistemology and to the theory of science. It has seen, according to Georges Gurvitch, as its task

the study of functional correlations which can be established between the different types . . . of knowledge, and . . . the social frameworks, such as glocal societies, social classes, particular groupings, and various manifestations of sociality (microsocial elements).[1]

The claim of the sociology of knowledge to confine its investigation to a mere examination of functional relations between types of knowledge and social frameworks is too modest, and has been difficult to maintain. It has tended to be violated in individual inquiries since this claim underestimates the social function of knowledge, its significance as an aspect of the social process.

To arrive at a sociology of knowledge concept of knowledge we proceed from the concept of the cultural reproduction of society. This refers to the reproduction of resources of social life not included in the mere material, biological reproduction of the human species. The cultural resources of society are the self-produced forms of human life as well as the results of an intellectual appropriation of nature. These cultural resources will be called "knowledge contents"; participation in their production will be called "knowledge" (as understood by the sociology of knowledge). In

this broad sense, the ability to read and open a door with a key, for example, is knowledge; participating in the musical heritage is knowledge as
much as proper conduct in traffic is knowledge. The central themes of the
sociology of knowledge are the result of such factors as unequal access of
members of a society to cultural resources, the formation of knowledge
strata and power structures, the development of subcultures by way of
shared access to specific knowledge resources, the latter's significance for
the sociality of such subcultures, their role in differentiating subcultures
from other such subcultures and in the formation of clienteles. The conflict between the carriers of different types of knowledge is a proper theme
of the sociology of knowledge. A sociology of knowledge which takes the
significance of knowledge for sociality seriously cannot remain a mere sociological specialty, but must be a sociology with a particular perspective,
which approaches sociality in terms of the participation in the cultural resources of society.

The sociology of knowledge has in fact been extended in this direction:
ethnomethodology assesses everyday knowledge in terms of its contribution to achieving sociality in general. But even the sociology of knowledge,
in its characteristic reference to "different types of knowledge" has already gone beyond its self-imposed limitation, for such a plurality of
knowledge types exists neither for its partner, epistemology, or for the theory of science. Epistemology appears as early as Plato as a field of demarcation, and its later descendant, our contemporary theory of science, is
little else: it determines what should be accepted as genuine knowledge
while rejecting all other types of knowledge as nonknowledge, as belief,
mere opinion, myth, metaphysics. It could be argued that by adopting a
neutral position in empirical matters, the sociology of knowledge has had
its own concept of knowledge all along: it has accepted as knowledge
whatever presented itself as such. Looking more closely, it will become
evident that the sociology of knowledge has not been neutral at all, but
has rather practiced an extremely commendable partiality. It has defended, for instance, knowledge claims by other forms of knowledge
against the absolute supremacy of science (e.g. Max Scheler's defense of
metaphysics against natural science); it has attempted, as a critique of
ideology, to break through the narrow-mindedness of certain forms of
knowledge (Karl Mannheim); or it has criticized certain knowledge contents because of their close affinity to their carriers (Sohn-Rethel, O.
Ulrich). In this way the sociology of knowledge has already entered into
the dispute about knowledge, that is, about the chance of participating in
society's cultural resources.

The sociology of knowledge assumes that all knowledge contents must
be reproduced socially. Differentiation between types of knowledge cannot

be achieved solely by cognitive structures.[2] Determining a particular type of knowledge requires a determination of the carriers of such knowledge — of a social category, group, community, or subculture. It must also determine what kind of participation in these knowledge contents takes place, and the function of this participation for a specific social framework, for instance for identification as a member of the group, interaction within the group, establishing the group's external boundaries, etc. It must further include a determination of the form of reproduction of the specific knowledge contents or the method of their production. In this sense, socialization, enculturation, teaching, may be regarded as subjects of the sociology of knowledge.

This comprehensive sociology of knowledge concept of knowledge can be made even clearer by comparing it with the narrower concept of knowledge of the theory of science. The theory of science is oriented almost exclusively toward the paradigm of the modern natural sciences, characterized by a separation of theory and praxis. The sociology of knowledge concept of knowledge resembles the French *savoir faire*, since knowledge as participation in the cultural resources of society implies by definition social knowledge. In following the paradigm of modern science, the theory of science has neglected both the participation of knowledge contents in favor of the production of new knowledge contents and reproduction in favor of innovation. The modern man of knowledge is no longer the scholar, but rather the scientist.[3] Finally, in the concept of knowledge of the theory of science, all structures of significance of knowledge have been removed. The sociology of knowledge concept of knowledge as participation, by contrast, assumes that knowledge is of significance to the knowledgeable individual.

Traditional epistemology and theory of science lack the wider basis required for a formulation of alternatives to the theory of science and to modern science itself. These disciplines were, in fact, developed to exclude such alternatives. Compared to scientific knowledge, knowledge of the life-world (*Lebenswelt*) has therefore hitherto been either simply seen as nonknowledge, or as a less exact, softer, and dependent kind of knowledge. Independence will not become evident until the knowledge carriers as a social group, hence the social functionality of this type of knowledge, are considered together with the historical struggles between knowledge carriers and their efforts to establish lines of demarcation.

Scientific Knowledge and Life-World Knowledge

The issue of life-world knowledge is most interesting in the search for alternatives to modern science, in particular to the modern natural sciences. The question here is whether in everyday life we continue to possess the kind of knowledge which enables us to independently cope with its demands. If this is not the case, coping is left to experts and is thereby removed from the context of everyday life. As a typical example of this process we shall examine the scientization of midwifery: childbirth no longer happens in the context of everyday life, cannot even happen there any longer since knowledge about midwifery has ceased to exist in that context. Instead, childbirth now takes place in the secluded sphere of medical science.

It is not our intention to deal specifically with the problems raised by the concept of life-world nor with the possible objections against such a contrasting of life-world and scientific knowledge.[4] Only this much for now: "life-world" can be a very vague concept if it is restricted merely to the diffuse mixture of the acts of daily living. This makes its relation to specific issues so important. In the case of the scientization of midwifery, for example, the life-world with which we are concerned is the vital nexus of the women who give birth. Another question may be whether the scientization of life-world knowledge is still possible once scientific knowledge has become diffused in the world of everyday life. It is our conviction that this diffusion does not take place at all, that scientific terms and isolated scientific data are merely sporadically used in everyday life, and that, quite to the contrary, scientization consists in delegating specific acts of daily living to scientifically educated experts. In addition, a contrasting of life-world and science can be turned into an ideological or political issue by asserting the presence of certain irrational or restorative characteristics. This line of argumentation presupposes from the start that rationality represents a kind of linear progress for the scientized spheres of life; yet this is precisely what must be doubted. Linear progress implies that scientization improves life-world knowledge, makes it more precise, eliminates superstition and error. The possibility that life-world knowledge might be simply different from scientific knowledge and perform a different function is thereby overlooked. But precisely this is a problem which should be examined.

We suggested earlier[5] an examination of the relationship between science and life-world knowledge for those cases where there are sociologically identifiable carriers of both types of knowledge and where the contrast between the two types is a real and not merely a theoretical problem. These conditions exist in the case of midwifery. Physicians and midwives represent typical carriers of the respective types of knowledge, and the scientization of midwifery is the result of their century-long struggle. Today this problem is more likely to confront us in a negative manner: the life-world has been practically deprived of knowledge about childbirth. In most European countries, hospital deliveries represent nearly all births.[6] Births are the responsibility of physicians, and midwives are left in the secondary role of mere assistants. Despite the extraordinary safety of childbirth which has thereby been achieved, the situation is experienced as unsatisfactory. Women encounter great difficulty in assimilating the experience of childbirth, which is set apart from the context of their lives. They complain about the loneliness and coldness of the overly mechanized delivery room. They experience their total dependence on specialists as disabling, as depriving them of one of the most important events in their life. The absence of a continuity between prenatal care, hospital stay, and postnatal care are objective deficiencies and affect in particular the socially deprived strata. The professionalization of natal care has, as elsewhere, lead to specialization, division of labor, and physical allocation of services, causing discontinuities and deficiencies. These subjective dissatisfactions and objective deficiencies warrant an inquiry into the problem, what life-world knowledge about childbirth actually used to be and what its achievements in fact were.

Midwives should be considered as the actual carriers of life-world knowledge about childbirth. It might be objected that they constitute an already differentiated professional group and that their knowledge is not the knowledge of the women affected by the life-world. This is indeed so. However, this objection applies, strictly speaking, only to the modern midwife. Originally midwifery was solidary aid, mutual aid of the individuals concerned, between the women themselves. The midwife was merely one among other women, except for the fact that she had been able through her individual experience to accumulate in a special way the knowledge possessed by all other women as well. In this sense we see the midwife as an expert of the life-world. Midwives of this kind still existed in Europe until 1800, in England even until 1900. From the beginning of the eighteenth century, there emerged a scientization of midwifery, a development which did not leave unaffected the midwives themselves, who were transformed from experts of the life-world into members of a modern professional group. This scientization of midwifery signifies the transfer of the power of decision making from midwives to physicians — from the hands of women into those of men. Scientization initiates a separation of the event of childbirth from everyday life, a transfer of childbirth into the synthetic environment of the hospital. There parturition itself is increasingly subjected to the conditions required for possible risky births. Advances in the scientific monitoring of childbirth transform the process from a natural, spontaneous event into a controlled process, into programmed delivery. In scientific midwifery, parturition is no longer perceived as an individual and personal experience, but rather as an objective and factual event.

When we inquire about the life-world knowledge of midwifery, we are apparently inquiring about knowledge which can no longer be examined by empirical methods. We are inquiring about a knowledge which existed in unadulterated form only before midwifery became scientized, in a period when midwifery, by contemporary standards, was poor and ineffective. What can this period teach us? The answer is twofold. On the one hand, the achievements of scientific obstetrics should not be minimized. The point is not to demonstrate that prescientific practices were superior to scientific ones. The question is rather whether the loss of life-world knowledge about childbirth has not created empty spaces which scientific knowledge has been unable to fill. For the sake of historical accuracy, it must be acknowledged that traditional midwifery failed only in those cases which today would be considered risks. However, in such cases men have traditionally been in charge, surgeons in particular. It may therefore be concluded that any inadequacies were in fact not the result of weaknesses in the traditional system of midwifery, but rather resulted from the absence of a scientific approach.

More serious is a methodological problem we must confront: how can we find out what the traditional midwives in fact knew? That their knowledge was not "scientific" means, among other things, that the majority of them could neither read nor write, but acquired their knowledge by way of observation and experience. The few books written by midwives cannot be used as clear evidence either since they reflect on the incipient process of scientization of their knowledge rather than report on its traditional contents. The two most outstanding figures, Louyse Bourgeois and Justine Siegemund, began their career in midwifery in an unusual way, by reading books on anatomy. Their own books must therefore be approached with caution if we are looking for an answer to the question of what midwives knew in those days. As source material they cannot be rejected altogether, especially since the process of scientization extended over a period of centuries, and since in the practice of midwifery both scientific and traditional knowledge were intermixed. The problem remains: how can a type of knowledge be studied which is essentially undocumented? Our answer is: our inquiry does not intend to reconstruct this knowledge in its details. Rather, we focus on the *type* of knowledge, on the relationship between the contents of knowledge and its carriers, on the manner of knowledge acquisition and its tradition, on the social significance of knowledge for its carriers, on the processes of defining proper knowledge for clients and other competing groups of carriers, in our case physicians. In this sense the traditional knowledge of midwives can indeed be reconstructed from the social history of midwives, which will be outlined in the following section.

The Social History of Midwives

In Europe the social history of midwives can be divided into four not very sharply separated phases. Certain aspects of one phase reappear, in less pronounced form, in the subsequent phase. These phases are: midwifery as solidary aid, as office, as traditional profession, and finally as modern profession.

Midwifery goes back to the early history of humankind. Precursors can even be found in the animal world, e.g. among dolphins. In its original form midwifery is mutual aid which women gave each other during childbirth. In our context, midwifery is of interest only to the extent that knowledge is one of its components, insofar as certain skills, rituals, and institutions extending beyond mere biological reproduction are present which must be passed on through tradition. Initially these skills were acquired solely through personal experience in life, through childbirth and observation. As a result, having given birth was considered a basic requirement for becoming a midwife — a notion which existed as late as 1800 and is partly present even today.[7] Philipp and Koch[8] give a characteristic description of conditions in the early phase of midwifery:

Every woman who had given birth to children and thus possessed a certain personal experience could assist other women in the capacity of a midwife. In addition, having gained some knowledge through practice they trained younger women in the necessary steps.

Among the experienced women who helped each other as midwives, some naturally stood out as particularly experienced and trustworthy. They were then considered wise women, *sages-femmes*, one of the oldest terms[9] for midwives. This first differentiation between midwives and other women, partly based on the fact that some women had accumulated special knowledge about childbirth and partly on the trust they had gained, led to that institution which Ackerknecht[10] has called "electing a midwife (*Hebammenwahl*)" — a prerequisite for the later development of turning midwifery into an office for a particular group of women without special training for this kind of job. This way of recruiting justifies at the same time our definition of the traditional midwife as an expert of life-world knowledge. The fact that a certain group of women is assigned the job of midwife by other women played a role until the beginning of midwifery as a modern profession. It necessarily required them to be older, experienced women. We must assume that this institution of the community midwife already existed before the office of midwife was created by official assent. Its basis was a kind of "midwifery democracy," as Gubalke[11] calls it.

The development of midwifery into an "office" is connected with the ritualization and ecclesiastical administration of life in the Middle Ages. An office is neither a trade nor a profession in the modern sense; it is rather the officially sanctioned administration of a specific aspect of everyday life. The midwife is now not only one who knows from personal experience and observation how a child is to be delivered, but she also knows how to organize childbirth as a sociocultural event. Philipp and Koch write about the first ecclesiastical regulations on midwifery in Schleswig-Holstein:

The main questions, the training, equipment, the physical work of the midwives during childbirth, their duties and rights are not mentioned at all, not even in later documents, although quite a few regulations on the customs and practices surrounding childbirth have been preserved. It is laid down, for instance, how much food, wine, beer and cake should be offered during childbirth to the large number of women who regularly gathered to assist, and according to a princely decree of the year 1600 the midwives were placed under the obligation to promise to watch over these things "under oath and under threat of losing their job."[12]

But it was not only a matter of organizing childbirth as a social event, but also of guaranteeing the newborn's spiritual salvation: the midwife was authorized to baptize. This meant that in practicing midwifery the midwife was required to know how to baptize, which words and gestures to use. It was the midwife's job to ensure that childbirth ran its proper course — that newborns were not killed, that no fraudulent substitution took place. She also had to ascertain the newborn's paternity, if necessary by questioning the mother while undergoing the torture of labor pains.[13] The midwife became the official witness of the birth; it is for the same reason that she was called "childbed inspectress" (*Kindbettbeseherin*).[14] In supervising one of the most important events of life, she was drawn into the universal struggle between good and evil. The more numerous her official duties to watch over the proper course of childbirth, the more she was exposed to the temptation of getting involved in the schemes of the eternal adversary, the devil. Regulations on midwifery dating from 1452 (Regensburg) regularly include prohibitions against witchcraft; and individual midwives were consequently frequently suspected of witchery.[15]

Official midwives were appointed and licensed by the church, and they were bound by oath to the regulations on midwifery after having been given an examination. Technical skills were not usually tested in this examination, as one would now expect. In some places, oral examinations by a group of specialists, physicians, surgeons, and midwives did take place (e.g. in Paris[16]). But as a rule, as Donnison[17] reports for England, the technical skills of the candidate were attested to by witnesses.[18] At least as important, if not more so, were character witnesses ("to testify to the rectitude of their lives and conversations,"[19] e.g. the parish clergyman. Licenses were issued to midwives primarily on the basis of their social and religious role.[20] Midwives were paid for their work, but were obliged not to make a profit. In accordance with the oath they had taken, they were committed to serve rich and poor alike, and to neither compete with one another nor to advertise their business.[21]

The transformation of midwifery into a traditional profession took place in the eighteenth century. This development had three main causes: the incipient secularization of all spheres of life, the introduction of a special training program and diplomas for midwives, and the emerging competition from male midwives. All these factors are interconnected. Until well into the eighteenth century, Christian ideology and ethics barred males from medically examining the female body, so that midwives acting as gynecologists dealt with many female problems other than those connected with childbirth. Apart from practical skills, the essential subject midwives had to study was anatomy. Anatomy, however, was taught by males. It was the appearance of "independently practicing" male midwives which finally forced female midwives to change their occupational approach. In spite of these developments, midwifery could not be called a profession by contemporary standards until well into the twentieth century. Being a midwife was just like being a peasant. The midwife took part in community life in her role as midwife. She was prepared to practice her profession any time. Her professional activities did not differ significantly from other activities in her life. Ackerknecht and Fischer-Homberger express this fact as follows: "The midwife oriented her activities more along those of a mother or housewife."[22] Even so, what she knew remained the special knowledge she acquired through practice; experience in life and the personal experience of childbirth were still prerequisites. Official training, usually in form of a three-month course, was rather theoretical in nature, more an additional instruction to the long apprenticeship of observing and assisting an older midwife.

How much the practice of midwifery remained bound to traditional patterns, despite the growing number of especially trained midwives and the increasing professionalization of midwifery, becomes clear only in comparison with the modern practice of midwifery.[23] Nowadays, after finishing school at the age of seventeen or eighteen, midwives are trained in special schools which are part of a larger hospital. Their work has nothing to do with their moral attitude and personal lifestyle. It is a matter of applying special, acquired skills in working hours set aside for that purpose and removed from the midwife's personal sphere of life, i.e., in the hospital.

This sketch of the changes in the occupational pattern of midwifery provides an outline of its social history. We would like to examine two points in greater detail which are essential for determining the type of knowledge involved in the transformation of midwifery into a traditional profession: on the one hand, the method of acquiring the skills of midwifery and the way of recruitment, and on the other hand the conflict between midwives and physicians. During the evolution of midwifery from a form of solidary aid to the office of a midwife and finally to a traditional profession, midwives acquired their knowledge through personal experience, observation, and learning in a teacher-student situation. Until well into the nineteenth century, marriage and the personal experience of childbirth remained generally accepted prerequisites for practicing midwifery.[24] Andräas provides an excellent description of the popular opinion on this matter in quoting a municipal document from Oberpfalz dated 1782:

She would prefer a woman who has given birth to several children to an *accoucheur* whose experience in ever having born a child is just as nonexistent as that of a medical man, whose advise is mere theory, who however in the course of his practice fills entire cemeteries.[25]

An attempt to explain this phenomenon can be found as early as Plato who, in describing the ancient art of midwifery in his dialogue *Theaetetus*, suggests that human nature is too weak to master the art of something in which it has no experience at all (*Theaetetus* 140 c). There have been opposing opinions, e.g. that of Soranos — a physician in the later part of the antiquity.[26] However, even such opposing views are little more than aspects of the prevailing general attitude, as shown for example in the statements of the famous Justine Siegemund: Justine had not borne any children herself and evidently felt compelled to demonstrate that this fact did not make her a less competent midwife:

At the very outset let me reply to the criticism of those wiseheads who think that a woman who has never endured labour pains cannot write accurately about complicated births and dangerous labour, and who therefore believe that my instruction has no basis. It is in fact not necessary that one should have personally experienced all such cases on which one wants to give advice or assistance to others.[27]

Simply through watching, every adult woman had some knowledge of midwifery, for, according to Philipp and Koch,[28] births were occasions for large "female gatherings," which were very lively and the number of whose participants were restricted by the authorities to a maximum of eight to ten.[29] Midwives rarely came alone to a childbirth, but were accompanied by other women who had the status of a midwife's apprentice, and that continued for years. The women were not only shown the necessary steps in handling the case, but were instructed verbally as well. Siegemund's book, written entirely in the form of a dialogue between an older experienced midwife and a younger one, may reflect this relationship. Quite frequently the knowledge was simply passed on from mother to daughter, so that just as the knowledge of childbirth was handed down in families, the practice of midwifery was frequently passed on from mother to daughter in the same way. Thus one part of the first modern book by a midwife, Louyse Bourgeois, is written as a letter to her daughter.[30]

How did one become a midwife? What recruiting methods were employed for this profession or office? In answering these questions one should remember that without exception only somewhat older women "became" midwives, that such a profession was not taken up at an early age, as is the case today. One method has already been mentioned: a woman succeeded her mother whom she had assisted for many years. Another method, which was adopted by Siegemund, may also have been typical: if one birth had been handled successfully, a woman was called on again by other women. Finally, there was the institution of electing a midwife, which meant that a respectable woman was either elected midwife by the community or that she was chosen by the authorities. Midwives were recruited from among the group of women with experience in childbirth or sometimes even with experience in midwifery. The majority of midwives were lower-class women, a fact which curiously contrasts with their otherwise respected position. Economic reasons may have been the cause for this: only lower-class women needed to turn occasional help between neighbors into a community service or business. The work of a midwife was hard, time-consuming, and required irregular hours. It was performed basically by married women, that is by women who needed the extra family income. The fact that midwifery was considered manual labor may also have deterred upper-class women.

"Poor but honest" is perhaps a characteristic motto for the traditional midwife.[31] The moral prerequisites for a midwife are repeatedly stressed by all authors and are also explicitly mentioned in the texts of regulations and oaths handed down through history.[32] As a sort of summing up of the many different formulations, we would like to quote from an article in *Zedler's Universallexikon*,[33] which defines the qualities required of a midwife:

Her most eminent virtues should be fear of God, respectability, knowledge and experience, which she has acquired partly by reading good books and partly through practical work; further, dexterity, agility, diligence and steadfastness, politeness, courage and understanding. On the other hand, she must shun and avoid ignorance, *Waschhafftigkeit*,[34] boozing, narrowmindedness, avarice and malice as the most abominable vices.

In concluding this sketch of the social history of midwives, we would like to focus on their conflict with physicians or men, because this conflict had the strongest impact on the transformation of midwifery from an assigned office to a modern profession. This conflict began in the eighteenth century but had its roots, as Esther Fischer-Homberger[35] has shown, as far back as the Middle Ages. In this conflict the issue was not so much the work of midwifery itself but rather the privileged legal position which midwives enjoyed because they alone had access to a complete examination of the female body. These privileges influenced the realm of forensic medicine in a particular way. Testifying to the legitimacy of a child and, as far as possible, identifying the father, were part of the midwife's duties. Similarly, midwives were expected to give expert advice on questions of virginity and pregnancy. Esther Fischer-Homberger suspects that, among other things, their partiality, or at least male claims of such, aroused male interest in becoming experts in this area themselves. In any case, at the beginning of the modern period physicians began to attack the role of midwife in court, claiming to possess a superior, i.e. anatomical knowledge of the female body.[36] This conflict with men in their capacity as physicians did not initially lead to any competition in the area of midwifery, but rather resulted in a certain degree of dependence. The notion that midwives needed to have some anatomical knowledge gained increasingly acceptance. This knowledge had to be acquired "from outside," since it was not part of the traditional knowledge of midwives. On the other hand, they could not extend their traditional knowledge in this direction because, being women, they were excluded from universities, the area in which this knowledge was produced and dispensed.

The actual conflict, which began at the beginning of the eighteenth century and focused on the area of practical midwifery itself, was between midwives and surgeons, barbers, and other free lance male midwives. As pointed out earlier, the mere fact that such free lance male midwives appeared on the scene put female midwives at a disadvantage, since they were constrained by the fact that their occupation was defined as an office.[37] Surgeons and barbers, who until the late eighteenth century were not regarded as physicians but rather as members of the broad spectrum of nonacademic medical professions,[38] had always on occasion been called in to assist in delivery, particularly in those difficult cases in which the delivery failed to take its natural course. Their assistance consisted of performing a Caesarean section or forcible extraction of the baby, which often was already dead. This division of labor was in turn indirectly safeguarded by regulations on midwifery which prohibited the use of instruments and drugs in the practice of female midwifery.[39] Male midwifery, which had in this sense existed for a long time, was significantly different from the female form of midwifery, since it consisted of the skilled use of instruments in dealing with the case, its responsibility extending to abnormal cases only. Two factors were crucial in turning this situation of a relatively well-balanced division of labor into a competitive situation.

As almost all other areas of human life, midwifery underwent dynamic changes in the modern period — it was increasingly affected by innovations. By relying on oral tradition, demonstration, and observation as different forms of transmitting knowledge, being bound by way of oath to the regulations on midwifery, and fulfilling the express duty as guardians assuming adherence to the rituals of childbirth, midwifery was incapable of undertaking these dynamic changes on its own. As a result, innovations occurred on the other side, in "independent" male midwifery. These innovations were in the area of the instruments used, later in the area of surgical midwifery, and finally in the area of antisepsis and anaesthesia. The invention of the forceps as an obstetrical instrument played a decisive role as early as the eighteenth century: it was the use of this instrument which extended the expertise of male midwifery to the normal case, for here was for the first time an instrument which permitted the survival of the child during risky births and facilitated delivery in difficult cases.

The second factor which favored the development of male over female midwifery was the fact that surgeons as a professional group succeeded relatively early in gaining academic recognition and in gradually obtaining medical status. As a result, the development of gynecology — medical science about women — coincided with the establishment of academic chairs for surgery.[40]

That the form of male or scientific midwifery became dominant is also the result of the emergence of maternity clinics, which were first introduced as training centers for midwives associated with academic chairs in gynecology. The formal education of midwives consisted of transmitting the very knowledge contents produced in the areas of anatomy and surgery but to which midwives had no access. From the outset, social relations between male and female midwives were different in maternity hospitals and in the outside community. Whereas in the community the physician or surgeon was only occasionally called upon by the midwife, within the hospital, on the strength of his institutional position, the physician was in charge of the delivery and had the authority to give instructions to the midwife even in the case of normal deliveries. Finally, the increase in the number of hospital deliveries in relation to home deliveries contributed in the long run to a loss of independence of the midwife, reduced her role to that of a medical assistant or, as in most North American states and provinces, caused her profession to disappear entirely.[41]

Conclusion: Differences between Types of Childbirth Knowledge

On the basis of the social history of midwives we shall now attempt to differentiate between the types of knowledge about childbirth characteristic of midwives and physicians. In this attempt, the midwife, as illustrated in the second section of this chapter, is considered an expert in life-world knowledge. In regard to the physician's knowledge we shall assume, without giving detailed proof, that it may be regarded as medical knowledge modelled after the type of knowledge characteristic of modern natural science. Scientization, as defined by modern natural science, is not the only possible kind of scientization. The leading role of this type of science is in any case not undisputed even in the realm of medical science. In the sphere of natal care this is a result of the fact that obstetrics originated in anatomy and surgery. Not until very recently have psychosomatic and anthropological approaches been gradually introduced.

Knowledge and the Individual

The knowledge of a midwife belongs to the type of "wisdom knowledge" characteristic of early medieval Europe.[42] This type can, for example, be encountered in Plato in the figure of the philosopher. A philosophical education cannot be successful by way of the transmission of knowledge alone, but must also include formation of character and the development of moral qualities. Similar observations apply to midwives: even such terms as *sage-femme* or the German *Alte* indicate that the midwife was expected to be a wise, experienced, mature woman. A mature personality was one qualification for working in a sphere which was not accessible to everybody (especially not to men) and which was considered a battleground between good and evil, salvation and damnation. The moral superiority of the midwife was not only a prerequisite for her office, but also a part of her qualification. She was a participant in a social drama and could play her part only if she gained the necessary trust of her client and of other women.

Modern scientific knowledge, in contrast, is characterized by a distinct separation between knowledge and the individual person. Since Galileo, moral superiority has not been a prerequisite and a part of scientific excellence, and, conversely, errors were no longer been attributed to moral deficiencies.[43] Truth and kindness are now autonomous qualities of knowledge contents. Knowledge itself is impersonal; age and maturity are no longer prerequisites for access to knowledge. On the contrary, age may even be detrimental, since it may be an obstacle in keeping close on the heels of the continuous process of innovation in knowledge. While scientific knowledge is in theory accessible to all, the formal thresholds which in fact prevent that "everybody" can acquire that knowledge, are steep indeed.

Types of Experience

In medieval Europe "knowledge of midwives" referred to empirical knowledge. The experienced person was one who had gone far, who had experienced much of the world. Experiential knowledge of this kind is bound to the individual — the experience must be personal and cannot be fully communicated. The fact that midwives were women and that it was generally required that they should have borne children themselves plays an important part in this type of knowledge. Such experiential knowledge naturally was especially significant in a period in which the science of anatomy was not well developed and anatomical knowledge not widely diffused. Experience derived from one's own body yielded the most reliable information. On the other hand, the midwife's experience as a woman who had borne children is distinguished in principle from experience gained through anatomy or surgery. The midwife's experience was self-experience, while the physician's is always experience of another, of the other body. This is a fundamental difference and has consequences for the practice of midwifery, at the very least in the psychological sphere. Whether the services rendered are based on a sympathetic understanding or on objective knowledge of the alien body is a difference that remains unbridgeable.

If the experience of the traditional midwife was self-experience, the physician's experience was objective. It is the experience of something not personally experienced, but rather viewed with the clinical eyes of the physician.[44] Scientific experience can be communicated because it is gained under standardized conditions. This makes it unnecessary that these experiences be reexperienced by everybody. The fact that they can in principle be reproduced makes their practical repetition unnecessary. The physician's experience, like experience in the natural sciences generally, gradually becomes less of a sensory and more of a technical phenomenon. Whereas as late as the nineteenth century the stethoscope was still an improvement and extension of the human ear, instruments such as the cardiotopograph now replace the ear.

The Context of Producing, Transmitting, and Applying Knowledge

The knowledge of midwives was acquired in the context of everyday living and remained tied to this context. The transmission of knowledge took place in the practice of everyday life, in which a separation of theory and practice did not exist. The knowledge of midwives was traditional, a knowledge whose contents remained essentially unchanged and which was continued in the teacher-student relationships of oral and craft traditions.

Scientific childbirth knowledge, by comparison, is clinical knowledge. It is produced in the hospital, an environment differentiated from that of everyday life. There is at least a partial detachment of theory from practice, even if, as elsewhere in medicine, this separation is never complete.

Nevertheless, a differentiation between school and theory on the one side and practice on the other has now been institutionalized. The physician's knowledge of childbirth, like all contemporary forms of knowledge, is innovative. To be a leader in an area of knowledge means to be progressive; whether the recent radical changes in the science of obstetrics should be regarded as improvements remains an unsettled question. Medical knowledge about childbirth has in the meantime produced its own problems no longer delimited by the practical concerns of childbirth. It now possesses its own sphere of meaning differentiated from the practical experience of those who bear children.[45]

Relationship to Nature

Implied in the traditional knowledge of midwives is an entirely different approach to nature than that encountered in the science of obstetrics. For midwives, birth was nature in the sense of the Greek concept of *physis*: nature is what takes its own course, that which unfolds, reveals itself. Correspondingly, midwifery was in the eyes of midwives nothing more than mutual help: support, watching, waiting patiently, helping to bear nature. Regulations on midwifery explicitly prohibited midwives from actively forcing or inducing delivery, for instance through labor-inducing drugs; they were also prohibited from using any instruments.[46] By comparison, the science of obstetrics sees childbirth as a process which must be initiated, and whose conditions and course can and must be controlled. For theoreticians of programmed delivery the concept of nature as "part of reality" no longer exists. On the contrary, there are only assumed optimal possibilities, which are of course never realized in nature as it actually is.[47]

Nature became an issue for scientific natal care — as is true for the natural sciences in general — only in terms of nature's oddities, its consequences, its "phenomena" which required an explanation. Just as Newton developed his theory of colors by looking at them as interfering with optical images, scientific obstetrics developed from a surgery which dealt with abnormal or risk cases. Medical obstetrics thus developed as "knowledge about avoiding interferences."[48] In modern obstetrics, even a normal birth is assumed to take place under the same conditions as a difficult birth or a pathologic case.

In conclusion we would like to return once again to the concept of knowledge developed in the introductory section. There we defined knowledge as participation in the cultural resources of society. Knowledge of childbirth would therefore refer to a partaking in the technical and social stock of knowledge on childbirth. It may be recalled that knowledge of midwifery was in its very beginning a collective type of knowledge. It was not an individual knowledge leading to self-help, but rather the knowledge of women as a group providing mutual help.

In the form of midwife knowledge this knowledge had already been acquired by some individuals; a certain privileged status was granted them by other women and by the authorities. Nevertheless, that the midwife's knowledge of childbirth remained women's collective knowledge was safeguarded by the recruitment practices of midwives and by the way in which knowledge was transmitted in women's gatherings.

The scientization of midwifery, in contrast, has brought far-reaching changes. The fact that since approximately the eighteenth century midwives had to acquire some of their knowledge in special schools, has made them partly dependent on another social group. The knowledge they needed, anatomical knowledge in particular, they could not produce themselves. As a result of this social dependence caused by their reliance on knowledge disseminated elsewhere, midwives were never able to become a "professional group" in the sense of administering their own bodies of academic knowledge.[49]

In addition, their social dependence on physicians gradually reduced their knowledge to a mere helper's knowledge. It became a knowledge of rules no longer constituted with the midwives' own area of expertise, and they lost control even of the application of their own skills.

Once maternity clinics had been established and childbirth had thereby been removed from the context of everyday life, knowledge of childbirth atrophied in the life-world. Women no longer were able, either individually or collectively, to "experience" birth. They found themselves helpless, dependent on experts, and the victims of fashions in science. Their ignorance in matters of childbirth and their inability to help themselves or each other collectively increasingly surrounded the event of childbirth with fear, thereby increasing women's dependence on hospitals and physicians.

Scientization of midwifery has resulted in an extraordinary specialization, increase, and improvement in the technical aspects of natal care. But the knowledge of childbirth as a biographical and social event has been lost in the process. Just as the exclusion of birth from the larger context of life has diminished the role of contextual knowledge, so the disappearance of knowledge about birth as a social event has contributed to a disappearance of the event itself: childbirth has become an inconvenient disruption in a life dominated by work and leisure.

Notes

Translated from German by Volker Meja and Barbara Stehr

1. G. Gurvitch, *The Social Frameworks of Knowledge* (New York: Harper & Row, 1971), p.16.

2. I purposely do not distinguish between types and forms of knowledge, a distinction introduced by Gurvitch. This distinction refers to a differentiation between (1) objective knowledge (knowledge of the outside world, knowledge of the Other, political and technical knowledge, etc.), and (2) knowledge of a certain kind (mystical versus rational knowledge, symbolic versus concrete knowledge, etc.). These distinctions refer to cognitive differences between contents of knowledge, whereas it is my view that a sociology of knowledge concept of knowledge should refer to the social differences in the relationship between carriers and contents of knowledge.

3. Florian Znaniecki, *The Social Role of the Man of Knowledge* (New York: Octagon, 1965).

4. Cf. the introduction in G. Böhme and M. v. Engelhardt, *Entfremdete Wissenschaft* (Frankfurt: Suhrkamp, 1979).

5. Cf. ibid.

6. J.M.L. Phaff, et. al., ed., *Midwives in Europe* (Strasbourg: Council of Europe, 1975), p.6.

7. Jean Donnison, *Midwives and Medical Men: A History of Inter-Professional Rivalries and Women's Rights* (London: Heinemann, 1977), p. 51.

8. E. Philipp and W. Koch, "Die Entwicklung des Hebammenwesens," in *Schleswig-Holstein bis zur Gründung der Universitäts-Frauenklinik und Hebammenlehranstalt in Kiel.* Festschrift zum 275jährigen Bestehen der Christian-Albrechts- Universität Kiel, ed. Paul Ritterbusch et. al. (Leipzig: Hirzel, 1940), p. 217.

9. The following is a list of expressions I compiled while reading the literature on the subject: *Hebamme, Hebmutter, Bademutter, Wehemutter, Kindbettbeseherin, Besechamme, Bademoene, Alter, sage-femme, ventrière, midwife.*

10. E.H. Ackerknecht, "Zur Geschichte der Hebamme," *Gesnerus* 31(1974):185.

11. Wolfgang Gubalke, *Die Hebamme im Wandel der Zeiten* (Hannover: Staude, 1964), p. 63.

12. E. Philipp and W. Koch, p.216.

13. J. Donnison.

14. Conrad Andräas, *Beiträge zur Geschichte des Seuchen- des Gesundheits- und Medizinalwesens der oberen Pfalz* (Regensburg: Mayr, 1900), p. 139.

15. Cf. Thomas Rogers Forbes, *The Midwife and the Witch* (New Haven: Yale University Press, 1966).

16. cf. Heinrich Fasbender, *Geschichte der Geburtshilfe* (Hildesheim: Olms, 1964). p. 83. Reprint of the 1906 original edition.

17. J. Donnison, p.6.

18. "They had also to bring to the hearing six 'honest matrons' whom they had delivered during their period of instruction and who were willing to testify to their skill."

19. J. Donnison, p. 6.

20. J. Donnison, p. 7: "Since this system of licensing was mainly concerned with the midwife's social and religious functions, it was not accompanied by any public provision for her instructions."

21. "Nemlich, dass sy alle zcyt, tag unnd nacht, willig unnd gehorsam seyen, dienen dem armen als dem reichen, von welchen sy ye zu zeytten am ersten berufft unnd begert werden, auch keine arme frauwe in nötten zu verlossen unnd an ander ordt zu gon umb merer gewins unnd lons willen . . . Item es sollen auch dieselben hebammen vy iren eyden kein schwangere frauwen bitten durch sich oder yemandt in iretwegen, sy zu kindts arbeit zu bruchen . . . ." *Freiburger Hebammenordnung* of 1510. K. Baas, "Mittelalterliche Hebammenordnungen," in (*Sudhoffs*) *Archiv für die Geschichte der Naturwissenschaft und der Technik* 6(1913):1-7.

22. E.H. Ackerknecht, E. Fischer-Homberger, "Five made it — one not: the rise of medical craftsmen to academic status during the 19th century," *Clio Medica* 12(1977):264.

23. For a distinction between traditional and modern professions cf. T. Parsons, "Die akademischen Berufe und die Sozialstruktur," in *Talcott Parsons Beiträge zur soziologischen Theorie,* ed. D. Rüschemeyer (Neuwied: Luchterhand, 1968), 2nd edition, pp. 160-79.

24. J. Donnison, pp. 3, 18.

25. Andräas, p. 143.

26. Soranus von Ephesus, *Die Gynäkologie*, trans. H. Lüneburg (Munich: Lehmann's Verlag, 1894), p. 31.

27. Justine Siegemund, *Die Königlich Preussische und Chur-Brandenburgische Hof-Wehe-Mutter,* 2nd ed. (Berlin: Christian Friedrich Voss, 1756) 1756), 2nd edition, B1 a2. Original edition 1690.

28. Ibid., p. 217.

29. J. Donnison, p. 3, also points out the instructive function of these female gatherings.

30. In a preface to the book of Justine Siegemund, Doctor Gohl also explicitly mentions maternal instruction. As the main prerequisites for pursuing the career of a midwife he names: (1) fear of God, (2) ability to read, and (3) learning from one's own mother or from another experienced midwife.

31. We are referring to the general, normal conditions of recruitment. That does not preclude that serious abuses did exist as well, that drunken midwives were not a rare occurrence, that they worked as *Engelmacherinnen* (abortionists) as well, etc.

32. Cf. for example J. Vollmar, "Geburtshilfe in Ulm: historischer Überblick," in *Geburtshilfe im Wandel der Zeit* (Ulm: Jahresveranstaltung der Scultetus-Gesellschaft, 20 October 1977), p.4, for the Ulm regulations on midwives. The midwifery license is reproduced in Donnison, p. 229. See further Philipp and Koch, p. 216 or once more the preface of Dr. Gohl in Siegemund's book.

33. Vol. 1, col. 1535.

34. A literal translation of this term would be "attitude of a washerwoman," meaning "being a gossip," which washerwomen were considered to be. This would have been a serious vice for midwives, who naturally were privy to many private affairs.

35. Esther Fischer-Homberger, *Krankheit Frau Und andere Arbeiten zur Medizingeschichte der Frau* (Bern/Stuttgart/Wien: Huber, 1979), p.85.

36. There may be a bit of historical backstairs humor in the fact that physicians erred in the very anatomical "findings" on which they based their case. The midwives had traditionally made the existence or nonexistence of the hymen the criterion of proof. Anatomists now disputed the existence of the hymen as a normal anatomical fact and at the same time the basis for the midwives' judgment (Fischer-Homberger, p.89). But this error actually goes much deeper than even that, since anatomy is a science of the dead body, a knowledge outside the biographical context.

37. Incidentally, as Donnison, (p. 22) has stated correctly, the market opportunity of men was not based on the fact that their fees were lower than those of the midwives, but higher: "In this, as in many other occupations, men generally received higher remuneration than women; it was therefore important to the aspiring tradesman to show his neighbours that he could afford the higher priced article." Thus the midwife tended to be called on by the poor (Donnison, ch. 5), whereas with growing prosperity male midwifery became more established.

38. Cf. Ackerknecht, Fischer-Homberger,

39. It would be worth examining whether these formulations in the regulations on midwifery were initiated by surgeons who, quite early, were organized in guilds and who in this way might have been able to protect their trade.

40. Hans H. Eulner, *Die Entwicklung der medizinischen Spezialfächer an den Universitäten des deutschen Sprachgebietes* (Stuttgart: Enke, 1970), p. 283.

41. Barbara Ehrenreich and Deidre Englisch, *Hexen, Hebammen und Krankenschwestern* (Munich: Ilona, 1979).

42. Florian Znaniecki, op. cit.

43. Niklas Luhmann, "Die Risiken der Wahrheit und die Perfektion der Kritik" (Bielefeld: MS, 1972.)

44. Michel Foucault, *Die Geburt der Klinik* (Munich: Ullstein, 1973).

45. Alfred Schütz and Thomas Luckmann, *Strukturen der Lebenswelt* (Neuwied/Berlin: Luchterhand, 1975).

46. "Item sy sollen auch keine frauwen nötten oder übertreiben zu kindes arbeit, es erschünen denn zuvor gewisse zeichen der nähin der geburt, unnd inen darin vlissigklichen dienen. . . . Item auch zu sollichen dingen keine grausamlich oder ungeschickt instrument bruchen kindt zu brechen oder usszuziehen als lang ysin oder hacken oder dessgleichen." (From "Freiburger Hebammenordnung 1510," Baas. Cf. more general description in Donnison, p. 22.

47. Definition of programmed delivery: "Programmed delivery refers to the complete and thorough planning of the best possible moment of delivery for mother and child throughout preparatory stages and the actual delivery stage for all individuals involved, as well as the organizing necessary for inducing delivery at the most favorable time." Hans G. Hillemanns and Heike Steiner eds., *Die programmierte Geburt* (Stuttgart: Thieme, 1978), p. 1. This is then later (ibid., p. 9) followed by the statement: "The programmed termination of pregnancy, or the 'timed birth,' consists in fact of inducing delivery, even before the 282th day of pregnancy, as a necessary step in the interest of the child; and even considerably earlier than that, especially in those cases where the mother shows hardly any signs of spontaneous delivery, including those cases where, for instance, dilatation has not even started."

48. Peter Janich, *Zweck und Methode der Physik aus philosophischer Sicht* (Konstanz: Universitätsverlag Konstanz, 1973).

49. On this issue of professionalization cf. Hans A. Hesse, *Berufe im Wandel: Ein Beitrag zum Problem der Professionalisierung* (Stuttgart: Enke, 1968). Storer's definition can make particularly evident what prevented the professionalization of midwives. According to Storer, what permits the establishment of a profession is the existence of a body of specialized knowledge and autonomy of access to that knowledge and in recruitment. Norman W. Storer, *The Social System of Science* (New York: Holt, Rinehart & Winston, 1966). Donnison points out that up to the present century midwives have been unable to form a guild or professional organization, and that the *Central Midwives Board* founded at the beginning of this century was subsequently run by physicians. J. Donnison, p. 179.

16

The Knowledge of the Eater

Marie-Noël Stourdze-Plessis and Hélène Strohl

Is the proliferation of reflections on food — especially on cooking — the same old story, a nostalgic resifting of a vanished art of living? The chefs who have made the prosperous shift to culinary discourse and to the vulgarization of *la grande cuisine*; the sociologists, historians, psychologists who are suddenly interested in a subject which, until now, could hardly be admitted to the canon of concepts; the increasing imperialization of dietetics on more and more aspects of daily life: are all these phenomena perhaps to cooking what the ethnologic census is to the cultures it describes, a frenetic attempt to render into discourse an already dead culture?

The pleasure of discourse indeed seems to entail a certain fading of the senses; and the more luxuriant and appetizing the analytic discourse is, the more banal and codified actual foodstuffs seem to become. Nevertheless, the very existence of a sociology of the alimentary, culinary "fact" (one which affirms itself to be an ever more vital branch of the sociology of knowledge) stands witness to the power of appetite, the passion for good eating — magical objects of study — which transform the serious sociologist into a refined gourmet, and enables a new "speech art" for the diner, the eater him/herself.

An Epicurean Outing: The Sociology of Cooking Evokes a Sharpening of All the Senses

The sociology of eating requires the rehabilitation of the senses as a method of social investigation. The sociologist of cookery must necessarily attend to taste, smell, form, color, atmosphere even before engaging in research and statistical studies.

How could one speak of markets without noting the bright, glaring red of the meat, the silvery wriggling of the fish, the lingering smell of the cheeses, the loathesome, nauseating odor of frying, the staccato hubbub of the vendors' cries which are the essential sounds of our epicure's outing?

How could one grasp the act of cooking itself, noting the changes and the continuities, the social connotations of the act, if one did not finally physically recall the feel of the dough, the monotonous motion of the pestle, the basic action of the kneading, the tedium of creaming the butter?

How could one reconstruct the meals and fashions of contemporary cooking if one had not been oneself moved by appetites, by gluttony even, if one had not experienced indigestion, or the pleasure of eating even when one is not hungry?

One must proceed by creating ever widening circles of illumination, starting with the food itself, which tempts us, decays, integrates itself into a chain, and gives its solidity over to a social definition of its situation.

One must become one with the field itself, as each word of the sociologist's discourse will be echoed by a savory fragrance. One must *read* eating as an invitation, its serious sociological study as a condiment to its flavor. One must speak in order to rediscover in the salivation that accompanies the word the pleasures of chewing.

Rather than desiring political change through one's discourse, one should find for it instead a modest yet grandiose place as an after-dinner speech. One could rediscover therein a genuine anthropology, one which approached social forms in all their physical concreteness, paying attention to the most trivial rituals, the most covert manias, to the behavioral secrets of the most banal acts.

The Sociology of Eating as a Total Social Fact

In the well-known terminology long utilized by J.P. Aron, Lange, L. Moulin, N. Chatelet, and others, to speak of a "total social fact" is to reconstruct in the act of eating its own logic, the grammar of the meal. One can only undertake a sociology of eating if one considers it as a total social fact, not limiting it to the area of reproduction or needs, nor seeing it as an indication of cultural problems, nor still yet as the experience of a general lifestyle. To use the words of Roland Barthes, one must realize that food knows none of the boundaries between politics and economics, economics and culture, etc.[1]

The acts of cooking and eating in their traditional or technical aspects, the meal in its functional or ritual aspect, the food chain in its economic or metaphoric aspect: all these are inscribed in the same forms of the imaginary and the real, of space and time, that continually shape all social behaviors.

Far from being a mere aside, a deviation or a sign, eating is that social act where memory and style, discourse and practice mix. References accumulate in it, behaviors define themselves in it, new differentiations establish themselves. Eating as a total social fact[2] is in this sense a "privileged sociological wager, a sociologist's joy," as Nicole Sansot put it in a systematic review of sociological research on the topic.[3]

To grasp eating as a total social fact is to renounce the concept of an unconscious basis for behavior; it is to treat the most commonplace and humble as persons with full status; it is to discover social life in all its lived concreteness; it is to pay heed to contemporary rituals, to explore the imagination of current mythologies — if not for their majesty, at least for their effervescence.

Eating is that activity which runs through all of social life, an activity in which the human being confronts his/her own body, others, fate. "From dust ye come and to dust ye shall return," in the proverbial phrase that covers both burial rites and the food cycle.

Approaching eating as a total social fact through the totality of practices surrounding food (spatial, temporal, age differentiations, ethnic and sexual variations), is a privileged mode in that it enables us to read, transversally, the reality of the contemporary imagination.

When one questions life directly one too often finds responses that are all too positive, only faintly rendering the texture of life, along with its imaginative nuances and half-tones.

The sociology of eating allows us to make a journey, to take a stroll in a space (urban, rural, road, apartment) in which the "field" is plowed not as research but as situation. By turns eater, cook, epicure, housewife, this gourmet traveler brings to light the impossibilities, the dreams, the discoures, the social bonds, the confrontations or complicities of alimentary social space.

The time and rhythm of the marketplaces, the code and rituals of meals, taxes, and means of distribution are so many readings which can overcome the oppositions work/leisure, male/female, public/private, past/present. The stylistic differentiations of eating accentuate regional, social, demographic diversity. They also undermine the classically accepted concepts of social divisions.

Tracing a pleasant fragrance may hardly be scientific, but it is imaginative; not a world-transforming sociology, but a sociology of pleasure. The pleasure of the table is for all ages, all conditions, all time; it can be associated with all other pleasure and remains the one taste that remains to console for the loss of all others.[4]

A Sociology of Cuisine Is a
Sociology of Communication

A sociology of cooking and eating is a sociology rooted in the pleasure of swallowing. Our era, which tends to restore to the table a place of honor, recognizes sociability in the meal: there are no "solitary protocols" as far as food is concerned; the table is the locus of "conviviality" par excellence.[5]

The locus of conviviality: locus of discourse and enunciation. If in the nineteenth century "gastronomic collectivity is essentially worldly, its ritual figure conversation,"[6] Florence Dupont has shown us (in her lovely work *Le plaisir et la loi*) that in ancient Greece the architecture of the banquet corresponds to the construction of a speech. But no matter what its rhetorical figure, pleasure is always its echo.

Behind the words of the banquet, the cosmogonic function of the meal can be seen in filigree. The meal models discourse, it gives information in the literal sense of "giving form." Likewise, elegy fixes the forms of the feast. Here language creates a world, founds a civil order; the table setting, the arrangement of the banquet bring us back to the law. The ideal form of the Athenian banquet is one legislated by elegy — and a certain use of wine.

It is the rule. The Law. On the private level, the counterpart to democracy on the public level. The Law, but a law indissolubly linked to pleasure. Nonetheless, the Atheneian banquet is not a place of laxity. At the other extreme, Spartan banquets are completely within the public sphere (one cannot drink wine there) and there are many coercions, means for submitting the entire life of the citizen to the social order. But let us leave the banquet — a drinking rather than an eating place — and return to the table.

A Sociology of Eating Is a History of the Table

The table: pretext for speaking, for discourse. It corresponds to another table marked essentially by the sign. It is that of the code, of the ceremonial table, the arrangement of dishes, the order of serving. The meal could be mistaken for a syntax, a kind of written word parallels the spoken word here. Let us look once more at these two different tables so well described by J.P. Aron and F. Lange. The French table service of the ancien régime was replaced by the Russian form. Two opposing conceptions, one that puts abundance on display, with an ever subtler and more decadent idea of excess, overladened tables, exorbitant, and in which one can follow the trace through the course of the meal, the decomposition of the food; another which substitutes a conception of the blank slate for the profusion of the other and in which one systematically removes leftovers from sight. It is the latter table that the bourgeoisie will choose for its own, and whose ritual will predominate, subsisting down to our day.

Let us describe, with the French style of service, the spectacle of abundance, exaltation, plenty. Let us imagine a table, upon the arrival of the guests, absolutely laden with dishes; a dinner for friends would be divided into three courses.

Now picture the same abundance in the centerpiece, flowers, figurines, ice-sculpture landscapes, and in the houses of the great, marvelous pasteboard pieces based on antique designs, not to mention all the dishes whose disparateness and diversity accentuate still more the lavish expenditures.

Certain showy menus served by Talleyrand and reported by Carême, by whose time serving *à la française* was only a mere shadow of its former self, still contain forty-eight different *entrées*. There are *hors d'oeuvres*, soups, pike, hens, meat pies, pâtés, etc; then in the next course, that of the roasts, large cold meats, vegetables, and side-dishes, the number of items served must equal that of the first course, with which it is symmetrical; and for the final sequence, that of desserts, the same holds true as well.

Such is the ceremony of the table, which within its three courses manages to accumulate a profusion of dishes at the same time as it also reveals scattered table scraps, scraps that pile up — the inverse, really, of the whole construction, when the work of decomposition, at first artistically hidden, progressively takes over.

Moreover, as the incredible descriptions tell us, the ice sculptures begin to melt and dribble on the tablecloth from the middle of the meal on: as if this time and space were that of the production of transitory artifices, of the revelation of the scene of decay.

The meal very quickly becomes the locus of the deployment of remains, leftovers, wastes. It is an entire protocol of the table that orchestrates the spectacle and unveils it for us. Now these piles, these heaps, these scraps, this obscene and immodest table of the princely and aristocratic household will disappear, displaced by the Russian style.

Judge for yourself: the table becomes a pretext for an entirely formalized organization. Ladies are served starting on the right hand of the master of the house; the dishes are presented on the left, then the plates are taken off, one after another, from the right. The "blank slate" table displaces the overladen table inundated with food. Procedures, identical to a set of algorithms, normalize the course of the meal. A normed time is created. The French meal had started with a rigorous architecture, a set of rules, and then had dissolved into a confused heap; the meal *à la russe* introduces a mechanical organization and a clockwork rigor into the alimentary ritual. It transforms it into nomenclatures, procedures. At the same time it allows decomposition to become a dialectic fact only of internal space. The table is therefore constituted as a place of passage, of transition, where nothing, not even leftover or crumb can subsist without scandal. The meal is like a kind of writing, the preparation of which is definitively "cooked up" elsewhere, offstage. Not even slicing and cutting. These operations of a fleshly, carnal model must be hidden from the eyes of the guests, taking place only in the kitchen, or at most in the sideboard in the dining room.

A Sociology of the Table
Is a Sociology of the Body

We have seen the relationship between the spectacle of decomposition being either displayed or hidden from the eyes of the participants in the meal. We have evoked the guest: we are brought back to this enigmatic space of solitary work where codes, like the sequencing and the arrangement of meals, tend toward dissimulation. Such dissimulation relates to the same kind of logic that camouflages the work that preparing the meal itself requires. But now what must be hidden here is the work of the body itself.

Witness those women who at Louis XV's table refrained from chewing.[7] A projective reversal, this, by means of which the body places itself outside the domain of transformations. Just as the noble would be sullied by engaging in work for pay, so, too, the body that admitted its own ingestive activity would be deemed ignominious. The idea itself of such a spectacle is insufferable. One can see why Vaucanson's duck produced such a scandal at court. The robot actually pecked, swallowed, digested, and as the bird was transparent, the entire process was visible. But if the work of digestion is censured at the level of the body it is put on stage, on the table itself.

The pleasure one has in seeing before oneself, for several moments, appetizing dishes, artistically set up and from which delectable aromas emanate, far from compensates for the disagreeable impression that the sight of these same dishes causes when, after having eaten one's fill, one finds oneself condemned to contemplate the shapeless detritus and to smell its faded odors. Noëlle Chatelet evokes the malaise one feels when facing "the biological functions of a compartmentalized, hierarchized body, from the cleanest to the dirtiest."

There are strange habits that escape this censorship, this death sentence, at the table, such as the custom that game be partially decayed in order to give it more flavor; Lévi-Strauss allows himself a charming reflection, linking this *faisandage* to the digestive action, both being the result of a patient work of decomposition, and *faisandage* comparable to predigestion. One should also note a custom of the Madans, who doted on dead beasts brought by the rising river, half-decomposed, in addition to the usual process of aging, or hanging meat outdoors. Predigestion by water, a medium favorable to putrefaction, the natural transforming of food from without akin to digesting it from within.

A Sociology of Cooking Is Also Prospective

The great ritual accomplishment of contemporary cooking is its elimination of this staging of the rotten. Rapidity, efficiency, cleanliness have replaced odor, slow ripening, the pleasure of touching — can one doubt it?

The transformation of kitchens is significant. The design of electrocookers (stove, processor, casserole, etc.) is essentially an aesthetic of preparation. In it, everything is conceived so as to hide the operation of the transformation of the foodstuffs: the pressure cooker cooks while closed up; the oven is self-cleaning, swallowing up grease drippings on the spot, smokiness is whisked away by vent fans. The blender automatically makes the transition from decomposition to recomposition, amalgamating the chronology of operations in a whirlwind of blades. Even the techniques of packaging food for cooking (boil-in-bags, etc.) reinforces the deterritorialization of the culinary art. The economy of the freezer itself tends to separate the kitchen operations from the meal itself, just as techniques for preserving food by sterilization (canning) separates harvest from consumption. Food preparation, the violence of culinary transformations, are stored and used in a forgotten timeframe (often a time that simply does not exist, when it is a matter of buying fully cooked foods), the forgotten time of planning. Mealtime is founded on the time it takes to reheat without bringing to a boil. Decomposition, culinary violence are voided, emptied out. Likewise know-how disappears.

Modern culinary machinery is a bastardization of old sophisticated techniques. Many of these have disappeared since they cannot be done by machine: keeping a stew going in the corner of the fireplace, pressing, using the pestle for grinding, etc. Only the kitchens of the grand restaurants still know the feverish activity of manual labor. Besides, with their equipment they look more like grandma's kitchen than a sterile laboratory. Copper, cast iron, wood, porcelain, and marble wear their nobility proudly: they are not enamel, plastic, stainless, or teflon.

A litany of the lost arts, a nostalgia for forgotten flavors would be interminable. But then a sociology of cooking would only be this backward-looking lament, an aesthetic of the past. It would be trapped in being either a patient ethnologic census or a pale reflection of the present, and the sociology of cooking would only be a pastime.

And yet a sociology of cooking could be a reading of resistances, ruses, by which we face the banality of both food and social life. It could find, even in their advertising, a return of the ancient, the natural, of qualities. It could dig into the painful themes of grand comedy as feast, of the rustic and the artisanal as supplements for a lack in the soul.

But above all, it could discover the fact that there will always be creative cooking and the pleasure of a repeated ritual. To disclose the modern forms of these prehistoric attitudes can be the prospective task of a sociology of eating. Michel Guérard, in his research into new tastes, new flavors created by new imaginative techniques, bears witness to the continuity of the desire for practical inventiveness, a breaking away from the automated, a resurgence of an old know-how. The purée, the mousse, puddings, chiffons — they are consistencies and flavors born from the mixmaster. It is not that they are "fake" purées, they are simply other.

Looking ahead, a sociology of cooking would consist of a repertoire of techniques, of their impact on the imagination, and of their ritual aspects: a reflection on the modifications of know-how, of tastes, of imagination stemming from new alimentary situations which in turn derive from new objects. In response to industrialization, which shrinks the culinary arts and narrows our bodily and imaginative relationship to food, a sociology of cooking could, through an avant garde use of new technology, be a means of redefining the eater's art of living.

Notes

Translated from French by Juliet Flower MacCannell

1. Roland Barthes, in his introductory essay "Introduction à Brillat-Savarin" to Brillat-Savarin's *La physiologie du goût* (Paris: Hermann, 1975) brings out this aspect: "In other words, discourse has the right to attack food from several angles; it is, in sum, a total social fact, around which one can group various metalanguages: physiological, chemical, geographical, historical, economic, sociological, political. . . ."

2. Nicole Sansot, "Un nouvel enjeu de la recherche scientifique, le fait alimentaire culinaire" (Master's thesis in sociology under the direction of Jean Baudrillard, Paris X, 1978).

3. Jean-Paul Aron, *Le mangeur du 19e siècle* (Paris: Laffont, 1973). Noëlle Chatelet, *Le corps à corps culinaire* (Paris: Seuil, 1977). Frédéric Lange, *Manger ou les jeux et les creux du plat* (Paris: Seuil, 1972). Léo Moulin, *L'Europe à table* (Brussels: Elsevier-Sequioia, 1975).

4. Jean-Anthelme Brillat-Savarin, aphorism vii in *Physiologie du goût*, op. cit., p. 37.

5. Léo Moulin, p. 7.

6. Roland Barthes.

7. This refusal to chew must have spurred the development of refined cuisine, of mousses, soufflés, purées, etc.

About the Contributors

Pierre Ansart is professor of sociology at the University of Paris (Sorbonne 7). He has also been a visiting professor at the universities of Montreal and Ottawa. His publications (on the history of sociology and on political ideologies) include: *Sociologie de Proudhon* (Paris: Presses Universitaires de France, 1967); *Marx et l'anarchisme* (Paris: PUF, (1970); *Les idéologies politiques* (Paris: PUF, 1974) and *Idéologies, conflits et pouvoir* (Paris: PUF, 1977). He is currently extending the analysis of political ideologies to the sociology of political effectiveness.

W. Baldamus is emeritus professor of sociology at the University of Birmingham, England. His present research interest is the growing internationalization of sociology, particularly in connection with the activities of nongovernmental scientific organizations. He is currently also engaged in extending cocitation network analyses from the sociology of science to social philosophy, sociology of knowledge, and systems theory. Among his major publications are *Der gerechte Lohn* (Berlin: Duncker & Humblot, 1960); *Efficiency and Effort* (London: Tavistock, 1967); *The Structure of Sociological Inference* (London/Oxford: Martin Robertson, 1976).

Barry Barnes was trained in natural sciences and in sociology before moving to the Science Studies Unit, Edinburgh University. Among his publications are *Scientific Knowledge and Sociological Theory* (London: Routledge & Kegan Paul, 1974); *Interests and the Growth of Knowledge* (London: Routledge & Kegan Paul, 1977); and *T.S. Kuhn and Social Science* (London: Macmillan, 1982). He is the joint editor of two collections of readings in the sociology and social history of science: *Natural Order* (Beverly Hills, Ca.: Sage, 1979), with S. Shapin, and *Science in Context* (London: Open University Press, 1982), with D.O. Edge. He has held visiting appointments at the University of Pennsylvania and at the Institute for Advanced Study, Princeton. His present work is on problems of reference and self-reference and on relations between the distribution of knowledge and power, themes developing out of a long-standing involvement in the sociology of knowledge.

David Bloor lectures in the philosophy of science at the Science Studies Unit, University of Edinburgh. His main interests are the sociology of knowledge, especially the sociology of scientific knowledge. He published *Knowledge and Social Imagery* (London: Routledge & Kegan Paul, 1976), in which he defended the so-called strong program in the sociology of knowledge. He has also just published *Wittgenstein: A Social Theory of Knowledge* (London: Macmillan, 1983), in which he analyzes and develops the later philosophy of Wittgenstein.

Gernot Böhme is professor of philosophy at the Technical University of Darmstadt, Germany. His previous positions include a research fellowship at the Max-Planck-Institute in Starnberg, Germany, a visiting professorship at the Institute for Advanced Studies, Vienna, and a visiting fellowship at Harvard University. His association with the Max-Planck-Institute resulted in the publication, in the Boston Studies in the Philosophy of Science Series, of *The Social Orientation of Scientific Progress* (coedited with W. Schäfer). Among his other major publications are *Zeit und Zahl* (Frankfurt: Suhrkamp, 1974), and *Alternativen der Wissenschaft* (Frankfurt: Suhrkamp, 1980). Aside from classical philosophy his main interests are history, sociology, and philosophy of science.

Juan E. Corradi is associate professor of sociology at New York University where, until recently, he was also director of the Latin American Center. Born in Argentina, he received his education in sociology at Brandeis University and subsequently lectured at the University of Massachusetts, the University of California at San Diego and at Santa Cruz, the Memorial University of Newfoundland, and the École des Hautes Études in Paris. He is co-editor of *Ideology and Social Change in Latin America* (New York: Gordon & Breach, 1977), and author of *The Making and Breaking of Argentina* (New York: Schenkmann/Halsted/ Wiley, 1984), as well as of articles on the sociology of knowledge. He is presently writing a book on the culture of fear.

Günter Dux is professor of sociology at the University of Freiburg, Germany. He studied law at the universities of Heidelberg and Bonn, and sociology and philosophy at the universities of Frankfurt and Konstanz. His main publications are *Strukturwandel der Legitimation* (Freiburg: Alber, 1976); *Rechtssoziologie* (Stuttgart: Kohlhammer, 1978); and *Die Logik der Weltbilder: Sinnstrukturen im Wandel der Geschichte* (Frankfurt: Suhrkamp, 1982). In his writings, which are based on philosophical anthropology, he attempts to connect the natural history of the human species with its cultural history. His research interests focus on socio-structural as well as cultural "process structures," especially in the cognitive realm. Presently he is concerned with cross-cultural studies of cognitive processes in developing and developed societies.

Norbert Elias is at present working at the Institute of Interdisciplinary Research, University of Bielefeld. Born in 1897, he studied medicine, philosophy (with Edmund Husserl), and psychology, and did postgraduate studies with Alfred Weber in Heidelberg. He taught at Frankfurt, where he worked with Karl Mannheim. After his forced emigration in 1933, he went on to posts in Paris, at the London School of Economics, and at the University of Leicester. He has also taught at the universities of Ghana, Amsterdam, Konstanz, Frankfurt, and others. In 1977 he received the Adorno Prize of the city of Frankfurt. Elias' human science applies historical, psychoanalytic, and sociological approaches to the empirical study of long-term social processes. Best known for his book *The Civilizing Process* (Oxford: Blackwell, 1979; 1982), which originally appeared in 1939, he has also published *What is Sociology?* (London: Hutchinson, 1978), *Die Höfische Gesellschaft* (Neuwied-Berlin: Luchterhand, 1969), and many other works. His books *Court Society*, *Involvement and Detachment*, and *Quest for Excitement* (with Eric Dunning) have recently been published.

Paul Forman is curator for physics at the Smithsonian Institution's National Museum of American History (sometime National Museum of History and Technology), Washington, D.C. His continuing interest in physics and scientific life in Germany in the early twentieth century has repeatedly been put aside to prepare exhibits on "Atom Smashers," "Einstein," "The Fall of Parity" and, most recently, "Atomic Clocks." His interest in the sociology of knowledge was greatest in the earliest stages of his scholarly career. Cp. his "The discovery of the diffraction of x-rays by crystals: a critique of the myths," *Archive for History of Exact Sciences* 6 (1969):38-71.

Joseph Gabel is emeritus professor of sociology and former department chairman at the University of Amiens, France. Born in Hungary, he received his university education in France and initially embarked on a career in medicine specializing in psychiatry. During his subsequent career in the social sciences he developed special interests in questions of ideology, utopia, false consciousness, and reification. His major publications include *La Fausse Conscience* (Paris: Éditions de Minuit, 1962) [English translation: *False Consciousness: An Essay on Reification* (New York: Harper, 1975)]; *Formen der Entfremdung* (Frankfurt: Fischer, 1964); *Sociologie de l'aliénation* (Paris: PUF, 1971); *Idéologies* (Paris: Éditions Anthropos, 1974); *Idéologies II* (Paris: Éditions Anthropos, 1978) and, with Bernard Rousset and Trinh Van Thao, *Actualité de la dialectique*

(Paris: Éditions Anthropos, 1981). He is presently involved in research projects on Socialism and Jewish Future; Modernity of Durkheim; and Karl Mannheim.

Karin Knorr-Cetina is professor of sociology and science in society at Wesleyan University, Connecticut. She is the author of one of the first ethnographic studies of scientific work, *The Manufacture of Knowledge* (Oxford: Pergamon, 1981), and has recently edited the *Sociology of the Sciences Yearbook*, Vol. IV, on *The Social Process of Scientific Investigation* (Boston: Reidel, 1980), with R. Krohn and R. Whitley. She has just completed a book, with M. Mulkay, on *Science Observed* (Beverly Hills, Calif.: Sage, 1983), which brings together recent analytical perspectives in the sociology of scientific knowledge. Her present work focuses on knowledge production and on the relation between micro and macro social phenomena in society in general. See her *Advances in Social Theory and Methodology: Toward an Integration of Micro- and Macrosociologies* (London: Routledge & Kegan Paul, 1981), with Aaron Cicourel.

Peter Ludes studied at the University of Trier and at Brandeis University. He is presently teaching sociology at the University of Wuppertal. In 1981-82 he was a visiting lecturer at the Memorial University of Newfoundland, St. John's, Canada. His main interest is in the area of the sociology of alternatives. He has published *Der Begriff der klassenlosen Gesellschaft bei Marx* (Frankfurt: Campus, 1979).

Niklas Luhmann is professor of sociology at the University of Bielefeld, Germany. He studied law at the University of Freiburg and sociology and public administration at Harvard University. Among his major publications are *Funktionen und Folgen formaler Organisation* (Berlin: Duncker & Humblot, 1964); *Zweckbegriff und Systemrationalität* (Frankfurt: Suhrkamp, 1973); *Soziologische Aufklärung. Aufsätze zur Theorie sozialer Systeme*, 3 volumes (Opladen: Westdeutscher Verlag, 1970, 1975, 1981); *Trust and Power* (New York: Wiley, 1979); *Gesellschaftsstruktur und Semantik*, 2 volumes (Frankfurt: Suhrkamp, 1980, 1981); *Ausdifferenzierung des Rechts* (Frankfurt: Suhrkamp, 1981); *The Differentiation of Society* (New York: Columbia University Press, 1982); *Liebe als Passion: Zur Codiering von Intimität* (Frankfurt: Suhrkamp, 1982). Adopting a functionalist approach to social organization, his main concern is the complex nature of modern society and the role of social institutions as means to order and control this complexity.

Volker Meja studied sociology, economics, and philosophy at the University of Frankfurt and at Brandeis University and is now associate professor of sociology at the Memorial University of Newfoundland, St. John's, Canada. He is coauthor of *Karl Mannheim* (London: Ellis Horwood; New York: Methuen, 1984), and coeditor of *Wissenssoziologie* (Opladen: Westdeutscher Verlag, 1981), *Der Streit um die Wissenssoziologie* (Frankfurt: Suhrkamp, 1982), and *The Sociology of Knowledge Dispute* (London: Routledge & Kegan Paul, 1984). He is also editor of the *Newsletter* of the *International Society for the Sociology of Knowledge*, and co-editor of the previously unpublished writings by Karl Mannheim now published as *Structures of Thinking* (London: Routledge & Kegan Paul, 1982) and forthcoming as *Conservatism* (London: Routledge & Kegan Paul, 1985).

Michael J. Mulkay is professor of sociology at the University of York, England. Among his publications are *Science and the Sociology of Knowledge* (London: Allen & Unwin, 1979); *Science Observed* (Beverly Hills, Calif.: Sage, 1983), edited with Karin Knorr-Cetina; and *Opening Pandora's Box: An Analysis of Scientists' Discourse* (Cambridge: Cambridge University Press, 1983), with G. Nigel Gilbert. He is at present working on various aspects of discourse analysis.

Gérard Namer is professor of sociology at the University of Paris, France. His special interest is the sociology of knowledge and he has published the following works on this subject: *L'Abbé Le Roy, essai sur le jansénisme* (Paris: Sevpen, 1962); *Machiavel: sociologue de la connaissance* (Paris: PUF, 1981); *Rousseau: sociologue de la connaissance* (Paris: Klincksiek, 1981); *Le système social de Rousseau* (Paris: Éditions Anthropos, 1981). Being responsible for the sociology of knowledge section of *L'Année Sociologique*, he contributed the article "La sociologie de la connaissance chez Durkheim et les Durkheimiens." His present interest is the sociology of memory. A book on "commemoration" is under preparation.

Nico Stehr is professor of sociology at the University of Alberta, Edmonton. His research interests center on the sociology and philosophy of the social sciences, the history of sociological thought, and the use of social science knowledge. He is one of the founding editors of the *Canadian Journal* of Sociology and has coedited (with René König) *Wissenschaftssoziologie: Studien und Materialien* (Opladen: Westdeutscher Verlag, 1975); (with David Kettler and Volker Meja) Karl Mannheim's *Structures of Thinking* (London: Routledge & Kegan Paul, 1982), and (with Volker Meja) *The Sociology of Knowledge Dispute* (London: Routledge & Kegan Paul, 1984). With David Kettler and Volker Meja he is co-author of *Karl Mannheim* (London: Ellis Horwood; New York: Methuen, 1984). He has held visiting appointments in Europe and the United States.

Marie-Noël Stourdze-Plessis is a researcher at the Université Paris-Dauphine.

Hélène Strohl is a former student of the École Nationale d'Administration of Sorbonne University where she is now professor of sociology specializing in the history of sociology. She coauthored (with Sansot et al.) *L'Espace et son double* (Paris: Éditions Champs Urbain, 1978), and is presently preparing a book on contemporary eating habits.

Johannes Weiss is professor in the Social Science Department of the University of Kassel, Germany, specializing in sociological theory and philosophy of the social sciences. Among his major publications are *Weltverlust und Subjektivität: Zur Kritik der Institutionenlehre Arnold Gehlens,* (Freiburg: Rombach, 1971); *Max Webers Grundlegung der Soziologie,* (Munich: Saur, 1975); *Das Werk Max Webers in der marxistischen Rezeption und Kritik* (Opladen: Westdeutscher Verlag, 1981). His other areas of interest are cultural sociology and social philosophy. He is presently involved in research projects on representation and deputyship and on social causality.

Index

DATE DUE